FORTS OF THE UPPER MISSOURI

FORTS OF THE

International Standard Book Number 0-8032-5762-7

Library of Congress Catalog Card Number 67-24466

First Bison Book printing: September 1972

Most recent printing shown by first digit below:

1 2 3 4 5 6 7 8 9 10

Bison Book edition reproduced from the first (1967) edition published by Prentice-Hall, Inc. by arrangement with the author.

Manufactured in the United States of America

To the
Memory
of
My Parents

Dakota
Pioneers

Preface

The American frontier was an elusive thing. It was a relatively undefinable line that constantly retreated as population moved generally westward. To each generation, particularly during the 19th century, the frontier was considered to be in some vague area just beyond the cutting edge of organized settlements. Frederick Jackson Turner, who was as baffled as anyone as to its location, said the frontier was to be found "somewhere between civilization and savagery." Both contemporary easterners, who viewed the phenomenon from afar, and westerners, who thought they lived on or near that magical line, were equally unable to give it a definite geographical definition.

However, in the general westward expansion that played a dominant part in American history after settlement had crossed the Appalachians, there were rare occasions when the military frontier and the frontier of settlement momentarily coincided, thus giving the word "frontier" a tangible characteristic. One of these developed along the Upper Missouri River during the 1860's when the Army began to erect its string of forts along that waterway. It became pronounced, and identifiable, during the Civil War era, as a result of the Sioux Uprising in Minnesota. Not only did the river serve as a specific line of demarcation, but the forts established on its banks underscored the specific nature of a fortified frontier. For a brief moment in history the line came close to representing the European type of frontier that sharply

Preface

The American Frontier was an elusive thing. It was a relatively undefinable line that constantly retreated as population flowed generally westward. To each generation, particularly during the 19th century, the frontier was considered to be in some vague area just beyond the cutting edge of organized settlements. Frederick Jackson Turner, who was as baffled as anyone as to its location, said the frontier was to be found "somewhere between civilization and savagery." Both contemporary easterners, who viewed the phenomenon from afar, and westerners who thought they lived on or near that magical line, were equally unable to give it a definite geographical definition.

However, in the general westward expansion that played a dominant part in American history after settlement had crossed the Appalachians, there were rare occasions when the military frontier and the frontier of settlement momentarily coincided, thus giving the word "frontier" a tangible characteristic. One of these developed along the Upper Missouri River during the 1850's when the Army began to erect its string of forts along that waterway. It became pronounced, and identifiable, during the Civil War era, as a result of the Sioux Uprising in Minnesota. Not only did the river serve as a specific line of demarcation, but the forts established on its banks underscored the specific nature of a fortified frontier. For a brief moment in history the line came close to representing the European type of frontier that sharply delineated two definite realms. This is the story of that frontier and of its influence upon the settlement of the West.

To write a book is to incur a good many obligations, none of which can be adequately repaid. Almost always those who lend their help do not ask anything in return, except a simple "thanks," and with that the account is closed. As one well-known historian once said to me, when I expressed my gratitude for assistance given: "If you are caught out on the range without shelter, you are always welcome to use my 'line' cabin; just wash the frying pan before you leave, will you?" I have used a great number of frying pans in this study and I would like to assure the owners that in each case they have been washed and hung back on the cabin wall.

I want to thank the University of Colorado Council on Research and Creative Work for a faculty fellowship that gave me time to write, and also to the History Department Chairman, Fritz L. Hoffmann who helped to lighten my teaching load when the going was heavy. Marilyn Winsor and Barbara Sublett, those willing and hard-working History Department "slaves," cheerfully typed and proof-read the entire manuscript at a time when other duties were most pressing. Bless 'em.

Without the enthusiastic help of those who run that documentary depository, the National Archives, my work would have been much more difficult. From the *bourgeois,* Robert Bahmer, who manages that post, to each and all of his *engagés,* "much obliged." I refer to Mr. E. O. Parker, Mr. Victor Gondos, and most especially to Sara D. Jackson. For nearly twenty years Sara has helped me with my work and has "mothered" a growing brood of my graduate students.

Librarians, that rare breed of individuals who "stand and serve" the frequently fussy and sometimes ungrateful inquirers who come to their doors, are the unsung heroes of most books that are published each year. Archibald Hanna, of the Western Americana Collection at Yale University, once again came forward with rich source material. Equally helpful were Will G. Robinson, State Historical Society of South Dakota; Margaret Rose, formerly of the North Dakota Historical Society, Ray H. Mattison and Craig Gannon, of the same place; Margaret Dempsey and Vivian Paladin, State Historical Society of Montana; Lucile Kane, Minnesota Historical Society; Lawrence W. Towner, Newberry Library; Andrew Hanson, Sioux City Public Library; Gene Gressley, University of Wyoming; and, of course, all the librarians at the University of Colorado. Special thanks go also to Professors Cedric Cummings and the late Everett Sterling of the University of South Dakota.

Wives, of course, always deserve an expression of appreciation, even if they offer no more than moral support. Mine is doubly deserving, for she not only lent critical assistance, but she was also helpful in other ways.

ROBERT G. ATHEARN

University of Colorado

CONTENTS

ONE

The Mysterious, Muddy Missouri

The war was over. From the outset it had been a very unsatisfactory affair, one whose outcome was constantly in question, and when it was finally concluded, the peacemakers at Ghent had, in effect, called the whole thing a draw. Historians gave it the rather unimaginative title "the War of 1812." But Americans nicknamed it the Second War for Independence, which meant they had won nothing, had failed to resolve the once-burning question of impressment, and were lucky to emerge with all the territory they had controlled at the outset. So they concluded they had maintained their independence, and returned to daily affairs unblushingly wearing that unaccountable air of optimism that for so long has annoyed and puzzled the British.

While there had been much excitement before the war about maritime rights, that subject tended to vanish from the discussions as peace talks proceeded during the conflict. More and more the Canadian-American boundary came into the conversations, with the British strongly implying that the Great Lakes were a part of Canada and that the area south of them would make a fine Indian buffer state between the two sovereignties. It was the possible loss of this vast stretch of country that made the American negotiators stand firm, stiffened Monroe's backbone, and stimulated more resolute taproom talk than patriots had been able to generate during most of the war years. Thanks to the stubbornness of the American peacemakers, to the complicated situation on the Continent, and to war weariness in Britain, the treaty wrought in 1815 was more satisfactory than many Americans expected, and it gave the lie to the often repeated statement that this country "had never lost a war or won a peace conference."

In postwar periods Americans traditionally have "turned within," have become preoccupied with internal problems. This was particularly true after 1815. Not only were settlers anxious to develop the Mississippi Valley and to probe Jefferson's fascinating purchase called Louisiana, but there was much talk about national defense. The recent war had underscored the weak and unprepared condition of the nation. Planners of the national destiny knew that the contest had been close, and rather than feeling more secure their apprehensions about Britain were as deep as ever. Theirs was a generation that genuinely distrusted the "perfidious Albion," and this lurking fear would persist on the part of some Americans for much of the nineteenth century.

It was only natural that apprehensive eyes were cast toward the northwestern country after 1815. British traders had cultivated Indian relations in the upper Mississippi and Missouri Valleys for years. Since neither the Spanish, the French nor the new American owners had shown a serious interest in developing trade in the region, there was no reason why the Hudson's Bay Company and others should not proceed as before. A decade had passed since Lewis and Clark had viewed the river country, but there was no sign of active American exploitation of the resources the explorers had observed. Americans knew almost nothing of the Indians of the area; it was the British to whom the natives most frequently turned.

The Madison administration showed its awareness of the problem in February 1815 when Secretary of War James Monroe recommended the erection of military posts along the upper reaches of the Mississippi River. Although national defense was the ostensible reason, the Secretary openly expressed the hope that Indian friendship, and exclusive commerce, would result. In the following year Monroe was elevated to the Presidency, and the pattern of northern defense spread farther across the map. The new Secretary of War, John C. Calhoun, shared the President's concern about British influence in the North. In the spring of 1818 he revealed a plan for the establishment of a post at the mouth of the Yellowstone River, where trade with the Indians could be cultivated. A few months later he decided that the elbow of the river's big bend, in Mandan country, would be a better location. As he told Andrew Jackson, it was the place nearest the British post on the Red River and the most strategic location from which to counteract both hostilities and Indian intrigue. He reiterated these views in a letter to the Chairman of the House Military Committee late in 1819, arguing the necessity of a military force high up on the Missouri River to control warlike Indians who were "open to the influence of a foreign Power." In addition to the dangers of subversion, the river tribes were independently powerful and "by the extension of our settlements, are becoming our near neighbors, [who] are yet very little acquainted with our power." He thought that additional troops should be sent to the northwestern frontier, especially to the areas where British trade could be stifled and, if possible, where warlike tribes might be overawed. Colonel Henry Atkinson of the Sixth Infantry was chosen to lead an expedition to accomplish these ends.

The plan was known as the "Yellowstone Expedition," although its anticipated goal was focused there only momentarily. It might better have been called the Mandan expedition, for this location, in modern central North Dakota, was the center of a tract of country "said to abound more in fur, and of a better quality, than any other portion of this continent," to use the words of Calhoun. Control of it, said the Secretary, would mean that "the most valuable fur trade in the world will be thrown into our hands." That section of the river offered natural advantages of communication to the Americans, who had both the Mississippi and Missouri river systems by which they could easily communicate with far-flung northern fur posts. Calhoun thought it proper that the military should protect entrepreneurs who wanted to develop the American fur trade and should evict British traders, some of whom had remained on American soil after the boundary had been established by the Convention of 1818.

The project was enthusiastically received by most Westerners.

St. Louis was delighted, of course, for it lay right in the mouth of the potential fur cornucopia. The *Missouri Gazette* agreed with the War Department that an outpost in Mandan country would protect the West from both Indians and British; also it would capture the fur trade, encourage immigration and settlement, open communication with the Pacific Ocean and, in general, increase geographical knowledge. In fact, suggested the paper, this would be a key move for it would open the way for possession of "the whole American Territory," presumably to the Pacific Coast. The notion that westward was the course of empire was already fixed in the American mind. This is seen in an enthusiastic letter published by the *Niles Register* in May 1819. Its author said the expedition would provide "a safe easy communication to China, which would give such a spur to commercial enterprise that ten years shall not pass away before we shall have the rich productions of that country transported from Canton to the Columbia, up that river to the mountains, over the mountains and down the Missouri and Mississippi, all the way (mountains and all) by the potent power of steam." [1]

The War Department, normally somewhat chary of such public optimism, especially that of Westerners who never missed a chance to sell supplies to the Army, was quite enthusiastic about the Yellowstone Expedition. Since the end of the war Congress had whittled away at the Army, cutting back appropriations and diminishing its size at every opportunity. Except for such emergencies as serious Indian outbreaks, the Regular Army had not been used a great deal for permanent defensive purposes in the West. Now, for the first time, the nation held title to land that was so remote it probably would not be settled in the foreseeable future, but that was of sufficient economic value to attract such outsiders as the British traders. Here was an exceptional opportunity to defend the nation, and the War Department lost no time in setting forth the necessity for its presence up the Missouri River. For a brief time there was talk of sending as many as a thousand men to the North. As Chittenden, the famed historian of the fur trade, said, Congress was somehow persuaded that the Government might save at least $40,000 a year by placing troops in a country where grass was free and the men could subsist on wild game. That the absolute reverse was going to be true only underscored the general lack of knowledge about this portion of Jefferson's purchase. The War Department was aware of its ignorance. The Secretary's instructions to Major Stephen Long, who was to lead the scientific part of the expedition, stated that one of the objectives was to gain more knowledge about a portion of the country that was "daily becoming more interesting, but which is yet imperfectly known."

Nor was this to be any small-scale ascent of the river. The steamboat, untried on western waters and not even thoroughly developed for use on larger rivers, was to be used in this rather elaborate venture. Five vessels were chartered; two of them did not even reach the Missouri, a third gave out before it had ascended the "Big Muddy" very far, and the others worked their way a little beyond the mouth of the Kansas River from which point they would return with the coming of spring. A sixth vessel, especially constructed for Major Long's group and appropriately named the *Western Engineer,* managed to tie up at Council Bluffs late in the summer of 1819. This unusual vessel, a stern-wheeler some seventy-five feet in length and drawing only nineteen inches of water, was designed not only for purposes of transportation but also for propaganda uses. It was equipped with a figurehead through whose open mouth excess steam was conducted, the hope being that its dragon-like appearance would terrify the natives. However, even the *Western Engineer* was not to have its chance to navigate the High Plains; when the expedition was called off it joined the other vessels in their retreat downriver. More than a decade would pass before the Sioux would marvel at the "fire that walks on water," and even without steam-snorting dragons the "fire boats" would duly impress local tribesmen.

As the expeditionary group passed the winter of 1819–1820 at Engineer Cantonment a few miles below Council Bluffs, Congress began to reconsider its generosity. The Panic of 1819, which dried up a number of tax sources, called for Governmental economy, and what Chittenden regarded as an extremely extravagant project about to be launched from Council Bluffs was one of the depression's victims. Instead, the taxpayers were offered a return of a few cents on each dollar invested by dispatching Major Stephen H. Long out to the Rocky Mountains of modern Colorado during the summer of 1820. Although he made no discoveries of any consequence, and accomplished little more than finding a mountain to bear his name, Long's account of the trek was much publicized. For the moment national concern about British aggrandizement from the North seemed to have been diverted. St. Louis traders, however, were determined to exploit the fur country of which Secretary Calhoun had spoken so highly, and they resolved to do it with or without the aid of protective military posts.

In February 1822, William H. Ashley, Missouri's first lieutenant governor, placed an advertisement in a St. Louis newspaper asking for one hundred "enterprising young men" to ascend the Missouri River to its source where they were to be employed. Since St. Louis was an important trading center and because furs were the only profitable economic resource of the country which Lewis and Clark had scanned, there was no necessity for Ashley to explain the nature of employment. By early April 150 hopefuls had been signed on and dispatched northward on that long, winding, keelboat journey into Indian country. It was largely a summer of sweat, aching backs and no excitement, except for a brief attack a little above the Mandan villages by some Assiniboins, who made off with some of the horses belonging to the land party.

By early October the main group reached the confluence of the Yellowstone and Missouri Rivers where the advance party of Andrew Henry had hastily erected a small log trading post that was to be known as Fort Henry. Both the land and water routes had been difficult; Henry's men had done part of their marching on empty bellies, and one of Ashley's keelboats containing $10,000 worth of goods had been sunk. As the traders made ready to spend the winter in a new, strange country, Ashley went back to St. Louis to make preparations for bringing up reinforcements the next spring.

Competition appeared when Michael Immel and Robert Jones of the Missouri Fur Company passed up the river, bound for the mouth of the Bighorn River in Yellowstone country, ready to join the race for riches among the beaver colonies. Characteristic of the trapping fraternity, both groups had penetrated a virgin land without benefit of any military protection. They could only hope the natives wanted to trade, not fight.

The spring of 1823 yielded a leaner harvest of "enterprising young men" than the Ashley-Henry outfit had found the previous year. Jim Clyman, in charge of recruiting, scoured the bars and brothels of St. Louis trying to gather additional forces, but he had had to confess that the ninety men he assembled made Falstaff's Battalion look genteel by comparison. Early in March they were herded onto two keelboats, the *Yellow Stone Packet* and *The Rocky Mountains*, to begin once more that agonizing journey into the wilderness. Their first goal was the Arickara villages where Ashley hoped to buy some horses. Andrew Henry had sent word from his outpost that operations were being hampered by a shortage of animals, and he had asked his partner to procure some from the Arickaras when the group passed their way.

The Arickaras, or Rees in the parlance of the mountain men, were rumored to be in a more disagreeable mood this year; consequently Ashley approached his horse-buying venture with extreme caution. Despite an outwardly friendly reception he remained vigilant, keeping his keelboats anchored in the middle of the river and sending trade goods ashore in small quantities. For two days, toward the end of May, the trading dragged on with only nineteen horses and some buffalo robes being purchased. Some of the crew thought their leader overly concerned about the Indians, who gave the outward appearance of warm friendship, and a few of them succumbed to the lure of Ree lodges after dark.

During the middle of the second night there was a commotion ashore, and those sleeping on their firearms in the boats learned that the Indians had just murdered one of the guests. In the morning there was an apology and an offer to return the remains of the unfortunate visitor, but it was explained that the corpse was in rather poor condition, the eyes having been put out, the head cut off and the body itself rather badly mangled. Negotiations were interrupted by a fusillade of shots from fortifications ashore, and the trappers scrambled for cover. After a few minutes of wild confusion, a portion of the shore party managed to get aboard the keelboats, and the two vessels quickly dropped downstream.

When the survivors found a defensible spot in a grove of trees about twenty-five miles away, they went ashore and took stock of their situation. On the second day after the fight Ashley wrote a report to Indian Agent Benjamin O'Fallon at Fort Atkinson (slightly north of modern Omaha) in which he listed the names of thirteen killed and ten wounded. His casualties amounted to almost a quarter of his total strength. However, had it not been for the coolness of such men as Jedediah Smith and Jim Clyman, the result probably would have been a good deal worse for, although the affair lasted only fifteen minutes, most of the boatmen were completely paralyzed by fright. Now, at their temporary refuge, Ashley tried to reorganize his force and talked of attempting to bypass the Indian village and reach Fort Henry. This suggestion was howled down by the demoralized rivermen. Only thirty men, some of them wounded, would even agree to stay on; the rest wanted to go south at once. Faced with this situation, Ashley dispatched Jedediah Smith and one of the others to Fort Henry to report the plight of the beleaguered party. Those who elected to wait for help turned *The Rocky Mountains* into a mobile fort, while the *Yellow Stone Packet* was loaded with wounded, recently retired voyageurs and unused trade goods and was sent back to Fort Atkinson where it arrived June 18.[2]

The arrival of Ashley's keelboat provided Colonel Henry Leavenworth, Fort Atkinson's commander, with the first news of difficulties up the river. He was so incensed by the account told by passengers aboard the *Yellow Stone Packet,* that he took the responsibility of ordering his Sixth Infantry troops to prepare for a campaign. As he said to General Henry Atkinson: "We go to secure the lives and property of our citizens, and to chastise and correct those who have committed outrages upon them." [3] Meantime, Indian Agent Benjamin O'Fallon delivered an impassioned recruitment speech to the forty-three men who had left Ashley's expedition, appealing to their patriotism and the Colonel's need for boatmen. Stirred by such oratory, shamed by their abandonment of brothers in need, and no doubt attracted by a chance to hire out to the Army as attractive wages, twenty of them agreed to try once more.

O'Fallon's feelings were not limited to sympathy for the unfortunate Ashley. The thirty-year-old Westerner, a nephew of the famed William Clark, soon would give up his position as Indian Agent and actively enter the fur trade. He was much exercised over British influence among the Northern tribes, and he shared the conviction of many Americans that Britannic intrigue was at the bottom of the trouble. Writing to General Atkinson a few days after the arrival of the *Yellow Stone Packet*, he lamented the barbarity of the Missouri River Indians. "They continue to deceive and murder the most enterprising of our people; and if we continue to forbear, if we do not discover a greater spirit of resentment, this river will be discolored with our blood." It was not merely the Ashley disaster, the Agent continued; this was only one chapter in the story. Hardly had reports of Ashley's defeat gone forward to higher Army authorities than more bad news came down the river. The Missouri Fur Company's expedition, commanded by Jones and Immel, had been attacked and both leaders, along with five of their men, had been killed by the Blackfeet. The same tribe also had killed four of Andrew Henry's men not far from his fort at the mouth of the Yellowstone.

The whole ugly business led straight to the Hudson's Bay Company door, said O'Fallon. He was convinced that the organization, barred from the American trade by the Treaty of Ghent, was exciting the Indians, either to drive out the Americans or to "reap with the Indians the fruits of our labor." It was the Agent's bitter conclusion that "they ravage our fields, and are unwilling that we should glean them." While such accusations were perfectly in tune with the mood of the day, they were probably somewhat overdrawn. Certainly British hunters were aggressive, and they were going to be accused of intrigue in the upper Missouri country for nearly a half century longer, but there is no evidence to show that their policy was one of destroying the fur trade from which they were barred. In general, the American public was apprehensive about the interest of any other power in the Trans-Mississippi region, and the War Department did nothing to allay these fears. Denied the chance to carry out its projected Yellowstone Expedition three years earlier, the Army lost no time in using the incident as a justification for sending troops upriver.

By June 22 Leavenworth's force was ready to move. It was comprised of 220 troops, 80 traders led by Joshua Pilcher of the Missouri Fur Company, and about 30 of Ashley's men. Leavenworth understood that he could also enlist the aid of 2,000 or 3,000 Sioux along the way, a tribe that never lost a chance to attack the Arickaras. As General Atkinson commented, it would be a combination strong enough to destroy any Indian force that the upper tribes could assemble. Governor William Clark, the explorer who had visited the country nearly two decades earlier, agreed that such a body of troops, equipped with cannon, would indeed reduce any concentrated force of Rees, but he doubted that they would be foolish enough to remain in their towns and submit to bombardment.[4] The campaign planners took this factor into account and decided that Pilcher's force, along with the Sioux, would comprise an advance party and the Rees, thinking they had only a handful of traders and some Indians to fight, would retreat to their fortifications. At this point Leavenworth's infantry-supported artillery would come up and cannonade the villages into rubble. The result would be humiliation for the Rees, plunder and prisoners for the Sioux and a lesson taught any other tribes of the region who thought they could wantonly attack American fur traders as they had Ashley's party.

General E. P. Gaines, commanding the Western Department from his headquarters in Kentucky, approved of the plan. He thought, however, that as allies the Sioux were "little to be relied on, without they are accompanied by a force sufficient to restrain, or, if necessary, to coerce them." Gaines agreed with others in the War Department that Americans should not permit themselves to be shoved out of the Indian trade and that the use of military force to protect it was entirely justifiable. "If we quietly give up this trade," he wrote to Secretary Calhoun, "we shall at once throw it, and with it the friendship and physical power of near 30,000 efficient warriors, into the arms of England who has taught us in letters of blood that this trade forms the reign and curb by which the turbulent and towering spirit of these lords of the forest can alone be governed." [5]

When the expeditionary force arrived before the Ree villages on August 9, Leavenworth's strategy was set in motion. In the initial skirmishing the Rees came forth, according to plan, and were met by the Sioux, but instead of retreating to their fortifications they began to drive away the attackers. The troops were now brought up and, upon seeing this, the Rees withdrew, but so many Sioux were scattered between the forces that the troops could not fire upon the Rees without endangering their allies. Leavenworth now brought forth part two of his plan. Six-pounders were placed in protected positions and began a bombardment of the villages that went on until midafternoon of the next day. "The Sioux were in the meantime busily engaged in gathering and carrying off the corn of the Ricarees," Leavenworth later recorded. Before long Ashley's hungry men joined in the search for corn, and military operations were temporarily suspended.

At this juncture Leavenworth's plan of action began to show further evidence of deterioration. He discovered parties of Sioux and Rees, on horseback, holding a parley on a hill near the upper town. As a result of the conference the Sioux announced that they were leaving. As Leavenworth explained it, the development came about "in a strange and unaccountable manner." The Rees now admitted that they had had enough of war, particularly of artillery fire, since it had blown to pieces one of their chiefs, "Grey Eyes." Leavenworth agreed to a treaty of peace. Joshua Pilcher, representing the aggrieved fur traders, was much opposed to this and did everything he could to disrupt the proceedings. He felt that the Indians had not done enough to restore Ashley's losses, and he wanted to resume the attack. The Indians asked that the troops be held off and Leavenworth issued the necessary orders, only to learn on the morning of August 13 that during the night the towns had been abandoned. Troops were sent in at once with orders that there be no looting; messengers were dispatched to recall the Indians, but none of them could be found.

The main problem now became procedural. The Sixth Infantry had marched forth to avenge Ashley, but the mountain men who had accompanied the troops were far from satisfied with the settlement. The military men had properly bombarded the objective, had occupied it, and now were perplexed as to the next maneuver. They had come to fight Indians, not to destroy towns, and apparently their mission had been carried out as far as was practical. Leavenworth ordered his command to load up and start downriver. As far as he was concerned, the campaign was over.

The trappers disagreed strenuously, and before the troops were out of sight they set fire to the villages. Leavenworth was mortified to think that his magnanimous settlement with a humbled enemy had been destroyed by the torch, and he predicted that the Rees would be excited to further hostilities. For Ashley and Henry, who still were interested in fur trade along the upper Missouri, the Colonel felt sympathy. But for the Missouri Fur Company, which, he understood, had withdrawn from that region, he had nothing but condemnation.[6] Joshua Pilcher, an acting partner in the Missouri Fur Company, had his own opinion of the affair. He charged Leavenworth with having caused trouble instead of restoring peace, of having come to open the way for the whites, but "by the imbecility of your conduct and operations [you have] created and left impassable barriers." [7]

The Government had shown its concern over the welfare of Missouri River fur traders ever since that area had come under American control. Calhoun had argued cogently for a strong military outpost deep in the river country, as an instrument to aid the peltry profession and to warn away British intruders. Despite the failure of Congress to respond, there remained an interest in this frontier among administrators in Washington. When Ashley's enterprising young men had entered hostile country on their own and had suffered sharply from Indian hostility, military aid was at once forthcoming. But it was led by a soldier who had no experience with the Indians and whose cumbersome efforts were regarded by mountain men as more harmful than helpful.

Despite delays and mismanagement that led in part to the abandonment of the Yellowstone Expedition in 1820, and despite the outcries that were heard after Leavenworth's puerile efforts in the "Arickara War," military men did not abandon their interest in the upper Missouri River. General Henry Atkinson, after whom the post at Council Bluffs was named, suggested that since no fort had been built in Indian country, annual trips upriver would serve as a substitute to impress the Indians. Congress responded in 1824 with an appropriation of $20,000, and in the following year troops were gathered at Fort Atkinson for another effort to put military power into Yellowstone country. The purpose of the movement was to effect treaties of peace and friendship with the tribes.

General Atkinson, who drew the assignment, was pleased by it. He was to have commanded the troops in the projected ascent of 1820, and its abandonment had cast some reflection upon his abilities to organize and carry out such a mission. Here was a chance to prove himself, and an opportunity to answer some questions of his own, particularly his paddle-powered keelboat theory. As his subordinates toiled over supplies and equipment for an expedition of nearly five hundred men, the General experimented with the mode of transportation that was to carry his men against the current of the treacherous river.

The problem of ascending the river had long challenged the imagination of men. The keelboat that was poled, dragged and on rare occasions sailed, had provided the only practical answer to date, and it was the prime method of water transportation used by the fur traders. The failure of steamboats to match the Missouri's tricks in the abortive expedition of 1819–1820 suggested that this modern method of propulsion was not yet far enough advanced for western waters. Henry Atkinson was therefore convinced that his idea of attaching paddle wheels to a keelboat was a compromise answer of practical value. He had been thinking about it ever since 1819.

After studying various sources of motive power, Atkinson decided that an inclined wheel geared to a shaft that turned paddle wheels would overcome the difficulties of navigating western rivers. Through experimentation he learned that a twenty-five-ton boat could be propelled twenty-four miles in a day by twenty-four men walking on a twenty-foot inclined wheel. This, he said, was a modest estimate, for the men he first used were "indifferent members of the First Regiment's band, and their output was minimal." He was convinced that with forty effective crew members, to serve in two shifts, a company of men could be moved thirty miles in a day. Such a vessel could be rigged for between $150 and $200.

By the time the 1825 expedition was ready to leave, the General had designed an advanced model: crew members sat on benches along the boat's gunwhales and with their legs pushed geared slides across a drive shaft connected to paddle wheels. The new power transmission was said to be an improvement on the inclined tread wheel that was subject to frequent breakdowns. It was officially accepted for use on the new expedition.[8]

On May 16 the expedition got under way. Into eight keelboats went men of the First Infantry commanded by Major Stephen Watts Kearny and troops of the Sixth Infantry under Colonel Henry Leavenworth. A group of forty mounted men, acting as scouts, moved along the river bank. While Atkinson was senior officer present, he shared the role of treatymaker with Major Benjamin O'Fallon, the irascible Indian Agent who had earlier evidenced rather strong ideas about management of the tribes.

For a time all went almost according to plan. The paddle-wheeled boats moved along slowly against the Missouri's spring-time current, running aground now and then, but largely proving the General's mechanical theories correct. A stop was made at the Ponca village, in present northeastern Nebraska, where medals and presents were handed out. After speeches by the visitors the Indians were given a treaty already drawn up, with the explanation that all they needed to do was sign. After that more presents were distributed, and the little fleet moved on toward Fort Kiowa for a talk with the several bands of Sioux. After some haggling these Indians also agreed to the general stipulations of the standard-form treaty: acknowledge American supremacy, submit to a regulation of the trade and avoid any traffic with enemies of the United States. In return for this the Government promised to protect the Indians, to provide them with licensed traders and to keep the peace.

During the early days of July the two treatymakers met with several more Sioux bands and, after a conference that featured boiled dogmeat and the smoking of a pipe that rested upon a buffalo dung when not being smoked, more treaties of commerce and amity were signed before the group moved on. At midmonth they reached the Arickara villages where Ashley had been so badly treated two years before. Because of their past conduct, the Rees gained only some tobacco in return for their signatures, and were given a stiff warning about future lapses of etiquette. Next on the itinerary was the Mandan village complex where the Gros Ventres and Mandans awaited.

Here the white diplomats came to a parting of the ways. During the afternoon discussions, accusations were made against the Mandans for having taken part in the Ashley attack, which the Indians explained away as acts of imprudence among their young warriors who fired into the white camp thinking they were Indians. O'Fallon, who had never recovered from his bitterness toward those who had attacked Ashley, was far from willing to accept the standard Indian explanation of past misdeeds. When Atkinson awarded them a generous portion of presents, O'Fallon objected strongly. The quarrel went on until dinner time, when tempers flared to a point where each grabbed an eating utensil and tried to stab the other. No blood was spilled, but O'Fallon made it clear that Washington authorities would hear about the General's bad judgment. As a witness wrote two days later: "They have not since spoken to each other, and how it will end God only knows." [9]

An air of bad humor lingered. A few days later when a large band of Crow Indians came in, there was more trouble. Atkinson demanded that the Crows give up two Iroquois prisoners, but he was told that these were prizes they had legitimately stolen from the Blackfeet and they would not be surrendered. The bickering dragged on over this and other minor items until Atkinson stepped out for a bite to eat. The fiery O'Fallon now took over and the tempo of quarreling increased. Finally some of the Indians decided to help themselves to a few presents. O'Fallon promptly grabbed a pistol and started clubbing heads. Atkinson returned in time to break up the brawl, although the situation remained so touchy that Major Kearny thought the question of war or peace hung on the toss of a coin. Both parties slept on the matter, and the next day the Indians reappeared ready for peace and presents. The General was generous with his gifts, and apparently the Crows were prepared to forget O'Fallon's pistol-whipping. However, the uneasy troops fired a number of rockets that night, hoping the display would leave the impression of strength and vigilance. They could not forget that the Crows outnumbered them. A few days later the expedition resumed its journey against the river's current, searching for more Indians with whom they might smoke the pipe.[10]

By mid-August the expedition reached the mouth of the Yellowstone River; a quarter of a mile beyond, on the south bank of the Missouri, they came to Ashley's abandoned fort. Some of the houses had been burned, but one remained standing, along with three sides of the stockade. Here the group stayed for a few days, calling their location Camp Barbour after the new Secretary of War, James Barbour. Just three years later, Kenneth McKenzie would locate the trading post named Fort Union across the river from the camp, and it would stand for years as the main outpost of the American Fur Company on the upper Missouri. But now, in 1825, there was no disposition to maintain a fur trading post in that hostile country.

Two days after Atkinson's expedition arrived, William Ashley and a party of twenty-four trappers came in, bringing a hundred packs of beaver skins. Atkinson offered Ashley an escort back to Council Bluffs if the trader would wait a few days until the expeditionary force probed the Missouri a little deeper. The invitation was accepted gladly. After Atkinson and his party of men reached the neighborhood of Porcupine River, which they guessed was 2,000 miles above St. Louis and 120 miles beyond the Yellowstone's mouth, they gave three cheers and returned to the encampment where Ashley and the others awaited. Twenty-three days later, on September 19, the combined party was back at Fort Atkinson.

From a tactical standpoint the Atkinson expedition was a success. The General had navigated approximately 2,000 miles of the Missouri, demonstrating to his satisfaction the utility of paddle-wheel keelboats, concluding twelve Indian treaties and returning without the loss of a man. Of more significance, however, was his conclusion regarding the value of a military post in upper Missouri country. During that summer General Jacob Brown had written to him from Washington, D.C., suggesting that if it appeared practical, the expeditionary force might take up station at the mouth of the Yellowstone or near the Mandan villages. When Atkinson made his report in November, he explained in some detail why this move, so long desired by the Department, was no longer worth consideration.

The British problem, he said, no longer existed. In recent years Canadians had shown little disposition to trade with American Indians below the great falls of the Missouri, and the Indians rarely went into the Red River country in search of British-made goods. Nor did the Indians themselves pose any real threat. Of all the bands east of the Rockies, only the Blackfeet were consistently hostile to whites. Traders associated with the others freely and without any need of protection from a military force. If, however, the Government thought a post desirable in the upper Missouri country, the mouth of the Yellowstone was still the most recommended of all sites. That location was the point of divergence for traders passing upriver and a junction for those bound for the states. Atkinson saw it as a resting place or rendezvous for traders, not as a defensive location. To give traders any practical protection the military would have to locate a post at the Three Forks of the Missouri, in present Montana. He did not recommend such an establishment, for it would be extremely expensive to supply and the men could not depend upon the mobile buffalo herds for subsistence. Nor did he believe that the Yellowstone post was justified; Council Bluffs was the highest point on the river that troops were needed. If the river Indians became obstreperous in years to come, a summer expeditionary force might well be sent upriver to discipline them. His own journey, just completed, demonstrated the feasibility of such a move.

Only a decade had passed since the Peace of Ghent, but in those short years much had happened in the West. The northwestern boundary questions had been settled in 1818, and the Florida Purchase of 1819 included a boundary agreement for the western extent of the Louisiana Purchase and a relinquishment of Spanish claims in Oregon. With both flanks apparently freed of immediate threat, Americans looked westward with increasing interest. Settlers pouring into the Mississippi Valley after the war forced the question of Indian removal, and in 1825 Monroe made his now-famous recommendations for that significant development in Indian policy. Removal of Indians beyond the states of Missouri and Arkansas would require a cordon of military posts and the establishment of a "permanent Indian frontier." Atkinson pointed this out in his report of November 1825, and he saw this development as a new and more significant duty for the Army than any needs on the upper Missouri River. It was a coincidence that, simultaneously, he also relayed a report from William Ashley, with whom he had returned downriver, stating that South Pass provided such an easy passage across the Rockies that wagons might traverse it. This was the direction in which Ashley was now to turn, and after the fur traders would come the Oregon Trail emigrants, trying out the easy accesses to the West. In that single year a military-Indian frontier was proposed and the method for puncturing it was suggested.

So fascinating was the idea that America spent the next generation probing the central High Plains. For three decades after Atkinson's expedition, the upper Missouri River country would have no military posts and the fur traders would, as the General suggested, carry on a relatively undisturbed commerce with the tribes. In the spring of 1827, Fort Atkinson was abandoned and its troops transferred to Fort Leavenworth. The river country was mentally set aside as pioneers talked of such exciting places as Oregon and California.

TWO

The Fur Forts

William Ashley's historic advertisement for "enterprising young men," published in March of 1822, marked the beginning of a fur trading career that excited the admiration of St. Louis businessmen for nearly a generation. But within weeks there occurred another event that was to carry deeper significance, although it was much less publicized. When John Jacob Astor's American Fur Company quietly established its western department at St. Louis, a competition began for the wealth in peltries deep in the river country that was to far outlive the efforts of individual traders. So great was the organization's success that a mere mention of "the company" was sufficient to identify it, and all rivals were to be disdainfully known merely as "the opposition." Long after Ashley's death, and after the demise of the Rocky Mountain Fur Company that grew out of his small advertisement, "the company" held sway, unchallenged and powerful, as a virtual sovereign over a wild and untamed land only vaguely known to most Americans.

Adopting a course that was to make it notorious, the American Fur Company began to buy rival concerns it could not kill through competition. One of them, the Columbia Fur Company, was absorbed in 1827 and henceforth was known simply as the Upper Missouri Outfit, or more popularly as the U.M.O. To stake its claim more thoroughly in the north country, Astor's firm directed Kenneth McKenzie to build a fortified post at some strategic point that would command a vast area rich in peltries. During 1828 his men selected a site on the north bank of the Missouri about five miles above the mouth of the Yellowstone, not far from where Ashley had placed his little outpost six years earlier. Construction began early in the following year, and it continued so slowly that nearly four years passed before Fort Union, as the post was finally named, was put into full operation. Its location, at the union of two important rivers, commanded a point where natural travel routes converged from the West and one that was accessible to steamboats. With the arrival of the *Yellowstone* in 1832, the fort assumed the significance company officers hoped it would have when they began construction.

For nearly four decades Fort Union stood as a great bastion of traders, and to those who paraded past it in the westward march of empire it became one of the principal landmarks of the Northwest. Prominent travelers who saw the place and went home to write of their adventures in the West inevitably recalled the impressive scene that unfolded as they approached this wilderness outpost.

Prince Maximilian, who stopped there in the spring of 1833, wrote in glowing terms of its setting "on a verdant plain, with the handsome American flag, gilded by the last rays of evening, floating in the azure sky, while a herd of horses grazing animated the peaceful scene." As his steamer came in view the fort greeted it with the thunder of cannon that was answered by a chatter of musketry from the vessel. As the explosive salutations died, the boat nudged against the river's muddy bank and its passengers crossed the gangplank to the massive double gates of Fort Union, only a few yards away. By now the establishment was ready to receive the vanguard of that army of visitors whose names would comprise a western *Who's Who* in the years that lay ahead. Damage done by fire a year earlier had delayed completion, but fortunately all that was destroyed was palisade timber and a thousand dried buffalo tongues. In 1833 no one worried about the supply of these commodities in a land of plenty; however, had the flames reached 2,000 pounds of powder stored in the magazine, the Prince would have found Fort Union's site quite as primitive as the countryside through which he passed on his river journey.

By the end of another decade Fort Union was in its prime. While one of the American Fur Company employees proudly called it "the principal and handsomest trading-post on the Missouri River," it was more than that. It was a well fortified fur emporium, as strong and as self-sufficient as many a medieval castle, and the Indians who traded there thoroughly understood its impregnability. A heavy wall of upright cottonwood logs, standing twenty feet high, enclosed an area that was almost 240 feet square, inside of which were the storerooms and living quarters. On opposite corners were thirty-foot stone bastions, glistening with whitewash, through whose gunports peered iron three-pounder cannons and brass swivel guns, loaded and ready. Atop secondary roofs reared two flagstaffs bearing American ensigns, and a pair of weathercocks, one representing a bull buffalo and the other an eagle. This wilderness bastion was well prepared to ward off any enemy not supported by artillery, and no Indians ever challenged it successfully.

The most attractive building within the compound was that occupied by the *bourgeois* or fur company officer in charge; in the 1840's Alexander Culbertson lived there. This long, narrow structure, which stretched for nearly eighty feet along one of the rough, palisaded walls, contrasted sharply with the rusticity of its surroundings. A clapboard front painted glistening white, set off by green shutters and capped with a bright red shingled roof, moved clerk Edwin Denig to characterize its appearance as "very imposing." At sundown favored employees gathered along a white-pillared veranda to combat the summer heat with refreshments cooled from a well-supplied icehouse. The building's handsomely papered interior, well ornamented with portraits and other pieces of art, gave visitors a sense of luxury that momentarily lifted them out of the primitive land that engulfed them. Nor was the illusion lost when the *bourgeois* led them into a nearby dining room and, taking his seat at the head of the table, served culinary delicacies to his guests and clerks who were seated according to the order of their importance.

Along the east side of the fort's interior ran an even longer building that was divided into storerooms, a retail store, a wholesale warehouse and, finally, a small room for storing meat and other food supplies. The widely known Charles Larpenteur, who ran the store, sold his merchandise under a strict price-control system "so that no bargaining or cheating is allowed," as Denig explained it. The pressroom, with a capacity of three hundred packs of buffalo robes, revealed to visitors one of the main stocks-in-trade of the upper country. Another building, of similar dimensions, was divided into apartments for clerks, resident hunters and various workmen. The kitchen, standing apart to isolate the sound and smell of cooking, constantly employed two or three cooks who labored to keep ahead of the little community's collective appetite. Still farther removed were the stables, a well-plastered henhouse, a cooper's shop, a milkhouse and a dairy. Near the front gate, where most of the trading was done, were shops for gunsmiths, blacksmiths and tinners. In short, the little stockade contained a village within itself, capable of defense, manufacture, commerce and self-sustenance.

From the center of the compound soared the pride of the fort: a sixty-three-foot flagstaff that bore an enormous American flag acquired from the Navy. Denig called it the glory of the fort and maintained that it offered "the certainty of security from dangers, rest to the weary traveller, peace and plenty to the fatigued and hungry, whose eyes are gladdened by the sight of it on arriving from the long and perilous voyages usual in this far Western wild." Upon the arrival and departure of boats the flag was raised, to the accompaniment of cannon fire, as a sign of welcome or of safe passage to some other destination.

Typical of trading posts, Fort Union had a double set of gates. Those on the exterior, brightly decorated with a painting that depicted a peace treaty between Indians and whites, opened into an area called the reception room. When the tribesmen came to trade the inner gate remained closed and they conducted their business through a window. At times the customers were too numerous or in a bad humor, and negotiations were carried on through a small opening in the fort's outer wall. In this way the fur company promoted its commerce protected from the treachery of the Indians, and was ever vigilant, but always willing to bargain for the wealth in peltries offered by the natives who came to buy the white man's goods and gadgets. Although the normal differences of opinion appeared between buyer and seller, some of which led to occasional violence, the system worked well; this and similar posts scattered throughout the upper Missouri country contributed the first great economic return from this portion of the Louisiana Purchase.

Fort Union was the American Fur Company's first permanent post above the Mandan villages, but it was not the largest operated along the river by that organization. Pierre Chouteau, Jr., who was anxious to strengthen his hold on the country to the south and west of Fort Union, decided to relocate and enlarge Fort Tecumseh which had stood on the present site of Pierre, South Dakota since 1822. The new post, named in his honor, was built on the west side of the river slightly above the old location. When Chouteau went upriver in 1832 aboard the company's new steamboat *Yellowstone,* he stopped off to inspect construction efforts. George Catlin, the distinguished western artist, accompanied the trader and witnessed the christening of a new link in the growing chain of river fur posts. It was here that Chouteau established his field headquarters, where all drafts and company papers were signed. Until 1855, when it had outlived its usefulness and was sold to the Army, Fort Pierre was a main "port" on the river and, like Fort Union, it drew comments from most of the travelers who passed its way.

The trading establishment was fortified much in the same manner of Fort Union. It had a protective enclosure of cottonwood log pickets that was nearly three hundred feet square, guarded by two large blockhouses that stood on opposite corners.[1] Upon entering the larger of two front gates that faced the river, visitors saw a little settlement of some twenty buildings. Two long, single-story structures, separated by a passageway that led into the compound, contained shops where tinners, blacksmiths, carpenters and saddlers worked. To the right and left ran even longer buildings, paralleling the fort's walls but set out about twenty-five feet. One of these contained a store where Indian trade articles were kept, and the other provided housing for the employees. At the rear was a large building complete with dormer windows, used principally as a dormitory. Thaddeus Culbertson described it, in the 1850's, as an impressive structure "with a porch along its whole front, windows in the roof and a bell on top and above it the old weather cock, looking for all the world like a Dutch tavern." Next door was "a neat log house with a pleasant little portico in the front . . . that is the boss house." Close by were the kitchens, a sawmill, an adobe powder magazine, stables and smaller buildings used for storing pelts. From the fort's center reared the traditional flagstaff from which the American colors waved their welcome to all friendly visitors.[2]

While this fur headquarters post was larger than Fort Union, it did not have as many refinements and usually suffered by comparison in the comments made by passersby. Nevertheless, it provided a welcome sight for those who reached it after a long and dangerous trip through the wilderness. As John Palliser remarked when he stopped there in the late 1840's: "The whole establishment has a most inviting look to a set of weary travellers on jaded horses."[3] Prince Maximilian visited Fort Pierre briefly in 1833 en route upriver, and stated, quite correctly, that it was "one of the most considerable settlements of the Fur Company on the Missouri." Palliser went beyond this praise and called it the finest post on the Missouri, but no one who had visited Fort Union could have agreed.

Whatever the relative merits of these outposts, they all suffered from one disability: loneliness. Even in later years the arrival of a steamboat caused a stir at such places, but in the infancy of that trade the rare visits induced a small celebration. After months of boredom that could be compared to virtual imprisonment, fur post residents were hungry for any scrap of news from the outside world, and the sight of smoke or the sound of whistles always precipitated an excited rush to the waterfront. The sounds of cannonading and cheering that inevitably developed were flattering to those aboard the arriving boats, and they rarely failed to comment on the royal greeting accorded them. When the *Yellowstone* approached Fort Pierre in 1833, fifty-one days out of St.

Louis, the commotion that followed was typical. Prince Maximilian recorded the event: "A great crowd came to welcome us; we were received by the whole population, consisting of some hundred persons, with the white inhabitants at their head, the chief of whom was Mr. Laidlow [William Laidlaw], a proprietor for the Fur Company, who has the management of the place." [4]

The passage of nearly two decades did little to alter the nature of such ceremonial greetings. In June of 1850, Thaddeus Culbertson wrote from Fort Pierre of the reaction to a report that a steamer had been sighted downstream. "This announcement electrified the whole establishment, and there were various opinions as to the hour she might be expected," he wrote, not mentioning if any of these estimates were backed by small wagers. Shortly after noon the *El Paso* came in sight. "Salutes were fired on the boat and the fort alternately, from the time she appeared in sight until her landing, and there was a great gathering of Indians and whites to welcome her." [5]

Passengers, always an object of curiosity, were equally fascinated by the forts and their inhabitants. Here was a chance to see a live American Indian, more or less in captivity, and to write about it. Thaddeus Culbertson, who visited Fort Pierre briefly, came away with a view that was superficial and quite common. "A number of Indians, men and women, with their robes or blankets wrapped around them, their bare legs, painted faces and curiously ornamented heads will probably be lounging in perfect listlessness about the gate, but don't be afraid, they won't hurt you." [6] A Frenchman, E. de Giradin, was equally attracted by the quaint natives in 1849. "A few steps from us on the shore, a group of Indians in holiday costume, their faces painted red, yellow and white, as motionless as statues, leaning on their guns, examine us with a somber and restless air. . . . We have scarcely landed when some fifty young warriors and women swarm upon our deck, enter the lounge, the kitchens, everywhere in fact, examining, touching and tasting everything, and in spite of the remonstrances of our Negro cooks, a huge kettle filled with boiled corn is emptied in an instant." [7] For nearly a century, passengers arriving at western points, whether by boat or rail, would remark about blankets, face paint and the curious customs of the red man.

Visitors who left their impressions in print usually were people of some importance or means, and as a rule they were offered the finest hospitality the forts had to offer. Consequently, what they saw did not always accurately reflect the living conditions of average residents. To them it appeared that the post was managed by "the boss," or *bourgeois,* under whose charge lived and worked a happy throng of white or half-breed employees. Actually, fur fort society was sharply stratified, and foreign travelers who talked much of America's classless society as seen in other parts of the land would have been struck by this characteristic.

Louis Letellier, one of the many French Canadians engaged in the fur trade, later wrote that the inhabitants of Fort Pierre were divided into three distinct classes. The first, and the most favored by the *bourgeois,* were the old half-breed traders known as "white Indians." They knew the Sioux language, moved freely among the Indians as well as the whites, and were "the big men" of the country. They were bound to appear in the guest list of any major Indian feast, and they stalked through the camps, plate of dog stew in hand, as self-assured as any Indian. That which they could not eat was cast to the less fortunate natives who hung around outside the lodges. While at the fur forts, these men sat at the same table with the *bourgeois* as favored members of a lesser nobility.

Beneath this class were those who had worked in lesser capacities for years, always hoping for admittance to the knighthood of the white Indians. They were reminded of their status each day at mealtime when they ate what was left over from the "high table."

At the bottom of the social ladder were the young men newly hired at St. Louis, "being deceived by some interested parties in the camp about the treatment they were going to be subject to," as Letellier wrote in bitter remembrance, and, as he added, "they had to submit themselves." Again, their badge of inferiority was culinary, and it was tossed to them in the form of a daily ration of dried buffalo meat whose arrival could be detected for some distance by its odor. It was dropped into a kettle of bouillon several days old, and when it was judged to be ready the cook opened the door to his room and let in the hungry men. But here again privilege appeared, for those who held seniority had an opportunity to fish out the best pieces with their wooden forks before the other probed the remnants. It was that or nothing. Prices at the post store were so prohibitive that the purchase of additional or substitute food was out of the question. In 1850 Letellier quoted sugar, coffee, flour and corn prices at Fort Pierre as a dollar a pound.[8]

Members of an all-male society, whether part of a military organization or of a corporate enterprise such as fur trading, tend to think and talk much about the low quality of food being served or about the painful lack of available women. One can assume that the food is extraordinarily bad if it becomes the major subject of conversation. At the trading posts, and later at military forts along the river, feminine company was always in fair supply, although it was generally held to be of doubtful quality. Men who shopped around for temporary mates or women who could solve immediate urges often felt that the need had to be of emergency proportions before they were willing to indulge.

But such men as Alexander Culbertson, who married a Blackfoot woman, did very well and were quite satisfied with native wives. Culbertson's wife was not only a source of great pride to him, but she was very useful as a translator and diplomat. Isaac I. Stevens, en route to the Territory of Washington where he was to become Governor, stopped at Fort Union in August of 1853, and there he met Mrs. Culbertson. Stevens explained the advantage of her presence, saying that it inspired local Indians with a perfect confidence. "The men and women were fond of gathering around Mrs. Culbertson to hear her stories of the whites," he wrote to the Commissioner of Indian Affairs. "One evening I heard loud shouts of merry laughter from one of the groups. Upon inquiring the source of the merriment, I learned that Mrs. Culbertson was telling stories to her simple Indian friends of what she saw at St. Louis. As she described a fat woman who she had seen exhibited, and sketched with great humor the ladies of St. Louis, it was pleasant to see the delight which beamed from the swarthy faces around her."[9]

The explorer John C. Frémont saw Indian women in an equally favorable light when he stopped at Fort Pierre in 1839. On this trip he accompanied the French scientist, Joseph N. Nicollet, who was making some geographical studies along the Missouri River. Frémont remarked, in his memoirs, that the Yankton Sioux girls were decked out in whitened, dressed skins heavily embroidered with beads and quills of many colors. He called them the best formed and best looking Indians of the plains. The Indians seemed to understand such appreciation of form and looks, for within a day or two one of them came to the fort with an attractive, well-dressed eighteen-year-old girl who was offered to Nicollet as a wife. The Frenchman explained that he already had been so blessed and by the customs of his people this was the limit; however, he suggested, young Frémont was still a free agent. The younger man was at a disadvantage, but he maneuvered his way out of the situation by explaining that he was going far away and did not have the heart to take the girl away from her people. But, to show his appreciation, he offered a present of scarlet and blue cloth, some beads and a mirror. All during the negotiations the object of the conference had leaned quietly against the doorway showing a pleased but almost detached interest in the proceedings.[10]

Such was the published description by a well-known American, written years later, and in it one sees the white man's fascination with what he regarded as the untutored mind of the unsophisticated native. Frémont's story suggests, however, that the parents of young Indian girls were not adverse to offering them for the use of visitors, the term "wife" having a number of shadings. Peter Garrioch, who lived with the fur traders and did not put down his thoughts for a nineteenth-century reading audience, painted a much less romantic view of interracial relations. It was at Fort Clark, a little fur post about a hundred feet square built on the banks of the Missouri a few miles below the mouth of the Knife River, that he watched his colleagues frolic with the native women.

His boat stopped at the little post one spring morning in 1842, and from the time it touched shore until nightfall the vessel was crowded with Arickara, Gros Ventre and Mandan Indians. As Garrioch explained, the visit was commercial rather than social, and the women come "not so much to cohabit with the whites for the pleasure of the thing, as the remuneration they expected after the rutting business was over." Parents brought forth their daughters and husbands offered their wives. "Never perhaps since the days of Adam, or since public markets were first instituted," wrote the trader, "did any species of animals or goods prove more marketable, or meet with more general demand and ready sale, than the hindquarters of these ignoble and prostitute females." That his colleagues regarded the situation as more a burning necessity than a casual pleasure is indicated in his comment: "If the object . . . bore the semblance of a woman it was enough, the reality was taken on chance to be discovered in the secret chamber." [11]

One of the difficulties in dealing with the Indians, whether the commerce was in pelts or sex, was that their attitudes were subject to sudden changes. Ashley's men discovered this among the Arickaras in 1823. A number of other traders made the same mistake over the years, and not a few of them died in the process. As the river trade increased and white men appeared in greater numbers, the natives tended to become more temperamental, and violence flared with increasing frequency. When the Federal Government tried to soothe them with gifts, they sometimes spurned the offer as being too paltry in quantity. By 1849 Little Bear, a Sioux, could refuse gifts at Fort Pierre with the charge that only scraps were being thrown to him. Not only did he want a hundred boatloads of merchandise and ammunition, but he sought compensation for all the female favors that had been handed the whites. "Behold," he said arrogantly, "you have lived with the women of our tribe long enough; we want in our turn a thousand young girls, virgin and of white skin." [12]

When the Indians were not awarded their boatloads of merchandise and white virgins, they showed their bad temper. Shooting at passing steamers, a practice that continued for years, provided them with both retribution and a form of recreation. Chittenden tells of one incident in 1843, not far from where Fort Randall later stood, in which a small band of Santees opened up on the *Omega* and added considerable excitement to the voyage. While no one was hurt there were some near-hits. One passenger, asleep in his bunk, was brought out of his slumbers by a bullet that passed through his pantaloons and flattened itself against a trunk. John James Audubon, the naturalist, added two of these spent specimens to his collection.[13]

Old-timers among the Indians, those French-Canadian "breeds" whom Letellier called "White Indians," moved among the tribes fairly well, although they also quarreled violently from time to time. In the early years important white visitors at the fur posts were the guests of selected local Indians, and usually were accompanied by an official of the fur company or someone chosen for knowledge of the native language and standing among the Indians. On his visit in 1849 De Giradin was invited to a dog meat dinner and he bravely accepted. He later reported that the meat was tender and fat like a mutton chop. Indian customs always intrigued visitors, and De Giradin was interested in the tradition of the hosts giving their guests leftovers from the meal, to be eaten on the spot or taken along for future use. However, he thought the closing ceremonies of the repast might have been eliminated. "At the end of a meal," he told his readers, "having the mouth full of whiskey, they pass the contents to the mouth of their neighbor, the greatest act of politeness and of good manners among the Sioux." [14]

Most of the Indians so visited were those who normally camped near the fort and were somewhat domesticated. Only a few of the hundreds who flocked to the forts to trade, as did the Assiniboins at Fort Union, were allowed beyond the trading pen or were the objects of fraternization. Normally the fur company employees did not trust the Indians, and the frequent killings that took place when whites, alone or in small groups, were caught and killed served as a constant reminder of the danger. That the traders tended to stay forted up most of the time and to transact their trade with the Indians through small openings in the walls or doors is understandable. But the success of the system was demonstrated by the number of furs that were received each year in St. Louis.

All along the river, far beyond Fort Union, deep into modern Montana and at dozens of other points flanking the river on both sides, lay trading houses of various sizes. Some were owned by "the company," while others represented efforts made by the current "opposition" to cut into the firm's stranglehold on the trade. Often the houses were simply log structures, intended only for a season's trade, and built wherever Indians happened to congregate or hunt. Together the companies fed their furs, ten robes to a pack, into the main stream of pelts that flowed toward the metropolis, St. Louis.

In 1850 Thaddeus Culbertson was told that some 100,000 pelts from the upper Missouri country would find their way downriver in a single season, and perhaps three times that number would be used by the Indians and others. He learned that each Indian needed at least two robes annually for clothing, and many more for replacements to maintain shelters. These figures were substantiated by the Indian Agent for the Upper Missouri Agency at Fort Pierre in 1853. "I have taken no little pains to ascertain the supposed number of buffalo annually destroyed in this agency," wrote Alfred Vaughan, and "the number does not fall very far short of 400,000."[15] There was, of course, a great deal of waste. Of the thousands of buffalo killed for their skins, whether for sale or domestic use, only a small proportion was needed to supply enough meat for daily use. Many an animal was slaughtered for its hide which, in turn, was used in building a lodge that was sold to some trader as a storage place for his peltries. While the Indians and a great many eastern humanitarians were to complain in later years about the wastefulness of the whites in their slaughter of the buffalo, the natives themselves often were guilty of it. Once the whites demonstrated that they were prepared to buy hides for hardware, cloth or whiskey, the Indians showed a willingness to kill the animals for the trade. There was also a demand for buffalo tongues, a delicacy to eastern palates, and many a shaggy animal died for the purpose of yielding only about four pounds of its total weight.

In the midnineteenth century, Indians in the river country were far more self-subsistent than they were a few years later when the herds began to diminish. While buffalo meat was the standard item of fare, some of the less nomadic tribes augmented it with agricultural produce. Those who lived along the river bottom land raised corn and vegetables in some quantity. In fact, the Gros Ventres, Rees and Mandans requested of agent Alfred Vaughan in 1854 that the Government send up no more corn. These Indians said they not only raised enough for their own use, but had a surplus for sale to other tribes.[16] Traders soon discovered that the river bottoms in the Great American Desert were capable of supporting small agricultural efforts. Experiments around Fort Union in the 1840's demonstrated that corn, oats, potatoes and most garden vegetables would grow. As was shown later all across the Northern Plains, this was true only if conditions were favorable. The soil around Fort Union was light and sandy, requiring an amount of rainfall that occurred about one year in three. In addition to this uncertainty there was the probability of destruction by grasshoppers and various other bugs. Nature provided such items as wild turnips, wild rhubarb, chokecherries, bullberries, service berries, red plums and grapes, but they were not much used by the whites. As Edwin Denig put it: "The natural productions of the country are few and such as no one but an Indian could relish." [17]

By midcentury great changes were taking place in the West, and the upper Missouri country, more or less passed by in the westward push, soon would feel pressure from the ever-widening white wedge being driven into the High Plains. The traders pursued their daily occupations much as they had for years, and relationships with the Indians seemed to have settled into a rather stable feeling of mutual distrust that still admitted a thriving peltry trade. But events to the south began to point toward the end of the uneasy calm that prevailed along the river.

By now the Oregon Trail was well traveled, the Mormons had laid their track upon the land, and the Argonauts had widened the highway with their gold-hungry hordes. In the great gathering of tribes at Fort Laramie in the autumn of 1851, the Indians had conceded the right of travel over a belt of land running westward along the Platte River, and the white negotiators mistakenly thought that they had effected a lasting peace. It was true, there would be no settlements of any consequence in that area for some time to come, but the initial thrust of the westward movement had penetrated the trans-Mississippi region and its force would be felt far beyond more populated areas. Minnesota and Iowa had achieved statehood, the burning Kansas-Nebraska question illuminated the political scene of the midfifties, and before the decade was out there came the cry of gold in the Pike's Peak country. Now the westward momentum became so great that its wake washed farther to either side than ever before, and the Dakotas felt the disturbance.

Since the history of the High Plains has such a strong association with cattle it is perhaps ironic, but not surprising, that difficulties between the races in that region were precipitated in part by a cow. In August 1854 a cow strayed or was stolen from a Mormon wagon train that approached Fort Laramie, and when the owners lodged a complaint against a band of Sioux Indians in the neighborhood, a small military force was sent to recover the animal or bring in the culprits.

The story of Lieutenant John Grattan's foolish foray with some thirty men against a large number of Sioux, and the resulting loss of the entire force, has been told many times. The significance of the event lies in that fact that it was like a rock thrown into a pond: The effects spread in ever widening concentric circles. Many of the Indians whom it touched would never hear of the young West Point graduate whose body was filled with so many arrows that he resembled a pincushion. The young man also was probably a stranger to Brevet Brigadier General William S. Harney, who was at that time enjoying an extended leave with his family in Paris. The case of the captured cow, out on the remote plains of the West, and the disturbance that followed, sent its shock waves all the way to France. On October 24 Harney received orders to report to Washington for an assignment which would take him to the scene of the trouble as the head of a punitive expedition. The action would commence, stated the orders, "as soon as the navigation of the Missouri river opens in the spring."

In Harney the War Department knew it had an experienced man. He had accompanied General Atkinson on his trip up the Missouri River in 1825, and he was a veteran of the Blackhawk War and the second Florida War (1837). He had also fought under Taylor in the Mexican War. And now on Christmas Eve, 1854, the General said goodbye to his family in their Paris residence and commenced a new assignment, one that would thoroughly establish his reputation as an Indian fighter. Harney, who was not a West Pointer, had a lifelong reputation for his understanding of the Indians, and he earned their respect as a hard fighter who was also just. As he left for the new assignment, some thoughts must have crossed his mind about young shavetails, fresh from "the Point," who hungered for a chance to make names for themselves fighting Indians on the American High Plains.

Experienced fur traders along the upper Missouri who learned of the Grattan affair probably shared his opinions. The demise of the cow, or "pinto buffalo" as the Indians thought of beef, was to disrupt a relative calm that had long prevailed along the river. Within a few years the Indians were to receive such military pressure and to find their domain so restricted, that they no longer could participate in the fur trade and, one by one, the traders would close down operations and abandon their outposts to the Indians or the ravages of the Dakota climate.

THREE

"We'll Never Forgive Old Harney"

In the spring of 1855 the upper Missouri country was once more a place of interest to the War Department. It was thirty years since General Atkinson had dismissed the necessity of troops in that region on grounds that the British menace was no longer significant and the Indians were not sufficiently hostile to be put in protective custody. But now the case of the Mormon cow stood as a symbol of new difficulties; the two races were colliding and bloodshed already had resulted in a number of minor instances. If white traffic were to flow westward under the terms of the Laramie Treaty, travelers and their property would have to be protected. This could be accomplished by military convoys or by sending troops against the refractory tribes. The latter course was chosen, and on March 22, 1855, General Harney was given command of an expeditionary force with orders to strike the Sioux. The day after his appointment he asked Major D. H. Vinton of the Quartermaster's Office at St. Louis for a report on the suitability of Fort Pierre, Nebraska Territory, as a main base for the coming operations.

The initial response to Harney's request was negative. Vinton had a long talk with John B. Sarpy, one of the partners in the American Fur Company, who expressed doubts that Fort Pierre was large enough to house a force of any size. Even if troops were encamped around the place, there was a very meager supply of grass, no soil suitable for raising corn or other fodder, and the nearest fuel supply was twenty miles away. However, said Sarpy, despite such limitations, he knew of no other point along the river better suited for a base from which to launch this particular operation.

This cautious endorsement was strengthened by a statement from Honoré Picotte, one of the old-timers of the fur company, whose attachment for the place probably was sentimental. Even so, Picotte's feeling strengthened the conviction of military officers that the location of Fort Pierre had some virtues. Harney liked the place because of its "many positive advantages for immediate operations," while Quartermaster General Thomas S. Jesup saw a chance to save money by shipping army supplies to Fort Laramie via Fort Pierre, utilizing cheap water transportation part of the distance. Major Vinton agreed with his superior that some savings in transportation costs could be effected by making the contemplated move. Boats of three hundred tons or less had to be used. They could travel from St. Louis to Fort Pierre, a distance of just over 1,500 miles, for approximately seventy-five days a year, and from there it was only 325 miles by land to Fort Laramie. From the standpoint of maintaining communications with Fort Laramie, Vinton acknowledged that there was no better location along the Missouri River. Despite Sarpy's honest advice and some misgivings on the part of Army men, the government bought Fort Pierre on April 14, 1855, for $45,000. The price included the buildings, the protective pickets and all other lumber on the premises, as well as the "land in the vicinity." Delivery date was June 1, 1855.[1]

Toward the end of April the Secretary of War directed Harney to plot out a military reservation around the fort, one that would include an arable island a few miles below the post, and to supply a map that would define its limits. Accordingly, Lieutenant G. K. Warren of the Topographical Engineers surveyed an area of 310 square miles; he said only about fourteen were of any value. The young officer admitted that the fort was the only one in that part of the country suitable for immediate purposes, but he warned that so much money would have to be spent on it that to remove it later would be "an affair of doubtful expediency."[2] Meanwhile, six companies of the Second Infantry were ordered to occupy the fort, and with that a long series of frustrations commenced. The problem of getting there developed into a logistical nightmare that cast grave doubts on the real value of utilizing river transportation and resulted in no little acrimony among the parties involved.

No sooner were the orders issued for a troop movement than Harney complained about the unusually low level of the Missouri River. The oldest river pilots, he said, assured him that there was no point in starting before the June rise, and even then only vessels of the lightest draft could be employed. The Government responded by buying two light-draft side-wheelers, the *William Baird* and the *Grey Cloud*, each drawing twenty-eight inches of water and able to move 350 tons in four and one-half feet of water. Every vessel available around St. Louis was chartered for the expedition. The "Big Muddy" answered the challenge so successfully that not a single vessel reached its objective with a full cargo. The Government-owned side-wheelers, heavy and cumbersome, did not reach Fort Pierre until August 20, while the others jettisoned portions of their freight along the way, trying to lighten the load enough to proceed. One of the chartered steamers, carrying troops from Fort Leavenworth, sank in nine feet of water. Although there was no loss of life, all the public stores aboard were lost. The first boat to arrive was the *Arabia*, which made Fort Pierre by July 7, carrying 109 officers and men. Other steamers turned up sporadically until late August. As the latter arrived they were joined by two companies under Captains Charles S. Lovell and Alfred Sully who marched their men across from Fort Ridgely, Minnesota.[3] That spring Indian Agent Alfred J. Vaughan went as far upriver as Fort Union, and he was struck by the condition of the river. It was lower, he said, than "ever had been known before by the oldest settler in the country." [4] For its summer campaign of 1855 the Army had selected an exceedingly poor year in which to utilize water transportation.

While Harney was unhappy over the maddening delays that plagued him, he was not at all surprised; he had been in the Army too long for that. In the early days of June he predicted that not much was going to be accomplished during the coming summer, and he lodged the blame in a familiar place. Congress, he said, had debated too much about authorizing the needed personnel for the expedition, and consequently the forces were not yet equipped or organized for their task. Gloomily he assumed that chastisement of the Sioux would have to await another season because the only other possibility, a winter campaign at the base of the Rocky Mountains, was far too risky to be considered.[5] Nevertheless, he felt that he had to make some kind of a showing, and in August he led a little army of some 600 men out of Fort Kearny, Nebraska, in search of hostile Sioux Indians.

By September 2 he came to a place known as Ash Hollow, along the Oregon Trail, where he learned that Little Thunder and his band of Brulé Sioux were camped a few miles away on Blue Water Creek. Remembering his own slogan expressed a few days earlier, "By God, I'm for battle—no peace," the General made ready to fight. Early the following morning, Lieutenant Colonel Philip St. George Cooke was dispatched to the enemy's rear with four mounted companies, and when Harney was sure escape had been cut off, he moved in. Quite sensibly, Little Thunder came forward with a white flag and expressed an interest in some talk, only to learn that the conditions were impossible. The Chief was asked to deliver all the young hell-raisers he could not control, those who had been raiding along the Oregon Trail, and white justice would deal with them. Unable to solve such a dilemma, Little Thunder decided upon the more honorable of the two solutions and returned to his men, ready for battle.

The result was a massacre, although in white annals it has been recorded as a battle. "I never saw a more beautiful thing in my life," wrote one infantryman, adding in mild apology, "We, of necessity, killed a great many women and children." More formally, Harney reported eighty-six killed, five wounded and seventy women and children prisoners; his losses were four killed and seven wounded. The score posted, he established a small place called Fort Grattan, and then moved on to Fort Laramie to talk with other Sioux chiefs.[6]

At Laramie he again demanded custody of young braves who

had recently robbed a stagecoach and the return of stolen animals. "They begged piteously to be spared and offered to comply with all my demands," reported the officer who had just insured his reputation as a tough Indian fighter at Ash Hollow. The ultimatum made, he marched his men in the general direction of the Missouri River, looking for any more Sioux who felt warlike.[7]

During the weeks that Harney was on the march hunting for Indians to chastise, elements of the Second Infantry straggled into Fort Pierre and tried to make themselves as comfortable as possible until they received further orders. According to one officer the resources of the embryonic community were not as advertised. Farm Island, carefully included in the military reservation because of its reputed agricultural capacities, was a disappointment. Instead of finding 500 acres under cultivation, Lieutenant Thomas Wright reported that only about five acres had been cleared, and only about three of them showed any signs of productivity. A few potatoes struggled for existence, but most had surrendered to the grasshoppers by the time the troops arrived. A scattering of cucumbers had survived the drought, but the corn was judged to be "of no account," and Wright ordered it cut green and stacked for cattle fodder during the coming winter.[8] It became clear at an early date that the men were not going to be able to live off the land and that food supplies, in quantity, would have to be hauled in at great expense. The logistical problem was growing.

Nor was the fort a haven for the weary. It was small, never having been intended for military use, and it was in an advanced state of decay. That additional quarters would be required had been anticipated in part, and the steamers had brought up a quantity of portable or prefabricated houses. Augustus Meyers, a young musician in the Second Infantry, remembered the housing problem vividly in later years. The flimsy barracks were one-room single-story houses whose floor beams sagged under their live weight, and whose walls were three-quarter inch boards set into grooves of two-by-three studdings. Into each of them some thirty men were crowded. There was no interior finishing, no insulation of any kind, and even the thin tarpaper roof invited cold. Each house had two wood-burning sheet-iron stoves with the stovepipes passing directly through the inflammable roof. But they were not enough to warm these cardboard houses, as Meyers called them, when the blizzards came. Painted red and perched on wooden posts two feet above the ground, the buildings looked like henhouses; in the words of the bitter musician, "The architect of these shelters was indirectly the cause of much suffering." About the only places of warmth were the log huts the men built as company kitchens, but since there were no messrooms even mealtimes were uncomfortable. Commissioned officers found that rank had few privileges when it came to housing, for their quarters were made in the same manner except that they were smaller and were divided into two rooms by a paper-thin partition.[9]

To add to the discomfort of the officers-in-charge at reconstituted Fort Pierre, General Harney arrived. The old campaigner left Fort Laramie on September 29 and marched along the White Earth River, through Brulé Sioux and Cheyenne country, without turning up any "Indian sign." Because it was too late in the season to venture into the Powder River country or along the Little Missouri, he headed for Fort Pierre where he hoped to winter his command. Upon his arrival on October 19, he learned that the place would not accommodate the four companies of dragoons and the ten of infantry present. It was much smaller than he had been led to expect, he told headquarters, and it was in a much more dilapidated condition than represented.[10] Worse than that, the officers who commanded the fort while he was out campaigning had done little or nothing to get it in shape for the winter. One can imagine his mounting indignation as he inspected what he found after a tiresome march from Fort Laramie.

A few of the portable cottages had been nailed together, but none of the kitchens were ready, and the latrine situation, so near and dear to the hearts of the military, was in a deplorable condition. In graphic terms he told the Adjutant General of the Army that the latrines were 250 yards from the nearest building, and that nocturnal trips were especially hazardous since "the surface of the earth was covered with human excrement and very offensive." The animals, as well as the troops, had been neglected; there was almost no wood or forage in the neighborhood, and no efforts to rectify the situation were in evidence. Not only were such supplies more than twenty miles away, but the river had to be crossed to reach them, and there was not even a rowboat available. Colonel W. R. Montgomery of the Second Infantry, who had commanded the post during the summer, had taken the fort's only two rowboats when he departed for Fort Leavenworth. "I have never visited a post where so little had been done for the comfort, convenience and necessities of the troops as at this place, when the length of time and number of troops present are considered," Harney wrote in bitter complaint.[11]

The General's wrath was impressive, and his junior officers must have kept their distances when they could. Young Augustus Meyers regarded the tall, powerfully built, always erect officer with awe. The white beard, the closely cut white hair, the fierce blue eyes, prompted the Indians to call him the "Great White Chief," and to enter his den was not a duty savored by the troops. "Whenever it was my turn as orderly at the adjutant's office," wrote Meyers, "one of my duties was to bring the general, in a sealed envelope, the 'countersign' or watchword for the night. When I approached him and saluted, and said 'General, the countersign,' he would reply in his gruff stentorian voice, 'Lay it on the table.' I was always glad to hustle out of his presence." [12]

While Harney's verbal assessment of the situation he found at Fort Pierre probably was quite colorful, he selected the word "unfortunate" when reporting to Army headquarters. "It was unfortunate that the steamers purchased to transport the troops here were entirely too large for the purpose; it was unfortunate the troops did not arrive in this country earlier; it was unfortunate they were stopped here; and most unfortunate of all, was the absence of a command of energy, experience and industry." [13] Major Montgomery, the object of the General's wrath, had been fortunate in the arrival of orders removing him from the unhappy scene.

Angered by delays and the dilatory tactics of those at the fort, Harney ordered the formation of an examining board a day or so after his arrival. It met from October 22 to 25 to determine the condition of the establishment as it was turned over to the Government. The officers agreed that the pickets on the north and east sides were rotted off at ground level and were falling down, that the mill was worn out and nearly valueless and that the place in general was in a bad state of repair. It was the board's conclusion that a sum of $22,022 would be required to put the fort in acceptable condition.[14] In addition to the survey of buildings and grounds, the whole question of suitability of location was reexamined. Captain P. T. Turnley of the Quartermaster's Department examined the land for eight miles above and below the fort, looking for building timber, fuel and grass and "found absolutely nothing worth hauling." [15] Captain Stewart Van Vliet, reporting to Turnley from the east side of the river—he called it the "civilized side"—thought the climate improved merely by crossing the river. "How the deuce any one in his sane mind can prefer the bleak plains of Fort Pierre, to the shelter of the woods, I cannot imagine," reported Assistant Quartermaster Van Vliet. "If I were the General, I would send every company away from the post with the exception of one or two." [16]

Charles E. Galpin, representing the American Fur Company, took exception to Army complaints about the purchased property. After examining Turnley's report on estimated repairs necessary to bring Fort Pierre up to Army standards, he remarked that his company had represented the place as being in good order only as a trading post. It was not meant to be a military post, and since twice the amount of supplies and the number of troops anticipated had arrived, there was, of course, some crowding. As to the rotten pickets and broken-down sawmill he said: "Certainly the Government did not mean to purchase a new fort." However, his company was willing to make an adjustment, and he agreed that existing structures on old foundations could be put in good condition for $3,000.[17] Turnley disagreed, and recommended that $20,520 ought to be deducted from the price the Government agreed to pay for the fort.[18]

Captain Turnley must have been disarmed by Galpin's response. The old-timer admitted that as a resident of the country for some sixteen years he could state: "Fort Pierre is a barren and exhausted place. It has long been established and everything like timber and fuel has been long since consumed." He admitted freely that aside from these limitations "it is the most inconvenient locality to get supplies to from other posts, that you can well find on the river." [19] By inference Army men were given to understand that the place was no better or worse than Sarpy had said it was, and that a deal was a deal. Major W. R. Montgomery, who had commanded the fort during the summer but was now at a safe distance from Harney, sympathized with Galpin's point of view and called the Quartermaster General's refusal to confirm the purchase as "the worst kind of taste, not to say want of good faith." Montgomery admitted the post was not in the best of repair, but thought it did not need rebuilding. He believed the establishment had served its purpose and had well returned the price paid for it. He strongly recommended payment as agreed upon, and even though eventually it might prove to be a bad bargain, "it is no time now to use it meanly." [20]

The season was getting late; there was not much Harney could do now but to get his troops through the winter. His men agreed that the Government's purchase was a typical military administrative blunder, and as they did their best to throw together makeshift shelters for the winter they sang a little doggerel to salve their feelings:

> Oh, we don't mind the marching,
>   nor the fight do we fear,
> But we'll never forgive old Harney
>   for bringing us to Pierre.
> They say old Shotto [Chouteau] built it,
>   but we know it is not so;
> For the man who built this bloody ranche,
>   is reigning down below.[21]

Six companies of the Sixth Infantry and two companies of cavalry were sent upriver about six miles where they built log houses on the east bank and managed to stay alive until spring.

They were better off than those who stayed at the fort and lived in portable houses. By the end of November the river was frozen thick enough to permit wagons to cross it, and the temperature dropped so far that the inside walls of the "portables" were covered with hoarfrost. By digging trenches around them and banking earth against the flimsy buildings the floors were made a little warmer. Because of the intense cold, inspections were held indoors. "To expose ourselves, even for ten minutes on parade out of doors without furs," wrote Augustus Meyers, "would have resulted in frost-bitten ears and noses." He documented his assertion with the case of three of his fellow soldiers who deserted and tried to reach civilization. "They perished before they had gone a hundred miles and their skeletons were found the following summer by a scouting party." Rude shelters of brushwood were built for the horses, but it was not enough to combat the bitter winter weather. Forage was so scarce the men stripped bark from trees as a substitute, but their best efforts were of no avail. The cavalry units lost more than a third of their animals that first winter.[22]

Soldiers at Fort Pierre soon discovered that theirs was a fight for survival, and the first goal to be achieved was to live until the coming of spring. Thin army blankets were no match for the cold, and as fast as possible the men bought buffalo robes from neighborhood Indians. These could be had for around $3, and a deer hide came to about $1 less. As the winter deepened the company tailor began to make fur clothing for those who had to stand duty outside. Buffalo coats, beaver skin mittens, buffalo skin boots, and fur caps with long earlaps became the uniform of the day. One trooper purchased a complete outfit of buffalo hide: boots, pantaloons, jacket and cap. His attire was so thoroughly of fur that the others dubbed him "Standing Buffalo." When they slept under their robes, the men too with them haversacks filled with rations for, if left exposed, the bread would freeze so hard by morning that only an axe would cut it. The necessity of buffalo for man's survival in Nebraska Territory was a fact that seemed to go without saying for the men of Harney's command.

When the weather moderated the soldiers, many of whom were quite young, visited the Indians encamped around the fort. As their fascination grew their tendency to imitate the natives went beyond copying their clothing. To amuse themselves they sometimes wrapped themselves in blankets and sat around council fires built behind their own quarters, "smoking the pipe" and delivering orations. From time to time imitation war dances, complete with painted faces and accompanied by chants and drumbeats, provided more activity than smoking or talking. When this was not exciting enough, imitation war parties were gotten up and prisoners were "scalped" and "burned at the stake," creating scenes probably gained from boyhood reading, for none of these men had yet seen a "wild" Indian.[23]

In late autumn three companies of the Second Infantry (including that of Augustus Meyers) were sent across the river and several miles upstream to build log cabins not far from the companies of the Sixth who also were spending the winter in temporary quarters.[24] About twenty lodges of Yanktonnais Sioux were camped nearby, and it was these Indians the troopers visited, imitated and came to know. "We soon had a well-beaten path through the deep snow leading to the camp," wrote Meyers. The soldiers watched Indian games with interest and then tried to teach the Indians a few of their own favorites. It was frustrating to learn that the natives simply could not understand the fundamentals of poker. The attempted games went badly astray because the Indians admired the jacks—which they dubbed "chiefs" —much more than kings, and took a firm stand that any card, even a deuce, could beat a queen, which they held to be a mere squaw. Therefore, the boys invented a simple game in which the greatest number of spots on a card took the trick, and since the Indians could count up to ten and no disturbing pictures were involved, they came to enjoy it.

When interest in card games flagged, the Indians showed off their favorite trophies, usually scalps. Courteously, the men admired the long black hair, the soft tanned texture of the skin, and were pleased that their hosts were diplomatic enough to hold back any white souvenirs. Often the Indians kept their prized possessions in a buckskin bag, and usually the most treasured was a paper, often provided by a white trader or guide, that served as an endorsement of character for the bearer. The documents would tell of the owner's faith, reliability and good habits. One of the Indians had several such papers, one of which he would show last because it always brought the greatest smiles and signs of pleasure from white readers. It said: "Beware of this Indian, Big Crow, he is a thief and a liar, and will murder you if he gets a chance. Take warning." [25]

By midwinter the paralyzing cold gained an ally in the form of scurvy. After nearly eight months of a saltmeat diet with no fresh vegetables or fruits, some of the men became pale and listless, their gums bled, their teeth loosened, body joints swelled and flesh softened. Serious cases were sent to the crowded hospital where lime juice was available from the medical stores. After great efforts, some potatoes were hauled in from "the States" and were administered to the sick in the form of raw scrapings mixed with vinegar.[26]

Despite Harney's dispersal of his men to points above and below Fort Pierre, the violent land gave a convincing demonstration of its unfriendliness, and the General redoubled his efforts to find a less difficult place for his men to live. His earlier convictions about Fort Pierre were borne out daily as he watched his men and animals suffer, and all during the winter, weather permitting, he continued his search. In January he thought he had found a better location near the Big Sioux River, but by February he was again convinced that Fort Pierre was the best place for a large depot. Within a month he was once again sure that the place had insuperable disadvantages because there was no good steamboat landing at that point, and he decided to move his command south to a point near old Fort Lookout below the great bend of the river. By the end of June 1856 he had changed his mind again, now favoring a location even farther south, some thirty miles above the mouth of the *L'eau-qui-court* (Niobrara) River, and on the west bank. If the War Department should approve, he suggested the new post be given the name Fort Randall in honor of the late Daniel Randall, Colonel and Deputy Paymaster General of the Army.[27]

Harney's search for a suitable location at which to establish a major supply base was animated by his conviction that such a fort was a necessary part of his plans to control the Sioux. He felt that his campaign of 1855 had given the Army an advantage it should retain, and that all the Sioux bands, treated as one Indian nation, should be kept in check by a single command designated for that purpose. Giving the War Department the benefit of his experience, he stated that the average Indian would struggle until every avenue of escape was closed, but once convinced that there was no alternative "he gracefully submits to his fate." Therefore, a treaty with the Sioux should be made and it should be enforced.[28]

The Secretary of War, Jefferson Davis, gave his approval to such a treaty in late December 1855. Stating an ancient principle that the President was disposed to treat kindly an unfortunate and untutored race, but that repeated outrages necessitated some kind of discipline, he advised Harney to proceed. The President, and Davis, understood that the several offending bands, now weak and dispirited, had thrown themselves upon the clemency of the Government, and in order to prevent further effusion of blood the American Government was ready to settle past differences.[29] By early March 1856, the weather had moderated sufficiently for the Indians to travel, and at that time nine bands of Sioux assembled at Fort Pierre, ready to talk.

On the first of March Harney addressed the assembled Indians. Considering their attendance record at later treaties, this one was well represented. About three thousand members of the Hunkpapa, Miniconjou, Brulé, Sans Arc, Blackfeet, Yanktonnais, Two Kettles, Yankton and Oglala bands came to hear what the "Great White Chief" had to say. Only Big Head's band of Yanktonnais and some of the Oglalas did not attend. Harney's talk was tough, so tough that afterwards Two Bears, a Yanktonnais chief, remarked: "Your manners are very hard, very severe." The white-maned officer sounded much as General William T. Sherman would a decade later, scolding, warning, threatening. Harney admitted that many of the young white men were unruly, but that they were punished for their bad conduct; he demanded the same of the Indians. If the Chiefs were not able to carry out such discipline, Harney offered to do it for them. "Every nation must have laws, and the people must obey them," he insisted. More scolding came for the shabby manner in which the natives had treated Indian Agent Alfred Vaughan, for the insults they had heaped upon him when he tried to help them. Now, said the General, the Great Father was much offended by such conduct, and he had ordered punishment which now would be meted out.[30]

Harney's erect figure and impressive white beard framing a fierce countenance might well have been enough to instill his listeners with awesome respect. But in his efforts to be convincing he tried to employ what educators later would call "visual aids," and in so doing he somewhat damaged his case. While discussing the great power of the American Government and the many sources of "big medicine" available to that organization, it occurred to him that he might take advantage of chloroform, just then coming into use. "I will show you the great power of the white man, I will show you how he can even kill and bring to life again," the General promised. There was a stir of interest in the audience as he called in one of the surgeons and ordered him to put a dog to sleep, cautioning him to use the anesthetic carefully. When the animal was soundly asleep, magician Harney invited the various chiefs to satisfy themselves that the victim had departed for another world. He then ordered the surgeon to perform a resurrection. To the great dismay of the management, the dog did not respond to treatment, even when the doctor nipped its tail with a pincers. With a show of amazement tinged with sarcasm, the chiefs clapped their hands to their mouths and exclaimed: "Medicine too strong, too strong."[31] Science failing, Harney closed up the laboratory and retreated to the forensic arena. The talks went on for nearly a week.

The Treaty of Fort Pierre, dated March 8, 1856, provided that the Sioux would deliver for trial to the nearest post any tribesman guilty of killing whites, and that they would promptly surrender any stolen property along with the thief. Indians henceforth were to stay clear of established roads used by the whites and to avoid Pawnee country. The chiefs were ordered to control their respective bands and to report to the military when they failed; to facilitate such discipline the Indians agreed to tell the Army authorities which chiefs they recognized as their leaders. In another effort to avoid trouble, the whites ordered that the Indian trade in horses and mules cease because "it encourages young men to steal." In return for these concessions Harney promised that the Sioux would be protected from the whites, that their annuities, withheld for disciplinary reasons, would be restored, and that all Indians currently being held for murder, robbery or other high crimes would be released upon compliance with the treaty. As an additional benefit, any Indians desiring to walk the white man's path even more precisely by engaging in farming, would be provided with draft animals, ploughs and seeds. By selecting a place near some post, ploughing service would be provided by the whites.[32]

The Secretary of the Interior asked Thomas S. Twiss, Agent for the Upper Platte Superintendency, to make an estimate of the money needed to carry out the treaty. Twiss reported that there were some seven hundred chiefs and designated soldiers in the nine bands, and that to provide them with arms, clothing and provisions would cost $63,000. An additional $1,000 per tribe would be necessary if agricultural assistance were to be provided. Viewing a total estimate of $72,000, Secretary Robert McClelland concluded that $100,000 was a good round figure that would cover all costs and take care of added contingencies.[33] Doane Robinson, South Dakota historian, later wrote that the treaty was never ratified, but that goods were provided "for a certain period."[34] Again, as in the Laramie Treaty of 1851, the Senate failed to support agreements made by treatymakers in the field.

Military planners apparently thought that the Sioux problem had been set at rest. The record showed that Harney had been dispatched to find and punish members of that tribe; had done this in a vigorous manner at Ash Hollow; had then searched the country for more warlike natives to chastise and, not finding them, had called the Sioux leaders into Fort Pierre where a treaty favorable to the whites had been wrung from presumably humbled warriors. On June 20, 1856, Adjutant General Samuel Cooper notified Harney that the objects of the Sioux expedition had been accomplished and, after sufficient troops were posted and supplied at points where the treaty could be enforced, he was to close his operations against the Sioux and return to Fort Leavenworth to await further orders.[35] Fort Randall, located in the southern portion of modern South Dakota, was to be the supply base for carrying out the treaty stipulations. Again, as in 1825, the War Department showed no inclination to advance the military frontier to the upper Missouri River country.

In accordance with orders, Harney began to move men and supplies from Fort Pierre to the new post. In late June Lieutenants D. S. Stanley and George Paige landed eighty-four recruits of the Second Infantry at Handy's Point on the Missouri. They began to build Fort Randall on a bench about 150 feet high and a half mile from the waterfront. The river at this point was nearly a thousand yards wide, and it provided a much more accessible landing place for steamboats. In the meantime Charles Galpin of the American Fur Company was hired to dismantle the portable cottages along with any other buildings at Fort Pierre that might yield usable building materials. He converted so much of it to his own purposes that the Government withheld more than half of the contract money, the remainder of the salvage finding its way to Fort Randall. When Galpin's demolition crew had finished its work, the Indians moved in and destroyed what was left. By mid-May 1857 when the last troops left, Fort Pierre was a ruin, noticed briefly by steamboat passengers as they passed and reminisced over its former role in the conquest of the West.[36]

Toward the end of July 1856, two companies of the Second Infantry and four of the Second Dragoons arrived at Fort Randall to make up the post's first garrison. The newly appointed commanding officer, Colonel Francis Lee, soon discovered that fort building could be as frustrating as chasing elusive Indians. There were so many desertions that construction almost came to a halt, and there were fears that the coming winter would bring as much suffering as that recently experienced by the troops around Fort Pierre. In early September Lee reported that in a ten-day period fourteen fully armed Dragoons had deserted, taking along their horses. The loss of animals was more an annoyance than a handicap for, at the moment, it was the manpower shortage that plagued the Colonel. He complained that during the summer "through some wonderful oversight" troops were sent from Fort

Leavenworth to Fort Riley, where there were few or no horses, and horses were brought upriver to Fort Randall by employed civilians, all of which resulted in confusion and needless expense. When rumors reached Leavenworth that desertions and discontent at Fort Randall perhaps led to the commanding officer's door, Lee answered with astonished indignation that "I have never seen more harmony, better content, and spirit of satisfaction pervading any similar body of gentlemen [his officers]. . . . All are entirely satisfied with this station." [37]

During these late September days more troops continued to reach the newly established paradise for commissioned officers. Lieutenant R. F. Hunter and Captain Alfred Sully brought in 114 from Fort Pierre. In a matter of only eight years the latter officer would have reached the rank of general and would be in command of an expedition against the Sioux of the Missouri River country. He would at that time bestow upon himself an honor usually reserved to brave officers who had passed on to their reward, that of having a fort named after them.[38] But now the problem was not so much the Sioux as it was a fight for survival against the climate and the loneliness along the Missouri.

In the summer and autumn of 1856, when Fort Randall was being built, there were few indications that the frontier of military posts would soon penetrate deeper into the upper Missouri country. The sectional issue was heightening, and the man on the street was much more interested in the national election in which a new party, called Republican, was asking voters to favor "Free Men, Free Soil, and Frémont." The words "Kansas" and "Nebraska" were on the tongues of men, but the connotation was political and symbolic, and even those who thought seriously about such places as homes for settlers tended to point their minds due west rather than north. Boosters of a young Iowa town called Sioux City talked about the coming flood of emigrants, but in middecade there was little evidence to show that it was more than Chamber of Commerce exuberance. For the moment, Army men viewed the situation correctly: There was not a sufficient number of white residents along the upper reaches of the river to merit troops in quantity.

The changing nature of frontier expansion was, in itself, beginning to alter the thinking of military planners. Jefferson Davis, the Secretary of War, commented upon this development in 1856, when he wrote that the frontier country then opening up was far different from that of yesteryear. From the time settlers began their westward advance from the Atlantic shores, they had found fertile land that readily yielded a living both to themselves and the military elements who came along to afford protection. Davis justified the expense of frontier troops on the ground that the national treasury was more than repaid by the productive results of the land put to the plough. But now the situation was different. The trans-Missouri region did not hold the same promise; indeed, its bad reputation as a desert had been long established. Posts in advance of settlement in this new country were expensive to maintain and usually were so small that they did little good. Worse, Davis thought, they could never be surrounded by a successful farming population. He firmly believed the Desert theory and held that reconnaissance reports of the preceding two years had substantiated his belief. He concluded, therefore, that the situation being what it was, the War Department had to revise its policy.

Instead of dispersing troops in small garrisons where the isolation and a hostile population would make them weak from the outset, Davis suggested the establishment of larger posts in more fertile regions, located near rail or water transportation. From such places strong mobile detachments might be dispatched to patrol the plains in the green season and to withdraw after rebellious Indians had been punished. This would give emigrants protection when they needed it: in the travel season. He argued that rather than being of any help, small, isolated posts were a detriment because their power radiated only a short distance, and the Indians developed a disdain for the Government instead of a fear of it. Also, the constant building and abandoning of small posts in a westerly direction took all the soldier's time and made him more a common laborer than a military man. Because of the continual movement, no trooper had any interest in improving his abode, for he knew that in a relatively short time he would have to abandon the place in favor of some new location. The Secretary thought that if the troops were quartered more comfortably, in more populated areas where there were more advantages of civilization, discipline problems would be much reduced.[39]

The whole plan reminded Davis of the French occupation of Algeria. The French, he said, wisely left the desert region to the nomadic tribes and established strong garrisons near cultivated regions from which troops might conduct expeditions. Strong columns had moved against troublesome tribesmen in Algeria, and the natives had been so impressed by French power that it was seldom necessary to punish a tribe more than once.

The desert theme was easily applied to the American scene, for these were the years when the Army was experimenting with camels in the West. As the 100th meridian was approached the aridity, distance and wild tribesmen of the region caused military men to make parallels such as those presented by the Secretary of War. From their vantage point in the passage of time, such conclusions were perfectly reasonable and understandable. The Great American Desert idea was firmly fixed in the American mind, and it would persist for another twenty years. Neither military men nor the average man on the street could know that the frontier movement, progressing at a walk as it had for years, would break into a gallop in the next few years. Just ahead lay the rush to Pike's Peak and the spread of gold mining throughout the Rocky Mountains, especially into Montana. With that development men poured westward, and then north toward the Canadian boundary. Suddenly the Sioux were surrounded, hemmed in by white men on all sides, and their reactions were the same as that of any people enveloped by the enemy.

In a few short years the role of the Missouri River in westward movement underwent an enormous change. For a generation it was pivotal in the plans of the military men whose job it was to guard the advancing northwestern frontier.

FOUR

Turbulent Tribesmen

With the establishment of Fort Randall in 1856, the Army not only physically retreated downriver, but it also indicated its apparent endorsement of the Desert theory. Colonel Francis Lee, who had held a commission for nearly thirty-five years, took a view widely accepted by his own generation that the High Plains region lacked many of the essentials sought by settlers. He admitted that the site of Fort Randall, which he commanded, was as good as any in that vicinity, but that it lacked timber, building stone and forage. Referring to the Secretary's recent recommendation that forts be placed nearer settled areas, he suggested that the upper Missouri River Indians could be controlled just as easily from the neighborhood of Sioux City, and that a post in that area could better protect the current westward emigration.

Lee argued that the availability of river transportation did not solve the problem of supplying posts farther inland because the river itself was unreliable. Not only was it frozen part of the year and too low at other times, but it was not well-suited to the steamers of the day. The Colonel cited the *Morton,* a side-wheeler, as an example of a vessel not suited to the Missouri's moods, and he charged that it was compelled to tie up with every puff of the wind. On one occasion when the *Morton* did arrive, Lee thanked the Quartermaster's office at St. Louis for the supply of corn "accidentally sent." Nonarrival of boats meant that wagons had to be used, and the Colonel was only one of many Army officers who complained about the high cost of wheeled transportation.[1] At this time civilians were asking $1.25 a hundredweight to haul supplies from Sioux City, a distance of about 140 miles.

Even though Fort Randall was not a great distance from Sioux City, its location was relatively isolated. Scurvy, the curse of many a frontier soldier, became a serious problem during the fort's first winter. The post surgeon reported that only the arrival of some potatoes from St. Louis, hauled the last hundred miles by wagon and in a frozen condition, had prevented serious illness among the men. By April, wild artichokes were available, and when made into pickles they served as a satisfactory antiscorbutic. Lime juice, green onions, dried fruits and molasses were used, although the doctor felt that in themselves they would not prevent the disease.[2] In addition to a limited diet the men were miserably housed, a factor that generated much complaint and some desertions. Colonel Lee told his superiors that there was not a single foot of plankage at the fort, and that the rude huts were covered with earth to provide some warmth. True, a sawmill had been dispatched, but low water had stopped its progress en route. Lee wondered what purpose it would serve when it arrived; the only available timber was green cottonwood and it made very poor lumber.[3]

In the best of military traditions the men cursed their situation and then philosophically settled down to the daily fight for survival against the elements. Since they were located fairly close to the frontier of agricultural settlement, and some distance from the more hostile Sioux, the assignment was essentially that of garrison duty. The day-to-day routine included the usual drills, with dress parades on Sunday. On occasion wagon companies asked for escorts to the village of Sioux City, and a few lucky soldiers enjoyed a brief escape from their exile. The nearby Yankton Indians were generally friendly, but from time to time there were minor disturbances that called for small detachments of troops, a duty that was welcomed as a means of escaping the boredom of daily routine. Those who were not called upon to adjudicate Indian difficulties or convoy wagons had to find their entertainment on the post. As usual there was a small band, including musician Augustus Meyers who came down from Fort Pierre with his unit. Commanding officers realized the morale-building value of these men and lent their unqualified support to the post bands. On one occasion Colonel Lee earnestly requested of the Adjutant General the return of one Thomas Gilmore, a deserter and a chronic drinker, on the ground that his musical talents compensated for his other deficiencies. "I would very much like to get him back," wrote the Colonel, "for I am informed that he probably is the *very best* Clarionet player in the Army and our Band needs that instrument badly." [4]

For those who wanted entertainment more stimulating than music appreciation, there was the inevitable bottle, a temptation that even talented clarinet players found hard to resist. As at other posts there was a sutler's store at Fort Randall, stocked with a wide variety of goods desired by the troops. The proprietor was permitted to sell a daily pint of ale or beer to each man, or, if the customer preferred, a gill of wine. The sutler was always under a great deal of pressure from his customers to provide something more stimulating, and in the end he yielded to the principle that the customer was always right. This necessitated a directive from Colonel Lee to sutler John B. S. Todd (a cousin of Mary Todd Lincoln), requesting that he import no more spirituous liquors than were required for private use (a figure that often reached startling proportions) and stating that subsequent consignments would be carefully examined as to alcoholic content. This effort to regulate morals generated a typical response from the enlisted men, and one of them later related the development: "An enterprising soldier's wife fixed up a small still in her quarters . . . and made a little corn whiskey which she sold to soldiers secretly; but she was informed on after a while and her distilling plant was destroyed." [5]

Fort Randall's period of loneliness was brief; even as it was being built the agricultural frontier was washing against the country which the fort was meant to guard. Sioux City journalists noted a surge in that village's commercial life during 1857, and particularly the brisk business done by the house of Frost, Todd and Company. In a single consignment that firm brought into town 7,567 buffalo robes, 739 beaver skins, 32 elk skins, 14 bear skins and 1 moosehide. Another index of activity was the increase in steamboat traffic, the figure having jumped from four arrivals in the 1856 season to seventeen by the end of July 1857.[6] Even more encouraging to local business interests was the news that Minnesota legislators had recently chartered an organization, known as the Dakota Land Company, which was interested in land along the Missouri River north of Sioux City.[7]

Captain John B. S. Todd, late of Company A, Sixth Infantry and more recently post sutler at Fort Randall, saw great economic possibilities in what soon would be known as Dakota, and he lost no time in launching his own campaign. In December 1857 he passed through Sioux City, accompanied by Man-Who-Strikes-the-Ree, Smutty Bear and thirteen lesser Sioux chiefs, bound for a conference with the Great Father at Washington.[8] Alexander H. Redfield, Agent for the Upper Missouri Agency, brought the Indians back to St. Louis in the spring and sent them upriver in mid-May aboard the *Spread Eagle*. He reported that by a treaty of April 19 the Yanktons had ceded to the Government their entire country, or about eleven million acres, "much of which is very fine for cultivation and grazing, and over which our bold and enterprising emigrants are resolved to spread." When the treaty was ratified by the Senate, a year later, Sioux City papers reported the size to be twelve million acres, at a cost of $1,650,000 or 13½¢ an acre, which was "a pretty good price for Uncle Sam to pay."[9] Meanwhile, in February, the Upper Missouri Land Company was organized by Captain Todd and his partner, D. M. Frost, along with several associates.

As the *Eagle* of Sioux City correctly predicted, "What a grand rush there will be across the Big Sioux at the first intelligence that the beautiful lands there are opened for squatters." The boomer spirit took over. Even before the treaty was signed, W. P. Holman, his son and others rushed to the future site of Yankton and built cabins, trying to anticipate the Missouri Land Company's desire to gain possession of that location. It took two Indian attacks, a warning from military authorities and a stern statement to the effect that no treaty of cession yet had been negotiated to persuade them to leave. In the next month, April, George D. Fiske and Samuel Mortimer, representing Todd and Company, claimed the right to settle and gained the honor of establishing the first permanent white settlement at Yankton.[10] The Holmans were only one of many families who tried to get there sooner. In June 1858 Agent Redfield found several squatters on Indian lands, busily trying to stake out the best property. They even moved into Indian camps, marking off homesites, and one group erected what Redfield called "a sort of a fortress for their protection" in the middle of a native village.[11]

As early as March 1857, Colonel Lee formally notified a "Mr. Stoker and others" that if they did not vacate the Indian lands upon which they were squatting "I will this spring send down a command of soldiers & *compel* you to leave, destroying every improvement you may have made." More than that, he said, the Yankton Indians would be told of the situation and they would be given more or less a free rein in running off the white intruders.[12] Despite such warnings illegal invasions continued. In the spring of 1858, after the treaty had been signed but during the one-year period in which the Indians were guaranteed undisturbed occupancy of their lands, Agent Redfield found it necessary to appeal to the Army for help. Major Hannibal Day, then in command at Fort Randall, promised to enforce the treaty stipulations, but the summer passed and the violations continued.

When Redfield arrived at Sioux City in September, having been upriver most of the summer, he learned that soldiers were waiting at Fort Randall with orders to take action against violators if the Agent would point out the squatters who were to be removed. He also heard that the Indians had commenced action on their own and had destroyed two or three squatter houses. Redfield returned to Fort Randall and began a march back down the river accompanied by fifty men commanded by Captain C. S. Lovell. In eight days they covered 120 miles during which Redfield "caused to be destroyed all the buildings and landmarks of the trespassers which I could find or hear of, and which could be destroyed. No resistance was met with, the intruders having all decamped." Most of the buildings were of little value, being only rude log huts with earthen roofs, and the only things of personal value that remained were a few haystacks which the troops burned. Redfield often found corner stakes, and promptly pulled them up, but he could do little to deface the ploughing that had been done.[13] As always, the squatters simply had fled in advance of the troops, only to return when the troops had passed through the country. Since the squatters left little to demolish, the re-establishment of their claims did not take long.

Redfield was deeply concerned at the turn of events. While the southern segment of the Yankton tribe seemed satisfied with the treaty, the others were quite distressed. On his trip downriver in September 1858, he tried to give presents to the Yankton Sioux at the site of old Fort Pierre, only to have the Indians refuse on the grounds that they feared punishment by tribesmen living to the north if they accepted. He met with the same refusal all the way down to Fort Randall; only Smutty Bear and Man-Who-Strikes-the-Ree were willing to take the proffered goods. It was a situation that had been growing for several years. Redfield had complained a year earlier that the abandonment of Fort Pierre was construed by the Indians to have resulted from fear. His predecessor, Alfred Vaughan, had found the Two Kettles band and the Upper Yanktonnais restless when he stopped at Fort Pierre in 1855. These were known as friendly Sioux, and the only way he could account for their surliness was the fact that troops were scheduled to occupy that place. The only Indians along the river who seemed to have no objections to military occupation were the Gros Ventres, near Fort Berthold, because they thought the troops would protect them from plains Sioux who periodically raided their villages. By 1856 Vaughan had correctly predicted the willingness of the Yanktons to sign a treaty, explaining that the game had been driven from their country and they had been forced to till the soil in order to live. Conditions, he said, had made them ready to yield to white talk. By doing so the Yanktons in effect joined the enemy and thus became victims of Sioux farther north whenever they were caught. It was this disregard by the whites for the docile Yanktons, and the growing restiveness of the other Sioux, that so worried Redfield and caused him to seek help from the troops at Fort Randall.[14]

Meanwhile, the situation in Mandan country was unsatisfactory, but it was not one that yet called for any large body of troops. North of the Mandans lay the trading post, Fort Union, where the Assiniboins, Crows and some Sioux still visited, although by the middle Fifties these Indians were becoming suspicious of the whites and were not as predictable as in former years. Rumors spread among them that presents and trade goods at that fort contained smallpox germs, and that to handle such items was death. Hundreds of Assiniboins had died from the disease. The Mandans also were declining in population, having numbered as many as five hundred lodges only a few years before and now mustering only thirty or forty. They wanted to join the Gros Ventres for protection, but were afraid that they might lose their identity when it came to doling out the annual annuity. The Rees, who lived near the Mandans and Gros Ventres, did not escape the smallpox. Redfield found their young men "wild and crazy with passion" from suffering, apt to do the most unexpected things and dangerous to be around. In June 1858, as Redfield was walking from the trading house to the river's edge, a group of braves accosted him and one of them placed the muzzle of his gun between the Agent's feet and fired. On the same visit one of the steamboat's passengers was fired upon by a young Ree.[15]

From the Yellowstone country all the way down the Missouri River to Fort Randall, there was dissatisfaction among the tribes. Captain Henry W. Wessells of the Second Infantry returned from detached service in the Yellowstone country in midsummer 1858 and furnished details. The Indians were unhappy over the growth of steamboating on the river and expressed the belief that it was to have been stopped north of Fort Pierre. As the Missouri River historian Phil Chappell later wrote, 1858 was a peak year for travel on the lower river—that is, below Sioux City—when some sixty regular packets and thirty or forty tramp steamers worked that territory, and the density of the traffic was beginning to make itself felt on the upper river.[16] As a form of protest, the seven bands of Sioux who normally received their annuity goods at Fort

Pierre now did so with great reluctance and would not sign receipts. The Upper Yanktons complained that goods were delivered to the lower villages and none were brought to them, whereupon Agent Redfield offered them tobacco, groceries and other provisions which they accepted only when he threatened to return the goods to the boat. Grumbling continued as the Indians received the goods, the loudest objection coming from those who held that the land being sold by lower Yanktons did not belong to them exclusively, but belonged to the Sioux nation as a whole. Henry Boller, who traveled upriver aboard the *Twilight* in 1858, described a stop that was made at Redfield's agency and a conference that took place aboard the vessel. "Those on shore indulged freely in remarks upon the deliberations of their chiefs; and among other pleasant suggestions, one fellow coolly proposed a general scalping of the whites! Although this humane project seemed to meet with universal favor, it was deemed inexpedient for the present." The vessel proceeded to Fort Pierre without any tonsorial ceremonies.[17]

Agent Redfield felt that he would not have been able to deliver his annuity goods safely in 1858 had it not been for the presence of a military escort. On that trip Captain Wessells, in command of forty soldiers from Fort Randall, accompanied him to Fort Union and back again. The Agent earnestly recommended the establishment of a permanent post in the heart of Sioux country, well up the river, where the warlike tribesmen could be disciplined and such weak Indians as the Arickaras, Gros Ventres and Mandans could be protected from their enemies.[18]

The increased restlessness of the Indians was a warning sign of coming national discomfort, a kind of muscle cramp at mid-continent, a growing pain, a puzzler for planners. The Desert theory, so recently reiterated by Jefferson Davis, was undergoing minor modifications in the late 1850's as settlement leaped across the plains to the mountain mining camps. Not only was the discovery of gold confirmed in Colorado in 1859, but in mid-July of that year the *Chippewa* moored a few miles below Fort Benton to establish a new head of steamboat navigation on the Missouri River. Colonel Alfred Vaughan, once described by a traveler as an amusing old man fond of exaggeration, stretched the truth only with regard to the river's length when he said of the *Chippewa's* feat: "The race was won, and the wished-for goal attained, and some six hundred miles added to the already almost interminable navigation of the mighty Missouri, a steamer having successfully breasted the current for a distance of thirty-one hundred miles from the Mississippi." [19]

John Floyd, Secretary of War, appreciated the significance of the waterway to Fort Benton. He fully believed that when the place was connected by road with Fort Walla Walla the Oregon country would achieve its desired connection with "the States." In his report of 1858, Floyd had described the area northwest of the Black Hills to the sources of the Missouri as a part of the country yet almost unknown to the whites. He recommended its exploration. Should this part of the West turn out to be suitable for road building, the combined land-water route, he predicted, "will be eventually one of the most important yet discovered between the Atlantic and Pacific for military purposes." [20] Any of the Sioux along the upper Missouri, whose literate friends were given to perusing government reports, would have found confirmation of old worries in Floyd's forecast. Even though white men were telling each other that Sioux country was a desert unsuitable for their kind of living, they had not taken into account the momentum of the frontier movement, a force that carried them westward in spite of their own doubts.

Army men had no illusions about the fertility of the soil on the High Plains, but they were aware that travel routes across that country would be used with increasing frequency, and they were cognizant of their role in protecting such roadways. In 1857, Lieutenant G. K. Warren conducted his explorations and reported to the Secretary of War that "the extreme frontiers of Nebraska are now near the western limit of the fertile portions of the prairie lands, and a desert space separates them from the fertile and desirable region in the western mountains." He acknowledged that the mountain slopes would be good for grazing, and he was convinced that small settlements would arise and would have to be supplied from the Nebraska and Missouri frontier.[21] This, inferentially, reiterated the old question of how best to meet these conditions in planning the advance of the military frontier. Residents of recently settled western areas, now safe from Indian attack, often were critical of continued occupancy of expensive forts long after the frontier had left them behind.[22] Floyd took the position, in 1857, that the present was a good time to select permanent locations on the Northwestern frontier because agricultural advance was now fairly well fixed, and there was little likelihood of such stations being overrun by population as in the past. These forts would become useless only when the tribes ceased to be a threat, or "disappear altogether." He thought that some policy of establishing western forts should be formulated, because the passage of each year made the importance of protecting long lines of communication to the Pacific Coast more important. Times had changed, he said; no longer did the hardy frontiersman venture forth on his own to take his stance in the wilderness, but instead he asked for Army protection. He suggested a "line of posts running parallel with our frontier, but near to the Indians' usual habitations, placed at convenient distance and suitable positions, and occupied by infantry." He thought five additional regiments would suffice.[23]

As the 1850's came to a close, there seemed to be general agreement among military officers that the country lying west of the Missouri River was unsuitable for agriculture as it was then practiced, but that as the more attractive lands beyond the "desert" were exploited by miners or grazers, certain travel routes would have to be maintained. When a traveler, Dr. Elias J. Marsh, examined the countryside along the Missouri in 1859 and commented that "The land is miserable and I think even civilized European farmers would find it difficult to draw their subsistence from it," he reflected an opinion long expressed by Army men.[24] Several possible routes connecting Fort Laramie with the river were examined, such as those along the Loup Fork, the Niobrara and White rivers, but none was found to be as practicable as that along the Platte Valley. In 1858, Captain A. A. Humphreys of the Topographical Engineers stated flatly that there were no good routes from the Missouri River westward to Fort Laramie or

South Pass above Fort Pierre.[25] By that time the War Department had decided in favor of connecting the headwaters of the Missouri and the Columbia by means of what was to be called the Mullan Road.

In the late autumn of 1859 Secretary of War John Floyd wrote that the military road from Fort Walla Walla to Fort Benton was half completed and that, except for the six hundred miles between these ports, steamboats could maintain a connection between the Atlantic and the Pacific. Theoretically he was correct. The Columbia was navigable in parts, but portages were necessary in at least two important sections, and the Missouri was navigable to Fort Benton only a portion of the year. Nevertheless, Floyd thought the route valuable to emigrants going west, and "in a military point of view it is of very great importance." He elaborated, saying that the most powerful Indian tribes lived at either end of the proposed roadway, and to keep them in a state of subjection would require facilities for transporting troops and materiel at a relatively small cost. He hoped that the river systems would provide a means of building up communities at their respective headwaters, which would lessen a need for troops and also would produce supplies for columns marching in that far country. He called the Mullan Road a necessity and a sound economy.[26]

It was a notion that found enthusiastic support at the stripling river town of Sioux City. A local editor admitted that a Pacific railroad was "a necessity of the age, and a work that will be accomplished in the present century," but he was also impressed by "what a magnificent route almost across the continent has nature provided in the Missouri and Columbia rivers." He thought a connecting railroad would link the Atlantic and Pacific oceans at a trifling cost, and provide a means of transportation that not only would give the military access to Indian country, but would utilize a "direct and safe" route to the Pacific in the event of foreign war.[27] Sioux City was, of course, the Gateway to the West.

Tribesmen of the Sioux nation did not share the enthusiasm of those who wanted to make the Missouri River a great avenue of commerce. Nor did they take kindly to the appearance of Army explorers and roadmakers. In June 1858 when Alexander Redfield stopped at Fort Union he heard similar complaints from the Assiniboins, who were alarmed at the prospect of a road through their country. "I assured them the Government would take nothing from them, nor permit them to be injured, without just compensation," wrote the Agent.[28] Such assurances did little to quiet Indian fears, and in the years that followed the complaints became more insistent. While at the Fort Berthold trading post in the summer of 1860, government explorer Lieutenant Henry E. Maynadier heard one of the Sioux chiefs address an assemblage in pointed language: "We are glad to have the traders, but we don't want you soldiers and roadmakers. The country is ours and we intend to keep it. Tell the Great Father we won't sell it, and tell him to keep his soldiers at home." Maynadier called it a tedious harangue and remarked that the Indians "richly deserve chastisement by the Government." [29]

While the upper river Sioux demonstrated their anger in a practical way, such as their heavy attack upon Fort Union in 1860, those farther downstream were only mutinous and insulting. Near new Fort Pierre, located in 1857 a few miles above the ruins of the original post, a river traveler watched the disbursement of Indian goods in June 1860. Some of the natives were dressed in bits and pieces of uniforms given them by General Harney, topped off by stovepipe hats, while the principal chiefs contented themselves with native dress. There were impassioned speeches, but as the visitor remarked "their eloquence turned principally upon pork; they want fat meat." [30] As a rule, sessions with the Agents were limited to eating and eloquence, but when the Sioux bands from the North came down to pick up their annuity goods, they excited their more domesticated brothers and caused a good deal of concern to disbursing officers.

Agent Walter A. Burleigh encountered such difficulty in 1861 while trying to dole out goods to his Yankton Sioux, not far from Fort Randall. About 150 warriors from the upper bands donned their war paint, piled hay around the warehouse and threatened to set the place on fire if they did not get all the powder in the magazine. Hoping to call their bluff, Burleigh told them to don another coat of war paint and call for more braves; he intended to stick by his announced policies. This occasioned a diplomatic stalemate, and the Indians retired for a conference whose lengthy deliberations led to a war dance. At that point Burleigh called for troops from Fort Randall; their appearance broke up the dance and sent the warriors fleeing upriver. Glad to be rid of the troublemakers, Burleigh commented: "The sooner the world is purged of these curses in human shape the better it will be for both decent white men and Indians." [31] While Burleigh did not make any comments about the conduct of the whites with whom he had to deal, he must have felt some doubts about the progress of that race, too. When he arrived at Yankton a month earlier, he reported that the *J. G. Morrow* had sunk within fifteen miles of its destination, carrying to the bottom some $30,000 worth of goods for the Yankton Agency, as well as a quantity of freight destined for Fort Randall. The Agent charged it to neglect on the part of the boat's officers and to the pilot who was drunk the entire trip.[32]

Despite complaints and threats from Indians all along the river and occasional examples of violence, the Commissioner of Indian Affairs did not seem to be perturbed. In 1861 he admitted that some of the old settlers were apprehensive and talked of a coming Indian outbreak, but, he said, "the superintendent is confident that it will be prevented." [33] Within a year, western Minnesota would be aflame with Indian violence, and the new Dakota frontier would be a shriveling thing, in danger of dying at birth.

One of the principal causes of Indian unrest along the upper river was the developing white encirclement. By the end of the Fifties, Iowa and Minnesota settlers were pressing from the East. At the same time a legion of prospectors was bound for the mountains, soon to spread northward along that craggy front and complete a giant net with which to trap the tribes against the Canadian line. Coincidentally, the Corps of Topographical Engineers was examining the interior of the Sioux empire, crisscrossing it with potential wagon routes, while steamboat men were poised on the threshold of the Golden Sixties, ready to capitalize upon the Missouri as a main artery of plains transportation. By 1859 more steamboats were leaving St. Louis for Missouri River ports than the combined number navigating both upper and lower reaches of the Mississippi.[34] In that year the peltry trade at St. Louis amounted to a record figure of $500,000; the largest item was 85,000 buffalo robes obtained from Indian country. In May of the next year, the American Fur Company sent three steamers upriver, carrying some four hundred men, in what was described as the largest expedition of its kind ever to depart St. Louis. One of them, the *Spread Eagle*, returned in early July with a cargo of 43,000 buffalo robes and 2,000 pelts.[35]

Such commerce excited Sioux City, whose merchants benefited from it, and the town's newspapers lost no opportunity to advertise the place as the Gateway to the West, particularly to the rich lands in what soon would be known as Dakota. When gold was discovered in Colorado, Sioux City papers discounted it, trying to divert emigrants to the Northwest. On April 23, 1859, the *Eagle* warned of the hazards in the Pike's Peak country and predicted that hopeful miners would find very little if they went there. On that same day the Denver *Rocky Mountain News* distributed its first issue, which included a number of advertisements from Council Bluffs and Omaha firms soliciting business from westward-bound miners. The golden charm of the Rockies thus siphoned off pioneers who might have gone up the river, and by 1861 a traveler commented that Sioux City was only a village of about two hundred inhabitants. "Lots which formerly were sold by the foot and inch at Broadway prices," he wrote, "are now begging purchasers for half acre tracts at rates upon which a farmer might thrive." [36]

Thus, on the eve of the Civil War, the military-Indian situation on the upper Missouri River presented a surface calm, and the Commissioner of Indian Affairs had reason to be optimistic. But a number of factors were shifting into a position that soon would disrupt that entire frontier and set the scene for over two decades of Indian warfare. The Sioux war in Minnesota, a spectacular gold discovery in Montana, increased river travel and, finally, the coming of the railroads provided a generation of Army men with the task of preserving domestic peace, and drew the nation's attention more closely to what was known as "the Indian problem."

The average soldier, carrying out his routine garrison duties at Fort Randall during that post's earliest years, had no notion that this place would become one of the largest and most important posts on the river in the days to come. Nor that, within a decade, a whole string of forts would dot the Missouri northward, welding together one of the most closely knit military frontiers in the American West. It just seemed that the Southerners Jefferson Davis and John Floyd had to be right about the Desert theory. And yet, so very soon, they would seem wrong, and about so many things.

FIVE

Rumblings North of Randall

Fort Randall, remarked a traveler in 1859, was no fort at all. Instead of formidable walls through which peered dangerous-looking cannons, he found "only barracks, log cabins occupied by the soldiers, and better ones by the officers, all facing an open square, in the center of which is a dial and a flagstaff, with a stand for the musicians." These log structures, twenty-four in number and longer than ordinary cabins, housed six companies of the Second Infantry, or about five hundred men. At first the only frame structure was the sutler's store operated by Captain John Todd, but by 1859 a hospital made of cedar boards and divided into seven moderately sized rooms gave the place a less primitive look. Part of the latter building was used by the quartermaster to house his stores. The magazine and guardhouse, both of which required sturdy construction, were built of hewed logs.[1] Since it was located relatively near a settlement and in a country of fairly peaceful Yankton Sioux, Fort Randall was the open cantonment type, similar to that of Fort Laramie, and many a visitor noted that, without the traditional palisades, it did not look much like a fort.

Typically, such an establishment attracted a number of Indian hangers-on who traded with travelers desiring such souvenirs as moccasins or bows and arrows, and solicited drinks or bits of food from anyone who wanted to contribute. As at any military post, in any generation, there was a demand for feminine company with no questions asked about degrees of pigmentation or racial origins. As one correspondent told his readers, "the papooses are many, bearing striking likenesses to officers and men of the army, who are proud of the issue of their loins. One half of the little ones hovering around the squaws are the offspring of white men." [2] Although it was the highest point on the Missouri River occupied by the Army, Fort Randall's garrison obviously had little occasion to have anything but the friendliest relations with the Indians.

In February 1859 President James Buchanan approved the establishment of the Yankton reservation, consisting of some 400,000 acres, within which was an agency, located twelve miles below Fort Randall on the east side of the river. These Indians, deprived of the hunt, were obliged to rely upon agriculture and governmental subsidies for their living. Sometimes they visited the fort to do a little begging; at other times they put on receptions for passing steamers, hoping for a few gifts. When Captain W. F. Raynolds visited the agency in 1859, he wrote that these Indians, led by old Smutty Bear, boarded the steamboats in full costume and were given the usual courtesy of hard bread and coffee. This band, he said, had recently sold its lands and was now "commencing to learn the arts of civilization." [3] By this he meant the Indians had been persuaded to till the soil. Their Agent, Alexander Redfield, saw no reason why the Yanktons should not prosper on the reservation, and to document his belief he cited the excellent results achieved by gardeners at Fort Randall. The potatoes, onions, tomatoes, broccoli and cabbage were "as fine as I ever saw in any country," he reported. With great care he measured some of the products and asserted that one rutabaga came to one foot and seven inches in circumference by one foot eight inches in length.[4] Such evidence, intended to demonstrate a happy, agrarian future for the Yanktons, was of far more interest to white farmers who heard about such results from the alluvial bottom lands along the Missouri.

While Redfield had great hopes for his educational efforts in the field of agriculture, he encountered certain difficulties with his charges in administrative areas. Particularly frustrating was the roll call, for rather than facing a problem of absenteeism, he was confronted by multiplying numbers and an apparent turnover that was astonishing. The count for 1860 was quite different from that of the preceding year because, as he lamented, many of the Sioux "appear to have no name, except such as is given to them at the time of counting, while others seem to have any number of names." He explained that the Indians sought a high count on the theory that greater numbers meant more money per band, and that each of the seven bands of Sioux with whom he was dealing also was anxious to appear larger for prestige reasons. "It was therefore impossible to entirely prevent them from coming up to be counted the second or third time, especially the women and children," Redfield complained. He appealed to the chiefs, who agreed to witness a second tally in order to reduce fraud, and this time the census of the Yanktons revealed a total of 2,053, a figure the Agent thought valid. The annual payment amounted to $10,000, or about $5 a head, and was disbursed in the presence of Fort Randall's commanding officer and several of his subordinates. Redfield was glad of their presence, and wrote that the "effect upon the Indians was evidently salutary." [5]

The boredom of peacetime garrison duty at the river posts was alleviated by such duties as witnessing the payment of Indian annuities or playing host to visitors who arrived on occasional steamboats. Lieutenant August Kautz, aboard the *Spread Eagle* on its 1860 ascent of the river—it was carrying troops to Fort Benton as a part of the Mullan road-building expedition—described the welcome accorded his party when it stopped at Fort Randall: "Some of the officers became quite merry on the occasion. . . . The Adjutant, who under the influence of wine became exceedingly agreeable, ordered out the band, which entertained us for an hour just before leaving." He concluded that the fort, which garrisoned five companies, "must be quite pleasant and gay for so isolated a post." [6] But the gaiety was largely contrived and except for the arrival of steamers, which generated a natural excitement, there was little about these posts that was festive. The social glass, referred to by Lieutenant Kautz, more often produced a court-martial for drunkenness or other related violations, than mere exhilaration.

In the spring of 1861 two events occurred that were to have an effect upon Fort Randall. The first of these was the creation of Dakota Territory, signed into life by President Buchanan on March 2, just before he relinquished the office to Abraham Lincoln. It signified governmental recognition of a new area, resulting in the arrival of more settlers and hence more troops to protect them. The second event was the opening of the Civil War, in April, and the resultant turnover in personnel at Fort Randall. When the hostilities began a high percentage of Regular Army troops were stationed in the West, and military necessities resulted in sudden and significant troop movements. Since June 1859, the headquarters and five other companies of the Fourth Artillery had been stationed at Fort Randall, replacing units of the Second Infantry, and now three of these were ordered east. All that remained at this time were two companies of the Fourth, under the command of Captain John A. Brown, a native of Maryland. He left his post without permission in July, and was not heard from again until the War Department received his resignation mailed from the Confederacy. Rumor had it that his wife, a southerner, persuaded the Captain to join his friends in the South. One of the men who came in as a replacement later wrote that six other officers of the Fourth pursued exactly the same course. The exodus reduced Fort Randall to one commissioned officer, Second Lieutenant T. R. Tannatt, and about one hundred enlisted men. This skeleton force held the place until mid-December when three companies of the newly organized Fourteenth Iowa Volunteers arrived, at which time the two remaining artillery companies were sent to Louisville, Kentucky.[7]

Although there were many changes at Fort Randall as regulars were replaced by volunteers, the war did not immediately affect the nature of the post's function. It remained a frontier garrison, an outpost at the edge of settlement standing watch over a lonely land, a place where newly inducted soldiers expected to watch the war from afar unless the War Department called them to the front. The new commandant was a recently commissioned resident of Iowa, John Pattee. Canadian born, he had migrated to Pennsylvania and then to Iowa where he had served a term as State Auditor. In September 1861, at the age of forty, he had enlisted in Company A of the Fourteenth Iowa, and because of his background, age and experience, he was elected Captain. Late in October the men of the Fourteenth Iowa were mustered into the Federal service at Iowa City and ordered to Fort Randall. The young farm boys were given a military baptism that amounted to total immersion; they marched the entire 540 miles and arrived so worn out and sick that the War Department was advised "it is feared some of them will never be restored to health." [8]

Once they were settled in their new assignments and had set up necessary housekeeping details, the recruits found Army life less rigorous. Amos R. Cherry, a sergeant in the Fourteenth Iowa, wrote that "The duty here is not very hard. Privates only comes on duty once in two weeks or once in fourteen days, corprals comes on once in nine days and the Sergeants once in twelve days." He explained further that when on duty he was not required to leave the guardhouse except at mealtime.[9] Captain Pattee took a paternal attitude toward the men, realizing that they were civilians in uniform, and as a result morale was high. Since most of his command came from the farm or workshop, he tried to keep everyone busy enough to keep out of trouble but still be gainfully employed. Incentive pay of twenty-five cents a day was offered for extra duty, and since this increased a private's income by fifty percent, a number of the men gladly availed themselves of the opportunity. As a result they willingly cut hay and wood or worked in the sawmill, which meant that there was no necessity for letting the customary contracts for these services. During the first year at Fort Randall, the extra-duty men manufactured 100,000 feet of lumber and provided all the hay and firewood the post could use.[10]

Life at Randall in the early days of the War continued to be routine, but most of the men there would not have traded their lot for service in the East. Amos Cherry, who thought the duty easy, was also happy about the table fare, an attitude that has not typified the enlisted man down through the years. "We get plenty to eat and more than we can eat," he noted one day as he contemplated a half a loaf of bread left over from his breakfast. "We have Beefe three days in the week and pork four days. When we have pork we have rice in our soupe; when we have Beefe we have Beans. . . . On sabath days we have warm buiscut roast Beefe and Pie and molassas; this is quite a treat to us but we all got it at home and thought nothing of it." It pleased him, too, that his long heavy overcoat "of a sky blue collor," with its large cape that came down to his waist, was in good condition and "my socks have not got a hole in them yet." Although the thermometer had fallen to −20° he had not suffered from the cold.[11]

Living quarters were much superior to those endured a few years earlier by the troops at Fort Pierre. Cherry called those at Fort Randall "comfertable and convenient," each of the eighteen-foot square rooms housing sixteen men. The rooms, well insulated "with matched cedar which makes them as warm as if they was plastered," were supplied with large stoves and a good supply of firewood. There were plenty of blankets for the coldest nights, an ample quantity of towels, water buckets, brooms, shovels, pokers and "a full kit of things to keep house with." In addition, the men were provided with mirrors, combs, brushes "and all things needed to make ourselves look slick." Considering the conditions at most frontier posts, this was an enlisted man's heaven.

Supplied with warm clothing and full bellies, and given a minimum of military duties, the men of Fort Randall found time to maintain the establishment and to have ample hours of leisure. The post had a theater at which no admission was charged, as well as the typical nineteenth century lyceum where all could participate. Sergeant Cherry found the latter very interesting and became an active member. One winter evening the question before the membership was: "Resolved that Wimmin should have the right of sufferage." The sergeant, who was assigned a place on the affirmative side, reported that the issue was "decided in favour of the negitave." However, he had hopes for the affirmative on the next issue: "Resolved that the Perusale of fictitious works is bennifical." Participants in the lyceum had a library of some two hundred volumes at their disposal when preparing for debates. Soldiers who had not developed a forensic interest passed their idle hours in the billiard room, playing on two excellent tables. The sutler's store was well stocked with goods Cherry thought reasonably priced. Purchases could be made with cash or by a payroll deduction system.[12]

On February 4, 1862, a small party of men arrived by team and threw Fort Randall into complete confusion. At their head was W. P. Lyman, a resident of Yankton, who announced that he was a major in the Dakota Volunteer Cavalry and the fort's new commanding officer. When Captain Pattee asked for authentication of the assertion, he was handed a document partly written and partly printed that he concluded was only a form used by the adjutant general's office to notify those appointed or promoted to office by the President. He told Lyman that as claimant he had failed to show a valid major's commission, and that since there was no Dakota Volunteers in existence, such an appointment was an impossibility. Holding that the documentation was irregular Pattee refused to surrender his command, only to have Lyman go to the post adjutant, take possession of the post order book and issue an order assuming command of the fort. Upon consulting some of his own officers, Pattee discovered that they did not agree with his interpretation of the situation, and he yielded to Lyman's request. The new commandant promptly placed Pattee under arrest.[13]

Captain Pattee remained under technical arrest until early May. During the intervening months he reported his situation to Governor Samuel J. Kirkwood of Iowa—his brother-in-law—and to one of the United States senators from Iowa, who conferred with the President and the Secretary of War. When it was established that Lyman never had received a commission in the federal army, the would-be major decamped, turning over command to Captain Bradley Mahana, next in rank below Pattee. Meanwhile Pattee, who had received no official confirmation of Lyman's reverse, made no effort to resume command. In early May he finally received a copy of the adjutant general's letter to Lyman, in which it was announced that there was no appointment, and on the tenth Pattee relieved Captain Mahana of command "by virtue of my rank."[14]

The struggle for control of Fort Randall makes an interesting story of territorial politics, and suggests a great deal about the problems of the War Department in maintaining frontier posts. The principal figure in this particular affair was John B. S. Todd, whose interest in Dakota dated from his service as a captain of Company A, Sixth U. S. Infantry, at Fort Pierre during Harney's regime. He resigned his commission in September 1856, soon to become sutler at Fort Randall and a member of the firm of Frost, Todd and Company, a company that traded extensively in the area. This firm had exerted its influence to gain the Yankton treaty of 1858, from which it gained the right to trade in Indian country and to scout future town sites. With the coming of the War Todd used his connections with the Lincoln family to gain a commission as brigadier general of Volunteers; he received this only four days before notification that he had been elected to Congress as a Dakota delegate. He reported to General John Frémont's headquarters at St. Louis and served there until November 26, when he returned to Washington to take up his congressional duties.

When Todd gave up the sutler's post at Fort Randall, he pulled the right strings and gained the position for his young nephew, George B. Hoffman, who antagonized Pattee almost as soon as the Iowan arrived to take command. Despite the fact that Sergeant Amos Cherry thought Hoffman's prices reasonable, Pattee was not at all satisfied with the way the store was conducted. He accused Hoffman of selling goods out of the same package at two and three different prices, of violating the prices fixed by the post's Council of Administration, and of selling liquor to the soldiers. "You have not the business capacity or moral honesty to qualify you for the position you hold and I do not believe that you owned in your own right the goods that you have already sold but have been acting for another [Todd]," he wrote to Hoffman.[15]

Pattee further complained that Hoffman and Postmaster J. Wherry, both Todd appointees, were corrupting his farm boys and were openly violating Army regulations. The center of this scandalous conduct was a small room behind the Post Office that also connected to the sutler's store which, said Pattee, "was a common resort of Soldiers, Citizens, Indians, and Squaws." While it was described as a working office, the Captain said he had never seen it used as such. Not only was it headquarters for card games, but it was alleged also to have been the post brothel. "I have never seen whoring at the office," Pattee admitted, "but I am certain that it was a regular habit to take Squaws into the post office, the store room, and the bed room for that purpose, and I have heard Mr. Geo. B. Hoffman, and others engaged to him, say that such was the fact." Wherry, the Postmaster, resigned under pressure, but to Pattee's dismay Hoffman was given his place. The commandant promptly suspended Hoffman for violating Army regulations, only to have Todd get him reinstated.

Pattee openly charged Todd with interfering with the control of the garrison ever since it was established. It was perfectly clear to the Iowa Captain that Fort Randall was the Congressman's domain, for good and sufficient reasons. "So long as Todd can control the commanding officer of the Post, he can be greatly benefitted in various ways. His family have been and are now [May 1862] being supplied with commissary stores, because of his holding an appointment as Brigadier General." It was Todd, said Pattee, who pulled strings to gain an appointment for Lyman, that "poor low-minded dissipated Indianized specimen of humanity, fit for neither savage nor civilized life." And what did Lyman do for Fort Randall, how did he spend his time? "In the Sutler's store drinking whiskey, playing billiards at the billiard room, or poker at his quarters, instead of laboring to improve the condition and discipline of the men over whom he was illegally appointed," charged the aggrieved officer. All of the blame was placed at Todd's doorstep for using misrepresentation and falsehoods to install a commanding officer whose abilities were inferior to any of the men whom he tried to direct.

It greatly distressed Pattee to think that Todd's insidious influence appeared to have turned some of the Iowa troops against him. In December 1862 a sergeant, a corporal and several enlisted men of the Forty-first Iowa Volunteer Infantry wrote to the Adjutant General, condemning Pattee who had resumed command. The writers called their commanding officer "one of the most accomplished villains in the volunteer service," and asserted that he knew absolutely nothing about military science. They further charged that he had been forced to leave Iowa as a swindler, that he had "robbed every man he had any dealings with," and now he was trying to get the Government to build another post, farther upriver, for which he would be the contractor, "so he could swindle Uncle Sam out of ten or twenty thousand dollars." General John Cook, then commanding the military district in which Fort Randall lay, called the round robin letter a forgery.

However, if Todd's charges against Pattee had any basis the troops at Fort Randall had some grounds for complaint. Early in 1863 Todd complained that Pattee had regained his command violently, by placing all the officers of one infantry company under arrest while he searched their quarters, seized private papers and then held his victims in confinement for sixty-three days. Todd countered cries of "corruption" with the assertion that Pattee's brother, Wallace, who was a commissary sergeant, had connived with the commanding officer in buying furs with provisions from the commissary store and transporting them to Iowa City in a government ambulance where they were sold. He added that John Pattee also had made money by charging from $1 to $1.50 per person for ferrying people across the river in government boats. Pattee denied participation in the fur trade, saying he had acquired but five buffalo robes and four beaver skins since his arrival, which he had purchased fairly from the Indians, and that he had sold four of the robes and had given the other to a needy Indian.

The Pattee-Todd quarrel touched the nearby Yankton Indian agency and further illustrated the involvement of local men in the fight for patronage in Dakota. Walter A. Burleigh, who succeeded Redfield as Agent, was one of Todd's enemies, and the new Congressman also tried to oust him in favor of a friend named Theophile Bruquier. In September 1862 Pattee found sufficient reasons for sending Captain G. H. Wolfe of the Fourteenth Iowa to arrest Bruquier and return him to the fort for confinement.[16] Burleigh, of course, was ever grateful to the commanding officer, and undoubtedly offered character references in Pattee's struggle with the Todd faction in Dakota.

Apparently Todd was not the only Dakotan who wanted to get rid of the Iowa officer. In late May 1862, about two weeks after Pattee had recaptured his position, Governor William Jayne wrote to Secretary of War Edwin Stanton offering to raise two companies of volunteers to garrison Fort Randall so that the Iowa Volunteers would be relieved, presumably for duty in some distant and more vital theater of war. The Governor, who was not entirely sure that Stanton had heard about such a place as Dakota, appended to his letter the following: "P.S. My address is Yankton, Dakt. Ter." [17]

During the months that the white factions battled over possession of Fort Randall, the Indians who visited fur trading posts along the river north to Fort Union, showed an increasing attitude of uneasiness. Agent Samuel Latta witnessed their sullen conduct on his trip upriver in the spring of 1862. Upon his arrival at new Fort Pierre, toward the end of May, he found between two and three thousand Sioux waiting for distribution of the annuities. He ordered the goods sent ashore in seven parcels, conforming in size to the respective bands who were to receive them, and then he called for a conference so that he might explain his mission. There were about a dozen Indians present who qualified as headmen, and they answered the call with extreme reluctance. Big Head of the Yanktonnais remained aloof and declined to take part in the proceedings. This came as no surprise to Latta who had entertained the Chief on board the *Spread Eagle*, and had given him coffee, bread, a spyglass and a supply of jewelry for his several wives, only to learn that unless the Government was prepared to pay off six years in back annuities, on the spot, Big Head was determined to refuse any goods. The council opened without him.

The oratory that ensued was delivered with such feeling that Latta regretted he had not recorded it. The various chiefs explained their own concern, and the extreme apprehensions of men such as Big Head, over developments since the days of 1856 when Harney had promised them aid and protection. Their dilemma arose from the fact that portions of the Sioux nation were growing increasingly hostile to the Government, and that the minority, still friendly toward the Great Father, stood in mortal danger. Since the Government had shown no disposition to establish military posts higher on the river than Fort Randall, the friendly Indians now felt obliged to break off intercourse with the white men and return to their respective bands. The annuities, too small to do much good, not only created discord among the recipients, but their acceptance brought threats of reprisal from the hostile elements. Therefore, said the chiefs, it would be best if no more goods were brought unless the donors were prepared to offer protection.

This was the consensus of the group with one exception. Bear's Rib, a Hunkpapa who had been designated a chief by Harney, arose and delivered an emotional address in which he told of his fidelity to the Government and of his repeated disappointments at not receiving the promised protection. He admitted that acceptance of the annuity would endanger his own life, but he resolved to do so this one last time with the request that this terminate the agreement. True to his premonition, he was killed a few days later by a band of Sans Arc Sioux who committed the act within the confines of new Fort Pierre. In reporting the event Latta stated that the Chief's 250 followers now were wandering outcasts, and it distressed him to think that the Government was about to lose the benefit of the years invested in currying that friendship.[18]

It was Latta's conviction that the Indians of his agency should be divided. He wanted to segregate the seven bands of Sioux, who numbered approximately 13,000, of whom only one-third could be considered friendly, to keep them from abusing the Mandans, Gros Ventres and Arickaras and from warring with the Assiniboins and Crows. He called the Sioux "a powerful and warlike people, proud, haughty, and defiant; will average six feet in height, strong muscular frames, and very good horsemen; well dressed, principally in dressed skins and robes; rich in horses and lodges, have great abundance of meat, since the buffalo, elk, antelope, and deer abound in their country." The Mandans and Gros Ventres lived together in villages along the river, and were described as "good people; peaceable, reliable and honest." They raised corn, pumpkins, beans and other hoe crops, but were very poor due to the constant raids by the Sioux and their reluctance to hunt very far from home for fear of being attacked. The Assiniboins also were endorsed as friendly, well-disposed people who were trying to abide by treaty obligations but they, too, were so harassed by the Sioux that they had abandoned their lands south of the river and now spent part of their time in Canada. All of these Indians demanded protection and, to afford it, Latta recommended a military post at the mouth of the Yellowstone River.

Another necessary reform, said the Indian Agent, was removal of the natives from the influence of fur traders. "This old American Fur Company," he charged, "is the most corrupt institution ever tolerated in our country." He accused the firm of involving the Government in its speculation, of enslaving the Indians, of cheating them out of their furs and of discouraging them in agricultural attempts by suggesting that if the white farmers discovered the richness of the soil along the Missouri they would at once take away Indian lands. Nor were the Indians the only victims, reported Latta. The company charged its own employees a dollar a pound for sugar and coffee and literally forced them to live on buffalo meat. He admitted the recent gold discoveries in Montana had somewhat alleviated their situation, for now the company had to offer better conditions to keep its men from boarding steamers passing to and from the mines.[19]

Charles Primeau, the *bourgeois* of reconstructed Fort Pierre, took the position that this and all other American Fur Company posts had a perfect right to operate in Indian country. He wrote to Pierre Chouteau, Jr., in June 1862, saying that the thirty or forty men at the post had spent most of their lives in Indian country and "everything we love and hold dear is here." The Government, he said, had been slow to furnish protection, but very shortly the course of events would force some kind of response from Washington, for the Montana mines were drawing prospectors in great numbers to what he termed "Blackfoot country." Primeau predicted "that the Government will, at a late day, establish military posts on the Missouri River, but in the mean time we daily run the risk of our lives." Typical of western businessmen, he assumed that authorized and established firms could fairly expect military protection in the pursuit of their occupations. The trader did not share Latta's sympathy with the poor, ignorant natives who were alleged to be the dupes of sharp practices, but rather he held that to do business with the Sioux involved a risk that merited high profit. When admitting Indians to the post to trade, it was hard for fur men to tell if their intentions were good or bad, and when the Sioux bought goods with pelts, they took the attitude that the customer was always right. "They not only insult and abuse us," Primeau complained, "but also the Government. The greater portion refuse annuities, hold council and advise with the English at Red River, and tell us every day that they do not recognize the American Government as having any control of them." He called it a "crying shame" that the Government was daily insulted by a handful of Indians.[20]

The unrest that manifested itself during the summer of 1862 reached all the way downriver to the bands living within range of Fort Randall. Late in May J. B. Hoffman, Agent for the Poncas, rewarded his Indians for having finished their corn planting by giving them permission to go on a hunt. On the second day out a group of warlike Brulé Sioux turned them back, and Hoffman appealed for military assistance. Pattee dispatched Captain Wolfe and thirty men to accompany a new hunting party that numbered about 250 Indians. When they had traveled about sixty miles they were again accosted by the Brulés, who informed the Captain that his entourage was in their country and the land was off limits to hunters. "They acted boldly and talked saucily," said Hoffman, who was annoyed because the Brulés loftily consented to refrain from any scalp-lifting if the intruders left at once. The hunters decided that there were other places where buffalo might be found and they veered off, as the Sioux began firing the grass to frighten away any game in the area. The Poncas stayed out twelve days and brought in only fifty-seven buffalo, a small catch for so large an expedition.[21]

Farther to the north, in the country around the fur-trading post of Fort Berthold, were the Hunkpapa Sioux, angry and as determined as the Brulés that the impending white invasion be stopped.

In July 1862 a group of that band's headmen petitioned the Indian Agent, demanding that a fur company steamer be turned back "as we don't want the whites to travel through our country." The authors of the work asserted that the Hunkpapas claimed both sides of the river above Fort Berthold, and although they had agreed to allow trade vessels to enter their country, they did not want any passenger packets or any land parties in their domain. "If you pay no attention to what we now say to you," said the signatories, "you may rely on seeing the tracks of our horses on the war-path." Nor did they want any more presents. Admittedly, some of the chiefs had fallen into the habit of accepting gifts, but this was not with the consent of the tribal leaders. Reference was made to the case of Bear's Rib who "had no ears, and we gave him ears by killing him." The lesson was to be applied to American intruders: "If your whites have no ears we will give them ears." Nor were the Hunkpapas impressed by recent threats that soldiers would come and punish them. Bring them, said Feather-Tied-To-His-Hair and his fellow petitioners, "All we ask of you is to bring men, and no women dressed in soldiers' clothes." [22] Rumbles of discontent from the hostile Sioux were growing louder, and the Government, deeply involved in a civil war, was threatened with a showdown at a time that was most inconvenient.

Agent Samuel Latta admitted the danger, but he was worried only about the Sioux. "No other Indians in the country will molest the white man," he wrote to the Commissioner of Indian Affairs. While such leaders as Feather-Tied-To-His-Hair and his friends refused to recognize him or any other Agent, Latta was on friendly terms with some of the Sioux warriors. They explained to him that none of the treaties to which they had agreed contemplated any emigration, by land or water, and on this point the Indians would stand firm. Experience had shown the Sioux that all the emigrants ever brought was disease and pestilence, and a countryside barren of buffalo. The Agent was convinced that the Hunkpapas and their allies meant business and he said so, quite plainly. "I am satisfied, from the bitterness they manifested, that no party of emigrants could pass overland through their country, and would not be safe on the river," he concluded after long talks with the chiefs.[23]

The main pressure against the northern plains empire ruled by the Sioux came from gold discoveries in the country soon to be known as Montana. Latta recognized this when he wrote that "a large emigration may be expected to pass up the Missouri River, as also overland, through the Indian country next season." Even in 1862, he said, steamers of the largest class had reached Fort Benton, not far from the diggings, and he predicted that the river "will become the great thoroughfare for emigrants to the gold mines."

Governor William Jayne of Dakota Territory made a similar report in which he said that the travel tended "to excite the prejudices of the Indian, and to alarm him with apprehension that his hunting grounds are to be invaded, and he too, perhaps, will soon be removed to other and distant lands." [24] In addressing the legislative assembly of Dakota, Jayne said the discovery of unusually rich gold fields "has made a highway through a part of this Territory never before marked by the footprint of the white man save an occasional hunter and trapper." [25] Part of the "highway" to which he referred was being marked off by Captain James L. Fisk who, that year, escorted a wagon train from Fort Abercrombie, Minnesota, to Fort Benton at the head of Missouri River navigation. Samuel Bond, who accompanied Fisk as a clerk and recorder, said the movement of the wagon train across the northern plains was inspired because "the recent and continued discoveries of gold in Oregon and Washington Territories have incited an extensive emigration to those regions." [26]

It has been suggested by an authority on river steamboating that the volume of river travel during the Civil War was not so great as the Indians supposed. In 1862 only the *Emilie,* the *Shreveport,* the *Key West No. 2* and the *Spread Eagle* were recorded as having arrived at Fort Benton, while in 1863 there were but two arrivals, and in 1864 the number was again four. Not until 1865 did the traffic increase appreciably, and only in the following year, when thirty-one vessels made the ascent, could the heyday of the upper Missouri River steamer be said to have arrived.[27] Nevertheless, the movement to and from the mines, whether by the Missouri River route or across the plains by foot or horseback, and including the numbers that filtered northward along the mountains from Colorado and returned to "the States" by floating down the Missouri in mackinaw boats, meant that an unusually large number of white men were on the move in or near Indian country.

There was unrealistic newspaper talk that some 100,000 miners would find their way into the mining country along the northern Rockies during 1862; nevertheless, the opening of new diggings in that country occasioned genuine optimism among the merchants of Sioux City and Yankton. "There is no abatement of the excitement in regard to the gold discoveries at the headwaters of the Missouri," reported the Yankton *Dakotian* on June 17, 1862. The editor announced the formation of a St. Louis company, capitalized at $100,000, whose founders intended "to explore and encourage emigration, by way of the Missouri River, to the mines." He referred to the ascent of the *Emilie* and explained that this was only the beginning of the boom; a line of packets was being organized to operate regularly between St. Louis and the falls of the Missouri.

While travel to the mines by land routes had some advantages, a great many people preferred to go by water because it was more comfortable and safer. Those who made the trip for business reasons were not apt to carry many possessions. The prospective miner who intended to buy his supplies after arrival also found the water route preferable. The steamboats carried a wide variety of individuals, ranging from preachers bound for the mining camps to save souls, to prostitutes, gamblers and saloonkeepers whose efforts helped to keep the clerics busy. Lewis Henry Morgan, the anthropologist, left a good description of river travel from notes made aboard the *Spread Eagle* in 1862. "The passengers are a mixture," he noted. "There are some fashionable young men in quest of health and pleasure. Some adventurers for the gold mines in Washington and Oregon. Some independent traders who reside in the Indian country and have Indian wives. Some traders and trappers in the service of the Fur Company. They play cards and smoke and chat and on the whole are well behaved and happy."

That the travelers were relaxed and content as they sailed across the plains is suggested by his comment: "We have a good table, and four excellent minstrels who at evening give us an excellent concert. . . . The boat is in a cheerful mood. There is some gaming going on but not of a serious character, and some drinking, but no drunkenness as yet." [28]

Gathered aboard the *Spread Eagle* was a rather distinguished company. Of the seventy-five who made the trip, about half were Missouri and Illinois men bound for the gold mines, but among the remainder were names that became very well known in western history. Father Pierre de Smet, the best-known Catholic on the plains, was returning to the country where he had gained his fame as a missionary. "He was at that time about sixty years old," wrote one of the passengers, "hale and hearty, of medium height, rather stoutly built, kind and friendly to everyone."

Another plainsman, who had made his reputation as a trader and now lived in Peoria, Illinois, was returning to visit his Indian in-laws up the river. Alexander Culbertson, described as a rather large man who appeared to be in his sixties, was accompanied by his Blackfoot wife, a woman some fifteen years his junior. Morgan, always interested in Indians, noted that the couple had with them two "fine looking half blood children," and he made an effort to cultivate the family. Mrs. Culbertson showed him a photograph of a daughter, then at home, who was eighteen years old, and after examining it he wrote: "It is a very beautiful face without a particle of Indian in it." The daughter on board was a child of twelve who, said the diarist, "will make, when educated, a woman to command attention anywhere. She talks the English only, having never learned Blackfoot." Malcolm Clark, another famed trader, was in the company. A fellow passenger saw him as a man with iron gray hair and beard, which made him look older, but he was a very attractive person who somewhat resembled some of the portraits of President Jackson.

Andrew Dawson would come aboard at Fort Union, bound for Fort Benton where he was in charge. He was rather badly crippled, and shipboard gossip had it that his condition was the result of dissipation. One of his fellow employees who also joined the group at Fort Union was Robert Meldrum, a fifty-seven-year-old Scot who had worked for the American Fur Company a number of years. Lewis Morgan sought him out at once, for Meldrum was accompanied by his Crow wife. The trader told Morgan that he could speak Crow better than English, and that he liked it better as a language. A passenger of some consequence was Henry W. Reed, Agent to the Blackfeet, who was characterized as a fifty-nine-year-old Methodist clergyman, "and a very agreeable gentleman." Morgan was a member of Reed's party, through an invitation extended him by the Secretary of the Interior. Of interest to the entire group was a youngster who sat on deck, day after day, holding copies of the Lewis and Clark journal as he checked off prominent landmarks in passing. He was the grandson of famed explorer Captain William Clark.

When the *Spread Eagle* reached Fort Berthold, one of the American Fur Company's posts, a large number of Indians from the Gros Ventre village assembled along the river bank. The vessel's steam whistle gave off a piercing shriek to acknowledge the welcoming committee, sending the women and children fleeing to the nearby slopes, which suggested that steamboats were not as thick along the upper Missouri as some of the natives had asserted. However, the terror was only momentary, and before long the Indians thronged along the gunwales crying "Whiskey." A. H. Wilcox, who was en route to the mining country, commented that the Gros Ventres "were ready to give anything they possessed, even their wives and daughters, for whiskey." Both passengers and boathands were prepared to trade, and before long a thriving business was being conducted, a quart of whiskey bringing a fine buffalo robe. Pierre Chouteau, Jr., who ran the American Fur Company's upper Missouri operations, was among the passengers, and when he discovered the commerce that had so suddenly sprung up he tried to stop it. Grabbing a keg of whiskey that belonged to one of the travelers, he hurled it into the river, only to watch a halfbreed who was standing nearby dive into the river and rescue it. Wilcox briefly noted the next sequence: "In less than an hour the whole Gros Ventres nation was gloriously drunk."

Before the vessel left Fort Berthold, one of the chiefs came aboard and attempted to conduct some business at a higher level, and with somewhat more subtlety than that carried on by his braves. He sought out Alexander Culbertson, and with a great show of generosity announced that he had on shore a fine pair of ponies that he wished to give to the distinguished westerner. As an old hand at the business the trader knew the price of Indian gifts, that is, it was customary to reciprocate with a present of even greater value. When he informed the chief that he felt too poor to respond in the proper manner, the Gros Ventre made a sarcastic remark about the "poverty of a man who had spent nearly all his life skinning Indians," and left the boat in a huff.

Upon resuming their travels the passengers returned to card playing, social drinking or just watching the landmarks go by. On June 6 they were treated to a few minutes of excitement not experienced on every ascent of the river, when they overtook and passed the *Emilie* owned by La Barge, Harkness and Company, an opposition fur company. Captain Joseph la Barge, of a famous family of river pilots, accepted the challenge and called for more steam; his was one of the finest vessels on the river, designed, owned and commanded by himself. Steamboat racing was an old custom on the Mississippi River and now, perhaps for the first time, a race was staged on the upper Missouri. Passengers on both vessels shared the excitement and cheered on their respective craft as the two vessels strained against the current, neck and neck, for more than a mile up a dangerously narrow channel. The space between the boats grew ominously narrow, and as the *Emilie* tried to gain the lead she swung into the other's path. Captain Robert E. Baily was unable to keep the *Spread Eagle* from ramming its rival, and when the two collided, the *Emilie* lost some of its guards. As La Barge watched timbers splintering on the starboard of his vessel—which carried his daughter's name—he "swore a big French oath," grabbed a rifle and aimed it at Baily's head. He regained control of himself when he noticed the muzzles of several rifles pointing at him from the decks of the *Spread Eagle*. There was no shooting, but a passenger on the *Emilie* noted in his diary that there was a good deal of angry talk.

When Baily returned to St. Louis he was charged with recklessness, and he lost his license for a time.[29]

By midsummer 1862, the restlessness of the Indians along the river was beginning to cause concern among the Indian Agents and among the white settlers who were moving into the fertile farming country around Fort Randall. The hostility of the natives to all travel through their country, by land or by water, coupled with the mounting pressures for safe transportation routes to the newly opened mines in the mountains, lent a strong feeling of uneasiness among those who feared the powerful Sioux. If the river were to be kept open, and if new land routes from Iowa and Minnesota were to be established, it was apparent that the Federal Government would be asked to extend its military power deeper into Missouri country. Legislative activities in Washington, D.C., suggested further reasons for Indian unrest. In that same significant year Congress enacted a free homestead law whose effect upon the entire West was to be enormous, and it passed transcontinental railroad legislation that shortly would spawn other western rail lines. By 1864 the Northern Pacific charter would point the "Iron Horse" directly at Sioux country.

In his annual report to the Territorial Legislature of Dakota that same year, Governor William Jayne stated that dissatisfactions among the Sioux, the increased use of roadways through their country and changing conditions to the west all foretold of trouble that could erupt into a general Indian war. Looking at the land north of Dakota settlements, he said: "I do not believe that peace can much longer be maintained in that section of Dakota without a sufficient force of United States troops to uphold and sustain the dignity, authority and power of the national government."

Agent Samuel Latta agreed, and strongly recommended that the first boats that ascended the river the following spring carry a regiment of cavalry to protect both the emigrants and the weak tribes from the Sioux. He suggested that the Army might also search out any secessionists lurking in that area, for the Sioux, already ill-disposed toward the Federal Government, might be easy targets for subversive elements. He thought the neighborhood of Fort Union would be a good place to establish a new military post, because the countryside in that area was fertile, well watered and had good pasturage. Troops in that vicinity would be able to keep an eye on British traders, who tended to disrupt relations with the northern Indians, and at the same time prevent the fur company post from harboring Confederate sympathizers. A discharged Union soldier, who had gone to work at Fort Union, assured Latta that "they were all secessionists at this post," and he had left, fearing for his life. Generously, Latta admitted that not all American Fur Company employees were dishonest and disloyal, but he held that the exceptions were few.[30]

Captain Pattee, writing from Fort Randall in July, made a similar recommendation. Referring to the pressures of the Sioux against the Arickaras, Mandans and Gros Ventres, he advised the establishment of a new post for their protection. "It may seem rather wild to propose to send two companies three hundred miles farther into the Indian country," he told General James Blunt, "but I assure you it is perfectly practicable and safe; at least I will gladly undertake it myself with my company & one of the others here." [31]

The Federal Government, faced by mounting criticism of McClellan's failure in the Peninsular Campaign in the early summer of 1862, and shaken by the resounding defeat of John Pope at Second Manassas late in August, was in no position to extend its military frontier farther up the Missouri River to satisfy the complaints of a few westerners who were nervous over Sioux restlessness. The preoccupation of the War Department with the pressing problem of civil war was such that only an Indian uprising of the first magnitude, one that resulted in widespread killing of whites and posed a serious threat to the agricultural frontier, would divert its attention from the main theater of war.

The precipitating event occurred on August 17 near Acton, Minnesota, when a small party of Santee Sioux got into an argument with a settler named Robinson Jones. Before the Indians moved on they murdered three members of the Jones family and two neighboring men. When they reported the deed to their fellow tribesmen, the more warlike faction took the position that the die was cast and the only thing to do now was to kill all the whites within reach. They commenced this project the following morning, and the famed Minnesota massacre was under way. Before the Minnesota Sioux were brought under control they had dispatched over five hundred men, women and children.

Although the "uprising," as it was termed, was not generated by the principal bands of trans-Missouri Sioux, the warfare that erupted in Minnesota drew attention to the Indian problem of the Northwest and demanded positive action of major proportions from both local forces and those of the national Government. For almost four decades after Henry Atkinson's recommendation that no forts were needed in the upper country, the War Department had refrained from extending its authority into that far land, but now it could wait no longer. Although the time was inauspicious for such a move, the situation was so dangerous that it could not be postponed. The ensuing military penetration of the river country began an advance that did not cease until the High Plains Sioux and other hostile bands were humiliated and relegated to reservations, a period in American history that became known as the era of the Indian wars, and one that found an important place in twentieth century literature of the West.

SIX

"It Is a National War"

Exactly a week after the murders at Acton, Minnesota, there was bloodshed along the river in Dakota. On August 24 Judge Joseph B. Amidon and his son were killed by Indians while working in a corn field on the outskirts of Sioux Falls. Since the violence took place within earshot of a Dakota cavalry detachment, there was great excitement among the other settlers who were now convinced that the area was no longer safe. They appealed to Governor William Jayne, who issued a proclamation, dated August 30, in which he ordered every male in the Territory between the ages of eighteen and fifty to enroll in a home defense company to be organized in each county. The men were directed to assemble, elect their own officers and then await distribution of arms the Governor had requisitioned from the commandant at Fort Randall. In addition, the Governor volunteered to employ a few reliable Indian scouts from the Yankton Agency.[1] He asked General James G. Blunt, commanding the district of Kansas at Leavenworth, for a supply of ammunition, three hundred muskets and three six-pounder guns, the latter to be used in defending blockhouses being constructed at three different points. Such help was absolutely necessary, he explained, to prevent the Territory from being depopulated. The Governor indicated the agitated condition of his nervous system when he told Blunt that his people, only a handful of settlers, were "at the mercy of 50,000 Indians, should they see proper to fall upon us."

By mid-September Dakota settlers in relatively isolated districts had moved their families to towns along the river, abandoning their homes, livestock and crops. Governor Jayne reported that Sioux Falls had been evacuated and that the Indians promptly burned the place. Iowans watched the turmoil north of them with growing uneasiness and prepared to defend themselves if the outbreak should spread farther southward. When Governor Samuel J. Kirkwood of Iowa was told that the only whites left in Dakota were at Fort Randall or the Yankton Agency, he resolved to fortify Sioux City. In a matter of days residents of that river town were working night and day to complete a fort three hundred feet square, complete with blockhouses, that would stem the oncoming red tide. The report of a riverboat captain, who warned that the whole Sioux nation was on the move intent upon exterminating all whites found along the frontier, drove the workers at Sioux City to almost frantic labors.[2]

The reports were somewhat exaggerated. While a good many people fled south to more settled areas, such places as Yankton, Vermillion, Elk Point and Richland were fortified and defended by groups of men who chose to remain and save their respective towns.[3] In a confused situation, with few available communications to serve a newly settled community, it is not surprising that rumors and overdrawn accounts spread fear along the river. Nor can one blame settlers for their apprehensions when men such as Captain John la Barge, a veteran of twenty-five years on Missouri steamboats, stated that never had he seen the Sioux so hostile. Nervousness increased on September 6, when word spread that the Yanktons were rising up and that they had commenced actual attacks. George Kingsbury, editor of the Yankton *Dakotian,* wrote that this development had persuaded settlers at Bon Homme to go to fortified Yankton, and those at Vermillion to leave for Sioux City. However, by September 15 Kingsbury felt that the public mind was calmer and he offered as documentation the fact that a number of settlers were beginning to return to their farms. This, he said, did not mean the danger had abated; he strongly recommended that more troops be sent for defense along the river since the force at Fort Randall was inadequate to cope with the new situation. The following week his paper published a column-long editorial underscoring the demand for troops, asking if the frontier was to be pushed back or if the Federal Government would send troops to protect the settlers.[4]

The feeling that the exigencies of the Civil War were bound to leave such places as the Dakota frontier to the mercies of the tribes was also felt in Minnesota. Early in September, Governor Alexander Ramsey complained to President Lincoln that the Indian outrages continued unabated in his state, and that a recent urgent request to Secretary of War Stanton for the Government purchase of five hundred horses had been refused. "This is not our war, it is a national war," said the Governor, and he demanded the return of Minnesota troops then fighting in Tennessee and Kentucky. Episcopal Bishop Henry B. Whipple, a well-known and influential religious figure from Minnesota, also talked with Lincoln, who was finally persuaded. He agreed to take up the matter with General Henry Halleck. In a matter of days, Minnesota was assigned to the Department of the Northwest, along with Iowa, Wisconsin and Dakota, a move that placed the militia units under federal army officers. General John Pope, disgraced at Second Bull Run in late August, was sent to St. Paul to take command.[5]

Events in Minnesota during September demonstrated the necessity of fielding a large number of troops, for this was no mere Indian scare. Highly excited by their initial successes the Santee Sioux twice attacked New Ulm, a town of perhaps nine hundred people, and threatened it so seriously that the place was evacuated at the first opportunity. About the same time Fort Ridgely was besieged until 1,400 men under Henry Hastings Sibley came to the rescue. Once a large military force was in the field, events moved rapidly, and the Sioux who were not captured fled westward. By October 9 General Pope informed Halleck that "the Sioux war may be considered at an end," and Governor Ramsey said much the same thing to Lincoln. But such sentiments were far from consoling to a nervous people who were unconvinced that danger had passed. Settlers in more remote areas, particularly in the West, howled their dissatisfaction at the statements, and the Democratic press ominously suggested that it was a purely political announcement, designed to keep Pope in his job as departmental commander. Pope quickly responded with the statement that five regiments would remain to guard the home front and only one would be sent to fight the Confederacy; Minnesota would not be abandoned.[6]

Residents of the sparsely settled portions of new Dakota Territory must have been relieved to hear that the military was not yet ready to leave unguarded the embers of discontent still smouldering among the Sioux of Minnesota. Recent events had placed them between warring Indians and bands whose unfriendliness could erupt into open hostilities on a moment's notice. Recognizing this, more conservative whites moved southward to escape the closing vise. Those who stayed on, taking a wait-and-see attitude, were further discouraged to learn that the Santee Sioux had fled westward from Minnesota to join the dangerous Yanktonnais, from whom they hoped to gain help. Late in September the *Dakotian* told its readers that two hundred Santees had turned up in the Fort Pierre neighborhood but, said the paper hopefully, they no doubt would move on upriver.[7]

In the heyday of Montana mining it became customary for prospectors to return to "the States" each fall by means of mackinaw (Mackinac) boats built quickly and cheaply for a single trip. In the late summer of 1862 some of these awkward, flat-bottomed craft made their way down the Missouri, bound for Sioux City or St. Louis. As they reached southern Dakota their passengers described the river as a gauntlet they had run between taunting, insulting Indians. One of these boats, which left Fort Benton September 22, was attacked by Yanktonnais of Big Head's band about 150 miles below Fort Berthold. At first the Indians signaled the vessel to heave to, and when that was refused they followed it for about thirty miles, firing at it all the way. None of the eighteen men aboard was killed, but one was hit in the thigh. Most of the passengers were men from St. Louis who had gone up the river on the *Emilie* that spring.[8] Pierre Chouteau, Jr., informed the Commissioner of Indian Affairs that these attacks were common and that the men who escaped were usually robbed of everything they had. Even Henry Reed of the Blackfoot Agency was said to have had a very narrow escape. "It is the hope of all our licensed traders," said Chouteau, "that these Indians may soon be punished by our Government." [9]

John Pattee, now promoted to major and back in command of Fort Randall, was concerned about the attacks, and he continued to recommend the establishment of a fort deeper in Sioux country, but he was little disposed to give any military protection to the traders. He was convinced that much of the trouble with the tribes was "the knavery of the American Fur Company under the leadership of Mr. Charles Choteau [*sic*] of St. Louis." He openly charged the company with fraud, stating that in the preceding year it pretended to have lost a large amount of goods on a steamboat fire, but "I have the best evidence the goods were left at Ft. Union, one of their trading posts, and then transported by land to their Post at Ft. Benton and traded off to the Blackfeet Indians." [10] Dr. Walter Burleigh, Yankton Agent, was more sympathetic. He talked with trader Charles Galpin, who came down from the upper Missouri country that autumn, and quoted him as saying there were, by now, some six hundred Santee warriors concentrated along the river one hundred miles north of Pierre. They had in their possession a number of white captives, a great many cows, mules, horses, wagons "and every other conceivable article and species of property," presumably plunder from Minnesota.

Frequently the Indian Agents were gentle men, who worked sympathetically among their flocks and avoided violence at all costs. Henry Reed, for example, went to the Blackfoot Agency as an elderly Methodist clergyman. Burleigh, on the other hand, stood apart from his colleagues, a man of action ready to take up the sword with anyone who chose to challenge him. He was not prepared for any nonsense from the Upper Sioux, particularly since they had threatened his Yanktons for refusing to join the others in their warlike ways. As soon as trouble showed itself in Dakota, Burleigh constructed an octagonal blockhouse, two stories high and twenty-six feet in diameter. The fortification was constructed of hewed timbers, twenty-two inches thick, loopholed for muskets and defended by one six-pound and two three-pound guns. Proudly, the Agent wrote that his stronghold controlled the countryside for two miles around. Now, he said, if the northern Sioux were "getting up a grand fuss," as he put it, and wanted war, they could find it at the place he had christened Fort Dole in honor of the Commissioner. "Let them try it," he wrote, "they will find the mettle of Fort Dole rather hard to digest. This is a place unknown by our eastern military men, but really the strongest fort west of the Mississippi river."

Burleigh was not one to rely solely upon defense. He begged Commissioner Dole to intercede with the President and to gain authorization for him to raise a regiment with which to march against "the villians." If this could be arranged, he said, "I will do so, and agree to retrieve every captive before the first day of April, with enough scalps to carpet Pennsylvania avenue from the Presidential mansion to the Capitol, if desired." Burleigh promised to find the men and supplies; all that had to be furnished was sufficient guns and ammunition. "Why will you not try to get the President to allow me to make a little military reputation?" he asked. And then, as an endorsement of his own case, he added: "I believe I am the only Indian Agent in this whole country who has stood his ground and not forsaken his post with his family." [11]

As the autumn of 1862 deepened, the Federal Government showed no further disposition to advance the military frontier farther into Sioux country. While Minnesotans found solace in the hanging of thirty-eight Sioux "war criminals" at Mankato on December 26, Dakotans heard no creaks of stretching rope in their part of the country. They were convinced, as settlers in many parts of the West would be each year for several decades to come, that "when the grass grew in the spring" the Indians would be on the move and blood would flow. During the months that followed the warfare in Minnesota, the Dakota press crackled with warnings of danger ahead. It angered Lounsberry of the Yankton *Dakotian* that a colleague in a more protected area had told his readers: "We look for no serious Indian troubles in Dakota this fall or winter." [12] To him it was obvious that a retreating tribe was marching straight into Dakota and, once there, would of course prey upon a relatively weak frontier. The editor printed a letter signed "Ajax," dated at Fort Randall, that recounted the attacks upon mackinaw boats and predicted a complete desolation of the frontier in the spring unless General Pope was willing to send help and thereby "imitate the example of Gen. Harney." Fur company men joined the chorus and did everything possible to attract the War Department's attention to the pressing need for protection. Charles Primeau wrote to Chouteau, from Fort Pierre, relating how Galpin had narrowly escaped death, of the number of white prisoners held by the cruel Santees, and of probable hostilities in the spring. Chouteau forwarded the correspondence to Commissioner Dole.[13]

The probability of Indian warfare in the spring bore heavily on the minds of the Dakotans during the winter of 1862–1863. In November James McFetridge, a member-elect to Dakota's Territorial Council, wrote to Minnesota's Senator Henry M. Rice urging that the Federal Government conduct a preventive winter campaign to catch the Indians in their camps. The writer expressed his conviction that once spring came and the Indians mounted up for a campaign, effective defense of the frontier would be an impossibility. Rice, who had known McFetridge for over a decade, read the letter thoughtfully and was impressed by its contents. He gave it his full endorsement before sending it on to Commissioner Dole.[14] Just before Christmas, Governor Jayne, Walter Burleigh and James S. Williams (an Associate Justice of Territorial Dakota) wrote a joint letter to Lincoln, warning that between five hundred and one thousand Santee and other Sioux were gathered along the river above Fort Pierre, practicing for the opening of activities in the spring by murdering all the whites they could lay hands on in that area. Prompt action would prevent much bloodshed in the spring, said the Dakotans, but only a firm blow, struck now, would prevent the subsequent carnage. They asked that General John Cook, a brigadier general who had shown his fighting qualities at the recent battles of Forts Henry and Donelson in Tennessee, and was currently in command of the Upper Missouri District, be given the men and the means to carry out the necessary task. General Cook, whose subdivision included Dakota and a section of northwest Iowa, was regarded by the trio as the ideal man to go up the river and take into custody these angry, dangerous Indians. "There is no time to be lost, if they are to be captured," warned the frontiersmen.[15]

Winter campaigns against the Indians were not regarded by the War Department as being practical, and none of any consequence would be attempted until Sheridan and Custer later moved against the Southern Cheyennes in 1868; however, in the autumn of 1862 Major Pattee gained permission to conduct a foray from Fort Randall. While even the Dakota press admitted that the season for campaigning was not propitious, the move was generally applauded as one that would at least show the Indians something of "our intent." Little Crow, a principal leader in the Minnesota uprising, had escaped trial and punishment and was said to be spending the winter somewhere in the country above Fort Pierre. Pattee's supporters thought it possible that he might flush the fugitive from hiding and bring him in. Another prospect was that of rescuing women and children said to have been captured in Minnesota, a project that sounded exciting to readers far and wide. When Charles Galpin arrived at Fort Randall he substantiated the story, saying that his Indian wife had learned of two women and six children who were being held by the Santees.

Pattee did not find Little Crow, and he did not challenge any of the Santees, but neither did he return empty-handed. On December 1, still two days from Fort Pierre, his force encountered two half-breeds named Frederick Dupree and Louis la Plant, who were escorting the women and children. The captives, taken at Lake Shetek in August, had been ransomed from the Indians through the efforts of Charles Primeau, *bourgeois* at Fort Pierre. Pattee later wrote that the purchase had been made at his behest, since he had only 175 men and did not think it safe to attempt a forceful rescue. He also recalled that the women had been accorded treatment that the American reading public had come to expect: they had suffered the indignity of being handed around among the braves as "wives," one of them having been traded on one occasion for a pair of pants and the other for a bag of shot. The women, Mrs. Julia Wright and Mrs. Laura Duley, along with their own children and three that did not belong to them, were taken to Fort Randall where they remained for several weeks before being sent on to their homes. Before they left, the men and officers got up a purse, the value of which Pattee set at $500.[16]

Evidence that the Missouri River frontier was on the verge of a major Indian war mounted steadily in the minds of the settlers. Governor Jayne expressed an opinion shared by his people when he said the only effective way to protect the people of southeastern Dakota was to establish a permanent military post somewhere along the Big Sioux River. "The valley of the Sioux," he wrote, "a most beautiful, rich and inviting section of the country, cannot and will not be settled up until the Government gives ample assurance that the settlers are to have protection to life and property." [17] Shortly the Dakota Territorial Select Committee on Indian Affairs asked President Lincoln for a post in that area. The committee report went on to say that a small settlement, commenced in 1856 about sixty miles north of Sioux Falls at a point where a westbound wagon road crossed the river, would have become a flourishing settlement except for the constant threat posed by the Indians. The required post was a minimum, the legislators maintained.

The year 1862 had also demonstrated the richness of the mines of the upper Missouri country, and the increased travel to and from what was then known as Idaho had been sufficiently contested by the Indians to make the whites all the more determined. The need for a string of forts between Minnesota and the mines was not only of value to the nation but also to Dakota. A territory that surely would be ready for statehood shortly was in danger of being throttled without the Governmental protection it so much deserved. Quite opposite from the current thinking of the War Department, the committee recommended a number of small posts, manned by few soldiers, as opposed to larger establishments, heavily defended.[18]

During January 1863 the Dakota Legislative Assembly addressed a memorial to Secretary of War Stanton, again expressing the fear that the coming spring would bring violence such as that recently seen in Minnesota unless the Government provided protection. Little Crow, who was yet at liberty, still posed a threat. The union of his Santees with other hostiles could point only to warfare; in fact, persistent rumors foretold of attacks upon the friendly Yanktons as punishment for their refusal to fight the whites. Meanwhile, each mackinaw that had found its way along the river the preceding autumn had confirmed and reconfirmed the magnitude of the new gold strikes in the mountains. Despite Indian hostilities, spring would see the river teeming with boats carrying "hardy pioneers and gold adventurers," as the document expressed it.

The legislators strongly recommended that Stanton put into action General Pope's recommendation of a strong expedition, at least 5,000 men, to crush the hostiles. After this was accomplished, permanent forts should be established along the river to protect growing settlements and the ever-increasing river traffic. The editor of the *Dakotian* not only reaffirmed such sentiments with great vigor and demanded that Fort Randall be garrisoned by at least a regiment, but he launched a typical western complaint against the ruling classes who resided safely in the East and who could well afford to sympathize with what he called an ignorant and degraded race. Dakotans, on the other hand, lived near the largest and most powerful Indian tribes in the country. They felt that peace would prevail only when the natives, who best understood military power, were thoroughly disciplined.[19]

Meanwhile, the Government's response to continued outcries from Minnesotans, who were certain their difficulties had not ended, was to remove from the state the Winnebagos and some of the Santee Sioux who had been involved in the uprising. Congressional approval of the plan came in February, and on March 3 a bill was passed that provided for a permanent reservation. Dakotans, who were complaining about having too many Indians, now witnessed the arrival of 3,250 Indians with all their belongings at a point only eighty miles above Fort Randall. Indian Agent Clark W. Thompson, assisted by Dr. Burleigh and some officers from Fort Randall, laid off the reservation at the mouth of Crow Creek, and then put to work a group of sixty soldiers who erected the agency buildings. The result of their labor, an establishment three hundred by four hundred feet surrounded by a stockade of cottonwood logs, looked so much like the typical fortifications of the fur companies that it was locally known as Fort Thompson. Officials at Washington called it the Winnebago or Crow Creek Agency. When the place was guarded by two companies of Iowa Volunteers and maintained by the usual number of white employees and their followers, a community came into existence that was for a time one of the largest in the Territory.[20]

Dakotans received the news about the new reservation with mixed feelings. Lounsberry of the *Dakotian* took the view that the arrival of more Indians placed residents at a dual disadvantage: first, they posed an additional danger to white settlers and second, the Santees had surrendered their annuities as a war debt and thus the people of Dakota would inherit hostile Indians "without reaping any of those benefits which generally accrue to settlers living in the neighborhood of tribes who are the recipients of Government annuities." Taking the long view, the editor concluded perhaps it was all for the best because the Government now would be forced to establish two or three forts housing anywhere from 1,500 to 2,000 troops. "This will secure for our people a ready and remunerative market for all the surplus products of their farms," and as a fringe benefit Fort Randall must, of necessity, become a principal distributing post. A letter-writer signing himself "Justitia" agreed with Lounsberry, but he warned that the benefits would accrue only if the Government agents were careful to bestow their patronage upon local merchants.[21]

Despite the prospect of Governmental largesse, Dakota settlers continued their pleas for military protection all during the spring of 1863. In April a resident of Yankton made a strong appeal to the acting governor, urging him to persuade General John Cook that a detachment of troops near their city was a necessity. He described the fire lights along the prairie horizon that sent settlers to bed each night with tingling scalps, and he predicted that unless some reassurances were made, any incident could touch off another southward stampede. So hesitant were farmers to plant their spring crops that, unless help came, he predicted "there will be no frontier in Dakota to protect by the 15th of June." Even if a rumored expedition materialized there would be danger of isolated attacks on small settlements; troops should also guard these places. The letter-writer closed by saying that "the very existence of our Territory hangs upon a chance, and it is but proper that he who is charged with our protection should be advised of the danger."

Acting Governor John Hutchinson responded by warning General Cook that "unless assurances can be given of early protection to the settlements, I have no doubt that the Territory will, within the next two months, be nearly depopulated." He was concerned because a single cavalry company that had patrolled danger areas in 1862 now was stationed at Fort Randall, and a new company then being raised might also be placed under Federal control and removed from the fighting frontier. If this happened, "the people would be deprived of most of their strength, and far more unable to protect themselves than last year." Receiving no reply, he wrote another appeal. Cook responded early in May, saying that the request already had been anticipated and troops were under orders to march.[22]

Military planners had been talking about the problem of the Dakota frontier most of the winter. In November 1862 departmental headquarters for the Northwest was moved to Milwaukee, and General Henry Hastings Sibley was left in charge of the District of Minnesota at St. Paul. During January and February, General Pope consulted with Secretary Stanton and General Halleck and convinced them that a two-pronged attack upon the Sioux was necessary to protect both the Minnesota and Dakota frontiers. He proposed to send Sibley's infantry westward to Devil's Lake as the upper arm of a pincers; General Alfred Sully, recently transferred to the West, was to move up the river with a large body of cavalry and intercept the fleeing Indians. Toward the end of February Pope told Sibley that as soon as the Missouri River was opened to navigation in the spring, General Sully would have about 2,500 men, mostly mounted, assembled at Fort Randall and ready for what he described as a vigorous campaign.[23]

As predicted, the spring of 1863 revealed a sharply increased interest in the mines of the upper Missouri. Those who had gone on ahead wrote to their friends, telling of the magnitude of the strikes and urging them to come before it was too late. Typical of these letters was one from George Detwiler, written at Bannack (then in Idaho Territory) to his friend Judge James Tufts of Yankton, in which he described a single pan of ore-bearing earth that paid $19, and how five men had panned $611 in a single day. One of the quartz mines, he said, was making as much as $500 a day. "You had better come, unless you now have a good thing where you are," urged Detwiler.[24] As fast as he could arrange passage, Tufts settled his affairs at Yankton and boarded the *Nellie Rogers* bound for the mines. It was about such men that Secretary of the Interior J. P. Usher wrote in 1863 when he reported the vast increase in "emigration to the newly discovered gold-bearing regions of the interior." The movement, said the Secretary, had now brought Americans into close contact with large and powerful tribes with whom the Government had only treaties of amity and friendship. He foresaw an inevitable collision of the two races.[25]

Agent Samuel Latta, who made an annual spring ascent of the river, could not have agreed more that the time of trouble was near. He told Commissioner Dole that on his last trip he was plainly warned by the Sioux against bringing any more annuities to them; the Indians were convinced such gifts meant an early demand by the Government for their lands in return for such favors. He was also warned that the occupants of the river country were determined to halt both land and water traffic. He cited attacks upon the *Shreveport* in August 1862 as an example of this determination, and he said that only by planking up the pilot house and forward quarters of the vessel was it able to fight its way through hostile country. The Agent recommended the use of military escorts for any Government property that was sent through Sioux country, adding that "they will destroy any party of emigrants and seize any Government property that may attempt to pass . . . through their country." [26]

The accuracy of Latta's prediction was borne out when the *Shreveport* and the *Robert Campbell* (No. 2) ascended the river in 1863. Indians struck the vessels at a point between the Gros

Ventre villages and Fort Union while one of them was taking on wood. The *Shreveport* at once pulled into midstream and the *Campbell* did the same, although a ball that passed through the wheelhouse nearly hit the wheelman. The attackers followed the vessels until they were stalled on sandbars about fifty miles below the mouth of the Yellowstone River, and then they loudly demanded provisions, arms and ammunition. Henry Boller, aboard the *Campbell,* estimated that there were at least two hundred of them, chanting derisive remarks about the whites being dogs, fit only to be killed, and of their intention to deal out such punishment. The passengers, mostly miners bound for the head of navigation, waited while the boats' officers decided what course they should take. Among the travelers was Colonel Alfred Vaughan, whose tenure with the Indian Bureau had ended when Buchanan left office and who was now aboard the *Campbell* with a large assortment of mining supplies he hoped to sell to prospectors. Mrs. Alexander Culbertson, an Indian, was aboard the same vessel, and when she learned that at Sam Latta's request Captain Joseph la Barge proposed to send a small boat ashore, she warned that its unarmed occupants would be killed. The boat was dispatched and as it approached the river bank it was fired upon. Only two of the six men escaped death. When the attack began both steamers set up a bombardment of cannonballs and rifle fire that finally forced the Indians to pull off, allowing the vessels to proceed to Fort Union.[27]

Those who made their way upriver on the spring rise of 1863 were constantly aware that the atmosphere was charged with hostility. When the *Campbell* stopped at Fort Berthold, its captain caused considerable rejoicing among the Mandans, Gros Ventres and Arickaras by telling them that troops were on their way to punish the Sioux. These river tribes had been so effectively shut out of buffalo hunting grounds that they were threatened by starvation. The pressure was relentless, the Sioux having driven off seventy-five of their horses only a few days before the boat's arrival. The Captain of the *Shreveport* noted in his log that the attacks had cost the friendly Indians a good many warriors and the loss, by burning, of some of their best lodges. He also mentioned that four of the La Barge and Harkness traders had been killed by the Sioux.[28]

At Fort Union, Henry Boller noticed the changes that had taken place since he had stayed there five years before. He recalled how one could stand atop McKenzie's Butte, named after the famous *bourgeois* at the post, and watch the approach of a steamer for nearly two days before she finally crabbed her way up to the Fort's landing. Not far away lay the ruins of old Fort William "and the mountaineers spoke regretfully of the good old times when both Posts were in the full tide of success, and the hospitalities that were so freely exchanged between them when the trading season was over." Formerly, he said, Fort Union had its own herd of cows and fresh butter was always available; the garden produced potatoes, vegetables and melons in abundance to supplement a diet of fresh buffalo meat; and the post stood as a mighty bastion at the confluence of two great rivers. But now it was merely a trading place for the Assiniboins—notoriously poor robe-makers—manned only by enough hands to keep the establishment open. The Sioux had become so persistent in their unfriendliness that the cattle herd was sent on upriver to Fort Benton, and the garden surrendered to the weeds; no one dared venture beyond the palisades and stone blockhouses.[29]

Conditions along the stretch of river between Fort Randall and Fort Pierre (where a military depot was established in early June) were not as threatening for the white population as they were in the neighborhood of Fort Union, but the discontent of the Indians was nevertheless quite apparent. The Minnesota Santees, held to be the ringleaders in the forthcoming trouble, were reported by the Dakota press as starving. During January and February the *Dakotian* described how the hungry Santees had come to Fort Pierre, ready to surrender, but since that place did not have enough food to help them they were refused admittance, after which they proceeded to Randall where they again offered to surrender. Early in February Major Pattee's men picked up three of them, about forty miles above Fort Randall, and took them back to the fort as prisoners. The Indians offered no resistance. In May Dr. Justus Townsend wrote from Fort Pierre that a large number of Indians were encamped nearby, and that if they were not fed, trouble would follow. "We are out of provisions," he wrote on May 19. "Tomorrow is issue day and we have not one day's rations on hand." Fortunately a small train of goods arrived just in time, and violence was averted.[30]

The ill humor of the Indians around Fort Pierre persisted, and in early June they literally held up one of the steamboats in order to get something to eat. Sergeant J. H. Drips of the Sixth Iowa Cavalry noted in his diary on June 9 that a vessel had discharged its freight and was preparing to cast off when "about 400 or 500 Indian warriors" seized the lines and refused to let go until the captain gave them presents. Despite their assertions that General Harney had promised such a toll from every boat passing by, the steamer's master refused to give them anything. At this point the Indians sent the women to their tepees and evidenced warlike preparations. John Pattee, now a colonel and in command of troops in the vicinity, advised the captain that diplomacy was better than war. Having no choice the unhappy skipper paid off with some crackers and tobacco. Sergeant Drips was much disappointed at the outcome, and he remarked bitterly: "Here was lost one of the finest chances for an Indian fight we had on the whole expedition through the cowardice, or lack of energy, or something else, of Col. Pattee, as all the other officers . . . went in for pitching in and clearing them out." Drips was confident that if the soldiers, whom he said were "anxious for the fray," had been ordered to fight they could have made the Indians "knock under."[31]

During the weeks that prospectors, Indian agents and others made their way up the Missouri River in the spring of 1863, General Pope attempted to put his grand pincers plan against the natives into operation. General Sibley gathered his troops at Camp Pope, near the confluence of the Redwood and Minnesota rivers. Toward the end of June he started for the vicinity of Devil's Lake, Dakota, where Little Crow was said to be (he had not been there for some months). The force consisted of about 2,000 infantry, 800 cavalry, 150 artillerymen and a handful of scouts. A small group of civilians, bound for the gold fields in another of Captain

James Fisk's ventures, joined the expedition for protection. As the men began their march and the wagons lined out on the Minnesota prairieland, the scene was one that would have impressed the Sioux who awaited beyond the Missouri. There were 225 mule-drawn wagons, filled with enough supplies for three months, and 100 wagons of ammunition, medical supplies, engineering equipment and quartermaster stores. A large herd of cattle, intended to keep the men supplied with fresh beef, milled along with the train. Never before had so large a body of troops moved against the Sioux of the upper Missouri River country.[32]

The activities of the troops that were to move up the Missouri River were much less impressive. In theory the river offered an excellent means of transporting large amounts of military supplies into Sioux country, but this was certainly the year of exceptions. Men who lived along the muddy stream searched their minds to recall a year when the river had been lower, and confessed that even the normal June rise would not provide enough water to make the navigation season of much value. The people of Yankton understood the problems nature had presented, but this did not lessen their growing concern at the continual delays of the long-promised campaign. The *Dakotian* of June 16 complained that the expedition should have been under way two months earlier, at a time when the Indians were still weak from the ravages of winter, but the editor still expected that the Indians were doomed to defeat in the near future and he tried to be patient.

To add to the public's growing concern, the Missouri River contingent of Pope's force experienced a change in command, an event that could well be used as an excuse for more delays. General John Cook was replaced by Brigadier General Alfred Sully, a Regular Army officer of considerable experience. Cautiously, the *Dakotian* stated that "the causes which have led to this change are unknown to us, and we therefore forbear comment"; the editor, who had been very enthusiastic about Cook, knew very little about the new man. News of Sully's appointment appeared in the Dakota press on June 2, and during the coming weeks readers learned more about him. A correspondent to the *Dakotian* praised the general for a Fourth of July speech he delivered to the troops at Fort Randall, an address that was mercifully short because of the sweltering heat, but one the writer called "affecting." One who signed himself simply "A" told the Yankton editor that "we have a real live General in command, one to whom nothing in the art of war is unknown. Nothing transpiring escapes his eye and . . . Dakotians may reasonably expect great result of his command during the fall." [33] The word from Fort Randall was that Sully expected to start after the Indians at once.

The effect of the Fourth of July oratory wore off during the next month as Dakotans waited in vain for action on the river frontier. Sully advanced his men to the neighborhood of Fort Pierre and there he went into camp, hoping each day that the expected steamers would bring him the supplies he needed to begin his campaign. The General's chief clerk of subsistence later wrote that the uncooperative Missouri River was only one of the hazards faced in furbishing an army. Early in June, about a week after Sully took command, George H. Rust was placed in charge of a large amount of stores aboard one of the river steamers, and given orders to get them to Fort Randall. As the vessel made its way up the river, the redoubtable Dr. Burleigh boarded it and demanded a portion of the goods for his hungry Yankton Indians. When Rust refused, Burleigh became insistent and said that as a Government Agent he had a right to the stores and he intended to take some. "I ordered the Lieut. in charge of the troops on board the boat to place a guard over them & not let any be landed at the agency," wrote Rust. [34]

By August Sully's position began to be critical. The campaigning season was slipping away and he was stalled at the starting line. The correspondent who called himself "A" was still confident, and in his dispatches to the *Dakotian* he asserted that despite the delays, poor grass that necessitated the haulage of grain for the animals, and other handicaps, "all that mortal man can do will be done by Gen. Sully, and it is his intention to make one bold strike at the Indians—grass or no grass." [35] A newspaper dispatch dated August 13 assured readers that the General proposed to move that very day, but another week passed before the troops began their march.

The repeated delays developed inevitable morale problems. Part of the troops were short-term enlistees who had signed up for as little as nine months' service, and discipline among them was poor. It did not improve as the weeks of inaction dragged on. Corporal Henry W. Pierce of the Second Nebraska Cavalry was ashamed of the conduct displayed by his outfit as it lay camped near Yankton late in the spring of 1863. "Tonight," he confessed in his diary, "whiskey displayed itself in all its meanness by some of the boys getting 'tight' & confiscating a peddler's wagon containing cakes & fruit. Such depredations on the kindness of the settlers will relieve us, to our mortification, of many luxuries." [36] Apparently other luxuries were being lost through abuses, for a Yankton paper announced that "the fair sex, with the exception of laundresses," had been directed to evacuate Fort Randall, by order of General Pope. The editor noted that the move "is creating quite a commotion within the crinoline circle," but he made no remarks about reactions from the soldiers who suffered the loss.[37] Some of the men, waiting at the encampment just north of Fort Pierre, were not burdened with the problems of liquor and women, but instead had to worry about finding enough food to keep alive. Amos Cherry wrote on July 10 that his commanding officer had decided to retreat to Fort Randall, without orders, "on the account of being out of rations and having only 6 days rations on hand." [38]

On August 19, a steamer carrying some supplies arrived at the encampment near Fort Pierre and was unloaded at once. Men who were too sick to travel and excess baggage of those who were to participate in the campaign were then sent a few miles downriver to the storage depot at Fort Pierre. But on the following day, just when Sully was ready to begin the long-delayed start, the troops were bombarded by the heaviest hailstorm the General had ever seen. Animals stampeded, rations were destroyed and the men were dispirited. At last, on August 21, the move began and the troops moved eleven miles over a road Sully described as "very heavy." [39]

In addition to all his other worries, Sully had to answer Pope's outspoken criticisms of the delays. Writing from Milwaukee on

August 5, Pope acknowledged a letter from Sully written on July 27, saying that "it both surprised and disappointed me." Pope expressed astonishment that "you could delay thus along the River," and once more he pointed out the supreme importance of coordinating with Sibley's movements. "I never dreamed you would consider yourself tied to the boats if they were obstacles in going up the River," said Pope. "As matters stand, it seems to me impossible understand how you have staid about the River, delaying from day to day, when time of all things was important, and when you had wagons enough to carry at least two months subsistence for your command." Sully was ordered to leave all baggage behind, to load his wagons with subsistence and to get started immediately, for if he failed in his mission "it will be impossible for you to explain it satisfactorily." Then Pope stung Sully with the remark that Sibley was faced by the same difficulties but had managed to move his men to Devil's Lake "and I should not be surprised to hear from him on the Missouri above you." Since Sully's force was largely cavalry, as opposed to Sibley's infantry, Pope could not understand "why you should not be able to execute the object of your expedition." [40]

Sully's march northward from Fort Pierre was laborious and uneventful, characterized principally by difficulties of marching over an unfriendly terrain. On August 24, he camped on the east side of the Missouri along a small creek named Bois Cache and, being now in buffalo country, he formed a hunting party to bring in fresh meat for his command. The results were so unsatisfactory that the disgruntled General said he had to call in the huntsmen "as they disabled more horses than buffaloes." The following day, after the troops had advanced another twenty-two miles, the hunters brought news that they had made a large kill and also had seen some Indians near the Missouri. Before the day was over a small scouting party brought in two Indian women and some children, from whom it was learned that General Sibley had engaged a sizable group of Indians and had routed them. Their reference was to a series of three fights made between July 24 and 28 northeast of Long Lake, in which Sibley estimated he had encountered approximately 2,200 Sioux warriors. Having killed an estimated 150 of them at a cost of only four dead, and having sent the rest fleeing west of the Missouri River, Sibley went into camp at the mouth of Apple Creek, just below the site of present Bismarck, where he waited ten days for Sully before moving on.[41]

A month later, on August 25, Sully was just approaching the general area in which the fight had taken place. On that date, at a time when Sully's men were questioning the captured Indian women, General Pope sat down in his Milwaukee office and wrote another biting letter to his snail-like subordinate. Again he expressed great disappointment at the lack of progress, and he expressed puzzlement at Sully's advance of only 160 miles when Sibley had taken his infantrymen across 600 miles of difficult country and had fought the Indians three times. Apparently despairing of any results from Sully's command during that fighting season, Pope talked of wintering the troops, specifying that they would be divided into groups small enough to be subsisted at Fort Pierre, Fort Randall and Sioux City. Due to the lateness of the summer Pope had almost written off the river campaign for 1863.[42]

Sully knew that the season was late, but he was determined to find some warlike Sioux before he ran out of supplies and had to turn back. Having talked with his Indian prisoners, he became convinced that hostiles were not out of his reach. Hoping to confirm his beliefs he sent out two companies of Nebraska cavalry "with orders to capture some Indians if possible," from whom he hoped to obtain more information. The weather was hot, good drinking water was in short supply and the progress of the main body of troops was slow, but they pushed forward. On August 27 Indian signs became more numerous, and during the day the soldiers found a lame old Indian hiding under a bush. He was identified as a "good Indian" able to supply more information. He substantiated the report that Sibley had been in the country to the northeast and had fought a series of three engagements about fifty miles from Sully's position, after which he had camped a few days along Apple Creek before moving eastward. The old Indian related that after Sibley had left, the Sioux returned to his campsite and inadvertently discovered a mackinaw making its way downriver, which they promptly attacked. The boat's twenty-one men, three women and some children were said to have been killed. Meanwhile, a small war party trailed Sibley until he had crossed the James River and was believed out of the vicinity.

Sully concluded that the report was "so much in keeping with the Indian mode of warfare" that he was inclined to believe it, even if it came from an Indian. His guides advised him that the west side of the Missouri was inhospitable for some distance, and that the Sioux had a habit of camping to the east along the tributaries of the James River, where the presence of lakes and springs meant fish, buffalo herds and grass. "I therefore determined to change my course toward the east, to move rapidly, and go as far as my rations would allow," he later wrote.

On September 3 Frank la Framboise, one of the scouts, reported a camp of over four hundred lodges nestled in protective ravines, apparently unaware that Sully had veered eastward. The scouting party report estimated that there were from 1,200 to 1,500 warriors in the camp, a body much larger than they had expected, and they returned to Sully at once with the information. They were Santees from Minnesota, Cut Heads, Yanktonnais, Blackfeet Sioux and Hunkpapas. It was four in the afternoon by the time word of the Indian encampment reached Sully, but when the bugle sounded a cheer went up and the men saddled their mounts in a matter of minutes. Leaving four companies of poorly mounted men to break camp and follow, Sully started off at full gallop with the Second Nebraska on his right, the Sixth Iowa on his left and the Seventh Iowa in the center. The troops covered the intervening ten miles "in much less than an hour," he said in reporting the battle.

Upon reaching the Indian camp, Sully discovered that the enemy was abandoning the place as fast as possible, leaving some of the tepees standing. Immediately he ordered Colonel Robert Furnas of the Second Nebraska to push his horses to the utmost and to circle around the Indians from the right in an attempt to cut off their retreat, while Colonel David S. Wilson and his Sixth Iowa cavalrymen carried out a similar maneuver to the left. As the two flankers disappeared into the dust, Sully charged the camp with one company of the Seventh Iowa and two companies of the Sixth Iowa, supported by a battery. As the General approached the camp's center he came upon a chief named Little Soldier, who had a reputation as a friendly and who was consequently placed in protective custody. Next the troopers encountered Big Head, notoriously unfriendly, along with some of his followers, all of whom were dressed for combat. The group, numbering about 120 when women and children were counted, surrendered and were put under guard. More resistance was encountered about a half-mile farther on, but small arms fire, supported by the battery, put these warriors to flight. Sully regretted that night was falling and pursuit was futile. He felt that another hour or two of daylight would have meant annihilation for the enemy. "As it was," he wrote, "I believe I can safely say I gave them one of the most severe punishments that the Indians have ever received."

On the following day, September 4, Sully went through the motions of sending out scouting parties to pick up stray Indians, but, as he suspected, the results were unrewarding. The men who remained in camp spent two days burning all the baggage and provisions at hand, some 400,000 or 500,000 pounds of buffalo meat and 300 lodges according to Sully's estimate. The martial scoreboard revealed twenty soldiers killed and thirty-eight wounded, as opposed to a guess of between 150 and 200 Indians dead and 156 prisoners, mostly women. Leaving the scene of battle, a place the Indians called White Stone Hill,[43] Sully struck off at once for Fort Pierre, his supplies so low that when he arrived on September 14 his food supply was nearly exhausted.[44]

The immediate demands of Dakotans had been met. At the height of the Civil War, and at a time when the Federal Government had been hard pressed, they called for help and were answered with a combined force of approximately 5,000 troops who spent the summer searching a parched land for hostile Indians. Between the efforts of Sibley and Sully perhaps three hundred warriors were killed and a handful captured. Both generals professed to think that the enemy had been soundly punished. The

Sioux took another point of view; rather than viewing the result as a defeat, they were highly irritated. For almost three decades after White Stone Hill they demonstrated their resentment in Dakota, and the Federal Government, having started a small fire, was now obligated to put out a major one.

SEVEN

"These Savages Block the Way"

Reactions to the Indian campaign of 1863 were varied. In general the western press was happy about it, not only because some warriors had been killed, but also because the appearance of a large number of troops in the region suggested Governmental interest in the western country. The Yankton *Dakotian* of October 13 devoted more than a column to praising General Sully for his efforts. The editor acknowledged the limitations under which he had worked—a late start, low water, poor grass and difficult terrain—and concluded that, under the circumstances, the expedition was a success. He admitted, however, that the Indians were still hostile and far from subjugated.

To a St. Louis newspaper the blows given the Sioux were of a very serious nature. "It is estimated that their loss of personal property is greater to them than the destruction of the city of New York would be to us," said that journal, whose correspondent reported at least three hundred Indians were dispatched to the land of their fathers.[1] As a further boost for Sully, who, it was hoped, would stay around to fight more Indians, the *Dakotian* tended to minimize the efforts of Sibley, the prominent Minnesotan. That paper quoted a letter written by a resident of St. Paul to the *New York Tribune,* in which the author said Sibley's efforts were far from conclusive, and that the only hope for a successful conclusion to the campaign lay with Sully's cavalrymen who, one day, would fall upon the Indians and "rout or kill them." For the mental comfort of its readers, the *Dakotian* stated that the General would remain along the river that winter, a statement that suggested another campaign in the spring.[2]

Dakota officials gave cautious approval to the recent campaign. In late September Acting Governor John Hutchinson, who was also acting *ex officio* Superintendent of Indian Affairs for the Territory, reported the events of that season to the Commissioner of Indian Affairs. While he had kind words for Sully, he also indicated that there was much more to be done: the Indians had to be defeated and humbled if the Missouri River, which he called "that great Thoroughfare," were to be kept open. For further protection of his people he asked for the establishment of a line of military posts running from Fort Ridgely, Minnesota, to Fort Randall, by way of Sioux Falls and Yankton.[3] The Territorial Governor, Newton Edmunds, expressed similar feelings when he addressed the Territorial legislature in December. As a man who would later engage in treatymaking with the Sioux, he was at this time much more anxious to administer punishment than presents. He was aware of Sully's problems and did not openly criticize the General, but he felt that the expedition's accomplishments were so ineffective that another strike would have to be made next season.[4]

Officials of the Indian Bureau were in general agreement with the Territorial point of view. Samuel Latta, Agent for the Upper Missouri Sioux, called it "bad policy" to force a large body of irritated Indians from their country and to antagonize anywhere from 25,000 to 40,000 of them who, up to that point, had been dealt with by the Government at a very reasonable cost. He doubted the wisdom of expending thousands of dollars on campaigns that would have to be followed by even more expensive efforts of a similar nature, when perhaps $500,000 spent upon food and housing for the natives, as well as the establishment of small military posts among them, would have accomplished much more. From the outset he had been convinced that the campaign of 1863 would accomplish nothing. It was apparent to him that the low state of the river that season, the poor condition of the grass, the willingness of the Indians to burn off the prairie for miles to prevent pursuit, all militated against success, and he predicted that "General Sully will not get within five hundred miles of any considerable body of hostile Indians this season." Sibley, he said, had done no more than to drive the Minnesota Indians into his Agency where he left them "as insolent and defiant as at any previous time." His new worry was that Sully might be withdrawn from the river country, leaving unprotected the agents, who would be unable to cope with highly aroused Indians; if this happened the military had done no more than aggravate an already dangerous situation.

Commissioner William Dole read Latta's report and came to the conclusion that the efforts of the two generals were "unproductive of any very favorable results," and he, too, felt the necessity for another expedition to rectify the damage already done. He raised once more a familiar argument, long used by his subordinates, that without military posts in the upper Missouri country there was danger not only to white residents, but also to a large number of friendly Indians who would be forced to side with the hostiles for their own safety.[5]

Henry Boller, who had gone upriver on the *Robert Campbell* in the spring of 1863, looked back upon the efforts of the military arm with considerable disdain. Referring to Sully's force, which he had passed as he proceeded toward Fort Union, he summarized: "The army took the field—the bugles were blown, the antelope badly frightened, sped over the hills, while from the distant bluffs 'the d——d redskins' defiantly waved their breech-clouts. Some few squaws were captured, and the army went into winter-quarters, the Indians having gone out of sight, and the safety of the frontiers thus being assured." [6] Sergeant J. H. Drips, one of Sully's men, thought the responsibility for failure lay elsewhere. On September 7, while encamped on Apple Creek during the return to Fort Pierre, he noted in his diary that the troops were not far from Sibley's "famous Camp 'Slaughter.'" The sergeant then remarked: "Here is where the General had a splendid chance to whip the Indians but failed to do so for reasons I suppose satisfactory to himself, if not to the whole country." [7]

General Sibley was not without his defenders. Before the end of August, Reverend J. A. André of Minnesota complimented him on his campaign and remarked that, aside from the other happy results, it "has undoubtedly disposed the mass of the Indians to offer their submission to the government." It pleased the cleric that Sibley had treated the captured women and children with such kindness, an act he said that "has touched the wild hearts of these barbarians, who in their own bloody wars devote to death all who may fall into their hands regardless of age or sex." [8] Joseph R. Brown, Agent for Minnesota's Upper Sioux, assured his friend the General that "the croakers about St. Paul" had been disarmed by the effectiveness of Sibley's expedition. Proof of this, he said, lay in the fact that the Indians had not troubled the frontier since Sibley had punished them, and even the very smallest raiding parties had not taken anything of great value.[9] Apparently the "croakers" at St. Paul had been of some concern to Sibley, who, during his march, had confided in his diary that one Major Hatch had been granted permission to raise two companies of cavalry and two of infantry to serve against the Indians. He had an explanation for such perfidy: "The whole thing I regard as a miserable scheme got up by [Senator Henry M.] Rice & others who hate Gen. Pope, and do not love me & who wish to annoy & humiliate us both. I have contempt for the whole humbug, inventors & all." [10]

Pope had only the strongest of endorsements for Sibley. On August 29 he reported to Secretary of War Edwin M. Stanton that Sibley had so effectively cleared the area west of Minnesota that "I do not suppose that there are now ten hostile Sioux Indians east of the Missouri River." In a letter to Sibley he was equally positive: "I myself have no idea that the Indians whom you drove across the Missouri River will ever return for hostile purposes, or in any other way, unless permission is obtained from Washington." [11] Stanton's only comment, in an otherwise objective report to the President, was regret that conditions had prevented the intended junction of forces, an occurrence he termed unfortunate.[12]

As late as the first of September, Pope clung to the faint hope that the Indians could be thoroughly punished that year. He urged

Sully to scour the Black Hills and the country to the north before cold weather set in, reminding him that it was his special mission to strike a final blow at the Indians Sibley had herded across the Missouri River. "The peace of the whole border, and particularly the security of the frontier settlements of Minnesota and Iowa, depend upon a vigorous campaign on your part until cold weather drives you from the plains," he wrote from Milwaukee.[13]

So far as General Sully was concerned, the fighting season was over. In mid-September he announced that his troops and their animals were in need of rest after the long march, and therefore he intended to order them downriver as far as practicable and into winter quarters. Part of the force would be sent to Sioux City, while the others would stay at Fort Randall and at a new post that was being built on the east side of the river a little above Farm Island. The island, located nearly five miles below modern Pierre, South Dakota, had long been known to the occupants of the original Fort Pierre as a source of wood and fuel as well as one suitable for raising garden vegetables. Sully knew the place for he had been stationed there as a Captain of the Second Infantry in 1857 under General Harney.[14]

On October 13 the new fort was pronounced ready for occupancy and the troops marched in. It was a typical cottonwood timber enclosure, 270 feet square, surrounded by a palisade twelve feet high and protected by the usual blockhouses. The principal buildings, made of unhewn logs, lay along the east and west sides. These low structures, roofed with cottonwood poles upon which brush and then dirt was thrown, were not as neat looking as the frame buildings at Fort Randall, but the earlier experience at Fort Pierre had demonstrated their practicability in sub-zero weather. In addition, the place offered some mental comfort to its occupants, for it was secure. Sergeant J. H. Drips described it as "pretty well fixed for defense and cannot be taken very easily by the Indians." As one who had helped to build the fort, he admitted that some of his fellow laborers placed the project in the category of sheer folly, but, philosophically, the Sergeant concluded it might well stand as a memorial to Sully's recent Indian campaign. Lieutenant Colonel E. M. Bartlett of the Thirtieth

Wisconsin Infantry, who served as the first commanding officer, was moved by the same sentiments. Upon assuming his new position he announced that the place would henceforth be known as Fort Sully "in compliment to our brave commander, Brigadier General Alfred Sully, U.S. Volunteers, now commanding the District of Iowa and Dakota." With christening ceremonies over, the troops settled down for the winter, an assignment in Dakota that often promised as much hardship as campaigning through the drought and heat of summer. The accommodations housed four companies of the Thirtieth Wisconsin, three companies of the Sixth Iowa and three of the Seventh Iowa Cavalry.[15]

The volunteers who forted up for the winter at Sully and Randall apparently were in no immediate danger of extinction from Indian attacks. The Yanktons remained peaceful; despite a virtual crop failure from the summer drought, they had a fairly good hunt that autumn. During the summer a detail of soldiers from Fort Randall, in search of some native horse thieves, came across a band of friendly Yanktons and killed seven of them before identification was made. Only promises of suitable reparations calmed the tribal leaders. On another occasion an unidentified band of hostiles from the north attacked the Sioux City-Fort Randall stage, killed one of the passengers and made off with the stagecoach horses. A group of Dakota cavalrymen chased them for over two hundred miles upriver.[16]

The Winnebagos, removed from Minnesota, found the Dakota country so inhospitable that they resolved to flee southward at the first opportunity. They had no crop in 1863, and by the first of November they had not yet received their annuity goods. On the third of that month the *Dakotian* admitted that "Their rations are already reduced to just sufficient to keep them above *terra firma* and ounce by ounce they are wasting away." Efforts of these Indians to reach their friends, the Omahas, where they hoped to find food, were temporarily frustrated by the soldiers. Toward the end of the month General Pope began to make inquiries as to the whereabouts of the supply train carrying annuities. One of his subordinates expressed his concern to Sibley, saying that Pope "fears that early storms will retard it, and make the trip unpleasant and dangerous." Apparently the Department's commanding officer was undisturbed about the Winnebagos who stood daily watch, waiting for the food that could save their lives.[17] Dakotans were critical of the supply system mainly because it originated in Minnesota rather than northern Iowa or southern Dakota. The Yankton *Dakotian* announced that local merchants were fully equipped to supply such necessities to the Winnebagos, and that they were ready to "coax powerful hard for the patronage of our Indian neighbors." [18]

During the winter of 1863–1864 the thinking of white residents of Dakota and Minnesota progressed from a genuine concern over the safety of their frontier settlements to a larger concept that encompassed both the protection of human life and the economic welfare of a growing commercial community. In his annual address to the Dakota Territorial legislature, Governor Newton Edmunds spoke of two principal routes to the mines: the first, of course, was the Missouri River, which he regarded as the most important; the second was the land route from Omaha by way of Fort Kearny, Fort Laramie and Salt Lake City, said to be six hundred miles longer. The river route was of great consequence to Dakotans, he maintained, because it flowed through the new farm communities and provided a ready market for farm produce at the site of production. Merchants also would profit "from the increased demands made upon their stocks and business occasioned by the immigration flowing constantly past their doors." [19]

Such sentiments met the approval of the area's newspapers. The *Dakotian* agreed that the river was "one of the leading features of Dakota," for it was a 2,000-mile avenue leading to gold country, one that soon would become a major commercial artery. The editor predicted that fifty steamers would not accommodate the needs of the coming season.[20] (He was not far wrong. By 1866 the number of steamboats on the upper Missouri exceeded fifty.) These vessels not only would serve the merchant, he continued, but they were an important part of General Pope's plans for future campaigns against the Sioux. The Yankton journalist spoke for his local readers when he maintained that unless the Indians were subdued by force, the economic development of the region would be severely curtailed; uninterrupted river commerce was central to the problem. To show that such sentiments had spread farther than the banks of the Missouri, he quoted the *St. Paul Press* on regional manifest destiny. "These savages block the way to the whole system of Northwestern development," the Minnesota paper contended, and quickly added: "Of course, the obstacle cannot be suffered to remain." To remove such annoying obstructions effectively, the editor recommended vigorous military action along the river, all the way to "the remotest spring of the Missouri," and he warned that the pacification of the tribes must be thorough even in the most remote parts of the country in contention.[21]

Sully was aware that his late summer campaign was only a beginning. As he went into winter quarters, he publicly warned settlers in outlying areas to be on guard and, where possible, to move to more defensible points until the danger had passed. He admitted that he had succeeded only in scattering the Indians, and that the destruction of their lodges, food supply and ponies meant that they would have to steal or starve during the winter. In an apologetic tone the General explained the difficulties with which he had contended, circumstances that prevented him from following up the murderers and ending their resistance, but he offered reassurance by announcing his intention to establish a new post on the river and to keep his troops there until spring.[22]

The establishment of Fort Sully marked the beginning of the Army's advance up the river beyond Fort Randall. For the next fifteen years the War Department continued to build new posts along the Missouri and its tributaries, gradually extending the military arm to the base of the Rockies. Fort Assiniboine, near present Havre, Montana and only a few miles from the international line, was built as late as 1879, to prevent Indians from moving northward into Canada.[23] This was the development that the residents of Minnesota, Dakota and what was to be Montana sought so anxiously in 1863.

Early in that year Henry Reed, Agent to the Blackfeet, joined with traders from the firm of La Barge, Harkness & Company to request the establishment of military posts on the upper Missouri. They asked for two companies of soldiers at Fort Pierre, one or two at Fort Berthold and the same number at Fort Benton, the head of navigation, pointing out that for over 1,800 miles between Fort Randall and Fort Benton there was not a single military post, not a soldier, not a civil officer, "indeed, no authority or government of any kind" except an occasional Indian Agent. In that great, intervening stretch of land lived the Sioux, hostile to whites and pro-white Indians alike, a powerful aggregation of the most dangerous Indians on the continent. Commissioner Dole publicly admitted that the failure to establish Army posts in that country had resulted in a loss of control over these Indians, and that the main route to the mines was therefore cut off.[24] Judge James Tufts, formerly of Yankton, wrote from Bannack reiterating the need for a line of military posts from Fort Randall to the Forks of the Missouri, while his friend, R. M. Hagaman, who had gone upriver with him earlier that year, also suggested the desirability of such protection when he told his Yankton friends that "the mines are much richer than I had anticipated." [25]

The idea of establishing permanent garrisons deeper in Indian country in order to control and, if necessary, to chastise the Indians severely, met with the complete approval of the general officers who had carried out the campaign of 1863. A St. Paul paper quoted John Pope as saying that he had, for years, believed in placing the forts in advance of settlement, a defense theory he had stated as early as 1849. He now regarded such forts as Abercrombie and Ridgely, both in Minnesota, as only supply depots, establishments that henceforth would support the new frontier Sully and Sibley had erected beyond the Missouri River.[26]

One of Sibley's subordinates, writing from Fort Abercrombie in January 1864, strongly supported the idea of extending a line of posts westward to the mining country. He doubted that any large body of Indians would launch attacks in the spring, but he advanced the notion that "no man who feels an interest in the future of Minnesota will willingly consent to leave them where they are in peace." Therefore, concluded the officer, the only way to secure a lasting peace was to occupy tribal lands, bring all redskinned murderers to justice and indoctrinate the subjected people with a respect for the Federal Government. Sibley, who only recently had been complimented by Reverend André for his humanitarian treatment of the Indians, lamented the fact that some of the hostiles had escaped into Canada where they had been saved from starvation by their British friends. Now, he said, the Government would have to spend several hundred thousand dollars running them down during the coming season "which would not have been required if they had been suffered to perish as they richly deserved." By every principle of international law and comity, said the angry General, this breach of etiquette was one that called for reparations by Her Majesty's Government. Forts along the upper reaches of the river would help to control Indian tendencies to flee across the 49th parallel to escape pursuing American troops.

Sibley's enthusiasm for a summer campaign grew during the winter of 1863–1864. In January he outlined his plans to General Pope, stating that he first wanted to strengthen existing posts along the Minnesota and Iowa frontiers to protect existing settlements, after which he proposed to send an expedition comprised of fourteen infantry and three cavalry companies, supported by mountain howitzers, into the heart of Dakota to seek out the Sioux. "I assume as a fixed fact that you will direct a formidable movement of troops up the Missouri River, to chastise the Teton Sioux, as to render safe the emigrant route to the gold regions of Idaho," he wrote to Pope. Sibley reiterated a view popular with the military when he talked of complete defeat and total submission of the Indians as the principal end in view. To make such a success permanent, he again recommended forts along the Missouri, to be manned principally by infantry elements because grain-fed cavalry horses were not only inferior to those of the Indians, but even infantry could outlast them on long marches.[27]

The American Fur Company, so long a power in the upper Missouri country, had some reservations about planting a line of forts across the land for the benefit of westbound emigrants. In late March Pierre Chouteau, Jr., wrote to Major General H. W. Halleck and suggested that the route from Fort Randall westward to Fort Laramie and then north along what would be known as the Bozeman Trail was a safer way for prospectors to approach the mines.

Describing a number of attacks made upon fur company traders in recent months, he concluded that "the Sioux are centering in large crowds in the angle formed by the Yellowstone and Missouri," or a section of country that lay directly in the path of the proposed roadway. Not only would users encounter heavy Indian opposition, said Chouteau, but the shortness of the travel season argued against the enormous governmental outlay of money that was involved. Further, he said, the country was often referred to as the *Mauvaises Terres,* or badlands, which correctly suggested a scarcity of grass, little wood and brackish water. The famed trader agreed that the Indians should be thoroughly subjugated, after which it would be a good time for the Government to think about locating forts to control the conquered race.[28] He did not explain, for obvious reasons, that a flow of immigrants through fur country would seriously disrupt a peltry trade that was already suffering from disruptions caused by the emergence of the mining frontier along the Rockies. He merely intimated that the argonauts of the Sixties would do well to approach the object of their endeavors by another avenue and give the dying fur trade a brief respite before it passed into history.

But the military had its own needs. The Civil War would end in the foreseeable future and the fraternity of army officers would have to find a place of occupation for its expanded ranks. At the war's outbreak most of the troops were serving in western commands; it was logical to suppose that this was the field to which they would return when the civil commotion had ended. Pope, who had failed in the East, sought to recover his lost reputation in the West. His subordinates, Sibley and Sully, were ready to try the Sioux again in 1864 and the Government, pressed by outcries from Minnesota and Iowa, apparently was committed to support the campaign with men and materiel. Sergeant Drips wrote that residents of these states "became clamorous for active operations," and in response to such pressure the Government determined to send another expedition up the Missouri to press the Indians back and to explore a route through to the Yellowstone River "as the excitement of the Idaho gold mines was then at a high pitch." [29]

Late in March Sully boarded a river steamer and went to St.

Louis to complete arrangements for what a Dakota paper called "the great Indian campaign of the ensuing summer." White residents along the upper river learned from the press that the General would have to charter at least a dozen light-draft steamers to transport his troops as well as some four thousand tons of supplies for the expeditionary force and the river posts that were to be built. It was understood that he would leave about four hundred men at each of several new posts and, with the support of troops sent overland from Minnesota, he would take about 3,500 troops westward on a "special visit" to some of the tribes. Much was made of Sully's desire to settle scores with Indians he had failed to encounter the preceding year, and once again there was enthusiasm for the projected strike against the enemy.[30]

Sully's most formidable opponent in 1863 had been the land through which he took his men rather than the Indians who lived there. The enigmatic Missouri had frustrated his efforts so effectively that the navigational season almost passed before he could get his force into the field. Now, in 1864, the river threatened him again. He admitted to Pope that the Yanktonnais and Sisseton Sioux were determined to stop ascending boats, and perhaps some force such as a small convoy would be required to overcome this threat. Yet the scarcity of transports that season obliged him to take whatever he could get. Pope was doubtful about sending single boats upriver, but he accepted Sully's explanation of the situation and agreed that the risk would have to be taken.[31]

As the campaigning season drew near, Pope became quite concerned about the lateness of the Missouri's annual spring rise. Low water had prevented a junction between the forces of Sibley and Sully in the preceding year, and he now began to worry about a reoccurrence of that regrettable development. At the end of April Pope showed his irritation over delays, this time nagging Sibley for his tendency to waste time with minute details when he ought to be moving out for the all-important union with Sully's forces.[32] Sibley countered by quoting an Army officer at Sioux City who said the *Benton*, carrying military stores to Fort Union, had consumed twenty-one days between St. Louis and Sioux City and had made only a few miles a day since leaving that port. The river was no higher than it had been during the preceding winter, and navigation was so difficult that he doubted there was any chance Sully would get off for the north in the near future. The *Benton* was thought to be the only boat working north of Omaha thus far in the season, and while there was a promise of others he did not believe they would reach Sioux City very soon. Sibley concluded that any movement of troops that season would have to move north of Sioux City by wagon, and he set June 1 as the earliest date the expedition might be expected to get under way.[33] Meanwhile he explained to Sully that he had sent General Pope information on river conditions and it should not be construed as any move to retard Sully's preparation. However, he added, his informants had told him that the Indians were ready for peace and he was sure that they would accede to the terms he had specified in the fall of 1863. In effect, he was telling Sully that the situation was well in hand—Sibley's hands—and that there was no need to hurry.[34]

Another reason for Pope's anxiety over delays was his fear that he would lose some of the troops at his disposal before he could get them into the field. On March 30, 1864, he wrote to General Henry W. Halleck at Washington, D.C., complaining about efforts being made to transfer part of his command to the Civil War front. He charged that those behind the move were persons "connected with our unfortunate Indian system, agents, Indians, traders, whiskey sellers, contractors, etc.," people Pope thought wanted to prolong Indian hostilities so that they might provide the goods inevitably promised in treaties that resulted from Indian warfare. "When the Indian war is really ended by driving the Indians entirely beyond reach of the settlements of Minnesota, the business of such people is brought to an end," he wrote. "They therefore do not desire to get rid of the Indians, nor do they favor any measures which will bring their connection with the Indians to an end."[35] Halleck admitted that General Grant had inquired about the availability of an Iowa Cavalry regiment in the Department of the Northwest, to which Pope responded that the Sixth Iowa, stationed at Forts Pierre and Randall, constituted a large part of Sully's force and that it was vital to the upcoming

Indian expedition. Within twenty-four hours Halleck telegraphed acknowledgment of the information and explained that there had been a number of unsuccessful efforts by members of Congress to get the Sixth Iowa away from Pope, and he thought it probable that this was where Grant was getting his information. "For some reason or other they do not wish this regiment to go into the Indian campaign, and hence their efforts to get it out of your command," explained the Chief of Staff.[36]

Efforts to appropriate part of Pope's troops failed, and as spring came to the river country the Indian expedition got under way. Sibley continued to comment about low water on the river and the probability that Sully again would be delayed as he organized his own elements of the expedition. He told G. S. Benson of Shakopee, Minnesota, who headed a group of emigrants readying themselves for a trip to the mines, that a column of his troops would leave Camp Pope, on the Minnesota River some twenty-five miles above Fort Ridgely, at the end of May. Colonel Minor T. Thomas and his Eighth Minnesota Volunteers would move westwardly to a junction with Sully, and the combination of forces would operate against the Sioux who were reported to be concentrated in the Fort Berthold area. Thomas' column, said Sibley, would be strong enough to protect emigrants as far as the Missouri, but no farther, until Sully's men had defeated the enemy and had cleared the country as far as the Yellowstone River. To Benson's inquiry if 250 well-armed men would be able to protect themselves, Sibley said "Emphatically, no!" He thought that the Sioux were so concentrated and powerful that no party of less than one thousand heavily armed and well-equipped men should venture into their country. Once the Indians were met and severely punished, he thought travel conditions would be safer. Then, cautioning one of his subordinates to prevent the men from scalping or cutting up Indian casualties, "for that is not like white men or Christians," General Sibley prepared to send his troopers forth to do their duty.[37]

Indian Bureau officials had mixed feelings about the new military expedition. Commissioner William Dole had not changed his opinion that a *little* punishment only antagonized the Indians, and he continued to doubt that the Army could come to grips with the Sioux conclusively enough to break their spirits. In March 1864 he asked Father P. J. De Smet to go upriver that spring and sound out the Indians with peace feelers. The Jesuit was to tell the Indians that while the Government wanted peace, it was ready to make war. Dole felt that no western man was better qualified for the mission. De Smet agreed to go and on April 16, accompanied by his interpreter, Zephyr Recontre, he left St. Louis aboard the *Yellowstone.* Six weeks later he was at Fort Sully asking the Yanktonnais and Two Kettles band of Sioux to pass the word that he would soon be at Berthold, ready to talk.[38] Agent Henry Reed, who was aboard the same vessel bound for Fort Benton, shared Dole's view that a force of fewer men, sent into the country to establish permanent posts, would have saved a lot of money and would have been of more benefit to the Indians. He was deeply disturbed that the Government was willing to discipline the Indians, but did little to punish those who brought in large quantities of liquor to arouse them. He charged that a large part of every cargo going to Fort Benton was whiskey, "and this leaks out astonishingly in going through the country." It annoyed him to think that when steamers were caught in sandbars it was not unusual for some of the goods to be left behind, in order to lighten the load, but to abandon any whiskey in such an emergency was almost totally unknown.[39]

Dakotans were not particularly worried about the infusion of whiskey into Indian country for that was an old story, but what bothered them was the slowness with which the military moved in beginning its campaign. On May 3 the Yankton *Dakotian* expressed its concern, saying that for two weeks "we have been anxiously waiting for some movement on the part of the military powers in this department," and expressing the hope that the promised forts would be established in the upper country. The paper agreed with the *Sioux City Register* that it was useless to send out annual expeditionary forces unless a line of forts was established between the settlements and the land of the hostile Indians. These would protect residents from raids by prowling bands while the main body of troops penetrated the interior.

Before May was over, word arrived that the long awaited movement upriver had commenced.

By June 12 Sully's troops had reached Fort Randall, where he was welcomed by Agent Walter Burleigh, who informed the General that he had organized about fifty of his Yanktons who would serve as scouts for the expedition. Not only would they be useful, said Burleigh, but since times were hard for the Yanktons it would give some of the men needed employment. Sully agreed to take them along and ordered that they be provided with condemned artillery uniforms and some rations. The arrangement proved less than satisfactory to the Indians, who were not only promised $75 each for their services (which it took them ten years to collect from the Government) but were given such meager rations that they had to forage for themselves on the marches that followed. On June 17 Sully moved his men forward, and within four days he wrote from an encampment above Fort Pierre that he had come upon a mixed camp of two hundred or three hundred Sioux who said they were friendly, but who warned that six thousand hostile warriors lay beyond, ready for battle. Sully, who had about 2,300 men in his force, approximately two-thirds of the troops then stationed in the Department of the Northwest, was perfectly willing to meet such a force.[40]

On June 28, near the mouth of the Little Cheyenne River, advance elements under the command of Captain Nelson Miner of the Dakota Cavalry gave chase to three Indians who had just killed one of Sully's topographical engineers caught while collecting specimens. When the raiders were overtaken and killed, Sully, whose temper was notorious, ordered that the corpses be decapitated and the heads stuck on poles as a warning to other warlike Indians.[41] He then pushed on to Swan Lake where the Minnesota troops—1,550 strong—joined him, and on July 3 the combined group took up the march northward. As the expeditionary force began its advance, Sully took one of the steamers up the Missouri to look for a good place to locate the fort that the War Department wanted to establish. Colonel Minor Thomas of the Minnesota column wrote gloomily to Sibley (who had remained at Fort Ridgely) that "We go from here to . . . establish a Post and then to have a big fight, so the Genl. says . . . and what else God only knows. Look out that we do not perish in this God forsaken desert this winter."[42]

From the steamer deck Sully studied the riverbanks, examining the foliage and stands of timber with great care. He thought he had found the most suitable place about fifteen miles below the mouth of Beaver Creek, which flows into the Missouri from the east, but he decided that it was too far south to suit the demands of the War Department. His next choice was farther up the river, on the west bank about eight miles by water beyond the mouth of the Cannonball River, and on July 7 he wrote to Pope: "I have the honor to report that I located Fort Rice this day." He noted that the location had several advantages: the sandstone banks would provide building material; the river was narrow at that point and it would be a good crossing place; there was a belt of timber just below the site and some above it, and there was grass along the river bottom to the north, although the forage in the general area was poor. The choice having been made, he sent scouts to guide his troops to the newly selected site, after which he sent the boats back to Farm Island where a thousand tons of freight and supplies lay waiting. After he had brought his troops across the river, and when the steamers had been dispatched southward, he planned to begin his search for the Sioux. "I shall strike west between the Cannonball and the Heart Rivers, to the enemy's camp," he wrote Pope, "and then to the Yellowstone."[43]

EIGHT

"Hell, with the Fires Put Out"

Before Sully could set his course for the Little Missouri country, where he understood some 1,600 lodges of Sioux waited ready to fight, he had to load his wagons and organize a rather large force for an arduous march. From July 7, when Fort Rice was laid out, until July 18 when Sully took up his march, the command was busy with campaign preparations and with initial construction of the new establishment.[1] Colonel Daniel Dill of the Thirtieth Wisconsin Volunteer Infantry was assigned the duty of constructing a ten-company post to be built along traditional lines, complete with palisades and blockhouses. Crews of Wisconsin boys who had worked at logging in civilian life were put to work cutting and hauling logs to feed two sawmills that ran day and night.[2] Buildings such as storehouses were made of unfinished logs, while the single-story barracks were built of sawed six-inch and eight-inch timbers. While the average western fort was not regarded as an architectural triumph by its occupants, Sergeant Drips thought Fort Rice "a beautiful place," well located on a tableland about one hundred feet above the river. He praised its location as being so well situated that, in his opinion, a hundred men could defend it against all the Indians in Dakota.[3]

The youngsters who were busy building an outpost in the Dakota wilderness were more concerned about their lonely assignment than they were worried about Indians. Theodore Powell of Milwaukee wrote to his sister that the men had seen but very few

Indians, and those who had come to the post were friendly Rees. Typical of troops at distant assignments, he was principally interested in the table fare and the prospect of mail from home. Late in July Powell noted that four boats had passed Fort Rice on the previous evening, but that they carried no mail for the Thirtieth Wisconsin. "I shall long to see next spring and the first boat," he sighed. But then, there was good food and that was a comfort. "Oh, I must tell you how we live," he told his sister. "Well, we have bread all the time, minx [*sic*] pies every other day and fresh beef the same. We have a brick oven to bake in. We built the first one. Oh, yes, we have pickles; I wish I could send you one. They are very nice and we have what they call desicated [*sic*] potatoes. They come in large tin cans. It looks like meel [*sic*]." Summing it up, he concluded that the fort was a good place in which to live, and he predicted that "we will have a city here before we know it."[4] When the construction was finished, Powell thought the troops would have a very easy assignment.[5]

As the Wisconsin troops initiated their logging operations and commenced to erect buildings, Sully completed his preparations for the march. The presence of a wagon train of gold-seekers from Minnesota worried him. "A large body of emigrant wagons and ox-teams and with women and children have followed the Minnesota troops to this point," he reported to Pope. "I wish they were away from here. I can't send them back. I can't leave them here, for I can't feed them, and they even have come to me for permission to purchase rations, which I cannot do, for there is danger of my not getting enough rations up here to supply the post on account of low water, and the river is falling rapidly." Since the oxen could not keep up with the General's mules, he detailed four hundred men to march with the emigrants, which left him a little more than two thousand troops with which to maneuver against the Sioux.[6] However, his consent to take the emigrants was not given unreservedly, as one member of the party suggested when he wrote: "Our train was crossed [over the Missouri River] on condition that we cut one cord of wood to each wagon for the steamboats." When the price was paid the argonaut confided to his diary: "One hundred and seventeen wagons make quite a pile of wood." [7]

On July 18 Sully's forces lined out and began the march westward, hopeful of finding the elusive hostile tribesmen and defeating them. Pope, who had just received Sully's reports to that date, wrote another of his pompous letters, urging the field commander to search out the enemy and punish him. "I trust you will not leave the upper plains until a definite and satisfactory arrangement be made with the Indians," he said. "After beating them, such an arrangement will probably not be difficult." [8] From his vantage point in a Milwaukee office, Pope had little idea of the terrain over which Sully was trying to take his men, and under what conditions, nor did he have a very clear conception of Indian warfare. As a military planner he expected his subordinates to do their duty, the details of the problem at hand being unimportant. After doing so, the deposed enemy was expected to recognize his status as the defeated party and comply with the victor's terms. Nineteenth century Army officers in the West were frustrated for years by their failure to indoctrinate the Indians in the proper rules of military gamesmanship.

Sully, whose experience with Indians was much greater than Pope's, struck off for the western part of modern North Dakota with much less confidence than that expressed by his immediate superior. At first his march was westerly, but along the way he learned that there were Indians in some force in the vicinity of the Knife River and he veered to a northerly course to find them. By July 23 he was encamped along the Heart River where he corralled the wagons and placed the emigrants under the care of Captain William Tripp, Dakota Cavalry, after which he intended to move rapidly against the Indians. At that point a series of annoyances began that accompanied Sully to the end of the campaign. When the men opened supply boxes they found no saddle blankets for the mules, and gunny sacks had to be substituted. They next discovered that the saddle cinches, instead of being wide duck webbing, were hard leather straps about three inches in width, which when tightened caused the mules to buck until their burdens were shaken loose. After the equipment was gathered up from the prairie sod, Sully pressed into service any light wagons he could find, from his own equipment or that of the emigrants, and hooked four of the more amenable mules to each of them, the rigs carrying about a thousand pounds each. The troops got away about 3 A.M. on July 26 and, after marching eighty miles in two long days, they reached the Indian camp. The natives were ready and waiting for, as Sully wrote bitterly, they had been given some twenty-four hours notice of his advance "by a party of my scouts falling in with a war party of theirs not sixteen miles from here. We followed their trail, which led me to their camp."

As Sully looked over the enemy force, well posted along the ravines and rolling hills that faced him, he concluded that it was composed of some 1,600 lodges or perhaps 5,000 to 6,000 warriors, largely Hunkpapas, Sans Arcs, Blackfeet Sioux, Miniconjous, Yanktonnais and Santees. To oppose it he had elements of Iowa, Dakota and Minnesota cavalry, two companies of Minnesota infantry, an artillery battery and some scouts, or a force of about 2,200 men. The cavalrymen were, as always, anxious to charge, but the terrain ahead was cut up by timber-filled ravines and not at all suitable for the traditional cavalry maneuver. In the face of this disappointment the men dismounted, closed ranks and moved forward with the Indians nipping at their flanks. At one point the painted warriors found the ground suitable for a charge of their own, to which Sully countered with one that drove them off. The Sioux tried once more that day, making a brief but unsuccessful attack on the column's rear, after which they galloped into the hills and left the soldiers to the quiet of Dakota's badlands. "We slept on the battleground that night," wrote Sully. It must have been an uneasy rest, however. Not only were the men excited over the events of the day and apprehensive of those to come, but as they lay thinking about death in the afternoon there were the sounds of new life at night. "One of Sully's squaws had a young brigadiere last night and judging from the fuss she made having it, it was a pretty good sized one," wrote one of the men the next day.[9]

As the troops arose after that long, suspenseful night, they wondered if they had hurt the enemy enough to keep him at bay for the moment, or if the battle had been no more than a curtain-raiser for something more serious.

Experienced Indian fighters knew that it was nearly impossible to judge the casualties inflicted upon the enemy for, invariably, they made every effort to remove their dead from the field of combat. Sully's figures for the battle of July 28 were couched in extremely general terms; for example, when the Sioux charged his column and were repulsed, he wrote that his men drove them back, "killing many of them." He guessed that from 100 to 150 were killed in the final foray of that afternoon, and admitted that "I saw them during the fight carry off a great many dead or wounded." Some of his subordinate officers thought the General's estimate too low and were sure that the figure was twice or treble his estimate.

The next day he took up the pursuit before daylight, but quickly discovered that his wagons and artillery could not pass through the rough country ahead and was thus obliged to give up the chase. From a hilltop he searched the countryside with a telescope and beheld, for what he judged was a distance of thirty miles, nothing but a sea of ridges and deep ravines that confirmed his decision. After he had destroyed what was left of the Indian camp, he pushed on for another six miles.[10] At this point the problem became more complicated. His Indian and half-breed guides told him that the country beyond was too rough even for a peaceful journey, and that he should swing south once more to skirt the Little Missouri country, and strike the Yellowstone near the Powder River. The principal objection to this plan was a shortage of rations. Sully found that he had enough supplies for six days, "by some mistake of my commissary, I suppose, for he is not with me to explain, as I left him back at Fort Rice." As he looked at the country ahead, the General admitted that he became alarmed "and almost despaired of ever being able to cross it," but one of the Indian guides told him that the passage could be made if the rough spots were leveled off.

The campaign, so bravely begun to search out the Indians and to punish them, now became one of survival and escape. Sully, the son of famed artist Thomas Sully and a man who dabbled with watercolors himself, was torn by his admiration for what he saw in the badlands and his awe at what he called "Hell, with the fires put out." As artists often admit, he confessed that he had not the power of words to describe what he saw, but he tried, calling it "grand, dismal and majestic." In describing the place to General Pope, he asked his superior to "imagine a deep basin, six hundred feet deep and twenty-five miles in diameter, filled with a number of cones and oven-shaped knolls of all sizes, from twenty feet to several hundred feet high, sometimes by themselves, sometimes piled large heaps one on top of another, in all conceivable shapes and confusion." As he viewed them at sundown, these formations that ranged from gray to a light brick color, free of vegetation, looked like the ruins of some ancient city.

Having worked their way down into the basin where they camped in the cottonwoods along the Little Missouri, the troops now were faced by the problem of digging their way out. Before they could commence that difficult project, some of the men spread out along the river, against orders, trying to find a little grass for their mounts, only to have a small party of Indians fire upon them and stampede the stock. Sully was obliged to report that most of the men ran when the shooting began, and only through luck were all but two of the mounts recovered. When the men were not trying to find wisps of grass with which to keep their mounts alive they foraged for fuel. During the march across the bleak Dakota prairie they had acquired the practice of collecting buffalo chips on their ramrods, saving them until it was time to make camp in the evening and then depositing their finds with the cook. One of the officers later recalled that the manure made a better fire than wood, and it was a good deal easier to find.[11]

During brief rest periods details were sent out to prepare a roadway for the ascent through the rough country that lay ahead. One detail, directed by Lieutenant Colonel John Pattee of the Seventh Iowa Cavalry, was sharply attacked as the Indians, having the quarry cornered, tried to take advantage of the natural trap into which the expedition had made its way. Disconsolately

Sully confessed: "I now knew I had come upon the Indians I fought a week ago, and in the worst possible section of the country I could possibly wish to encounter an enemy."

As the situation became more serious Sully's concern deepened. His men, many of whom were green, watched him as he stalked about camp dressed in corduroy pants stuffed into long boots and an old slouch hat jammed over his head, a most unmilitary figure. But they told themselves that he had no superior as an Indian fighter. He was no dude, said one of them; he was an unpretentious man of ordinary build "and rather past the vigorous days of the prime of manhood," but his mind was sharp and more than once his intuition had smelled out an Indian location.[12] At the moment, however, he knew where the Indians were and his worry was that of getting his men and the emigrants out of a tight spot. The long civilian train, heavily laden and moving behind oxen at a snail's pace, strung out for three or four miles in a single line as a most inviting target. This heightened the General's irascibility, and the men who knew him kept their distance. "If he was crossed or criticized he would fairly foam with rage," wrote Sergeant Drips, recalling that when Colonel Samuel M. Pollock of the Sixth Iowa Cavalry made a sneering comment about the folly of chasing Indians with ox teams, Sully was furious, and "he never lost an opportunity of venting his spite on the Colonel." [13]

Flanking the emigrant train with a protective cover of troops—a very difficult thing to do in the rough country—Sully edged forward, blasting with his artillery at Indians hidden in the rocks, hopeful of working his way into more hospitable country. After crawling forward for some ten miles, the little army came to a spring where the Indians struck with greater energy, trying to keep the troops from getting the only water available to them that long hot day. The attackers succeeded in cutting off and cornering one company in a small hollow; a rescue party fought through and brought the men out with few casualties. Sully's sense of relief over the happy outcome of this potentially dangerous situation was shortlived. During the action his Indian guide wandered too far in advance and was shot. Sergeant Drips recalled the day's events in his diary: "The red whelps harassed us all day, but they done us but little harm with the exception of wounding our Blackfoot guide and the only one we had that knew anything of our whereabouts. He was pretty badly wounded through the left shoulder." [14]

Resolutely the General pushed on, facing at times what he judged to be at least a thousand Indians who swirled around his flanks, probing for weak spots and attacking the rear in the hope of picking off stragglers. At last the train broke into open country and the Indians pulled off at a high gallop, leaving a trail of dust visible for six or eight miles. "They were better mounted than we were," said Sully with his usual frankness.

As the expedition made its way toward the Yellowstone, Sully looked back over the events of the past few days and concluded that, by and large, the men had behaved well. There were some incidents that deserved criticism, but they were more easily forgiven in the light of feats of individual bravery under fire. In general the Indians kept a respectful distance from the artillery and long-range rifles, contenting themselves with hit-and-run tactics. The men found that the only way to counter this kind of warfare was to use an old Indian trick: dash at the enemy with a small force and encourage pursuit that led into an ambush. It worked for Sully's men several times during the running fight. When the lengthy engagement was over, Sully admitted freely that he had no idea as to the probable number of enemy dead. It was a moot point; the fight was over, the Indians had left and he could not pursue them. Because of his situation—short rations, the encumbrance of the emigrant train and weakened animals—the stance of the troops had been purely defensive. Typical of plains warfare, the natives had picked the time, place and duration of the fight.

On August 12 the worn, hungry column approached the Yellowstone River. All the way from the Little Missouri the men had marched through a land laid bare by grasshoppers and supplied only with nauseating alkali water. Behind them lay a trail of dead horses bloating in the sun, animals that had given out by the hundreds and were shot to stop their suffering. As the troops straggled forward, their tongues swollen from the lack of water, their bodies aching from the agonies of the summer heat and the ravages of dysentery—Sergeant Drips called it the "Dakota Quickstep"—an Indian scout came running toward Sully, holding a chip of wood in his hand. "It did not need words to tell what the chip meant," wrote one of the officers. "It had been cut by our steamboat men and was floating down the sweet, cool waters of the longed-for Yellowstone." [15] One of the General's orderlies carried the find along the winding line of bleary-eyed men, holding it up as a message of hope and succor, and silently they trudged forward, now provided with enough additional resolution to complete the march. Sully's sense of relief must have been as great as any in his command, and without doubt every man shared his view when he later wrote that it was a section of the West that he never wished to try again.

Two steamers, ordered to meet the force, were waiting when the tired and hungry expedition trailed down out of the badlands to the water's edge, not far from modern Glendive, Montana. The *Chippewa Falls* and the *Alone*, small, light-draft stern-wheelers, each carried about fifty tons of freight. The corn supply, however, was scant, for the *Island City*, bearing most of that supply, had sunk near Fort Union. Under the circumstances Sully abandoned all plans for further pursuit of the Indians and for building a post along the Yellowstone that season. Instead, he moved down the river to its mouth and went into camp near Fort Union.

By the time he reached the Yellowstone, Sully had learned a great deal more about campaigning in the West than he had known before. In that wild country from which he had just emerged, one that looked "tumbled to pieces," a terrain that was, in his view, a worse place than the swamps of Florida to hunt Indians, the army had found more than its match. The General admitted freely that he overtook the Sioux bands only because they wanted to be overtaken, and that they used the countryside well in the actions fought. One of his officers added the thought, some years later, that a loss of nine killed and perhaps a hundred wounded represented nothing but good fortune. He offered the opinion that if those Indians had been as well armed as the ones who fought Custer "the result would have been disastrous." [16] Sully would not have disagreed. At the time he made his report to Pope, he stated that the only way to "finish up" the Indians was to establish forts in their own country "and keep after them until you run them down." He admitted that he had fallen far short of the Government's goal of bringing the Indians to their knees, and that he had not built the posts desired by the War Department at that time, yet he had done all that any mortal could have done under the circumstances.

Despite his frank appraisal of the shortcomings of his campaign, Sully convinced himself that the presence of such a large body of troops in Indian country had impressed the natives, and he did not believe they would ever again present an organized resistance to a force of that size. He concluded from this: "I do not therefore think it will be necessary to have another expedition." In any event, the old Indian fighter had no desire to carry out a campaign such as the one he had just concluded.

The emigrant train accompanied Sully's men down the Yellowstone and went into camp near Fort Union. As they organized for the remainder of their westward trip, one of the civilians noted: "Prospects are poor and we are afraid of the Indians. No more military protection." [17] The parting was not mutually tearful, for Sully was glad to be free from the impediment, although it would be some time before he would forget his civilian friends. As a final compliment, the emigrants made off with a number of horses, mules and oxen, as well as a large quantity of pistols and other small arms. Some sixty-five of the troopers, anxious to try their hand at mining, deserted and joined the westbound argonauts. Upon learning of the appropriation made from his supplies, the General's well-known temper flared and he sent a detail after the "Idaho gentlemen," as he phrased it. The post trader noted the affair in his diary and accurately predicted the outcome. "There will be no catch to them," he wrote. "They have stolen the pick of the horses and the best of rifles & revolvers." [18] The cavalrymen overtook only part of the departing prospectors, and found recovery of the goods impossible because the wagons were spread out all over the prairie. As Sully commented caustically: "Twenty Indians could have captured them." Those who were queried about the missing Government property acknowledged that some of the lower elements in the group had traded whiskey for a sizable amount of equipment, but they were quite vague about the present whereabouts of the missing men. The wild country of what is now eastern Montana had swallowed up the travelers, and Sully's bluecoats were in no mood to hunt for needles in a haystack. After listening to expressions of great regret from what professed to be the higher type of emigrants, and apologies for their misfortune of associating with rascals, the detail returned to Fort Union empty-handed.[19]

For four days Sully kept his troops at Fort Union, which he called "an old, dilapidated affair, almost falling to pieces." [20] Company I of the Thirtieth Wisconsin Infantry was there awaiting him, having been sent upriver earlier to guard a supply of stores intended for the new post which Sully intended to establish on the Yellowstone. That plan had been shelved due to circumstances, but before going downriver the General took a final look at the possibility of such an establishment. He concluded that Fort Union, on its last legs as a fur post, was not a desirable place for troops because it was too far above the mouth of the Yellowstone and it was frequently inaccessible to steamers. He decided upon a location at the mouth of the river where there was a body of timber, and here he marked off a reservation four miles square. Two years later Fort Buford would be built in that vicinity.

The troops who had gone to that strange, forbidding land of the upper Missouri as military pioneers were the first group to be stationed that deep in the river country. Almost at once they felt the isolation, and as they looked at the rolling sod and broken terrain around them, they thought of the sea, as so many others had done before them and would do later. "We are out of the land of civilization, and as far as hearing what is transpiring on earth is concerned we might as well be in the heart of the Atlantic ocean," wrote one lonely soldier.[21]

Ever hungry for some kind of communication, the men of Company I tried to answer the need in a way their civilian counterparts would do in hundreds of embryonic cities in the West. They started a newspaper. On July 14 Fort Union's *Frontier Scout* appeared, and its first issue dramatized the major problem: Under the heading "Latest News," the editor explained there was none, because no boats had arrived from below. Trader Charles Larpenteur noted the emergence of the paper that day and lamented the lack of publishable material, saying of the editors: "It is a pitty [*sic*] that they have not more to keep them busy for they appear to be quite competent for the publication." [22] Having no national news to print, the editors contented themselves with items of local interest. They made mention of gold discoveries in the mountains to the West, but cautioned their enlisted readers that the Sioux had made prospecting a very dangerous business, the inference being that life at Fort Union was much safer. Small advertisements appeared, one asking for a "good milch cow" for which the advertiser promised to pay cash. In the best tradition, the paper engaged in an editorial effort to uplift the community, the first issue lodging a complaint about the awful smells about the fort and asking Larpenteur for improvements in sanitation.[23] As an old-time fur handler, the trader probably had become immune to smell; however, he took no exception to the suggestion and welcomed the press to Fort Union.

Before the summer was over there was more news. On July 25 two steamers were attacked as they approached the Fort, and there was cannonading on the river as the vessels hurled canister at the horsemen along the riverhead. The troops welcomed the embattled steamers, and then were astounded to see two more tie up at their landing. The editors of the *Frontier Scout* admitted that they were "startled nearly out of our senses by the arrival of four boats laden with government stores." Had it not been for an accident that sank the *Island City*, resulting in a total loss of the cargo, the fleet would have numbered five. But even four was a gold mine that yielded news from below and a good many cigars handed out by the prairie sailors, who were glad to make port.[24]

By mid-August there were more events to report. Sully had arrived with news of his expedition, and the *Scout* gave the account a full page. "The whistle of the steamer, the shouting of men, the passage of boats, the fording of men and of animals belonging to the North Western Indian Expedition has furnished a sight never before witnessed on these shores," said the editor, happy that the monotony of garrison life at last had been broken.[25] Larpenteur, noting that the *General Grant* had come downriver after having encountered the returning expedition, spoke less enthusiastically, saying that the vessel "brought but little news, reported that Gen. Sully had had a fight with the Sioux killing about two hundred and destroying their camp." In a laconic afterthought he jotted down: "Weather delightfull." [26] A few days later the trader was even less complimentary of the army. "From the reports so far it seems that they have done but little or nothing with the Sioux. It is said that they saw them in overpowering numbers and the army consisting of five thousand strong, the Sioux followed them until one day's march from the Yellow Stone. Something strange in this affair." [27] But then, as an old hand in Indian country, Larpenteur was not given to excitement over Indian fighting. From the traders' point of view, all that the presence of the military could accomplish would be to stir up the Indians and hurt the fur business. He was quite accustomed to forays at the post because the various tribes had fought with each other for a long time.

In late July, about the time of Sully's first encounter with the Sioux in the badlands, there was an alarm at Fort Union that Larpenteur concluded was no more than an effort by a Sioux party to steal Assiniboin horses. Some of the friendly Indians around the post, accompanied by soldiers, gave chase, but with the usual lack of success. Larpenteur noted that two of the Assiniboins were wounded, one suffering a flesh wound in the arm and "the other was shot with an arrow through the stern. . . . None of the wounds considered dangerous." [28] It was all a part of the business; Larpenteur had watched the natives squabble and rob each other for years and the presence of the Army would not change the pattern.

After the Northwestern Expedition moved on, the men at Fort Union settled in for the winter, fighting only monotony, bedbugs and liquor. Larpenteur noted that on one occasion, when a steamer stopped momentarily, the boat's captain gave strict orders to the "barr keeper not to sell liquor to no one," with the result that "no boddy was drunk at the Fort today."[29] Efforts to enforce prohibition were made somewhat more difficult by the arrival of the soldiers who, according to the trader, "always make out to have a little of the old Barly Corn on hand." He noted that Christmas of 1864 "passed off rather dry" except for celebrations among the troops whose commanding officer "got a few degrees beyond Gloriously drunk," but the day closed without any resultant violence.[30] The Indians who traded at the post had less difficulty in coming by their supply of liquor because they always had something to trade for it. Larpenteur one day watched "some gentlemen Crows" enter the place, two of them aboard a single pony, bottles waving, both passengers drunk, and he commented that the tribe "have fell into the beautyfull habbit of using liquor, that accomplishment introduced by the whites," in their business dealings. When they could not make a deal that involved the stimulant, they stalked out in what he called "a bad humour."[31]

Sully marched his troops away from Fort Union on August 21, and a week later he arrived at the Fort Berthold trading post. Here he was met by large delegations of Arickaras, Gros Ventres and Mandans who were very glad to see him and who told the General that his arrival was tantamount to freedom from Sioux slavery. For years these Indians, who lived in earthen huts along the river and farmed the bottom land, had asked for military protection and, at last, it was given to them. Sully ordered Company G of the Sixth Iowa Cavalry, commanded by Captain A. B. Moreland, to garrison the trading post and to remain during the winter. It was a move he thought necessary, not only as a protection to friendly Indians, but also to help keep open river communication. Father De Smet, who had arrived at the Fort aboard the *Yellowstone* on June 9, strongly recommended the establishment of a military post in the vicinity to protect the village Indians. He had been sent into Sioux country by the Government as a peacemaker, but after conferring with Sully at Fort Rice, on the eve of the General's departure, the famed missionary concluded that to talk peace while the soldiers were conducting a punitive campaign would put him in a false position.[32] Although he remained convinced that many of the Indians were disposed to listen to his overtures, he felt that the military's mission made his own "bootless," to use his words, and after baptizing a large number of Indian children, De Smet returned to St. Louis with the admission that his assignment had been a failure.

Fort Berthold, a successor to Fort Clark, had been built in 1845 and, like Fort Union, it was nearing the end of its usefulness. John Buchanan, en route to the gold fields by steamer that year, described the place as a typical palisaded structure, complete with the usual bastions on opposite corners, and situated on the east bank of the Missouri. Within the enclosure stood the usual log buildings: warehouses, trading rooms and living quarters for the employees. Nearby was the Indian village, about a hundred dirt and pole houses, each capable of sheltering three or four families. Buchanan found the houses comparatively clean inside, and said they were cool in the summer and warm in the winter. It amused him to watch the soldiers en route to Fort Union engage in a spirited trading with the Indians, who were anxious to acquire any surplus uniforms for sale. Speaking of the typical villager, he wrote: "He is fond of brass buttons, as much so as some of the galls in the States. A red or blue blanket he admires, but will give but little for a grey one. He wants heavy, coarse cloth, being in this matter a good judge." The visitor, who perhaps engaged in some bargaining himself, commented that some of the natives were "shrude traders." [33] On September 3 the Iowa troops moved into the palisade, but their stay was relatively brief. Due to some disagreement with the resident Agent, the troops moved out in the early spring, and during April 1865 they took up quarters in log buildings erected adjacent to Fort Berthold.[34] Two years later nearby Fort Stevenson was erected, and it served for a number of years as another link in the chain of river forts.

By September 1 Sully was on the move again, bound for Fort Rice and glad to get his men away from Fort Berthold, where the Indians appeared to have an unlimited supply of whiskey for sale. Setting up portable saloons in their tents, they hawked their wares to the whites in a reversal of the usual procedure in Indian country. Aside from the temptations of strong drink, there were other reasons for getting the boys away from the Fort Berthold vicinity.

The morals of the Indians, said Sully, were "in a terrible state," particularly those of the Rees, which he thought were "as bad as it is possible for a human to be."

On the way downriver his men picked up signs of Pembina carts, whose owners had established a well-known traffic out of the Red River country, and he concluded that the Indians had moved across the international line with their British friends. His trip had been an arduous one and Sully himself was not feeling well, so he was not particularly disposed to put his large force in motion against Indians who had already shown a tendency to disappear into the hills. Instead, his men reveled in a buffalo hunt, now being in an area where meat was easily found. The expedition's dwindling food supply was quickly replenished. On September 8 Sully reached Fort Rice, and there learned of events at the new post since his departure in mid-July.

Colonel Daniel Dill of the Thirtieth Wisconsin, in command of Fort Rice, was pleased by General Sully's compliments over the progress of construction during his absence of nearly two months, and was flattered to hear him say that, when completed, it would be one of the best posts in the West. But the happy reunion was short-lived. In the course of conversation the General learned that, about two weeks before his return, Captain James L. Fisk, Assistant Quartermaster of Volunteers, had arrived at Fort Rice with an emigrant train of eighty to a hundred wagons. Fisk was proceeding westward under the terms of a congressional appropriation approved March 3, 1864, part of which was to be used for protecting the emigrant route from Fort Abercrombie, Minnesota, to Fort Benton. When he arrived at Fort Rice he requested a cavalry escort, and Colonel Dill provided it, although Sully said later this was against his orders. According to those at Fort Rice, the Captain was arrogant and highly critical of the Army's efforts against the Sioux, boasting that he could go anywhere in the country with only fifty troops, and that he was asking for an escort only to quiet the fears of the women and children in the party. Sully was furious when he heard the story and asserted that the Government was spending a lot of money just to escort a group of draft-dodgers westward. Fisk followed Sully's route for about

The awesome-looking General William S. Harney, whose violent disposition terrified young officers and enlisted men. *National Archives, Brady Collection*

Meriwether Lewis. *Year, Inc.*

General Alfred Sully as a young officer. *Minnesota Historical Society*

Early river travelers were impressed by the magnitude of the country through which they traveled, and by its native population. In this Bodmer painting of Fort Pierre both elements are emphasized. *State Historical Society of North Dakota*

An interior view of Fort Pierre sketched by Alfred Sully in 1856. *Gilcrease Museum*

Fort Pierre, looking south, 1856, by Alfred Sully. *Gilcrease Museum*

Fort Union, 1864. From a drawing by a soldier of General Sully's command, expedition of 1864. *State Historical Society of North Dakota*

Part of General Sully's Army near Fort Berthold. 1864 is the probable date of the photograph. *Minnesota Historical Society*

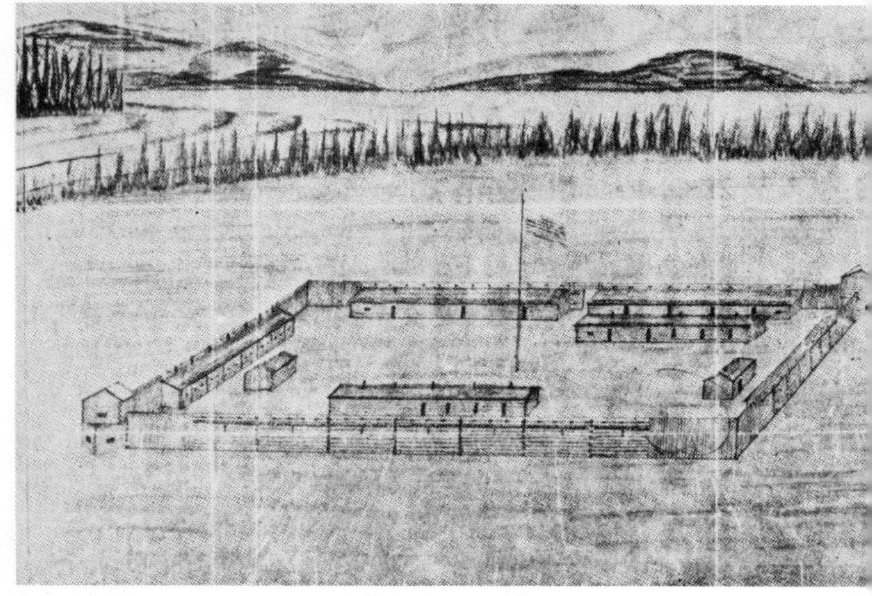

This sketch of Fort Sully, by an unidentified artist, depicts the loneliness and isolation of the river forts. Typically, the flagstaff is the dominating feature. *National Archives*

Living conditions along the river were crude in the early years. This was the building assigned to the Post Surgeon and Post Commandant at Fort Berthold, 1865. *State Historical Society of North Dakota*

Campaigning in Dakota required an enormous amount of supplies. These slow-moving trains rarely found any Indians; the Indians found them. This is part of Sully's force. *Minnesota Historical Society*

The Upper Missouri River fur traders were the first to exploit the economic resources of that country. Frederick Francis Gerard of Fort Berthold typified the group. *State Historical Society of North Dakota*

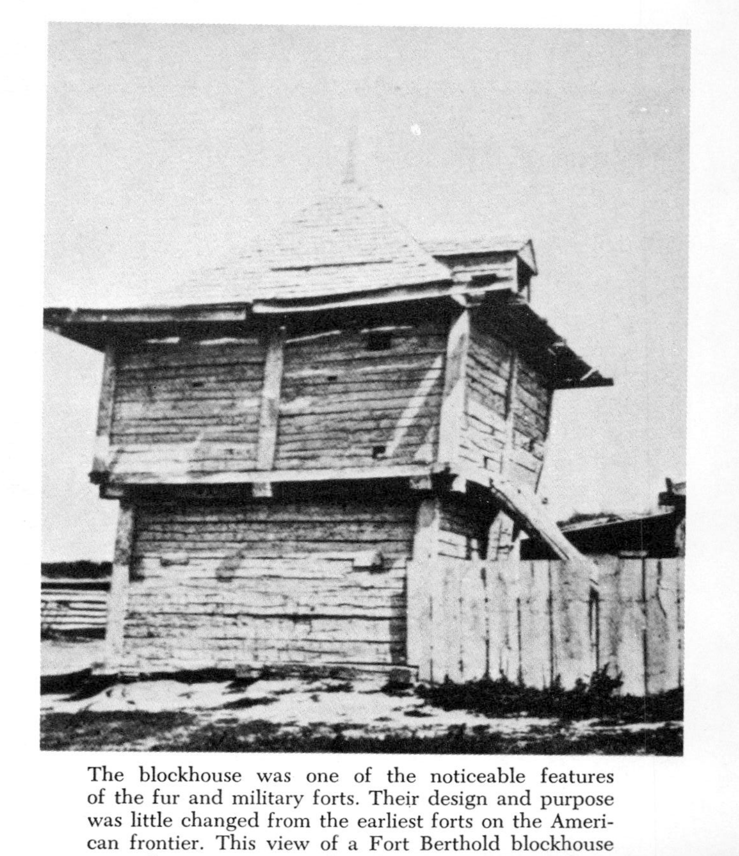

The blockhouse was one of the noticeable features of the fur and military forts. Their design and purpose was little changed from the earliest forts on the American frontier. This view of a Fort Berthold blockhouse

Colonel Philippe Régis de Trobriand found time to paint during his days at Fort Stevenson. Nearby Fort Berthold is the subject of this artistic effort. *State Historical Society of North Dakota*

Army officers stationed in Dakota never failed to be impressed by the Siberian qualities of its winter. In this 1868 scene at Fort Stevenson, Colonel de Trobriand dramatized the "white death" with his brush. *State Historical Society of North Dakota*

The typical picture of a peace conference is one of Indians and whites squatting around a fire in a tepee, smoking the pipe. This view, taken at Fort Berthold in 1870, looks much more relaxed and comfortable. *State Historical Society of North Dakota*

As the years passed the buildings at the Forts were built of milled lumber. The occupants, however, did not always improve in their appearance as the garb of the second man from the left indicates. The photograph was taken at Fort Buford. *State Historical Society of North Dakota*

This drawing shows Fort Buford looking south from the guardhouse. The Missouri River is in the background. *National Archives*

Fort Buford, like the other river forts, was supplied with water from the river. Its "tanker" was kept busy furnishing the daily needs of the soldiers. *State Historical Society of North Dakota*

The *Far West*, built in 1870 for the Coulson Line, played a dramatic role in the Custer campaign of 1876 and, through it, became one of the river's most famous steamers. *Montana Historical Society*

Troopers who were sent upriver to build outposts found the land a lonely, barren place with the steamboat as their only connection with the outside world. *F. Jay Haynes—Photographer, from collection of Montána Historical Society*

The flat-bottomed, ungainly-looking Missouri River steamers supplied the river forts for over three decades. The spars on the foredeck were used for "grass-hoppering" over sandbars. The name came from the resemblance of poised grass-hopper legs. *Montana Historical Society*

The early river military establishments were crude affairs, made of logs and roofed with dirt. This is Fort Rice, about 1865. *State Historical Society of North Dakota*

During the latter part of the nineteenth century life at Missouri River posts became much more "civilized" as this view of Fort Buford's officers' quarters suggests. *State Historical Society of North Dakota*

eighty miles and then left it in favor of a more southerly route. About 165 miles west of Fort Rice he was stopped by a force of Indians at first reported to be one thousand, but which the returning soldiers said amounted to perhaps three hundred.

Cursing Fisk and the trouble he had caused, Sully ordered Colonel Dill to take six hundred infantrymen and three hundred mounted troops into the country he had covered and rescue the emigrant train. He wanted to send only cavalry, but his mounts were so weakened by the 1,500-mile circle which they had just completed that they were in no condition to travel. While the General had little sympathy for Fisk, he could not risk the lives of the emigrants; also, he feared that an Indian victory over the train would so raise the morale of the natives that it would be doubly hard for him to make peace with them. He wanted to keep the command at Fort Rice, but he was short of supplies due to the sinking of several boats, and because many of the rations he had on hand were not fit for use. Therefore, he sent Dill out to make the rescue and to bring back the train as rapidly as possible before sending his troops downriver. With that he called the summer campaign to a close.

Sully was anxious to get out of the river country before winter set in and killed off his weakened animals. There were other reasons for the move. "I am very anxious to get away from here before cold weather, for I am not well," he told Pope. "I have had a severe attack of my old complaint—rheumatism near the heart—and I fear being overtaken with a storm on the prairie. Another such attack might pop me off. . . ." [35] By the first week of October Dill had brought in the Fisk party and General Sully was on his way downriver, stopping briefly at Fort Sully where he stayed a few days, and then moving on to Sioux City where he spent the winter.

As he concluded his efforts of 1864, Sully summarized the situation and expressed his views on the Indian problem. He felt there was a large number of Indians who would come in and live a peaceable existence if they could, but the hostiles in the bands constantly threatened them when there was such talk. If they came in, he theorized, the Indians would have their horses and property taken away, leaving them as beggars or at least a people depending entirely upon the Government for their support. This was not a very attractive prospect for an independent people. Since he had not enough stores to feed large numbers of Indians, Sully recommended supplying them for a brief period, then lending them horses and guns with which to hunt. The country still had sufficient game to support the tribesmen, and he thought they could subsist satisfactorily. He did not believe in a war of extermination for, as he said, this would make it necessary to "shoot everything that wears a blanket," and it would be a very expensive project. If the Government really wanted to solve the Indian problem by extermination, Sully proposed a more economical means than fighting them: "The cheapest and easiest way to exterminate the wild Indian is to bring him into a civilized country in contact with the white (the women would soon become prostitutes and the men drunkards)." [36]

Father De Smet, a man who had studied the Indian problem for years, agreed upon the futility of a major Indian war. The Sioux warriors, he said, were five or six thousand strong, well mounted and always ready to fight, for fighting was more than a business to them; it was "the occupation *par excellence* of their lives." Quite correctly he said: "They are here to-day and somewhere else to-morrow." Highly mobile, the Indians moved quickly, now striking at an emigrant train, now attacking river steamers, engaging the soldiers when and where they chose. "The Indian has the gift of being everywhere without being anywhere," wrote the priest. Without forts, unembarrassed by baggage or supply trains, he picked his battle site and chose one that invariably gave him the advantage of numbers and position. Thus, the use of strategy in operating against the tribes brought meager results, for the opposition never performed in a manner expected of it.[37]

Sully thought there was reason to consider the practicability of using Indians as troops. During 1864 he organized a small group of Yanktonnais as auxiliaries and even sent them against their own people to retrieve some stolen horses. The Indians followed orders, and although they brought in only one horse, they also produced two scalps to show their sincerity. As he left Fort Rice he enlisted fifty Indians from a friendly Yanktonnais band and ordered them to camp during the winter near the fort, with their wives, so that the post commandant might use them as scouts. The native troops were to receive two rations per day along with a small amount of ammunition. By doing this, he thought, the Indians would become dependent upon the garrisons and would accustom themselves to the ways of the whites. He felt that ultimately these Indians would make "the best frontier troops we could find," and he was sure they would respond to military discipline, for his experience with them had shown this to be the case. "I have no trouble in making them obey my orders strictly," he remarked, as he wrote a report to Pope from Fort Sully, and he added: "I have now in front of my tent an Indian soldier on duty as sentinel." [38]

By the autumn of 1864 Dakotans had watched the Army conduct campaigns in the Territory during the preceding two summers and, as might have been expected, there were various shades of opinion as to the effectiveness of the operations. The businessmen of Sioux City, Iowa—a place that served southern Dakota and regarded itself as the coming entrepôt of Missouri river trade—shared the feeling of their fellow merchants around Yankton. They had complained about Indian dangers in 1862 and had welcomed the soldiers during the next two campaigning seasons, but instead of satisfying them, the Army apparently did too much: It moved northward beyond their environs. When a Yankton editor was accused of criticizing Sully he denied it, but he pointed out that he thought the General had been sent to protect his neighborhood rather than to afford protection to emigrant trains moving from Minnesota to the new Territory of Montana. Eyeing the developing westward trade to the north, the Dakota editor commented bitterly that "if the object of the military movements in the Northwest was to open this route to the gold mines, and give it ample protection, it has been very successfully accomplished," but, he added, very few Indians had been punished.[39]

General Pope apparently felt some of the criticism even before the 1864 campaign. That spring he explained to Governor Newton Edmunds of Dakota that Sully's mission was to protect the Territory's frontier settlements. To do this he wanted to establish posts deep in Indian country, far beyond the settlements, and he did not deny that their presence would afford a passage from East to West through Dakota.[40] As he explained it to General Henry Halleck, the posts were designed to cover both the Iowa and Minnesota borders, as well as the infant settlements of Dakota, and were so located that they could threaten the Sioux at enough points to prevent any concerted action by the Indians. Confidently, he told his superior officer that the campaigns had been so successful that the Government could dismiss all fears of any more Indian wars in the upper Missouri country. Yes, he said, there would be small raids as there has been in the past, but now that the forts were in process of establishment, a relatively small force of soldiers could control the tribes and protect emigrants. He asked only that the military arm be left in charge and that all trading be placed in its control "without the interposition of Indian Agents." If these suggestions were carried out, he was ready to "cheerfully guarantee peace with the Indian tribes in this department." [41]

Men of the Indian Bureau, of course, took another point of view. Governor Edmunds, who was *ex officio* Superintendent of Indian Affairs for Dakota and who was sympathetic to the business community that traded with the tribes or supplied annuities, thought the recent campaigns not only expensive but positively damaging to the Territory's economy. The soldiers had, in his view, so stirred up the Sioux that white settlement must necessarily be confined to a narrow strip along the river. Rather than go out and kill Indians, he thought the Government should restrict their trade to authorized whites and patrol their country with Indian scouts. He praised Walter Burleigh's Yankton scouts and thought that the Doctor had a very good idea.[42]

The outspoken Burleigh expressed himself in terms as blunt as ever, decrying the Army's efforts in the most sarcastic tones. "If the object of the expedition and the construction of the chain of posts from Minnesota to the mouth of the Yellowstone was designed to benefit a few speculators, and drive the hostile Indians of the Missouri down upon our settlements, it has been most admirably attained," he wrote to Dole. Burleigh's own interest in the economic future of southern Dakota was indicated when he complained that instead of placing the troops between his neighborhood and the tribes, the Government had constructed the posts between the hostile bands and the Rocky Mountains. He reacted sharply to Pope's theories regarding the solution of the Indian problem, and he criticized that officer for making generalizations that, with a stroke of the pen, swept into oblivion a system Burleigh thought had worked well for a quarter-century.[43] For the moment he excused Sully's failure on the ground that the whole plan was defective, but within a few months he openly attacked him personally. He not only accused Sully of being unfit to command troops in Indian country, but charged him with habitual drunkenness that rendered him unfit to perform his duties. George Rust, a clerk in the Northwestern Indian expedition's subsistence department, came to the General's defense, admitting that "like almost all officers Gen. Sully is daily in the habit of taking liquor," but at no time did he believe the effects sufficient to have impaired the commander's judgment.[44]

Samuel Latta, then Agent at Fort Sully, joined his colleagues in the Indian Bureau in their view that Army intervention had far from solved the Indian problem along the upper Missouri. Of the seven tribes of Sioux under his charge, numbering about thirteen thousand, he thought that at least ten thousand remained hostile. While he was ready to admit that some of these certainly were bloodthirsty savages, he was sympathetic to the dilemma in which the whole group found itself. The land had been transformed, he said, from a place once regarded as a desert to one that had become a useful thoroughfare to the mines, and in the transformation a number of Indians had been "cheated, robbed, and driven from every desirable locality." He did not deny that force would have to be used in rounding up the warlike natives, but when that was carried out he felt they should be placed on reservations capable of growing crops. Those around Fort Sully had not been able to farm successfully and their subsistence, such as it was, came from occasional fishing, berry picking and Government handouts. He called their situation in the autumn of 1864 "destitute."[45]

The wide variety of opinions expressed during the autumn of

1864 indicated a transition in the military-Indian situation of the Northwest that was to affect the area for the next quarter-century. The Army's mounting dissatisfaction with the Interior Department's control over Indian affairs, a status awarded it in 1849, was emerging as an open interdepartmental fight. Pressures from the settlers' frontier in southern Dakota as well as that in Minnesota, coupled with the suddenly increased importance of the Missouri River due to Montana's spectacular rise as a mining community, brought sufficient pressure to bear upon authorities at Washington for troops to be assigned to Indian fighting in the area at the height of the Civil War. After two campaigns of questionable value, the Army's role along the upper Missouri stood in jeopardy. At stake was the future of General John Pope, who was trying to give some lustre to a tarnished reputation; the political ambitions of General Henry H. Sibley, who sought to enhance his name through a military career; and the professional name of the old Indian fighter, General Sully, whose recent efforts had been frustrating to say the least. As the year came to a close, Sibley was deeply angered that Pope had recommended Sully for a promotion and ignored him, and there ensued a hotly worded correspondence between them. Meanwhile Sully was busy, writing to Pope in an effort to keep his command intact for another campaign. Pope, in turn, was relaying the pleas to Halleck in Washington, D.C. As the letter-writers worked furiously, a group of former Confederate prisoners of war, lately enlisted in the U. S. Service, made their way through the deepening cold of Dakota as replacements for those to be sent to the front in a larger conflict that was reaching its climax.

NINE

The Galvanized Yankees

By the summer of 1864 the Civil War was approaching its climax, and the Federal Government was gathering all available troops for the final effort. By then the threat to Minnesota's frontiers was stifled, at least temporarily, and the force of approximately five thousand men that comprised the Sibley-Sully expedition of 1863, which had been kept in the Department of the Northwest to be used, in part, for the 1864 campaign in the Dakota badlands, was needed elsewhere. Attempts to transfer part of Pope's command to the South had met with loud protests from Minnesota and Iowa, and the War Department was obliged to yield to the political pressures. In their search for more fighting men, Lincoln and his Secretary of War, Edwin M. Stanton, listened with interest to the proposal of General Benjamin F. Butler for the enlistment of Confederate prisoners of war who were willing to take the oath of allegiance and to serve out their time in service rather than in prison. Lincoln approved the plan despite Grant's open opposition, and when Grant was obliged to accept it, he suggested that the men should be sent to the West.

The Confederates who exchanged their gray uniforms for those of blue were described in a number of ways, as Dee Brown has explained in his volume about them, but the term most widely accepted was "Galvanized Yankees." The expression apparently meant to imply that the men were temporarily clothed with an outer layer of Yankeeism, just as iron is coated or "galvanized" with zinc to protect it from the elements.

On August 9, 1864, Grant ordered the First U.S. Volunteers, comprised of about a thousand men, to Pope's command in the Northwest, remarking that it was not right to expose them where they would be treated as deserters if captured.[1] These men were part of the prisoners enlisted at Point Lookout, Maryland, and they were intended to replace troops such as those of the Thirtieth Wisconsin then stationed at Fort Rice,[2] as well as other regulars on duty throughout the West. On August 15 the First U.S. Volunteers left their prison stockade and went by ship to New York, where they boarded a twenty-nine car New York Central train that took them westward. At Chicago the group was divided, four regiments being sent to Pope at Milwaukee and the remaining six to St. Louis for Sully's use.

Pope forwarded the replacements with some misgivings. He explained that they were "refugees and rebel deserters," and although he was sure many of them were good men, he warned that the others would require strict discipline. He urged Sully to select the very best officer he had to command Fort Rice because "It will probably require a man of resolution and character to command such a post."[3] The officer in charge of the troops in transit, and the one who was to meet the requirements suggested by Pope, was Colonel Charles Augustus Ropes Dimon, a twenty-three-year-old New Englander who had been promoted to that rank only a few days earlier by his sponsor, General Butler. On August 22 the young officer brought his "Whitewashed Rebs" into St. Louis, and there he found further orders from General Pope directing him to place his men aboard a river steamer and take them at once to Fort Rice. Four days later the troops were aboard the *Effie Deans*, captained by famed riverman Joseph la Barge, and on their way to Indian country. It was a week since they had left Maryland; it would be seven more before they reached their destination.

As the steamer fought the river's current, its engines straining to turn the great stern paddle wheel and making the whole craft "shake like an old rattle box," Colonel Dimon had time to contemplate his new assignment. He was aware that his men were volunteers only in the sense that they had chosen western duty in preference to prison, and that unless he maintained the strictest control, disobedience easily could turn into mutiny. Despite his youth Dimon was a seasoned officer, having enlisted in a Massachusetts regiment in the spring of 1861, after which he participated in the capture of New Orleans and the siege at Vicksburg, rising to the rank of major before being forced out of action by disabilities. His fellow townsman from Salem, Massachusetts, General Butler, brought him out of retirement for the unusual assignment with the Galvanized Yankees, and he thought highly enough of Dimon to see that he was raised two grades in rank. The young man was flattered and pleased by such favor and he resolved not to disappoint his benefactor.[4] If necessary, he intended to take the most extreme measures against any Southerner who exhibited any symptoms of recurring rebellion.

Before the *Effie Deans* reached Sioux City Colonel Dimon had to make good his resolve. Within the first week several of his men slipped over the side and were gone for good. Precautions against desertion were increased, and on September 5 the first man was caught. On that evening one of the corporals reported that Private William C. Dowdy from Tennessee had flatly stated that "he would be damned if he would not take the first opportunity to desert the Regiment." The outspoken redhead was just twenty-two, a year younger than his colonel, and was known to have a quick temper. Undoubtedly a number of his fellow soldiers had made remarks equally offensive, but Dowdy was a victim of unfortunate timing. Dimon was ambitious and anxious to make good; he was also concerned about escorting six hundred of his former enemies into a strange land, ever fearful of possible mutiny. Dowdy was quickly brought to trial, charged with seditious language, and on the flimsiest evidence was convicted and sentenced to death. On September 9, not far above Omaha, the *Effie Deans* stopped along the Iowa side and the men were marched ashore to witness the execution. At three in the afternoon, to the slow roll of drums, the firing squad, four men bearing a coffin, and the prisoner took their positions. Moments later Private Dowdy was dead and Colonel Dimon's prediction made a few days earlier—"Shall shoot one of my men for desertion next week. It's hard but an example must be set"—came true.[5]

Had Dowdy been a gentleman by an act of Congress, or even an ordinary soldier unmarked by the blight of secessionism, his punishment would not have been so severe. About the time that he was reported to have made the alleged threatening remarks, Colonel Dimon reported to his superiors that Second Lieutenant Conrad Kimmel had deserted the regiment at New York, but he had caught up with it at St. Louis, "acknowledging drunkenness to be the cause." The officer was also charged with converting $68.77 of Government funds to his own use. For this Dimon recommended that the offender be made to pay back the money and to lose his commission. Meanwhile, Kimmel proceeded with the regiment and later, in mid-November, Dimon had to send him back, saying that in his brief stay at the new post he had been drunk twice and he was also guilty of selling liquor to the enlisted men.[6]

A week after the execution the group reached Fort Randall, which Dimon called "a *very pretty* place." Typical of travelers viewing their first western fort, he described the log structures, the octagonal blockhouse complete with loopholes, and other physical details of interest. The young bachelor, bound for a lonely winter vigil to the north, made special note of the fact that "The officers had their wives with them who done all the cooking &c and they did look cozy." The stay was brief, for Captain la Barge was concerned about the low state of the Missouri River. In fact, the *Effie Deans* did not make another hundred miles beyond Fort Randall; she went aground below the mouth of the White Earth River and Dimon was obliged to unload his command at this point. It was here that the real suffering of the Galvanized Yankees began.

Hoping to find some wagons at the Crow Creek Agency, about forty miles distant, the regiments started off, marching across a country so barren, windy and cold that Dimon doubted he could stand the hardship. The men plodded along, through hail, rain and raw winds, stopping only long enough to eat a little hardtack and salt pork toasted on a stick, washed down with coffee. On the second day Dimon got off his horse, went down to his knees, and fainted for the first time in his life. The forlorn group reached the Agency on September 30 and rested there for three days while a few wagons were collected; then they moved on to Fort Sully, another sixty miles. General Sully, en route downriver for the winter, met them there and provided additional equipment for the remainder of their journey. He sympathized with the newcomers, commenting to Pope that they were in poor condition to make a march at that time of year without shelter or suitable transportation. He gave them some surplus tents and hired as many wagons as he could find. Sergeant Drips, in Sully's command, commented that "The Alabama fellows looked rather seedy. Their marching and different climate accounting for that." [7]

After meeting Sully's command Dimon pushed on, anxious to complete the 170-mile trip to Fort Rice before the weather turned any colder. Now he had thirty-two sets of six-ox teams and, at night, he very carefully placed them within the circled wagons, aware that he was in Indian country where "pinto buffalo" were regarded as an acceptable substitute for the real thing. After the regiment was settled for the night, the Colonel sat by an open fire smoking his pipe and studying the next day's route. On the ninth of October he noted in a diary-form letter that "I am getting tough." But he was also getting careless; that night the Sioux made off with four of his teams. During the next few days the hard march, bad water and poor food began to take their toll. On the twelfth Private John Blackburn died of dysentery and near Bordache Creek the following day, another succumbed; in all, Dimon lost four men of the sickness on the ten-day march to Fort Rice. By the morning of the seventeenth they came in view of the fort and "What a cry of joy burst out, as we saw its unfinished battlements!" [8]

There was little time for the men to rest if ample quarters were to be completed by the time the Dakota blizzards came. Dimon estimated that the fort was about a quarter finished, and the first task at hand was to complete the troops' barracks. As a conscientious officer, the Colonel moved into a tent where he stayed until his men were housed. While he was not disappointed in Fort Rice —any kind of shelter looked good to him after the grueling march— Dimon wrote to his sweetheart that the site was "out of the United States" and he assured her that "you never saw such a forsaken place as it is here for five hundred miles." However, there was timber enough to provide housing and fuel, and he estimated that about two years' supply of provisions were in storage. In his short stay in Dakota he was already tired of buffalo meat, but he accepted it as the traditional local fare, and within a few days after his arrival he negotiated with one of the Indians to make a pair of moccasins for him. The New Englander was trying hard to adjust to his new conditions.

On October 12, before the former Confederate troops arrived, Colonel Daniel Dill started his Wisconsin boys southward, followed a week later by part of the Sixth Iowa troops. Lieutenant Colonel Edward M. Bartlett, who remained with a few men, officially transferred the command of Fort Rice to Dimon on November 1. By then the Southerners had been at work for nearly two weeks and had completed the work in progress on six buildings to be used as troop barracks, a second hospital building, a stable and two blockhouses, and were nearly finished with the headquarters building. The stockade was ready except for the main gate, yet to be hung. At the end of the month a magazine and one officers' quarters would be usable.[9]

By the time winter came in earnest to Dakota, the men at Fort Rice were well fortified against its blasts. Toward the end of November Dimon assured his parents that he was quite comfortable; the logs in his cabin were well chinked, the buffalo steaks and rabbit pies were excellent, and although the countryside was desolate, he was happy and he had much for which to be thankful. "All is ice and winter about us," he admitted, yet this isolation had its virtues, for "we are free from temptation here." In a vein that would have met the approval of his New England forebears, he explained that "We have to work to live. God has given us lumber, water and game and the Government has given us provisions for two years, mechanics, tools, and left us to work our way." It was a sentiment worthy of a Pilgrim Father.

All available evidence indicates that the young Colonel, who stood just under six feet tall, with gray eyes, a light complexion and dark hair, was extremely serious and strait-laced. His letters to his sweetheart and to his parents suggest a touch of vanity, but they also reveal a deep sense of responsibility. When he commented upon the freedom from temptation at Fort Rice, which, in fact, was far from true, he was not thinking about himself, for he was not easily led astray. His thoughts were about his brother Ben, a Captain in the First U.S. Volunteers, who apparently was much in need of a change of scene. Charles reported to his parents, with great pride, that Ben was winning his fight against the bottle and his success had been so spectacular that fellow officers had dubbed him the "temperance man." In fact, the post surgeon had expressed fears that Ben's reformation was so sudden and so violent that it might be injurious to his health. When he recommended a more gradual course toward sobriety, Ben answered: "No, I have made a fool of myself for so many years and now I commence to live." Charles was delighted, and he fully believed that this time the cure was permanent. "It makes me proud to see my own brother so independent and manly and at last *a man*," he wrote home, assuring his family that "I have learnt to love him and revere him." [10]

Resolved to spend the long winter nights profitably, Dimon wrote to publisher D. Van Nostrand of New York City and ordered eleven books that cost a total of $28. Among them were two volumes of *Scott's Military Dictionary, Manual of Engineers, System of Military Bridges, Hints on Preservation of Health in Armies* and *Manual of Instructions for Surgeons.* The chance that his order would ever reach New York was highly problematical; the Dakota mail service was in the hands of breeds or "trusted Indians" who carried the pouches from post to post for a fixed amount. In one instance, Dimon placed his confidence in "One-Who-Don't-Eat-the-Goose," who collected his fee and threw away the mail en route, much to the Colonel's dismay. This time, however, the native mailman was conscientious and, presently, Mr. Van Nostrand acknowledged receipt of the order.

During the snowy months, when the garrison had little to fear from Indian attack, the principal enemies were disease and the cold. While their Colonel studied, wrote letters and made out the usual reports, his men carried out routine duties, but even this was far from comfortable or safe. In mid-December Dimon wrote that the thermometer had ranged from −29° to −34° for the past ten days and that the guard had to be relieved every fifteen minutes. Despite such precautions, several men suffered from frozen faces, feet and fingers, one of them having lost a foot and a hand from the cold. Years later Dimon recalled the bitter cold and how "the snows sweeping along the plains, drifted against our log huts and palisades, completely covering them, so that sentry boxes with stoves in them were mounted on top of the buildings." [11] During a particularly severe blizzard, one of the sergeants took pity on the guards and sent them indoors. Dimon, the strict disciplinarian, promptly reduced him in rank for "exposing the garrison to danger from attack and from fire." There was a danger from overheated stoves, as more than one frontier post discovered, but the possibility of attack in that kind of weather was not substantial. The Colonel, however, took leave of his quarters from time to time, wrapped in a coat, vest, mittens, cap, boots and leggings made entirely of buffalo skins, and saw to it that the guards kept a sharp eye on the white desert around his lonely little post.

The fight against dropping temperatures and swirling snow was one that buffalo robes, ample firewood and certain precautions could combat, but the slow, agonizing effects of diarrhea and scurvy took a heavy toll. By April the command had lost fifty men, including a hospital steward, and the post surgeon, George H. W. Herrick, was among twenty then on the sick list. The doctor, a Harvard graduate who was appointed while the troops were en route to Fort Rice, had taken the position because of its obvious opportunities for extensive practice. He lost his wife the day the regiment arrived at the Fort, and before spring came to Dakota there was a prospect that he might join her. Captain Enoch Adams, a young Yale graduate with a literary bent, who would become Dimon's leading critic, wrote a poem about Mrs. Herrick's passing, the first four lines of which commented upon the loneliness of death in Dakota:

> May the angels guard and guide thee
> O'er the trackless plains Dakotian
> Where no human mark is beside thee
> Like the limitless waste of ocean.[12]

Dimon and Herrick did their best to provide a balanced diet for the men, but the supply of anti-scorbutics was limited and there was little opportunity to replenish them. When a few potatoes were hauled in during a break in the weather, they were frozen so badly as to be of little use. Complaints about the fare were answered by surprise inspections of the kitchens. Although there was a strong suspicion that the cooks had been diverting food supplies to local Indian women in return for favors, there was insufficient proof and, in typical military fashion, the Colonel was obliged to satisfy himself by issuing orders threatening the most dire punishment for those found guilty in the future. To underscore his sincerity he reduced two cooks to the ranks, removing them from further temptations, culinary or sensual.[13]

Herrick's health measures also affected nonmilitary personnel at Fort Rice. William Larned and his wife, among the Fisk expedition members who elected to remain for the winter, decided to turn their idle time to profit and began to sell pastries to the soldiers. There was a ready market since the hungry men had brought some $20,000 with them, but ingredients for manufacture were in short supply. The Larneds sold pies at thirty cents each, ginger and molasses cakes at fifty cents a dozen and milk at ninety cents a gallon. The latter was a mixture of fresh cow's milk and condensed milk thinned with two gallons of water to a can of concentrate. Bread sold at five cents a slice, with biscuits in "demand heavy" bringing seventy-five cents a dozen. Boiled rice was offered at ten cents a saucer and boiled beans (no meat included) at twenty-five cents a plate. Butter, very scarce, did not sell readily because the proprietors asked $1.50 a pound. "Money changes hands freely," proprietor Larned wrote in October, but within a few days he reported that Governmental regulations had stifled private enterprise. "On the recommendation of Surgeon Herrick an order was issued today forbidding the sale of pies to soldiers," he noted on November 8. "This is a good order, but hits my business about six dollars a day." He felt better when he learned that the regulation also applied to Major Charles Galpin, post sutler, who, although he was taking most of the soldiers' money for other items, had decided to enter the pie market. His rival, said Galpin, was "sore" about the restriction, but he had "rallied" from the setback and had decided to sell cakes instead. "These may be tolerated by the Surgeon," admitted Larned, "but are not more wholesome than the pies he has condemned." The pie order was not as severe a reverse as Larned hinted, for at the end of four months he reported a gross on all sales of $3,170. Marooned in a wilderness outpost for the winter, he had applied his ingenuity and his wife's talents to a market that proved to be quite lucrative.[14]

There were demands for other commodities that neither the sutler nor the Larneds could furnish. Enoch Adams, who wrote a good deal of poetry that long, cold winter, spoke for the troops when he said:

> All we lack in this vicinity
> Is a stock of feminity
> Sutler bring it to Fort Rice,
> It will fetch an awful price.

Admitting that "In this Fort we are like Adam, Ere he had obtained his madam," the Captain wrote wistfully that "Butter, cheese and woman's eyes, would make this place a paradise." By "femininity" Adams apparently meant fair ladies, for any soldier who wanted to satisfy his male urges had but to cross the river and visit the tepee of ill-fame operated by Fool Dog, a native who also sensed the economic opportunities offered by an injection of Federal money into the Dakota economy. According to Dimon, in charges he made the following year, Fort Rice's poet laureate was one of Fool Dog's regular customers.[15]

As the men fell sick and grew restless, Dimon tightened his control, ever fearful that they were not sufficiently "galvanized" to maintain a continuing loyalty. Whenever those who were bold enough, or perhaps completely desperate, had the opportunity, they took their chances with Dakota's winter and fled. Dimon nagged the commander of Company H on this subject, urging him to exercise a more strict discipline and to take extreme measure at the slightest sign of mutiny. When Sergeant R. A. Edwards of Company H called Dimon's Adjutant "a God Dam Son of a Bitch or words to that effect," the Colonel promptly preferred charges in which it was suggested that the Sergeant's attitude was "prejudicial to good order and military discipline." On the trip to Fort Rice Private Dowdy had talked himself into an early grave and, if necessary, the Colonel was prepared to mete out the most severe punishment for lapses in conduct. But when his own officers were disrespectful, the problem became more complicated. Before spring came he was obliged to reprimand Captain Adams, the post's second-ranking officer, for "complaining and mutinous language." Stating flatly that such complaining was "the result of a diseased imagination," Dimon threatened Adams with immediate arrest if he heard any more from him.[16]

No disciplinarian expects affection in return for his efforts and so, when Colonel Dimon learned that his men had raised $1,000 to purchase an ornate sword for him, he was pleasantly surprised. Formal presentation took place on the President's birthday in a hollow square of troops assembled by Dimon's old friend, Captain William Upton, against whom he would soon prefer charges. When all was ready the Colonel was called for, and a sergeant stepped forward to deliver a prepared speech. "We the enlisted men of this command that were once your enemies, and now your friends, present you with this sword knowing you will always prove worth the trust our country has reposed in you and never draw save in the cause of liberty, justice and right," intoned the Sergeant. The recipient was much moved, and he later confessed that "I felt so completely worked up I could not hardly speak. My cold allowed me only to make a short speech." He must have had a vision of Private Dowdy as he stood there talking, for he made reference to the "painful duty of taking one of your numbers life not long since," and said he was glad his listeners understood the necessity of obedience. After admiring the sword, with its silver-plated handle decorated with the Goddess of Liberty on one side and a shield of rubies on the other, he retreated to his quarters. As he left the men cheered and threw their hats in the air until the emotionally aroused young man was out of sight. He admitted to his sweetheart that he was unable to control himself before the men, and a tear had rolled down his cheek in full company.[17]

Typical of extremely conscientious young officers, the Colonel was overly zealous in his desire to satisfy his superiors. In addition to the localized command given him, he assumed suzerainty over the entire country ranging from Fort Sully to Fort Benton in central Montana, and issued all manner of orders from his stronghold in the heart of Dakota. On December 23 he issued General Order Number Seven that proclaimed his domain under martial law and directed all those arriving at its capital to register their names, places of residence and reason for visiting, and to take the oath of allegiance, all within twenty-four hours, or render themselves suspicious characters subject to arrest and confinement. None of such visitors were to go near any of the Indians or try to trade with them without the commandant's specific permission. He was convinced that traders harboring traitorous sentiments were selling powder and ball to the Indians and perhaps engaging in other conspiratorial activities. On Christmas day he apprised Sully's office of his concern over a "large number of citizens arriving at this Post without any visible means of occupation and who I firmly believe to have entertained disloyal sentiments." He enclosed a list of local residents who had been purified by taking the oath.

By February Dimon confessed to Sully that his attempted purge of subversive elements in Dakota had met with some opposition. The presence of remnants of the Fisk party and a "number of unknown characters from 'Idaho' and other parts in the immediate vicinity of the Fort" had moved him to issue Order Number Seven, in response to which these suspects had marched into the establishment, drums beating, and confronted the commandant. They took the oath, stating that it was done with mental reservations, and they used the occasion to insult the post adjutant, after which they apologized for their intemperance. But Dimon was not satisfied. "Some words they dropped led me to think they were not very friendly to you or to the U.S. Gov't," he told Sully. "They labored for some time under the delusion they were to govern this Post this winter, but upon my positive assurance that upon the least exhibition in the future of that bravado they would be acquainted with my Guard House and have the benefit of outdoor exercise on the Gov't works till spring, they concluded to become peaceable citizens amenable to martial law." [18]

Locked in the winter fastness of the high Missouri country, the civilians in and around Fort Rice could do little but comply with Dimon's loyalty oath requirements. However, when spring came and the steamers once again broke the silence of that frozen land, the Colonel discovered the weakness of military edicts among a people unaccustomed to such restraints. When the *Yellowstone* stopped at the fort on May 10 it displayed not only a cargo of Indian goods, but, in Dimon's mind, it also carried the seeds of sedition. The vessel brought word of Lincoln's assassination and an incorrect report that Secretary of State William Seward had been killed. Such news sent a wave of excitement through the little community, but this was quickly overshadowed by the tensions created when Charles P. Chouteau, Jr., who was aboard the vessel, let it be known that he had no objections to such violence. "I am sorry to say that some high words passed between Mr. Chouteau and some of our officers," Dimon admitted, but since it was apparent to him that the St. Louis trader was a Rebel, such men did "not deserve the aid & esteem of any officer of the U.S. Army." Typically, the Colonel took vigorous action, requesting all passersby to purge themselves of sedition before proceeding. So far as Chouteau was concerned, Dimon had no doubts as to a correct course of conduct: "I regard him as an unprincipled man and disloyal citizen and shall treat him accordingly." In an effort to more fully explain his policy to Sully, he said he stopped boats and administered the oath only at the request of the respective captains, and that he had not held over any passengers. In one instance pastors on board complained that they were being persecuted by the majority for their Union sentiments, and Dimon felt obliged to "galvanize" the travelers in the interest of God and country.[19]

The *Frontier Scout,* locally managed by Captain Adams and Lieutenant C. H. Champney, editorially supported Dimon's loyalty program. Adams warned that "Treason, dislodged from its home in civilization, is putting out like Jeff Davis for the brush," and part of it was seeping toward the new mountain territories. "The boats are crowded with the debris of the Rebellion," he warned, "putting for up the river, trying to out run their reputation. . . . Missouri is emptying its Border Ruffians into the lap of Montana." Annoyed by the "ladies singing 'Stonewall Jackson's March' and 'Bonnie Blue Flag' as they sail, like wild geese northward," he wondered if the Government could be too strict with such people. "Will it allow the Missouri to be the sewer to float such a population off, bidding them 'God-speed,' and giving them gold mines for worn-out plantations, not even allowing their feelings to be hurt by requiring them to take the oath of allegiance?" To Adams, the soldier, the answer was no. "Let the bayonet and the sword propel civilization into the Territories," he recommended. And, if taking the oath "makes them pucker their mouths worse than a dose of castor oil," so much the better, for these people were "worse than brigands." Unless treason was stamped out in its early stages, he felt it might take root, and "assisted by the natural character of the country to the West it would make us a vast amount of trouble." [20]

Incensed by the spread of secessionism in Dakota, Dimon took the bit in his teeth and plunged forward. Aware that both Sully and Pope were at odds with the Indian Bureau, particularly because its representatives were thought to be lax in the matter of controlling trade among the natives, he now sought to cooperate with his superiors by putting the trade under military control. The authority for such a move originated in a letter from Pope to Sully, dated February 1, in which the District Commander stated that Indians who were willing to be peaceable could live near the posts, but they would be regarded as prisoners of war and there would be no trading with them. Nor would they receive any annuities as before. Realizing that such Indians would have to be fed in some manner, Pope gave permission for the issuance of a limited amount of rations. To augment this meager fare, he supposed that the tribesmen could help themselves by "hauling and trading at the Military posts." [21] In late March Dimon referred to letters from Pope and Sully on this subject and said he was much pleased "as it assures me of a change I have been wishing for, viz: the transfer of affairs in a measure from the Indian Bureau to the War Dept." He interpreted the letters to mean that he had authority to stop every steamer coming upriver and seize all goods not consigned to the Army.[22]

In his eyes this also had the virtue of controlling some of the Red River breeds who had been furnishing the Indians with guns and ammunition, presumably with the aid and counsel of Confederate agents. Explaining to Sully that "I lay the most of my trouble with the Indians at this post to the influence of the traders," he reported that he had revoked the license of Hawley and Hubbell's Northwestern Fur Company—successor to the American Fur Company—and, to enforce the order, he dispatched part of his command to Fort Berthold and to Fort Union. The first of these men were placed upon the *Yellowstone*, over Chouteau's vigorous protest, and sent on their way. "I have gained an enemy in Gov. Edmunds and the Indian Agents by refusing to recognize his license . . . but at the same time fear nothing from them," he said with his usual resolution. As he rationalized to Sully: "I act always as I deem it my strict duty to my country, and as near as possible covered by the Army Regulations and Customs of War—with these and 'Military Necessity' I think they will find it hard to kick against the 'Pricks.' " This hint of defensiveness was underscored by an additional comment, in which he suggested to the General that after nearly four years of service he would welcome a transfer closer to the main theater of war because "I am inclined to chafe under this exile and wish for active work."

To command Fort Union Dimon selected his friend "Billy" Upton, a Captain, and gave him instructions to be strict with his men but to treat the natives kindly. The new commandant arrived on May 19 aboard the *Yellowstone* and reported that the place was in fair condition, but "far from up to our mark." He promptly evicted a group of fur company employees from their homes along the west side of the fort, only to find that the lodgings were so full of bedbugs that they were uninhabitable. For the moment the men pitched some tents inside the fort and laid plans for exterminating the pests. Upton took over the headquarters building, allowing Charles Larpenteur to live in one end of it.[23] On May 29 the Captain reported that the *Benton* had put in two days earlier, only to find the high life of the village closed down. "They say here that it is the first time boats ever came here without all the Fort hands and all the Indians round getting drunk and keeping so for a week," he reported to Dimon.

On June 10 the *Twilight* and the *Lillie Martin* arrived at Fort Union, bearing Indian goods assigned to the Blackfoot Agency at Fort Benton. Upton, who had heard that these Indians were unfriendly, ordered the goods put ashore and impounded. Colonel Dimon, meanwhile, ordered the *St. Johns* to disgorge its goods for the Blackfeet at Fort Union because some members of that tribe were reported to be encamped in his vicinity. He may not have known the difference between the Blackfeet Sioux and members of the Blackfoot nation who lived in north-central Montana. Removal of the annuity goods was not accomplished without vociferous dissent. Agent Gad E. Upson, en route to Fort Benton, relieved his mind of a number of uncomplimentary sentiments about the Army and its ways. Billy Upton wrote that "he was pretty fiery at first and commenced talking about the imbecility of the Military and Gen. Sully." When the Captain objected to such talk, Upson "then toned down and fizzed out as quick as he had foamed, like a glass of soda." When the Agent was able to control his temper, he confessed that he had nothing against Dimon personally, but that Sully was going too far; worse, he was trying to "throw off" on the Colonel at Fort Rice.[24]

For command of Fort Berthold Colonel Dimon selected his brother, Ben, and gave him a set of instructions similar to those issued to Upton. To help his brother carry forth the high ideals he was now practicing as a reformed reprobate, Charles sent along ninety testaments, ninety hymn books and 153 tracts to be distributed among those needing moral succor. Illicit Indian trade was prohibited; Ben was to allow no one but D. W. Marsh, sutler to the regiment, to engage in such commerce.

The latter subject was one that had worried Charles for some time. Rumors persisted at Fort Rice during the winter that half-breed traders from Canada had arrived in the neighborhood of Berthold with ten sleigh-loads of goods, and that they had gone into camp with the English flag flying at the head of their procession. The visitors reportedly said: "This flag will not be put down for anybody, only for God Almighty. Those who join us will not get hurt. Those who join the Americans will get hurt. We will return the last of the month with more powder, ball arms, and some Santees, and will take Fort Berthold and then Fort Rice." The speech was followed by a feast and the presentation of five kegs of powder and a few sacks of bullets. Encouraged by such hospitality, Man-Who-Strikes-the-Ree got up and promised, "As long as I live I shall never shake hands with the whites." Not to be outdone, Medicine Bear told the gathering, "I am the man to make war with the Americans; kill all you can, I will say nothing against you." In reporting the story, Dimon told Sully that despite such warlike talk he felt that the peace party was still the stronger among the Indians; however, the influence of the traders was dangerous and he advised strict control over them.[25]

Even more disturbing was the rumor that Captain Moreland, placed in charge of Fort Berthold by Sully, had developed some commercial interests. Chouteau accused Moreland of appropriating Government goods and trading them to the Indians for his own profit, not to mention his encouragement of the liquor trade among the natives. F. F. Gerard, who worked for Chouteau at the post, stated that Moreland not only had dealt with him, but that he regularly exchanged powder and ball for Indian robes in secret transactions. Gerard complained that, after about two months, Moreland broke off relations, took away his keys and "treats me more as a prisoner than a host." To compound the crime, in Gerard's eyes, Moreland permitted another trader, F. D. Pease, to continue operations.

At the end of April Colonel Dimon appointed Captain Alfred

F. Fay to investigate Moreland's conduct and to learn if Pease had been trading ammunition to the Indians. Fay had the authority to stop such trade, but in Moreland's case he was reminded that his assignment was strictly that of investigation and only a court-martial could determine the officer's guilt. By May 17, when Fay made his report, Ben Dimon was in command, and he had not only decided that Pease was guilty of illegal trade but he had thrown the trader into the guardhouse to await delivery to Fort Rice. However, Pease had a half-breed brother-in-law who was rumored to be acting as his representative during his confinement. In order to prevent further commerce, Captain Dimon ordered the relative to report to him three times a day. Ben was not sure what the military code said about someone who was about to do something illegal, and he asked Charles for his advice in the matter. It was a moot point, for by mid-July Captain Samuel G. Sewall of the Fourth U.S. Volunteers notified Sully's headquarters that a military commission had concluded there was not sufficient evidence against Pease to make any charges.[26]

Colonel Dimon's war with the traders and the Indian Bureau was not long in generating loud complaints from his opponents. When Mahlon Wilkinson, Agent for the Upper Missouri Indians, reached Fort Rice that spring, he discovered that the Colonel had not only extended his power from Fort Sully to Fort Benton, but he "had assumed control of Indian affairs in that country, and had determined that the Assiniboins should have no goods this year, for the reason that he had been informed that parties of them had smoked with the Sioux." A greater surprise awaited Wilkinson at Fort Berthold, where Ben Dimon was carrying out his brother's orders with a vengeance. "He held a long council with the chiefs, after my arrival," complained the Agent, "at which I was not permitted to be present. I was not permitted to talk with the Indians except in his presence." Wilkinson was told that all trade had been stopped except that carried on by the sutler or his representatives. Helpless to do anything about it, he moved on to Fort Union where he found matters in the same condition.[27] Fort Rice's official organ, the *Frontier Scout,* scorned the traders, charging them with wanting to make all they could in the shortest time, and it lamented the fact that "Troops are kept here at vast expense to the Government, to act as a body-guard and menials for these men, generally disloyal and always rapacious." It dismissed the Indian Bureau as the "Slave Power of the Territories." Dimon complained to Sully that the traders were trying to undermine his discipline by advising his men that he had been too strict with them, and he said he would like very to prefer charges against them, especially Chouteau, but he could not "get below" to do it. "My great fault," he confessed, "is introducing a little whole discipline in the upper country and interfering with unauthorized traders." [28]

General Sully, preparing for another summer campaign, discovered that Dimon's military satrapy, deep in Indian country, was beginning to complicate his own plans. Both he and Pope had the strongest feelings about the Indian Bureau's role in controlling and trading with the tribes and, in all probability, they privately sanctioned the young Colonel's actions. However, the Bureau and the fur company interests had powerful friends in Washington and they were making their influence felt. Dr. Burleigh and Governor Newton Edmunds also were men of influence, and their outcries against military aggressiveness were being heard. Sully had no recourse but to disavow Ben Butler's protégé; he did so in an order of May 23, 1865.

Pointing out that the commandant at Fort Rice had no right to interfere with steamers unless their masters were breaking the law, and that the conduct of Indian affairs was lodged with the Secretary of the Interior, he told Dimon that his duties were limited to the management of a single post. The Colonel was directed to revoke all orders regarding the *Yellowstone* and other steamers, since the "Territory of Dakota is not to be considered as a disloyal State." Furthermore, said Sully, his subordinates were not to act upon mere rumor, but rather they were to report all irregularities of trading to him.[29] Dimon acknowledged the order—ironically his letter was sent downriver on the *Yellowstone*—but he confessed that he was "pained to know my conduct has not been approved by the Genl. Comdg., but must say that I think it has been wrongfully represented." He explained that rather than harassing steamboat passengers, he had helped them in a number of ways, including the loan of ammunition. However, he promised, "I will confine myself in future entirely to this Post." [30] Even before he penned his letter to Sully, the chastened commander wrote to Ben and to Billy Upton, revoking his orders and directing them to refrain from any more interference with licensed traders or with Indian annuity goods. Charles Galpin was handed a similar communication which explained the changed situation and advised him that he was to confine his trading to Forts Berthold and Union.[31]

Sully felt that Dimon was a good officer, always willing to obey orders, but his youth, ambition, and lack of mature judgment worried the General. On June 10 he wrote a confidential letter to General Pope in which he spoke "unofficially, just as I would talk to you if I could see you." The subject was Colonel Dimon who was "making a good deal of trouble for me, and eventually for you, in his overzealous desire to do his duty." Sully admitted that "I admire his energy and pluck, and determination with which he carries out orders; but he is too young—too rash—for his position and it would be well if he could be removed." There was no question of Dimon's friendliness to his superiors or his willingness to carry out all instructions, said Sully, but he recalled that the young man was one of Ben Butler's appointees, "and he is too much like him in his actions for an Indian country." The writer expressed his intention to have a fatherly talk with the energetic Colonel, in the hope that "I can change matters and curb him," but if this failed, perhaps a change of command was in order. Sully suggested Minnesota. "I do not wish to hurt his feelings," he confessed, "but I think the interests of the Government would be advanced by having an older and cooler head at Fort Rice." Within a few days Sully had Pope's permission to "act as you think best," and with that reassurance he resolved to look into matters at Fort Rice when he arrived there during the course of his coming campaign.[32]

TEN

The Politics of War

Part of the Indian problem, as it developed in the latter half of the nineteenth century, was the presence in the West of young army officers who were more interested in personal advancement than in promoting race relations. Charles Dimon was typical, in that he was young, ambitious, a strict disciplinarian and quick to make judgments. His professional life was governed by "the book," a reference work cast in black and white with no gray areas, from which he drew the sources of his decisions. He and his fellow officers felt that Indian policy was in the wrong hands, and that their team could do a much more effective job in furnishing what the natives needed most: discipline. In one of his first letters written from Fort Rice, he said his most important task was to be with the Indians, a people he could treat with force or kindness since he had the necessary men to do either, but he was inclined to offer the latter until it proved to be ineffective.

The young officer also typified his generation in that, as an easterner, he was outwardly sympathetic to the Indians and amused by them as savages and inferiors whose habits were quaint. When he learned that some of the neighborhood Hunkpapas had eaten about sixty of their horses to keep from starving, he handed out a few rations in the interest of humanity and better relations with the tribe. "The Indian chiefs are very sharp and are very eloquent," he told his sweetheart. "You would laugh to be present at some of our councils. They come in making friendly signs and express a desire to see the 'great Captain' as they call me to have a council." He then described procedures familiar to eastern readers, those of the natives greeting their host with "hows," of sitting in a circle solemnly smoking, and of their long deliberation before speaking. He described their oratorical methods, and how they began with lengthy prefatory remarks that outlined the whole history of their race before they discussed the problem at hand, their present misery.

The "Whitewashed Rebs" were at Fort Rice for nearly six weeks before their commander's enchantment with the natives was marred. One Sunday late in November, a small detachment from the fort was attacked while taking rations to a herding party not far away. A lieutenant and a sergeant were brought in suffering from arrow wounds. In response the Colonel quickly sent out a detail to find the guilty and to administer punishment. The soldiers found nothing. The wounded lieutenant, who was unable to distinguish one band from another, had thought the Indians belonged to either the friendly Two Bear or the Fool Dog Yanktonnais who were camped across the river. It disappointed him that the unidentified natives had made friendly signs just before they attacked, conduct frowned upon in more formal warfare. "In order to guard against such mistakes in the future," said Dimon, "I have ordered the 'Two Bear' and all friendly Indians to keep on the East side of the River and shall treat all on the West bank as enemies." It was a simple, clear-cut decision. Of course, the arbitrary delineation would result in the deaths of some friendly Indians in the future, but that was the misfortune of war.[1]

The general situation along the river in the fall of 1864 was one of uncertainty and of an uneasy peace. During the same month that Dimon's men were wounded, a soldier was killed within three miles of Fort Randall. As usual, detachments of cavalrymen took up the chase only to discover that, after a few miles, the trail frayed into confusing fragments and there was not a warrior in sight.[2] Dimon was anxious to talk peace but it was hard to effect a meeting. Stormy Goose and Look-for-His-Horses, along with about fifteen others from the Two Bear band, brought word that

Black Catfish was interested in coming in but he did not trust the bluecoats. The Colonel understood that there were about 650 lodges of Santees camped in the Mouse River country, and in order to establish some communication he tried, without success, to get Black Catfish to meet on the neutral ground of Two Bear's camp. "I think the opportunity is offered to effect a peace this winter with the hostile Indians," he wrote to Captain A. B. Moreland at Fort Berthold, "which with proper management will be lasting, and which will save the Government the services of troops which will be needed further South next spring." [3]

In letters to Generals Butler and Sully he took a much more outspoken point of view. He told Butler, who had promoted the plan for using Galvanized Yankees, that the Army had been deprived of an unnecessarily large number of men during the past summer while it engaged in a rather fruitless Indian campaign. Much of the trouble with the tribes, he said, came from the "clashing of the Departments at Washington," and he was highly critical of the Interior Department's Indian Bureau for the way it granted trading licenses, dispensed annuities and carried out the intercourse laws, all without being able to control its charges. He thought the answer to the problem fairly easy: the Indians could be controlled through fear. To do this he recommended to Sully that "for every soldier killed by treachery kill twelve men or squaws and meet any hostile acts with immediate punishment." There is no record of Butler's response, but Sully, who was immediately responsible for the Army's conduct on the upper Missouri, lost no time in commenting upon the stern measures Dimon proposed. In prescribing less violent treatment he pointed out that "The Indians are not governed by as strict laws among themselves as the whites," and he suggested that the natives might not take well to such reprisals. Nor would the method meet with approval among government officials, for "The treatment of Indians in the present state of affairs is a very delicate subject." Congress had recently appointed a committee to look into Indian matters, he explained. Meantime, both he and Pope had been reporting the situation to the authorities at Washington, for which action the generals had "met with very violent opposition from certain citizens whose interests would thereby be affected." In short, he was telling Dimon to proceed with great care for the situation was fraught with danger not only in Dakota but also in more civilized parts.[4]

In early March 1865 the Indians struck again, this time killing a herder of Government cattle not far from the Cannonball River. The soldiers who discovered the body with four arrows in it concluded that the Santees were guilty. When he reported the death, Dimon told Sully that he had decided to give all Indians in the area until May 1 to make peace, after which he intended to treat those who had not come in as enemies.[5] However, on March 30, when a war party of twenty Santees boldly rode past the post, across the river, the Colonel ignored his own deadline and sent ten mounted soldiers after them. The Indians quickly scattered, two of them fleeing to the Yanktonnais camp of Two Bears, who promptly surrendered them to the soldiers. The prisoners said they were from the upper James River and they had simply come down to hear the latest news. They carried English guns. Dimon locked them up and then asked Sully what he should do with them.

Before Sully could respond, the commandant at Fort Rice found his own answer. In mid-April a party of about two hundred Santees and hostile Yanktonnais came down out of the hills behind the fort and attacked civilian herders guarding cattle belonging to Charles Galpin and resident members of the Fisk party. The civilians ran, giving up thirteen horses, nineteen mules, thirty-five cows and one ox. A group of soldiers protecting Government livestock stood their ground, and paid a price of two dead. The attack both frustrated and infuriated Dimon. Since he had no cavalry to pursue the hit-and-run attackers, offensive action was out of the question; even more humiliating, about a quarter of the warriors wore cavalry jackets and pants "traded at Berthold this winter." When the mutilated bodies of his men were brought into the fort, the Colonel took the only retaliation he could. The two Santee prisoners were hauled out of confinement and executed.[6]

About ten days later a force of three hundred Indians returned and made off with two horses and two mules before they were driven away. The engagement took place less than a mile from the fort. Dimon, who was able to watch the entire engagement, was proud of the way his Southerners withstood several charges, "cool, calm and collected—determined not to give up an inch of ground. They carried out implicitly my orders and instructions to them in regard to Indian fighting." Eight Indians were believed killed; one soldier was wounded.[7]

The month of May was one of continuous harassment. On the fifth, hostiles attacked the mail carrier and sent him fleeing back to Fort Berthold. Three days later they raided the horse herd at Fort Rice and captured three mounts before the troops could get into action. On May 19 the attackers closed to within four hundred yards of the fort and severely wounded one of the pickets. This attack was followed by another on May 22 in which the Indians tried to capture the sawmill. The next night they struck Two Bears' camp, across the river, but were again driven off. The raiders were back in four days, this time ambushing a logging detail led by Lieutenant Benjamin S. Wilson. A flight of arrows knocked the officer from his horse, but before the Indians could collect a scalp, Charles Galpin's Indian wife rushed out of the Fort and drove them away with a torrent of Sioux expletives. The pace was quickening, and all reports indicated that the 1865 fighting season would be an active one along the river. Dimon reported to Sully on May 21 that he had been gathering all available information and it told him that nearly three thousand lodges of various Sioux bands were ready for an all-out war. The Indian plan, he said, was to concentrate on the upper Missouri country, to level forts Rice, Berthold and Union, and then to hold the region against all comers.

The constant attacks convinced Dimon and his officers that there was truth in the rumors of a major offensive. Thus, when Indians appeared at five different points around the fort on the morning of June 2, it seemed obvious that the visitors had not come for peaceful purposes. Taking no chances, Dimon sent out infantrymen with instructions to occupy the bluffs to the rear, and as they advanced the Indians fell back in typical fashion. Tired of being limited to a defensive posture, the Colonel this time mounted men on all his available horses and augmented the force with warriors from the bands of Two Bears' Yanktonnais and of Bear's Rib's Hunkpapas. The appearance of this group, supported by a mountain howitzer, sent the strangers on their way; they were, as it later developed, only curious passersby. Even so, they made one stand, but as Dimon wrote, "A few shells thrown among them scattered them, they leaving robes and throwing clothing off in all directions." As the angry Indians retreated they taunted Dimon's auxiliaries, saying that in a few days a much larger group would return and reduce the fort. He had no idea how many of them there were "as every ravine and knoll for two miles contained squads of hostile Indians," but, he promised, "I shall keep everything compact and guard against surprise." [8]

A few days after this engagement the steamer *Twilight* arrived, bound for Montana. Hiram D. Upham, an Indian Bureau clerk, wrote that there was much excitement and apprehension at Fort Rice, and that the boat's passengers were warned of the dangers ahead. "The night before we got to the Fort one of the pickets had been shot by an Indian who crawled up on him in the grass and killed him within two hundred yards of the Fort," he told one of his friends back home. The travelers were anxious to buy some fresh beef, but none was available. "They have plenty of cattle back on the hills—but having no cavalry they did not dare go after them." It angered Upham to think that the military had been placed in such a helpless position. "The fact of it is the soldiers in all these Forts on the River are kept penned up by the Indians like so many cattle. All the good they do is to keep the River open for Steamboats and protect traders and Indian Agents." Nevertheless, the *Twilight's* occupants took warning, and after leaving Fort Rice "we took extra precautions and kept a double guard on nights." Before they left they witnessed the death of Lieutenant Wilson, wounded during the affair of May 26. It was a thought-provoking scene.[9]

During May, as the spring rise of the Missouri opened that great avenue to the mining country for another season, traffic through Sioux country increased sharply. During an eighteen-day period, fourteen steamboats arrived at Fort Rice, most of them en route to Montana. "All were well loaded with passengers and freight," said the post newspaper, the *Frontier Scout.* "After taking in ice &c. they started for above, and we wish them a speedy and pleasant trip. The passengers think this is the speediest and safest routes to the mines." [10] During the next month the editors were obliged to report that the river was far from safe. The *St. Johns,* en route downriver, was fired upon below Fort Berthold. The suspects again were Santees, and their efforts resulted in the death of one crew member and the wounding of another. "The iron-clad about the wheel house was all that preserved the pilot." As the dead sailor was laid away in Fort Rice's cemetery, the *Scout* said solemnly: "His funeral procession was a sample of what life, as well as death, is on the frontiers." [11]

The coming of spring necessitated a decision among military planners as to whether there was to be peace or war that season. Constant attacks on the river forts and on passing steamers dramatized the necessity of an early answer to the question. Sully, who was most directly concerned, gave the matter a good deal of thought. Early in May he wrote a long letter to Pope, reciting the events at Fort Rice as Dimon had reported them and concluding that there was substance to the rumors of an impending Indian offensive. The Cheyennes, he said, had been driven from the Platte River country during the preceding autumn, and now they were in the Black Hills trying to ally themselves with the Santee and northern Yanktonnais Sioux. Sully remained convinced that the Sioux with whom he had made peace earlier were still faithful to their agreements, and that they should be given some small token of esteem by the Government to strengthen their resolution in the face of threats by the hostiles. He was anxious to use this friendship, and regarded it as an important element in his plan to subdue the warlike tribesmen. "I would get the friendly Indians to fighting the hostile party," he told Pope, "assisting them with all my troops, and by presents of provisions, blankets and ammunition, with the promise they should have the exclusive right to hunt over the lands they now live in." [12] The old warrior even suggested offering these allies a bounty of fifty dollars per hostile scalp.

In the first days of June Sully wrote to Major General Samuel R. Curtis at Milwaukee, repeating much of what he had said to Pope and reiterating his belief that the bands were gathering to the north for a major campaign. He believed that the Indians driven away from the Platte intended to abandon the country south of the Big Cheyenne River and retain the buffalo-filled land that lay to the north of it. "In order to do this they are going to commence to clean out all posts, commencing with Rice." Sully was not so sure he disagreed with the policy of concentration, with some modifications. "If these Indians will only remain in the country north of the Cheyenne and let the posts and passing boats alone it would be a blessing to all, for I do not think a sane white man will ever want to go into that country." [13]

Curtis agreed that "very little of the country is cultivable," but he held that the Indians of the upper Missouri probably "will be there for centuries" and "we may therefore regard our military arrangements in that quarter as more likely to remain fixtures than elsewhere on our national frontier." On this assumption Curtis wanted to determine a location for a permanent fort where troops could be wintered and could guard that segment of the river. "If you agree with me as to Fort Rice being the best point for a main depot you will concur in the propriety of securing ample stores for any occasion at that place." He recommended a large garden "and perhaps a considerable corn field," as well as extensive hay-fields to feed livestock that could not easily be brought downriver each autumn. Sully favored the idea of reinforcing Fort Rice, but he was concerned about supplying it with troops as well as provender. It worried him that Dimon had lost eleven percent of his command through fatal illness during the terrible Dakota winter, and that it was further weakened by a sick list of over two hundred, not to mention the loss of those dispatched to Fort Berthold and Union. Unless he could find more troops, Rice would not be as strong a post as the situation demanded, "and the battalion of the Fourth U.S. Volunteers is fast mustering itself out by desertion. I have caught a great many of them, and have them in the guard house." [14] He asked Pope's permission to execute those found guilty of desertion.

In addition to keeping Fort Rice strong, Sully wanted to strengthen the other links in the chain of river posts. Demands for troops at Rice and at proposed new forts threatened to drain manpower from older stations farther downriver. While Curtis had mentally moved deeper into Indian country and wanted to make Rice a main base of year-round operations, Sully was concerned about the fact that he had only a few troops left to garrison Fort Randall and the post near old Fort Pierre. "This latter post I consider the most important post in the district on account of its position in regard to the Indians," he said to Pope. "It has always been for years a great point for the Sioux Indians to congregate at. I would, therefore, like to have some infantry to garrison these posts." He suggested the four companies of First U.S. Volunteers then stationed in Minnesota. Randall, he said, was "more like a village than a military post." Its barracks, storehouses and stables were so scattered that it required about forty-five men just to post the required sentinels.[15]

Although Randall was much closer to the settlements it, too, had suffered from scurvy. During the winter of 1864–1865 the men had purchased potatoes, onions and other vegetables from Sioux City from company funds, and they were so hungry for them that they often paid as much as five cents apiece for an onion or a potato. As it was in other forts, the men at Randall found plenty of amusement, even as they yearned for antiscorbutic food. The billiard hall, recalled one soldier, was always well patronized, and for those who wanted a more active amusement there "was the tenpin alley, kept by a Jew down at the ferry boat landing." The library, well supplied with books, "mostly fiction, but some good standard works of history, travel, etc., was presided over by a one-legged soldier named Jim. "Uncle Billy" Shaver, an old time Army man who had nearly ruined himself through intemperance during earlier days, headed the local Order of Good Templars "which had a good membership and was the old man's darling." As the reminiscing soldier summed it up, "taking it all together Randall had some good points, while there were some disadvantages." [16] General Sully knew this and he was anxious to eliminate the disadvantages, particularly the large amount of sickness at the forts caused by poor dietary conditions, but it constituted a problem for which he had not yet found a solution. As he prepared his 1865 campaign he thought about it a good deal, as his correspondence reveals.

Before June was out Sully was on his way up the river, resolved to continue his campaigns of the two preceding summers; but now, it appeared, there were new worries. The Interior Department, he wrote to Dimon, had been given $30,000 with which to make peace, and although Pope had "very wisely" forbidden its use in his realm, "I very much fear they may succeed in getting orders from higher Military authority to carry this out, i.e., paying the hostile Indians to behave themselves." This, he thought, would have a very bad effect upon the peaceful Indians who had been ill-paid for their good conduct. In order to avoid disappointing the faithful tribesmen, Sully was ready to act firmly and quickly. He would get to the hostiles before the Indian Agents could spend their appropriation. "I wish therefore," he wrote to Dimon, "if you can do so to send someone to the hostile camp, tell them I & others are after them, if they wish to fight; if they don't, to meet me and we will talk the matter over. If after we talk they don't like what I say I will give them my word they can go back to their camp & get ready to fight me." Meantime, he advised Dimon, hunt up the friendlies and ask them to assemble at Fort Rice in two or three weeks where they could hear from their sponsor. As he waited at Fort Sully he wrote: "I leave here as soon as the boat arrives which I expect soon. I may cross here & march up but don't know yet." [17] Each year before he had waited for steamers, and then he had marched.

While he waited at Fort Sully, the General must have mulled the entire Indian-military situation as it applied to his district. For the third consecutive year a sizable body of troops would move against the Sioux of the upper river country, attempting to sufficiently subdue the natives so that travel routes to the mines would be safe and the Minnesota frontier absolutely guaranteed. One thing Sully knew from past experience was that this was indeed a sparse country, a land as yet seen by relatively few whites and having few attractions to them as settlers. In the early months of 1865 he told Pope that there were no settlements save those along the Missouri and a scattering of farmers about thirty miles up the Big Sioux. "In fact," he said, "taking the forty-third parallel of latitude as a boundary, there are not over three or four white settlers north of it." [18] He mentioned the lack of settlement to Curtis a few days later and added, "nor do I judge there is much likelihood of there being any for many years to come." [19] He thought that if the posts to the north were kept up, a few soldiers could protect the Yankton and Vermillion area; his major force, meanwhile, would take station along the Missouri and maintain that line as a physical frontier and as a more or less permanent barrier between the white and Indian populations.

In this barren land through which the Missouri flowed, and generally west of it, Sully had met two kinds of Indians: hostile and generally peaceful. Those who were destitute, or near it, usually were those most anxious to make peace. The river Indians around Fort Berthold had been friendly for some time; now some of the Miniconjou and Sans Arc Sioux were ready to talk, as were the people of Two Bears who were camped across the river from Fort Rice. The latter could field about three hundred warriors. Black Catfish, the Yanktonnais who was so reluctant to meet with Colonel Dimon, was said to be far less hostile than before, but Medicine Bear was opposed to any immediate concessions. The Santees were believed to be the principal instigators of the war policy, and at their door was laid most of the blame for recent depredations up the river.[20]

The problem of 1865 was a continuing one. The Minnesota uprising of 1862 had generated the original campaign in the Missouri River country and, despite the large expenditures of money and men since that time, Minnesotans were not yet satisfied that the danger had passed. Or so they said. In May General Pope wrote to General Henry Sibley at St. Paul, saying that one of the missionaries had suggested resettling certain of the Minnesota Sioux upon their old lands. Pope professed to agree, provided the people of Minnesota were willing to have these Indians "located in contact with their frontier settlements and will themselves be responsible for the results." However, he warned, the policy of maintaining groups of Indians "inside the line of posts" was both unwise and dangerous. Sibley telegraphed his answer at once: "I do not believe the people will consent to have Indians so near the frontier."[21] Governor Stephen Miller not only opposed the plan, but he urged General Curtis to move immediately against hostile Indians said to be in the vicinity of Devil's Lake, for "they will attack by raiding parties, if not more formidable, our entire western frontier." He talked of a possible repetition of the 1862 situation when western counties were depopulated and hundreds were driven from their homes. "Much of the panic which would ensue would doubtless be baseless and discreditable to the men who ought to stand by and defend their homes," he admitted, "but I must take matters as they are; and the repeated raids upon our borders have so alarmed our people that in too many instances whole neighborhoods abandon their homes upon the first appearance of a raiding detachment of savages." He urged a continued vigilance at the edge of these settlements and a "prompt, vigorous, and continuous campaign against the savages . . . wherever they may be found."[22]

By the time Miller made his appeal, both Curtis and Pope had responded to Minnesota pressures. On May 23 Pope ordered Sully to abandon his proposed march into the Black Hills, and on the same day Curtis telegraphed Sully that "in consequences of the recent troubles in Minnesota," Sully would carry out his campaign under him.[23]

Pope's unhappiness at having his plans altered through political pressures was revealed in a letter to General U. S. Grant, in which he said there were more than enough troops in Minnesota to protect it and that this was no more than the annual spring scare. He saw little point in attacking the Sioux who lived around Devil's Lake, for they invariably fled into Canada at the first sign of Federal troops. Under the circumstances he felt that "there is not and cannot be anything like an Indian war." This led him to one of his periodic essays on Indian management or the lack thereof. The Plains Indian tribes, he told Grant, "are now reaping the harvest of bad management and bad policy which have characterized our Indian systems for so many years." Under existing policies the natives had not been slow to discover that hostilities were followed by treaties, and treaties inevitably produced presents. Now, with travel to the mines heavy and small groups of prospectors wandering farther afield each day, the chance of depredations by parties of young braves increased sharply. The answer, as Pope and many other high military officers saw it, was to restrict the Indians to large reservations and support them outright as an alternative to ultimate extinction through continued contact. It was his hope that such segregation would protect the Indians from the whites and provide them with an opportunity to learn a "new way of life." Grant agreed that to colonize Indians in Minnesota would only aggravate an already touchy situation. He offered to send Pope some of General George Thomas' troops, if necessary, and he added that it might even be necessary to use them to protect some of the Indians from white aggression.[24]

As Sully prepared for the march to Fort Rice, the tugging among elements in Iowa, Dakota and Minnesota increased. Sully's plan to scour the Black Hills had met with great approval from business people at Sioux City because they were financially interested in the road westward along the Niobrara to Montana, to be surveyed shortly by Colonel J. A. Sawyer.[25] Judge A. W. Hubbard of that city assured Pope that there was a large concentration of Indians along the route Sawyer intended to cover, and he attached great importance to the necessity of Sully carrying out his campaign as originally planned. He was concerned about rumors of impending change in military plans for the summer, and he discounted the effectiveness of campaigning against the Indians of northeast Dakota until the troops had permission to pursue the enemy into Canada.[26]

Sully based his opposition to the Devil's Lake proposal on the same ground, saying to Pope that the troops should fight the Indians where it would do the most good instead of futilely pursuing Indians to the international line beyond which he could not go. He much preferred the Black Hills region as a locale for his penetration of Indian country; according to his information there were around ten thousand warriors gathered just north of that point, a figure he held to be greatly exaggerated, but whatever the number "they feel confident they can whip me." Worse, they were taunting him by spreading the rumor that Sully was going north to get away from the Cheyennes, reputed to be extremely brave warriors. The frustrated old Indian fighter made known his wishes and then yielded to higher authority with the comment: "My troops will be ready to march for Devil's Lake, or anywhere else, as soon as boats arrive here with commissary stores, wagons &c." [27] Sully told Pope that he had little hope of finding any Indians in the area Curtis had designated. "Of course," he added, "I will go where the general orders me," but he was reluctant to maintain the silence about his movements Curtis had advised. "This I don't dare to do, for it would raise such a howl with the Dakota people that the world would hear it, but so far as the fear of the Indians knowing it, this they will know as soon as I strike north." [28] Thus the Minnesotans, who very much wanted the northern wagon route opened and protected, had made their Indian scare gambit work, and Sully's forces would serve their needs during the summer of 1865 rather than going to where he thought the main force of the enemy lay.

As Sully predicted, Dakotans did not take kindly to the itinerary of the latest expedition. Those living around Yankton, who had earlier demanded troops, now discovered that the "front" was so far beyond their locality that the economic benefits distributed by the military were most disappointing. The editor of the *Union and Dakotaian* concluded that all these expeditions accomplished was to stir up the Indians and impede settlement. "It is an advertisement to the whole country that there is danger in Dakota." Resentfully, he remarked that Minnesota had its line of frontier posts, "but here we have nothing of the kind." By the time Sully was on his way to Fort Rice, the same editor expressed criticism of the Army's plan "to fit out an immense expedition . . . at a cost of $40,000,000 to establish posts for frontier protection. The truth is, about one half of the sharpers about Sioux City are getting rich out of these expeditions, and they will of course defend and excuse them, while the honest, reliable and disinterested citizens of Sioux City pronounce them ruinous humbugs." [29] The honest and reliable citizens of Yankton did not like being left out of the Government's program for western development.

By July 3 Sully was finally ready to march his men northward. He wrote to Dimon on the preceding evening saying that he was, at last, ready and asked the Colonel to "tell the Indians I am coming but don't tell them on which side of the river." [30] Once again, his faith in the utility of the Missouri River had been shaken, for, as he explained to a fellow officer, four of his boats had sunk before he could get the supply flotilla under way.[31] By now travel along the river bank was routine and he expected no trouble. He told Curtis that small parties could pass that way without molestation, whereas when he first came to the country such a thing would have been impossible. "I mention this to show the great improvement in Indian affairs," he explained.[32] Apparently, conditions in the far north had not yet improved, for Larpenteur related that three of the soldiers stationed at Fort Union were attacked near the post while bear hunting. Two were wounded and the third was riddled with eleven arrows, scalped and stripped. The day after the event the trader recorded, in his laconic way, that the troops buried the soldier and then "hung the Sioux," who presumably had failed to make his getaway after the attack.[33]

The march to Fort Rice was without serious incident except for a mishap to Lieutenant A. R. Fuller that probably diminished his interest in the post's social life upon arrival. The young officer was, according to Sergeant Drips, "thrown forward on his saddle, his horse having stumbled," and the rider "got a pretty hard bump in a very tender spot. Afterwards he had to have the pommel of his saddle covered with buffalo skin to make it more easy riding." The jolt must have been impressive to the accompanying witnesses, for the Sergeant speculated that "whether the effects are going to be permanent remains to be determined in the future." [34] Fortunately for Fuller, the party was only one day out of Fort Rice; on July 13 it approached the post from the opposite side of the river. The arrival of the troops, including two companies of the Fourth U.S. Volunteers (also Galvanized Yankees), generated a good deal of enthusiasm, and the traditional salute was fired as a welcome. The Indians, who had gathered to witness the event, thought they were being fired upon and they fled in all directions, returning only when Sully sent out messengers to assure them that the commotion was purely ceremonial.[35]

Shortly after his arrival, Sully conferred with the Indians who had gathered in the neighborhood. The editor of the *Frontier Scout* ventured an opinion that the natives "like the Rebels, seem anxious to take the amnesty oath." He referred to Bear's Rib, Two Bears, Black Catfish, Little Soldier, Medicine Bear, Two Heart and others who had earlier opposed Sully but who now asserted that they were tired of war and of being driven from place to place. "The remainder of Indians west of us are still of the opinion that they can whip the whites, encouraged by the success of the Cheyennes on the Platte," he added. Editor E. G. Adams, however, assured his military readers that the General "if not interfered with by meddlers and busybodies, will accomplish more than a hundred thousand dollars expended in annuities to the hostile tribes."

Dimon talked at length with Sully about the situation as he saw it. His earlier letters had indicated a belief that the Hunkpapas wanted to continue the war, but that they would be at Fort Rice to talk it over. Ben Dimon came down from Fort Berthold to give his report, looking "a little care-worn from his responsible duties," according to editor Adams. If Ben's condition had resulted from a return to his old weakness, the editor, of course, could not publicize it. Charles Dimon wrote to his parents that the General was anxious for him to stay on, but he thought he would try to get a post farther south next winter. In fact, the Colonel's health was much worse within a week after Sully's arrival. On July 21 Surgeon George Herrick certified that he had examined that officer carefully and discovered that he not only suffered from chronic laryngitis, but that he was also debilitated from scurvy. "I believe that it is absolutely necessary that he should leave this section of the country both on account of its climate and absence of vegetable diet," he testified. Colonel John Pattee, who was later to command Fort Rice, wrote that Colonel Dimon, whom he called a "down-east Yankee from Massachusetts, and that is all that need be said," applied for a leave of absence for twenty days. Sully granted Dimon permission to go to St. Louis and thus "got him out of the way." On July 24 Pattee assumed command of the post.[36]

By the time Sully arrived at Fort Rice, the health of the command was much improved and the General was pleased by the appearance of the men. Only a few months earlier Dimon had made a desperate plea for "Sour Krout," pickles and desiccated potatoes to better the dietary conditions. He also tried to explain the disappearance of one thousand gallons of whiskey at the post between October and March, swearing that no issues of the stimulant had been made "without caution by me." [37] By late June the post surgeon reported that the sick list had decreased with the appearance of wild onions on the hillsides and there were only eleven cases of scurvy, all convalescent. He expressed hope that a "messenger of mercy" in the form of a steamer would turn up, lamenting the fact that the *Fanny Ogden* had brought potatoes that were all in an advanced state of decomposition. He hoped sufficient antiscorbutics would be furnished so that "whoever may be so unfortunate as to be exiled here the coming winter may not suffer as we have." Bitterly he compared the men at Fort Rice to a man in a well, dependent upon someone at the top for sustenance. "If our pleadings are not responded to from down the river, and the means of self-preservation furnished, we must die." [38] Those who had spent the winter at Fort Rice would never forget the experience.

The talks at Fort Rice were not particularly fruitful since a number of Indians Sully wanted to confer with did not show up. On July 23 he moved out with around 840 fighting men and enough teamsters, herders and others to swell the force to 1,000, marching in a northeasterly direction toward Devil's Lake where he arrived on July 29. "It seemed like starting out on a sea voyage as we left the Fort and set forth on the wilderness of Dakota plains," wrote one of the expedition's members. Along the way they encountered large buffalo herds, and some of the men obtained permission to do some hunting. After their arrival at the Lake they explored its shores but found little of interest. Part of the days were spent in camp, around fires, for the weather had turned as cold "as a New England November day." As had been reported, there were half-breeds in the neighborhood. Sully described a camp of them, at which there were some 1,500 carts; the half-breeds were butchering buffalo and drying the meat. They freely admitted that they were from Canada and that they had been on the hunt for about two months. Sully's queries about their presence in Dakota brought no satisfactory explanations. "They answered me they knew no line or frontier . . . that they paid no taxes, had no laws; but that each colony or camp made their own laws, appointed a chief and two councilors, police &c. They handed me a written copy of their laws, among which I saw it was a fine of $5 to sell ammunition to Indians." [39]

After staying long enough to assure himself that there were indeed no enemies in the vicinity, Sully led his men to a campsite near Fort Berthold. "We have thus marched a distance of 275 miles without seeing a hostile Indian, though every means in the power of the General commanding has been used to find their camp," said an expedition chronicler. In disgust he added: "The Expedition thus far shows the folly of a Commander sitting quietly in his office at Head Quarters, and ordering an expedition under command of an experienced Indian fighter to a certain point (as Devil's Lake for instance) in this vast Territory. If he is sent here to fight Indians let him have the privilege of going where the Red-Skins are, and not tie him down with orders from Head Quarters, a thousand miles away, telling him to fight the Indians, but to be sure and not go where they are!" [40]

If Sully had hoped to find out more about the disposition of the Indians for peace or war when he arrived at Berthold, he was disappointed. He had designated this as the meeting point after he was told that the bands did not want to meet at Fort Rice. His own explanation of this situation was that the traders, having far more freedom at Berthold, had persuaded the Indians this would be a safer place to meet, the real reason being that here the half-breeds had a much better chance to profit from the gathering. A few nights before Sully had marched out of Fort Rice, an event took place that strengthened his suspicions as to its reputation among the Indians. One of the steamers transferred some supplies across the river and someone—said to be white or half-breed—had spread the word through the Indian encampment that the vessel was dispatched to bring soldiers with which to kill the Indians. "In a moment the lodges were struck and there was great confusion," Sully reported to Curtis. "Colonel Dimon, the commanding officer, and some of the chiefs went to the camp and succeeded in quieting the disturbance, but not before some of the young bucks mounted their horses and were off." [41] This kind of nervousness, said Sully, made the problem even more complex; it tended to swing over some of the more peaceably inclined to the war group. He related how one of the pro-war chiefs capitalized upon the excitability of the Indians by going through camp cutting himself with a knife, crying out that he had just escaped from Fort Rice where all those who had surrendered were being slaughtered. "In consequence of this five hundred warriors went with him to Rice to see if it were true and avenge the massacre." [42]

On the morning of July 28 a body of Sioux and Cheyennes, estimated at about six hundred in number, appeared on the northwest and south sides of Fort Rice and tried to cut off the herders. It was a familiar maneuver, and Colonel Pattee responded by moving his men out and lending support to the herdsmen. The Indians picked the site upon which they wanted to fight, about two miles southwest of the fort, and engaged the troops in close combat for about an hour and a half before pulling off. It was a typical Indian battle, with the painted horsemen swirling around groups of infantrymen, launching slashing attacks at full gallop and then moving out of range before striking again. Private Andrew J. Burch of H Company, one of the few mounted infantrymen, told of the color of the engagement in an account he supplied for the *Frontier Scout.* In describing how he had emptied his revolver at one Indian, without any effect, he explained that he should have hit the target but his horse was frightened by the opponent's war-rigging. "His pony was hung with red tassels; he, himself, had a red blanket around his waist, his shoulders were naked and painted red, his hair was hanging loose, two feathers fluttering in it. He had a rifle or shotgun in a fringed covering hanging on his back, and in one hand his bow and arrows. His horse was streaked off with red paint over his haunches." Apparently there was a good deal of inaccurate firing on both sides, for the troops reported but one killed and two wounded while the Indians' loss was estimated at only ten.[43]

Except for a brief foray against Fort Rice on July 30, there were no further Indian attacks of any consequences on the Missouri River posts during the 1865 season. In the July 30 engagement no troops were injured, the attackers being driven off by the post's heavy guns. After one native was blown to bits by a cannonball, the Indians fell back and then drifted away in search of less dangerous adventures. After his stop at Fort Berthold, Sully moved his men down to Fort Rice where he stayed until September 5 and then, as the *Scout* put it, the expedition started downriver "on its winding way to civilization." Another campaign was over, and it was the least successful of the three Sully had conducted. Ordered to march away from the Indians rather than to the place where he thought they were, the General had been obliged to spend thousands of dollars in a futile effort to hunt down the defiant Sioux. Regardless of whose shoulders carried the responsibility of the misadventure, the campaign was completely fruitless, and that alone gave the growing humanitarian groups of the East and the ambitious businessmen of Dakota fresh evidence that the military force had done little to solve the "Indian problem" along the river. The failure of war is frequently followed by the resumption of diplomatic efforts, and that would be the course of events in the region during the coming months.

ELEVEN

"Sully's Case Is Peculiar"

The autumn of 1865 was a time of readjustment and reappraisal along the upper Missouri River. Sully's third campaign immediately followed the close of the Civil War, and it coincided with the confusion that resulted from the disbanding of a Union army of nearly a million men and officers. The troops at the river posts were principally volunteers, almost all of whom were more than anxious to be mustered out, and if the forts were to be maintained an almost completely new infusion of personnel was needed. During the summer James Hubbell and Alpheus F. Hawley, who had recently purchased the Chouteau interests in the name of the Northwest Fur Company, took over their newly purchased property which included Forts Union and Berthold. With the departure of the troops, except for a few that remained at Berthold, the Army retreated downriver to Fort Rice. In addition to these developments, there was renewed pressure from eastern "peace policy" advocates and from western trading interests to reexamine the role of the military on the northwestern frontier.

The men at Fort Rice were deeply disturbed by the state of flux in which the military found itself. Their restlessness over the uncertainties of the future typified the attitude of civilian soldiers at the end of the major war. When Colonel Dimon left toward the end of July, the *Frontier Scout* announced that the First U.S. Volunteers and other similar regiments were to be mustered out of service. Since Captain Adams was the paper's editor, the item suggested that the information was authentic and from official channels. Anticipation turned to consternation when some of the post's officers handed around a private letter from Dimon inferring that, on the contrary, Pope did not intend to discharge the volunteers. "To no one except those that have spent such a winter of death and suffering at that advanced Post as we have done can the effect of such a report on the officers and men be imagined," Dimon later wrote. In their despair over the prospect of another winter at Fort Rice, the officers sympathized openly with their men, absented themselves from roll calls, and staged drunken orgies in their quarters. The men responded by refusing to muster and by ransacking the bar of a visiting steamboat, after which thirty-eight of them deserted with about $5,000 worth of horses, saddles and arms.[1]

While Dimon was ready to admit that volunteer troops were of little use in such a state of discipline and that they should be mustered out, he had no sympathy for the conduct of his subordinate officers at Fort Rice. Captain Adams, who had been a thorn in his side for some time, now received the full force of Dimon's anger. The Colonel charged him with a long list of infractions. The first alleged that Adams had accused Dimon of trying to keep the volunteers in service for his own selfish ends and that, rather than trying to stop the mutiny, he had assured the men that their commander was trying to persuade Pope to keep them from being mustered out. In addition to such subversion, said the Colonel, the offender had a very bad set of morals. On one occasion, when the Captain failed to answer roll call, a search was instituted that ended in a local tepee operated as a brothel by Fool Dog. On at least two other instances, the Captain was accused of trying to force Indian women, and when he was not so engaged he had embraced the bottle, once being so drunk he had to be carried to his quarters by fellow officers. Not even Dimon's old friend, Billy Upton, escaped censure. He was charged with openly supporting mutiny by agreeing to go downriver with his men if they were not discharged, and of drunkenness while on duty.[2]

There is no record of counter-accusations against the commanding officer at Fort Rice. His concern over brother Ben's fondness for strong drink suggests moderation on his part, and as for the availability of women, Dimon admitted to his uncle that Two Bear had tried to make him a present of an Indian girl, which he refused, much to the Indian's surprise, since the market price of the article was one horse and one blanket.[3]

The report about the probable mustering out of the First and Fourth U.S. Volunteers was more than rumor. On July 23 Sully told Curtis that he had just received the order, and he objected to it in his usual strong terms. He argued that the water was now so low that, in all probability, no boat could ascend the river to Fort Union; consequently, both Fort Union and Fort Berthold might have to be abandoned because there were no troops to garrison them. He said that he had a small body of cavalry that would stay on, but he did not think it practical to station such units at the upper river posts because there was not enough forage to sustain the animals. Looking toward the postwar years when the Army would seek to justify larger appropriations to support its work in the West, Sully predicted that "if the posts are abandoned the injury to the service will be very serious." [4]

But the order stood, and although the mutinous troops along the river did not know it, their terms of service were virtually over. Orders went out to Captain Upton at Fort Union to start his men southward. "Quite a sudden change," Charles Larpenteur wrote in his journal on August 13. "Twenty soldiers will remain until the Steamer returns, but there will be no troops here during the winter." [5] The rumor reached Fort Berthold, where Sergeant Drips commented that "the talk in camp today is that the fort is to be abandoned." [6] As it developed, Berthold was used by the army until 1867, for which the Government was billed $14,020. The figure included rent on the premises, the use of oxen and "40 large sticks of timber." [7]

With the departure of troops from Fort Union, the last of which left August 21, the old fort was again in the hands of the traders. It was not the same as before, however; there were only ten men at the place, including Larpenteur. Gone were the days of grandeur when "King" McKenzie of the American Fur Company held sway; gone was "the Company" itself. In March 1865 the Northwest Fur Company, organized by Minnesotans Hubbell and Hawley, as mentioned, and by James A. Smith of Chicago and C. Francis Bates of New York, bought out the Chouteau interests and secured a license from Governor Newton Edmunds to trade with the Indians along the river from Fort Sully to Fort Union. Within four years the outfit would sell out to Durfee and Peck.[8] "Quiet times about the establishment," sighed Larpenteur as the troops left. "Weather extreamly [*sic*] hot, musquitoes [*sic*] very bad for the first time this season." The dull, hot weeks were enlivened somewhat by quarrels between the Crows and Assiniboins, and occasional drunken brawls in which the women participated freely. "Great row among the Squaws at night having smuggled down a five gallon keg of whiskey upon which they immediately commenced, a search was made but nothing was found," he noted one day in September. "We turned them all out and on making another search we found the five gallon and one bottle which was put away into the cellar. Very little which after having been turned out they became sober and turned in again, thus ended row No. 2." [9] In a small way, it was almost like the old days.

Meanwhile, the troops at Fort Rice waited out the sultry August days. As elements of the Fourth U.S. Volunteers left on the *Big Horn*, editor Adams moaned: "When will the deliverance come for the 1st U.S.V. Infantry? How long, O Lord, how long?" He might have asked General Sully, who arrived at the fort August 25, had he dared brace the gruff old campaigner. Instead, the officers of the First tendered the General a dinner described as "a happy reunion," at which the guest of honor was "in his best humor, and, like a harvest moon, shed happiness on all present." As the toasting progressed Sully complimented the officers present "for their energy in their efforts to make life even pleasant in such a waste as this," but he did not tell them how soon they would reap the rewards of their good works.[10]

Even as he joined his fellow officers in the festivities of the evening, Sully was probably aware that his days along the

Missouri River frontier were numbered. As far back as December, Dimon had mentioned rumors of efforts to remove him, in a personal letter he had written to the General. Always hopeful of gaining favor, Dimon had assured Sully that he had spoken to "a prominent friend of mine" [Benjamin Butler] in his superior's behalf.[11] Enoch Adams made reference to rumors when he blamed the failure of the summer campaign on "the mercenary motives of the men by whose representations the season's operations have been controlled" and confessed that "we have been long convinced that the little knot of self-constituted guardians of this country were animated by the sole desire of effecting the removal of the District Commander and securing a successor less disposed to interfere with and expose their nefarious Indian transactions."[12]

Sully's removal had been a subject of official discussion before he left Fort Rice for Devil's Lake. On July 20 Grant suggested to General William Tecumseh Sherman that the end of the war had freed a number of experienced officers, and he thought one of them should replace Sully. Sherman showed the dispatch to Pope, who wondered if perhaps there was confusion—it must be Sibley who was suggested for removal. Or at least this is what Pope apparently wanted it to mean. Although he had criticized Sully sharply for his slowness, it was Sully and not Sibley whom he would recommend for promotion, much to the latter's indignation. Besides, Sibley was not a member of the regular establishment. Grant lost no time in explaining himself. On July 21 he telegraphed to Pope: "I meant Sully in my dispatch to Sherman. The order for a change is not imperative, but the complaints against Sully and the management of the quartermaster's department in the Northwest are such that whilst we have too many generals of known ability, I think a change can do no harm and may do great good."[13]

The *Frontier Scout* at Fort Rice was quick to toss editorial bouquets to General Sully, for he was the commanding officer and the editors were his military subordinates. But in one issue there appeared a remark that the General regarded as censorious and his well-known temper flared. The issue of August 3 carried a story entitled "Affairs at Fort Rice," signed by S.P.Y., whom

Sergeant Drips later identified as a "certain Surgeon of the Seventh Cavalry." While it professed to discuss the foolishness of sending forth an army to fight to nonexistent Indians at Devil's Lake, and to comment upon the utter uselessness of the Indian race, not to mention Dakota itself, the writer remarked that the uniforms Sully gave to some "friendlies" later appeared prominently in the front line of an attacking Indian force that struck Fort Rice. Although the writer hastened to correct any inferences about Sully's lack of judgment, and swore that this was the farthest from his intention, the damage was done. "When the General saw the article he fairly boiled over with rage," said Sergeant Drips. " 'S.P.Y.! Yes, he is a spy! I'll spy him! What, a damned spy talk that way about me, and in the newspaper at that!' And so on, but the Doctor was right all the same and the General had to take his medicine." [14]

Other editors did not have to tiptoe around an irascible General, for they had no promotions or comfortable assignments in jeopardy, and when he touched tender spots they reacted. The *Union and Dakotaian* of Yankton, once a Sully supporter, took offense at some comments he had to make about Dakota. In describing the ravages of grasshoppers, the old campaigner recalled how they had destroyed his grass supply, had eaten holes in wagon covers and even chewed a sleeping soldier until such exposed places as his throat and wrists bled. Fearful of the effect of such accounts upon prospective settlers, the editor discounted the story and remarked that "The Munchausen" was a common characteristic of military officials. He admitted that some gardens had been slightly hurt by locusts, but in Yankton many of them were said to be completely untouched.[15] The great grasshopper scourges of the Seventies lay just ahead, and Sully would be more than vindicated, but in 1865 his frankness was regarded only as knocking the country.

Pope described the situation ably when he told Grant that "Sully's case is peculiar." He explained that "he is complained of by persons whose personal views and objects he will not promote at the expense of the public interests." His reference was to men holding official positions in the Indian Bureau and to the traders and contractors connected with them. Pope, who was completely antagonistic to this group, wanted to retain Sully on the ground that his dismissal would tend to justify the charges of his enemies. An investigation made by the inspector general of Pope's department revealed that the main source of criticism came from Walter Burleigh, recently the Agent at Yankton, and in the fall of 1865 a delegate to Congress. When approached, Burleigh could not be induced to elaborate upon his accusations or even to talk about the subject.[16]

More of the economic and political web in which the military was entangled is revealed in a letter from Major J. R. Brown, written late in 1864 from Fort Wadsworth (in the northeastern section of modern South Dakota) to General Sibley, with whom he corresponded regularly. "I will admit for the sake of argument," said Brown, "that Gen. Sully is an Indian man and has been long enough on our frontier to understand its wants, and the best mode of meeting them, but he lacks that intimate knowledge of the Indian character which a *long and intimate business connection* with them has given you." Touching upon the politics of military life, Brown continued: "He could not command the confidence of the people East of the Missouri as you can and whatever position he might occupy would most probably lead to unpleasant relations between you, or a condition of affairs that would result in your acting the part of an automaton. In fact, your ranks are too closely assimilated to leave the district of country East of the Missouri large enough to hold you both as one military district." [17]

On August 25 Pope ordered Sully to reduce the forces in his district to one infantry regiment and six companies of cavalry, relieving the six companies of U.S. Volunteer infantrymen who were to be mustered out of the service. He suggested that only enough horses be kept at the posts to carry mail and dispatches during the winter, due to the expense of providing forage for a larger number of animals. In Sully's response he confirmed the rumor that had circulated along the river all summer: "I cannot issue such instructions to the commanders of Forts Rice and Randall, as General [Grenville M.] Dodge has assumed command over these posts."[18] Hobbled by political considerations in his efforts to fight Indians, the crusty campaigner had been shot down from behind by his white enemies.

As Sully prepared to leave his command, he set down some thoughts about the Indian-military situation along the river as he had watched it change during his three summers in that country. He was convinced that the Indians had been shown what they had previously refused to believe: They could not oppose the Government with any hope of success. Recalling the days before 1863 when the tribes controlled the country above Fort Pierre and made life hazardous for small parties, or even steamboats, to traverse it, he said that little groups of three or four soldiers could travel by land to Fort Rice without any great risk. Admittedly there were, and would be for some time to come, occasional hostile Indians who would steal and murder despite all treaties, but they were growing fewer in number, "and their number will grow smaller every year by proper treatment, which is, by killing them off or forcing them in the manner already suggested."

Despite his feeling that recent campaigns in Indian country had shown the natives the power of the Government, he had come to doubt the value of sending forth large bodies of troops. "In fact," he admitted, "I think it is better to compromise than make war any longer for the present." He proposed maintaining the existing garrisons as a means of showing intent, but he opposed further large expenditures of money. He suggested one means of economizing when he wrote: "I would offer a reward for every hostile Indian captured, or for his scalp. This would be cheaper and more effective than sending large bodies of troops." In any event, whether the future course was war or peace, he thought the results would be much the same; that is, small war parties of young braves who had nothing to lose by war would continue to raid when the opportunity presented itself. His main desire was to make peace with the major portion of the Indians and then stamp out the small brush fires of opposition as they appeared.[19]

During the spring and summer of 1865, as Sully prepared for and then engaged in his futile march, warfare had broken out on a second front between General Pope and Governor Newton Edmunds. Both sides professed to want peace with the Indians, but there was sharp disagreement over who was to effect it and what kind of a settlement would be the best.

Edmunds, who had been appointed territorial governor in 1863 and also acted as *ex officio* Superintendent of Indian Affairs for Dakota, wanted to negotiate in behalf of the Indian office. During the winter of 1864–1865 he went to Washington, D.C., and talked to President Lincoln, who referred him favorably to Commissioner William P. Dole. Edmunds estimated the cost of the negotiation to be $20,000, but Dole thought it would come nearer to $50,000; they took their respective viewpoints to Senator James R. Doolittle (Wisconsin), Chairman of the Senate Committee on Indian Affairs. The Senator, who thought the efforts of the previous river expeditions fruitless and a waste of money, agreed to help provided the peace treaty cost no more than the figure Edmunds had suggested. Early in March he attached the proposal to the Indian appropriation bill then in Congress, recommending it on the ground that it would save money and release troops for duty at the front "where they can do something for the benefit of the country."

When Pope learned of the move he pushed his own plans as rapidly as possible, hoping to send an expedition into the Black Hills and crush the Sioux, said to be gathered there, before the Edmunds forces could get an appropriation from Congress and use it. It was his belief that if the Indians could be sharply defeated, the Army could write its own treaty. Meanwhile, Pope informed Edmunds that the Indian war was still on and there could be no treatymaking for the time being. The natives, he said, were openly hostile and he intended to deal with them forcefully. "This arrangement the Indians thoroughly understand and it furnishes them much stronger inducements to keep the peace than can be offered by presents of goods and money annuities." Sully was instructed to make no agreements without Pope's express permission. The Minnesota Indian scare that caused Grant, at the request of Curtis, to divert the expedition to Devil's Lake was a development Pope had not expected and, in the end, it severely disrupted his plans for an "Army peace." [20]

Edmunds promptly appealed to Secretary of the Interior James Harlan, quoting a letter from Sully who said he also wanted to make peace, but that Pope was for war, and orders were orders. "From the above it is clear that the military commander of this department has his face firmly set against making peace with these Indians, notwithstanding the evident desire of Congress to consummate this very desirable object," wrote the Governor. "A revocation of the military order above quoted seems necessary before any action can be taken on my part to treat with the Indians, and I trust that such action may be taken by the War Department as will cause the military commander of this district to cooperate." [21] To hurry the cooperation, Edmunds reported to Dole that there were a number of irregularities occuring at the river posts, such as the sale of contraband articles of war to the Indians in exchange for their peltries. He hoped the Commissioner would relay the news of such scandalous conduct to Secretary Harlan and others who might use their influence to correct military misconduct.[22]

While Edmunds bombarded Washington administrators, Dakota's frontier press rolled out its editorial guns and set up another barrage. During May the Yankton *Union and Dakotaian* criticized the military arm for its lack of cooperation with civilian authorities, charging that various officers wanted to continue the Indian war for fear of losing their present ranks now that the big war in the East was over. "The Confederacy has 'busted,' and 'generals' are a 'drug in the market,' " said the little western sheet. The press, once so anxious to have troops in the region, now held that "the fact of an Indian Expedition, or even the appearance of danger which the military display in this department naturally begets, will keep the emigrant aloof. Our prosperity is identified with Peace." Perhaps word already had reached Dakota of Dole's promise to send $11,000 of the appropriation to Edmunds and Burleigh to be used at their discretion.

Several years earlier southern Dakota had cried for protection, which it was granted, but there was no longer any Indian danger in that section. The area to the north, alarmingly close to Minnesota supply houses, had gained the soldiers, and now people at Yankton showed no reluctance in expressing the wish that the Department of the Northwest soon would be "gathered into oblivion—though we are painfully conscious that history will perpetuate its folly."[23] The countryside around Yankton was witnessing the passing of the military frontier, and its sentiment typified the reaction demonstrated in later years in other communities farther west.

Harlan responded to Edmunds' plea by taking the matter to Secretary of War Edwin Stanton. He mentioned the desire of Congress to restore friendly relations with the Sioux, some four thousand of whom were said to be near Fort Pierre, ready to talk, but he said that these desires were being frustrated by the unwillingness of the military authorities to cooperate. "Indeed, they evince a settled determination to oppose the negotiation of any treaties with those Indians."[24] In his annual report of 1865, Harlan charged that "the policy of total destruction of the Indians has been openly advocated by gentlemen of high position, intelligence, and personal character." While he named no names, it was generally understood that these sentiments were strongest among military men, including those of high rank, and the Secretary strongly condemned the attitude as one unbefitting an enlightened nation. Besides, he added rather naively, "financial considerations forbid the inauguration of such a policy." To liquidate some 300,000 people apparently was not only uncivilized, but it was fiscally unsound. Harlan urged that Pope's policy, which he either misunderstood or purposely misinterpreted, be overruled.[25]

The General's counter-argument was that Edmunds and the Indian Bureau were simply trying to execute the same old treaty: Namely, to gather up the Indians and to give them presents in exchange for promises of better conduct. "In other words, the Indians are bribed not to molest the whites." Such agreements, he held, were always looked down upon by the Indians, who showed no reluctance to break them at the first opportunity. As he said to Grant, whose support he sought, it was a well-known fact that whenever the Sioux needed powder and ball all they had to do was to go down along the Overland Trail and kill a few emigrants, shortly after which they would be accorded a new treaty that supplied their immediate wants.[26] Pope was willing for Sully to make peace with the Sioux and Cheyennes who ranged that road, hoping to keep them north of the Platte River, but he cautioned his subordinate not to give them any money or goods in the fashion of the Indian Bureau. Presumably Sully was to use force and intimidation rather than presents. It was in this spirit that the summer campaign of 1865 was planned.[27]

While Sully was making his march to Devil's Lake, Colonel John Pattee took charge of Fort Rice and made an effort to resume peace talks with the Indians. The new commander, an Iowan who had been on the Dakota scene since the days of the Minnesota outbreak, was regarded as one of the local boys by Governor Edmunds, who called Dimon's removal and the appointment of a man known to the Indians as "Big Heart" a favorable omen.[28] To him it meant the replacement of an officer who had "by his unfortunate management seriously complicated matters in the vicinity" with one who had been in the country a long time and had gained a reputation for honest dealing among the Indians. Pattee's comment that "the primary object of my being stationed at Fort Rice was to open communication with hostile Indians on the west side of the Missouri River, and try to make peace with them," coupled with Edmunds' warm endorsement, suggests the influence of local political pressure upon the military in early post-Civil War days.

To carry out his mission Pattee dispatched Charles Galpin, the old-time fur trader, to Fort Berthold, where he was to find out all he could about the prospects for peace. Galpin spread the word throughout the Indian camps that a conference at Fort Rice was desired and, at the same time, Pattee sent a friendly Indian directly to the tribes, reiterating the invitation. The emissary met with an icy reception; in fact, he was told that he ought to be killed for deserting his own people, but he was allowed to go back to Fort Rice and report his failure. Twice more Pattee sent him forth, and on the last visit one of the old tribal leaders said: "This is the third time this man has come and told us these same words, and I am getting tired of this fighting and I think we ought to go and hear what he has to say." It was agreed that a delegation would go to the hill back of the fort's cemetery, in full view of the place, where Galpin and Pattee were to come forth for a council. In the talks that took place, the Indians made it clear that they deeply resented the establishment of Fort Rice and the road west of there to the Yellowstone River. Fire Heart, a Blackfoot Sioux, complained that past treaties had given his people the land between the Cannonball and Heart Rivers and the whites had no business in that part of the country. To the Indians there did not seem to be much to negotiate, and they were very little disposed to talk about revisions in policy.[29]

On August 18 Pope informed Sully that a Commission had been appointed to treat with the Indians of the upper Missouri River. While the military was represented by Generals S. R. Curtis and H. H. Sibley, the naming of Superintendent Edward B. Taylor, Reverend Henry W. Reed (both of the Indian Bureau), Orrin Guernsey (a Wisconsin political figure) and Newton Edmunds to the body signified Pope's defeat in his contest with the Interior Department.[30] On September 6, the steamboat *Calypso* left St. Louis and began gathering commissioners along the way. It picked up Guernsey at St. Joseph, Curtis and Taylor at Omaha, Sibley at Sioux City and Reed at Yankton. Inching through low water and struggling over numerous sandbars, the boat finally tied up at Fort Randall on August 29. Its destination had been Fort Rice, described by Pope as a good place to talk with some of the Indians who had separated from the hostile bands and who were in a mood for peace. Now it was getting late in the season and the going was hard; Sully suggested that the conference be held at Fort Sully because it was a more convenient place and also because the Sioux had a particular distaste for Fort Rice.

The representatives of several Sioux bands that Pattee gathered at Fort Rice were not enthusiastic about Sully's efforts to spare the Commissioners more river travel. They told the Colonel that the 180-mile trip would wear out their horses and ruin them for the fall hunt. "Big Heart" must have used a good deal of oratorical effort upon them, for he eventually got their consent to start off on foot, a mode of travel not at all popular with the natives, taking along several of his horses in case they found buffalo along the way. Down to Fort Sully they went, through blustery weather and occasional snow, where they joined members of other tribes in the deliberations which had been in progress since October 6.

The peace commissioners spent most of October talking with representatives of the Lower Brulés, Two Kettles band, Sans Arcs, Blackfeet Sioux, Hunkpapas, Lower Yanktonnais and Miniconjou Sioux, the last of which they called "one of the most numerous, warlike and mischievous subdivisions of the great family of the Teton Dakotas or Sioux." On October 10 the first of a series of treaties containing the traditional provisions was signed, in which the Indians promised to cease all hostilities, to dissuade hostile warriors from making attacks and to withdraw from travel routes established or to be established through their country. There was great objection to the latter provision; it was argued that new routes would endanger the buffalo supply. In answer to this, the white diplomats promised $30 a year for each family, as compensation for such losses already suffered. There was some disposition on the part of the Commissioners to suggest agriculture as a means of supplementing tribal diet, but they soon noticed that any mention of farming brought audible grunts of discontent from their listeners, and they quickly turned to more interesting subjects.[31]

J. Allen Hosmer, the son of Montana's first territorial Chief Justice, stopped at Fort Sully on his way to "the States" in mid-October and witnessed some of the proceedings. After the speeches were over and the proper documents signed, the distribution of presents began. Hosmer watched the Two Kettles band receive theirs, and he wrote of the wagonloads of goods brought from the fort for distribution among the encamped Indians. First came some two hundred boxes of hardtack or "pilot bread" and large quantities of sugar, coffee and hams, followed by coats, hats, calicos, blankets and, finally, the all-important powder and bullets. "After the goods were all landed," wrote the traveler, "the squaws came and opened the boxes that contained the goods, and took what was given them . . . , and then started with their packs, some of which weighed over a hundred pounds, but these women seemed to shoulder their loads very easily and would carry them . . . without stopping to rest, the men would stand around and tell the women what to take." [32]

As the deliberations proceeded at the maddeningly slow pace that characterized Indian negotiations, the Captain of the *Calypso* watched the river drop two or three inches every day. He grew nervous. On October 24 three inches of snow fell, and two days later ice began floating by the moored vessel. Faced with the prospect of being frozen in for the winter, the Commissioners asked for a delay of one more day, hoping that straggling remnants of those bands not yet signed up would arrive, after which they agreed to leave. On October 27 the steamer pulled out into the channel and, as Superintendent Taylor expressed it, "took its departure for America." [33]

As the meetings with the Indians broke up and each side departed for winter quarters, the affair left behind a story which the Army officers passed around as being an example of the way treaties were being made by the Interior Department. It told of an Indian of the Two Kettles band who wanted to visit a woman in whom he was interested at the Yankton Agency below Fort Randall. Accordingly, he applied at Fort Sully for a safe-conduct pass. Upon hearing of the conferences taking place, he pocketed the pass and, enlisting fifteen agency Indians, he presented himself before the Commissioners, claiming that the group represented fifteen lodges of recently hostile, but now humbled, warriors. The listeners were so impressed that they doled out presents and supplies for the ninety persons claimed as dependents, and the shrewd native collected his profits before resuming his romantic pursuits at the Yankton Agency.[34] If the story were correct, it lent weight to Pope's contention that the natives were more interested in material gain than in the higher motives of peace, and that their objectives often were of a more immediate nature.

A treaty of sorts had been signed, but it was by no means adequate or conclusive. Governor Edmunds explained that, due to the lateness of the season and the presence of only scattered representations from part of the tribes, the efforts of the Commissioners were inconclusive at best. "I see no remedy for this matter," he told the Commissioner of Indian Affairs, "but for the commission to adjourn with the important work but half commenced, to be called together next spring, when it can easily be fully completed. . . ." Taylor, who headed the Northern Superintendency, was more optimistic. Despite the difficulties of negotiations, there seemed to be a disposition for peace upon the part of the Indians, and although scattered raids could be expected in the future, he said: "I am fully satisfied that the great Indian war is substantially at an end." [35] It was hopeful predictions such as this that infuriated Army men and caused them to talk darkly about the plains warriors being Indian Bureau pets. Sully, who had marched and countermarched through the Dakota country, and Pope, who had directed the operations, both felt that a start had been made and that the Indians had seen a demonstration of power, but it was also their conviction that, unless such pressure was continued, only an uneasy peace could be maintained.

TWELVE

A Military Frontier

Under different circumstances, the unsuccessful military campaigns in the upper Missouri country that followed the Sioux uprising in Minnesota might have resulted in the abandonment of that country to the Indians as it had, in effect, some forty years earlier after General Atkinson's expedition. The disappointment of those living in southern Dakota at the lack of economic gain from the campaigns, the rising humanitarian sentiment in the East toward the Plains Indians, and the normal American lack of interest in the military which occurs at the close of every great war did not promise much enthusiastic support for the Federal Army in the peacetime days that lay ahead. Those of the Regular Army establishment who watched the magnificent fighting machine of 1865 disintegrate were aware that a large number of commissioned and noncommissioned officers would choose to stay in the service until retirement. In order to find employment for them, as well as to maintain the organization itself, every possible justification for appropriations would be needed. As the Volunteers moved southward, bound for civilian life, and the Indian Bureau strengthened its hold on the destiny of the tribes, the future of the Missouri River posts was questionable.

At the close of the Civil War the land along the upper reaches of the river was not considered agriculturally desirable, and there was little disposition for farmers to look in that direction when they sought to take advantage of the new homestead law. Certainly none of Sully's veterans, who had struggled through the badlands of Dakota on their way to the Yellowstone River, had any inclination to return as civilians. In the public mind the American Desert was still very real, and almost no one who traversed this section envisaged the possibility of farming in the foreseeable future, even though advocates of the Indian cause constantly suggested the idea to the natives, who also regarded it as ridiculous. The agrarian focus of that day was upon Kansas and Nebraska, where the Union Pacific Railroad was being built. Even though the Northern Pacific was chartered before the war's end, the man on the street did not yet believe in this route as one which crossed a potential American breadbasket. The "new Northwest," as it became known, was still looked upon as the land of the Sioux which, in fact, it was.

If the expanse that was Dakota and the plains of Montana was still considered desert and a place to be traversed, not settled, the northern Rocky Mountain country was beginning to be looked upon as an important part of America's treasure chest. The convincing strikes at Bannack, Virginia City and Last Chance Gulch developed increasing excitement. Each suggested the possibility of bigger and richer finds in the future, the total impact of which contributed mounting evidence that this was the biggest gold field of all. By the autumn of 1865, as hundreds of miners floated down the Missouri in their mackinaw boats to spend the winter in "the States," word spread of the heavy pokes they carried, and of their intention to hurry back in the spring to where more treasure lay waiting for the taking. The early months of 1866 were filled with suppressed excitement over the mother lode that was said to be hidden in the Montana mountains. Many war veterans resolved to take the first boat going that way, when the river shed its coat of ice and sent forth that great wash of muddy water upon which the tiny river steamers crabbed their crooked way northward to the diggings.

Although General Sully had almost reached a point of despair over the inefficiency of steamboat travel, the war years saw an increasing use of the lower part of the river by the awkward-looking vessels. During that time the Montana mines began to yield impressive amounts of gold, and there was a rising demand for heavy machinery for use in lode mining. Yet very few vessels had ever reached the head of navigation at Fort Benton. Prior to the 1866 season only four boats had made such a trip, but in that season the picture changed very quickly. It was now known that Fort Benton could be reached successfully, and the reward for doing so made all the efforts and risks worthwhile. The prairie sailors were ready to meet the challenge. Now began what one historian has called the golden era of steamboating on the upper Missouri, as thirty-one cargos reached that difficult destination and deposited in central Montana 4,686 tons of freight, exclusive of Government supplies.[1]

Even before the spring rise of that season, there was a throb of anticipation along the river. St. Louis newspaper readers noticed more frequent advertisements for river passage to Montana, and a Nebraska daily predicted: "The emigration promises to revive the scenes of California emigration of '49–'50." [2] Montana, it was said, had sent eastward over $70,000,000 in gold dust in its short mining history, and the prediction for the coming year alone was nearly half that total. The excitement was reflected also in the recommendations of the military planners, who talked of Montana in their reports and called for additional protection of the routes leading to the mines. In a lengthy and detailed report of February 1866, General John Pope spoke of the growing population in the mountains and pointed out that it would require more transportation than land vehicles could then offer. Although he erroneously believed that the miners would always depend upon the Missouri and Mississippi valleys for "the necessaries as well as the luxuries of life," he correctly assumed that the immediate needs of that remote area would be very great. His statement that the intervening region was "utterly unproductive and uninhabitable by civilized man" found ready agreement among the troops who had wintered along the river and, for the time, the contention was yet to be disproved. Less subject to argument was his assertion that the most numerous and warlike of American Indian tribes inhabited the region, and that their presence would pose serious problems to travelers, although not all of his colleagues agreed with him that this condition would prevail until the natives were either exterminated or Christianized.

Pope concluded that there were three principal practical northern land routes to Montana, all of which included the Missouri River and its forts in some manner. The first ran from St. Paul, Minnesota, to Forts Rice and Union and on to Fort Benton. A second began at Mankato, Minnesota, crossed the river at Fort Pierre, and then followed the valley of the Big Cheyenne to the Black Hills and on to the Powder River country where it picked up the Yellowstone River. A third possibility was the route beyond the Missouri, up the Niobrara to the southern Black Hills and from there to the Powder River. He felt that no more than one of these could be properly guarded for the time being, and, therefore, some choice would have to be made. He recommended the second, or Big Cheyenne, route because of its suitable terrain and because he did not think the country west of Fort Union could be made safe for travel until the Indians in those parts were under better control.[3]

Although the Sioux who lived between Fort Pierre and the Black Hills had strong objections to the choice, the merchants of southern Dakota and northern Iowa approved. Minnesotans argued that a more northerly approach was shorter, and in January 1866 Congressman Ignatius Donnelly offered a resolution asking the House Committee on Military Affairs to recommend the establishment of a series of posts from Minnesota's western boundary to the Montana mines, by the most direct line.[4] The Commissioner of Indian Affairs admitted that wagon trains already were using the road by way of Forts Wadsworth, Berthold, Union and on to Montana, and he concluded: "It seems likely that a route following up the Missouri on the east side of the river will hereafter also become a great highway."[5]

General William Tecumseh Sherman, commanding the Military Division of the Missouri, studied Pope's report, balanced it against other recommendations, and came to the conclusion that the troops at his disposal could protect no more than a total of two or three routes to Montana. These, he wrote, would be guarded by "lines of blockhouses, and small patrols . . . and trust to cavalry expeditions to maintain a general condition of security on the plains." [6] In April he ordered Colonel Delos B. Sacket to inspect the Missouri River country, saying that he believed the Montana-bound traffic would flow along three principal routes: (1) By way of the Missouri River, (2) up the Platte River to Fort Laramie and then along the Bozeman Trail into Montana and (3) over the Big Cheyenne roadway recommended by Pope. Two of these involved the Missouri River, and their existence pointed to the further establishment of posts along that waterway.[7]

Colonel Sacket, a West Pointer with more than two decades of experience, had spent a considerable portion of his career on the frontier. During the Civil War he served as an inspector general, with the rank of colonel, during which time he made a number of inspections of the type he was now asked to perform.[8] Although remote outposts were nothing new to him, his more recent efforts in the wartime army must have accustomed him to a set of standards which would make the scenes which he was now to see appear to be those of another world. As he headed upriver early in May 1866, he no doubt had little idea of the conditions under which the men of this forgotten front had lived during the more exciting days that had recently ended for the Federal armies at the front. Fort Randall was to be his first stop.

An army wife, Sarah Canfield, who visited Fort Randall shortly before Sacket's arrival, called the place a rude affair on the edge of civilization. Her description of its physical features typified that of most of the visitors who came upon these river posts. She mentioned its log blockhouses fitted with loopholes and swivel guns, and its lookout post, from which a soldier constantly scanned the countryside with his telescope. To Mrs. Canfield, such vigilance was important, "for we are now in the Indian country and they are very hostile." Despite its crude appearance, she admitted that she had spent a very pleasant afternoon at the post, visiting with the army officers and their wives.[9]

Colonel Sacket viewed Fort Randall as a place that had outlived its usefulness and should be abandoned. The soft cottonwood logs had rotted away, leaving the quarters so filled with vermin and rats that the men slept out of doors, weather permitting. Colonel Charles C. G. Thornton, the commanding officer, lived in a frame building "erected at an enormous expense," but not in complete comfort. "While sitting in the commanding officer's quarters two bugs dropped from the ceiling upon me," wrote Sacket. Even more unsatisfactory, he said, was the establishment's location. It was built on the wrong side of the river, where no roads led to it; most of the hay and wood had to be hauled from the northeast side and ferried across on flatboats at great expense and effort. "I can see very little use of a six-company post at this point—in fact can see very little use of a post of any kind," he concluded. Instead of sharing Mrs. Canfield's concern about the Indians, the Colonel thought Randall's troops should be transferred to Fort Benton where the Indians were really hostile. If the Government thought it needed a fort in this area, he suggested the erection of a new one some nine miles north, on Pease Creek.

The men did not present a much more attractive appearance. Colonel Thornton admitted that he had not held a drill or a dress parade in months, and when he brought his force out for inspection, its appearance was quite unmilitary. The soldiers stood before the visitor dirty, ragged, unshaven and long-haired, without knapsacks (which had been condemned and destroyed), their carbines, revolvers and ammunition boxes in poor condition. Colonel Sacket did not request that this sorry lot be drilled, "being fully satisfied that they knew little or nothing about it." The cavalry units, dismounted because they had no horses, did not know how to come to an inspection of arms. Sacket did not request target practice, probably in the interest of the safety of all.

Despite personal appearances the men appeared to be healthy; their food was well prepared, even though the kitchens were not very clean, and the hospital was rated as "good." There were only four sick men at the post, and the death rate from illness was very low. As the weather warmed "summer complaint" took its toll, and Dr. C. C. Gray, post surgeon, reported that by August the command was in a very weakened condition. He blamed it on bad bread and too much salt meat.[10] Under such conditions the men were inclined to desert, but many of them were too weak to leave and, worse, the Government owed them as much as ten months' pay.

The post had only twenty-three horses, twenty-one of which were unserviceable because "the hay and grass the horses must eat, grown upon these lands, causes their hoofs and tails to drop off, and in many cases kills them." Nor was there much prospect of raising food for man or beast because of the alkaline soil, the soldiers being able to make a garden only about once in five years. Sacket did not think any settlements would grow in such a place, and the advance of civilization surely would pass it by.[11]

On Sunday morning, May 20, the *Lillie Martin* slowly approached Fort Sully, its crewmen constantly probing the river bottom to find a passable channel. Daniel Weston, a passenger bound for Montana, wrote in his diary: "There was no sign of a living inhabitant and the farstretching slopes grass-green and fair looked like a pleasant place for human beings." About five o'clock he looked out his stateroom window and there lay Fort Sully, flanked by an enormous encampment of Indians. Unable to make a proper landing, the boat tied up at the opposite bank and a yawl was put out to carry Colonel Sacket across the river where Lieutenant Colonel John Pattee awaited him. The former Commander of Fort Rice, long accustomed to the wilderness, was dressed in shirt-sleeves, civilian trousers and Indian moccasins.[12]

Pattee, of the Seventh Iowa Cavalry, was now a veteran among Volunteer troops and, like many others who spent much time at frontier posts, he had gone more or less native in his dress. Neither U. S. Grant nor W. T. Sherman was any more fastidious, but since they were the two highest-ranking American Army officers they, like the rich, could afford to dress with studied carelessness. Sacket viewed the casual attire of the post's commanding officer with great distaste and noted in his report: "Lieutenant Colonel Pattee may be a most excellent man, but he certainly has not the first element of a soldier in his composition."

An inspection of the troops commenced, and Colonel Sacket's concern turned to cautious hope. Second Lieutenant L. O. Parker of the Fourth U.S. Volunteers brought forth a company that looked almost military. The men were long-haired, but otherwise their appearance was neat, their clothing, arms, belts, knapsacks and canteens were in good repair, and the company's general condition indicated what an attentive officer could accomplish. Then the Colonel came upon the next company of the Fourth, commanded by Second Lieutenant William H. Vose. Here was a shuffling line of long-haired, dirty, ragged individuals, without knapsacks or canteens and carrying cartridge boxes that barely passed inspection. Vose also commanded a small detachment of mounted troopers and this, too, presented a picture of neglect and carelessness. Their horses, poorly cared for and without any hay for some time, were housed in ramshackle, badly ventilated stables. Sacket abandoned any hope of conducting drill or target practice "knowing it would be time and ammunition thrown away uselessly." The men had not indulged in either activity for more than a year. "It will be a great thing for the service, and for the Indians, when all the volunteers at these posts are mustered out of service, and replaced by regular troops," growled the academy-trained Colonel.

As at Fort Randall, the means of transportation at this post were also quite limited. Twenty-one mules and five horses were in good enough condition to pull the nine serviceable wagons. This motive power was supposed to be supplemented by a small herd of oxen, but those animals had been placed on Farm Island for the winter, and when they ran out of forage, the high water of the spring runoff and the loss of the post's only flatboat prevented them from being rescued. The animals had nearly starved to death. Lieutenant George Strong was responsible for providing livestock feed, but, commented Colonel Sacket, "he has not the least conception of what his duties are, and is totally disqualified for the position he holds." When asked why he had made no official reports, the young officer exclaimed that he had no blanks. With painful sarcasm Sacket suggested that he rule off some plain paper and use that until printed forms arrived. Sacket also complained that hay at nearly $30 a ton was much too high a price to pay, and he was highly critical of Pattee who had allowed 2,500 sacks of corn to sit out in the open where rats, soldiers or Indians could help themselves to it.

There was little about Fort Sully that was acceptable to Colonel Sacket. He could not find "a stick of wood, a bush, or a blade of grass" within two miles of it. Firewood was a luxury, and there was no lumber available for any purpose, not even enough "to make a coffin should any one die." The well water was so alkaline that the muddy product of the river, hauled nearly three-quarters of a mile, had to suffice for drinking and cooking purposes. The officers' quarters were dark, poorly ventilated log structures with little headroom above the mud roofs. The floors were of dirt, the walls were so filled with cracks that dust sifted in constantly on windy days, and the structures were overrun with rats, mice and fleas. The men's quarters were so bad that Sacket did not think human beings should be permitted to live in them, and the kitchens were even worse. The guardhouse and the hospital, also dark and filthy, were unsuitable for human use by any standards. In fact, he did not see a structure at the post that was of the least value, except the flagstaff "and it is only a tolerable one."

Under such living conditions the men struggled for their very survival and paid little heed to appearances. Colonel Pattee kept books, in a manner of speaking, but the results were far from complete. Occasionally Lieutenant Parker, or any enlisted man who could write legibly, assisted him, but for the most part, Pattee worked out post reports in his own hand. The post sutler, who was supposed to cater to the needs of the troops, kept little or nothing in stock, for he was little interested in their patronage. The far more lucrative Indian trade occupied nearly all of his attention. "I came to the conclusion that all military duty was performed in a very loose manner," wrote Sacket, as he prepared to leave Fort Sully for posts higher up the river.[13]

The relations between the men at Fort Sully and the neighboring Indians were quite friendly. Within a ten-mile radius of the post lived some 1,900 Sioux, composed mainly of Brulés, Miniconjous, Yanktonnais, Sans Arcs, Two Kettles and Santees, and also including some 300 Oglala Sioux widows and children. Pattee issued rations to them three times a week and, on one occasion, distributed nearly 18,000 pounds of food. The local Indian Agent reported that a good deal of hard liquor also passed from the steamers through the post and into the Indian camps, and he warned of its "dangerous and blasting influence" upon the natives.[14]

The Sioux around Fort Sully had earlier been promised a large supply of goods and presents by the Indian Commission, and they had waited impatiently for the arrival of a Commissioner. They mistook Sacket for the promised representative, and gave him the warm welcome accorded to all bearers of such gifts. The Colonel complained that he "was compelled to shake hands and be hugged by every dirty buck I met." When he explained to them that he bore no gifts and that he belonged to another branch of the Washington tribe, their unhappiness was great. He then listened to a recitation of misdeeds on the part of the whites, of broken promises, of the many steamboats that had passed the place without depositing a single trinket, and of their great dissatisfaction with white travel along the Big Cheyenne road.[15]

Colonel Sacket's recommendation with regard to Fort Sully was clear: Abandon the place. He conceded that, at the time of its location, the choice might have been defensible, but now it was impossible to find one good reason for its site. He suggested that Lieutenant Colonel George S. Andrews, who was shortly to assume command of the post, be authorized to select a location farther upriver. Two months later Andrews reported that he had found a suitable spot about thirty miles above the old location, and that he had founded what was to be known as New Fort Sully. Located on the east side of the river, the place had a fine steamboat landing, a good supply of grass and timber, and was located at a point where Sacket felt the Montana road would cross to the west bank. Four companies of the Thirteenth Infantry commenced the construction of the new post, determined to make it more habitable than its predecessor. Before July was out Andrews had collected eight hundred logs, and he called for a sawmill and a shingle-making machine, determined to build quarters that would not attract rats and vermin as had the old dirt-roofed buildings from which the men had moved.[16] It seemed apparent that the War Department recognized the Missouri River frontier as an integral part of its western defense system, and that it was prepared to keep troops there until they no longer were needed.

Colonel Sacket started for Fort Rice toward the end of May, and on the last two days of the month he conducted his inspection of that post. As he penetrated Dakota more deeply, the land became wilder and more bleak. Mrs. Canfield, who passed along the river a month earlier, wrote that "This is a worse country than I ever dreamed of. Nothing but hills of dry sand, with little streaks of short shriveled grass in the hollows and on the river bottoms." [17] Daniel Weston called Fort Rice, located in this desolate land, the finest post he had passed.[18] Colonel Sacket, aboard the *Lillie Martin,* partially agreed with him, admitting that the place was certainly better than Randall or Sully, "which is not saying a great deal." He praised the commanding officer, Colonel John G. Clark, who had installed floors, windows and ventilators in all the quarters, which made them much more comfortable. However, he noticed that the roofs were of dirt and the floors were not raised enough to permit proper ventilation. The mess rooms were low, dark and without sufficient air space. A two-story building, plastered within, with exterior clapboards and a shingled roof, served as a headquarters building, and with this the visiting Colonel was pleased. Also worthy of praise was a row of well-built storehouses and a set of stables and corrals placed upon high ground and well drained. Sacket was critical of General Sully, who had told Clark to tear down some of the new buildings, commenting that it was a pity such orders were issued. However, said Sacket, before the Government proceeded with its improvement program at Fort Rice, it should consider moving the whole place downriver about a half mile where there was a better steamboat landing and boats could land easily even during low water, thus eliminating unnecessary haulage to the post.

Colonel Clark was highly praised for his management of the men. He commanded nine companies of the Fiftieth Wisconsin Volunteers, a unit that took up its duties at the post in September 1865. Since their promised date of discharge was four months past, Sacket thought Clark had done a fine job in controlling 450 men who were understandably discontent. The men of Fort Rice knew no more about drill than those at the posts downriver, but Sacket passed over this deficiency, saying they had received their discipline through hard work. "I did not think it worthwhile to try and make a one-year regiment drill when it had not had a drill during its term of service," he explained, adding that the buildings erected during the winter probably contributed more to the service than if the time had been spent in military exercises. The Wisconsin boys, many of whom were used to logging or other outdoor work, had been generally healthy, yielding but one of their number to the ravages of scurvy. The hospital was clean, and Surgeon John W. Vivian had made every effort to keep his men available for duty. Despite his best efforts, and those of Colonel Clark who worked his men hard, it was impossible to keep soldiers away from Indian women. "At all the posts on the Missouri River I find there is a great deal of syphillis," Sacket reported, but even though he suspected a very high incidence of disease among the natives around this post, its venereal rate was below average. The problem was recognized as being common, so much so that the surgeons normally did not excuse men from duty on its account. Still, the Inspector worried about the numbers of what he called "these creatures" around the forts, and he predicted that, unless easy mingling with them was stopped, many of the men would be rendered unfit for duty.

An inspection of the men elicited a number of compliments from the visitor. The companies were uniformly neat in their appearance, their clothing clean and free of holes, their arms and accouterments in excellent order, and even the long haircuts did not give the impression of shagginess. As Sacket went over Clark's books, he was pleased to find them carefully and correctly kept, all, he said, "in very nice order." In addition to the regularly employed soldiers, the post had one interpreter, Frank la Framboise, who was employed at a salary of $50 a month, and forty-two enlisted men who were assigned to special duties as herders, stable hands, carpenters, blacksmiths, saddlers, warehousemen and clerks. Colonel Sacket thought this number none too large for the size of the establishment.

As at Fort Sully, this post had several thousand Indians living around it and they, too, anxiously awaited the arrival of Indian Commissioners and presents. Here he learned that, soon after his departure from Fort Sully, the Indians had become quite troublesome and had sworn a number of threats based upon a supposed deception by the Commission. No doubt the same would be the case with Fort Rice's suburban residents. Typical of the military fraternity, he took the view that civilian peacemakers generated nothing but trouble, and he commented sourly that, in all probability, the present Commissioners would have to call upon the Army to get them safely out of Indian country.[19] William Larned, who spent the winter of 1865–1866 at Fort Rice, did not regard the 3,500 natives who lived in the neighborhood as sufficiently dangerous to bother the Commissioners or anyone else. He said they were quite poor and so near starvation, "owing to their Supreme Shiftlessness," that they had little inclination to fight. Instead, they resorted to stealing on a large scale, having recently made off with thousands of pounds of corn, hay, tools, peltries, chickens, young cattle, clothing, halters, ox bows, bridles and "in fine, everything they can lay their hands on." [20]

Having completed a two-day inspection of Fort Rice, Inspector General Sacket moved on to Fort Berthold, the temporary post that had been used by the Army since 1864. It was one of several river fortifications that claimed the name "fort" both as a furtraders' stronghold and as a military bastion. The original buildings were erected in 1845 by F. A. Chardon for the American Fur Company, and named in honor of Bartholomew Berthold, a prominent trader. Located on the north side of the Missouri River, it presented the typical picture of a quadrilateral stockade, and it served until 1862 when the Company moved its occupants to nearby Fort Atkinson, which it had purchased from the opposition, and renamed that post Berthold. At the time of Sacket's visit the place was still used by the Army, but, within a year, the troops would be removed to newly built Fort Stevenson, located not far downriver.[21]

Colonel Sacket arrived at Fort Berthold on June 3 aboard the *Sunset,* along with the famed fur trader Charles Larpenteur who was bound for his place of business at Fort Union. He took one look at the place, situated on a high bluff on the river's north bank, and concluded that it was no place for a military post. As usual, there was no hay supply, wood had to be hauled two miles, and the site was not near enough to the waterfront. Worse yet, there were too many begging Indians nearby. It was situated among the Ree, Mandan and Gros Ventre villages where, as Sully had explained to Sacket, a company of troops had been left to protect those helpless natives. The Colonel thought this a very poor reason, for the villagers merely used the soldiers as a shield to protect them after they conducted horse-stealing raids against the more powerful Sioux bands, and such protection made them very brave indeed. "I hardly believe in using troops to protect Indians from Indians," he remarked, "as we have as much as we can do to protect white men from the Indians." He thought it best to send the Berthold soldiers on up to Fort Union and let the Indians around the former post "use each other up."

There was not much to inspect at Fort Berthold. A single company of the Fourth U.S. Volunteers was stationed there—only sixty-nine men in all—and none of them had engaged in either target practice or drill for more than a year. As Volunteers went, they were fairly neat, and the company books were in good order, but their quarters left much to be desired. The dwellings were the usual low, dark, badly ventilated rooms; there was no mess hall, the men having to carry food from the tiny kitchen to their quarters and eat as best they could. The officers' quarters, the dispensary and the storerooms all presented a similar picture of overcrowded housing. Dr. Washington Matthews had three men down with scurvy, none of whom Sacket thought ill enough to be in bed. As usual, he was surprised that men living under such conditions could stay as healthy as they did.

Sarah Canfield, the army wife who preceded Sacket by only a few days, presented a somewhat more attractive picture, writing that "our two rooms are very neat and cosy." One of them was used as a sitting room, an army cot covered with a buffalo robe serving as a sofa, with three chairs, a shelf of books and a writing desk completing its furnishings. The other room, a bedroom, was described as being neatly but plainly furnished; both rooms were carpeted.[22] If she expressed such views to the Colonel, it did not alter his soldierly judgment; the place was not owned by the Government and no loss would be incurred by abandonment. He did not like one-company posts, and if the Army wanted to strengthen its hold on that part of the country, another more commodious post would be needed. In those years there was plenty of room in Dakota to find a better place to build.[23]

Since the days of Lewis and Clark, the Mandans had welcomed white visitors and, in later years, when the Rees and Gros Ventres joined them for protection, the latter tribes also were more sociable. To many an eastern visitor, the Mandans, in particular, represented the Indians of which they had read in Longfellow or Cooper, perhaps because they hunted, fished, farmed and lived a more diversified life than the fierce horse Indians farther to the northwest. Daniel Weston expressed this sentiment as he described the approach of the *Lillie Martin* to Fort Berthold in the early days of June 1866. His boat stopped for wood a few miles below that place, "and while there a Mandan Indian came on board full of gesticulations and sign talking." As he boarded what the Indians sometimes called "the fire that walks on water," the native displayed a great curiosity about the vessel, as did his fellow tribesmen who galloped along the river bank and watched its progress up the muddy stream. When a clump of trees forced them away from the shore, "they dashed off with streaming hair on their wild ponies, a fine picture of barbaric picturesqueness." Weston was thrilled to see the Mandan village "where Catlin abode so long and whose story so charmed me in my boyhood as I read his volumes. It seemed a dream that I was passing and viewing . . . the place that seemed a wild romance to me when reading Catlin, little thinking that the time would ever come when I too should look upon the romantic home of the Mandans."[24]

Mrs. Canfield, who saw the villagers at close range, was less affected by the romantic aura, but she was no less fascinated. As she watched one family prepare its meal in a large kettle suspended over the fire, she guessed that soon it would be set upon the dirt floor "when the family will gather around and snatch such pieces as they want or can get." She noted that her hostess wore a much-soiled calico gown, and her children pranced around in "less than even the traditional fig leaf," but generally kept well in the background for reasons, she thought, of either propriety or timidity.[25]

Sacket also mentioned the Indian villages and commented upon their agricultural effort, saying that in normal years they raised large quantities of corn along the river bottom. While he conceded that the land would produce gardens for soldiers, he did not believe there was enough of it to induce farmers to come and settle. Nor did he hold out much hope of any of Dakota being so utilized by his countrymen, remarking sourly that he would like to give every foot of the Territory to the Indians and pay them to live on it.[26]

As Sacket moved on toward Fort Union, the country grew even wilder and more forbidding. He viewed it from the standpoint of an Army officer, always considering the feasibility of locations for forts and worrying about the problems of transport and supply. Daniel Weston, on the other hand, did not have to concern himself about such things, and his impressions were those of the many travelers who had passed that way for years. He marveled at the country's emptiness, the great distance from civilization and the loneliness. It was impressive that there were "no human beings for thousands of miles but wandering and scattered savages or a few soldiers at widely separate and solitary government posts." Here was a land where there were only wild animals ranging "almost trackless leagues on leagues" of desolate stretches, "yet it seems but yesterday since I left the old civilization of New England, and sat in the pew of a rich Boston church. How strange it seems, too, that the great civilizer steam is carrying us through this vast wilderness. Here we sit on easy chairs or walk with slippered feet on rich carpets thousands of miles from any civilization and glide our easy way through thousands of miles of unsettled wilderness." [27] Sacket viewed all this, too, and wondered where it would be best to locate a strong military post deep in this hostile land of the Sioux.

Fort Union was not regarded as a good place for a military establishment. At the moment it was only a storage point for the stores Captain William Greer had left there at the close of the preceding season. Among the items owned by the Government were kegs of nails, horseshoes, a sawmill, a mowing machine, two six-pound iron guns and a twelve-pound brass howitzer. Sacket recommended that these be moved downriver a few miles to a point near the old site of Fort William, where there was wood, water, building stone and a good steamboat landing. Here, he said, should be located a new post capable of housing from four to six companies, for this was a great crossing point to the Yellowstone country used by all the tribes living north and east, and it would offer a commanding position.

As he examined the country around Fort Union on June 11, he admitted that he did not know what choice had been made for the location of the new post. That information was not long in being divulged, for, two days later, Captain William G. Rankin of the Thirteenth Infantry began to build a fort named after Major John Buford, an assistant Inspector General who had died in December 1863. When completed, the 360-foot square structure enclosed living quarters, a mess room, a warehouse, a bathhouse and stables. A pair of blockhouses, armed with twelve-pounders capable of raking the area, reared two stories high above the palisaded walls.[28] Charles Larpenteur, who paid a visit on June 15, noted that the soldiers already "were very hard at work hauling their stuff and also plowing to plant potatoes &c &c. Too late." [29]

In his report on river forts, Inspector General Sacket emphasized two principal points: First, that the general condition of each of them was so poor that it should be classed as uninhabitable; second, that every one of the existing posts should be moved to a more suitable location, to be supplemented at a later time with new units to fill the intervening gaps. If the War Department decided to act upon these recommendations, a considerable amount of money would have to be allocated for the strengthening of the Missouri River frontier. Such construction would not be of brick, but neither would it be of soft cottonwood logs as before. Frame buildings came to typify the new forts, and although much of the labor was performed by troops, the reconstruction program was far from cheap. Some of these structures lasted for three decades, until they weathered away or were torn down; almost nothing was preserved for posterity. But they served the purpose of guarding an established military frontier until they were no longer needed.

In 1866 the line of posts was regarded as necessary and useful. During the latter part of that summer, an even larger number of miners floated downstream in mackinaw boats, and a good many others headed for home aboard steamers. In August the *Omaha Republican* reported the arrival of the *Gallatin* from Fort Benton, bearing an amount of gold estimated in value at between $600,000 and $1,000,000. Even such guesses on the part of editors made exciting news, and postwar America tingled at the prospect of finding hidden riches in the new California. The year 1867 promised to be even more fruitful and the War Department, anticipating a growing traffic along the Missouri River, prepared to strengthen the defenses of that popular route westward.

The Sioux nation, disappointed in its dealing with Indian Commissioners and far from cowed by Sully's campaigns, resolved to meet the challenge posed by the hated forts along the river. For the next few years places such as Fort Buford would be under repeated attack, as the whole river road became a contested land.

THIRTEEN

The Fight for the River

In his report of 1872, Commissioner of Indian Affairs Francis A. Walker put into words what the Indians had tried to dramatize by action in the early post-Civil War years. "Had the settlements of the United States not been extended beyond the frontier of 1867, all the Indians of the continent would to the end of time have found upon the Plains an inexhaustible supply of food and clothing." Even the great loss of land which the Indians had suffered in the intervening five years, he thought, had not extinguished their "hope of life," but it seemed certain that another such period of white advance would "see the Indians of Dakota and Montana as poor as the Indians of Nevada and Southern California; that is, reduced to an habitual condition of suffering from want of food." [1]

As the Sioux bands watched the river traffic grow after 1865 and learned of the many demands for roads through their country, their apprehensions turned to alarm. Sherman's talk of defending specific routes, particularly the Cheyenne River road, was supplemented in early 1867 by General Alfred H. Terry, commanding the Department of Dakota, when he promised that he would recommend the construction of a line of army posts from Minnesota to the Sun River country in Montana.[2] Captain C. W. Howell, who examined the Missouri River for the army engineers, admitted that railroads would, someday, solve the western transportation problem, but until that time the river would continue to serve as a major avenue to Montana. In 1867 he guessed that five-sixths of the Territory's products reached the East by way of the river, and at least 10,000 persons used it during the travel season, paying an average of $150 for passage. As a means of transportation it was expensive, slow and often uncertain. The *Miner*, on which the Captain made his trip, burned twenty-four cords of wood daily—thirty cords of it were dry cottonwood—paying $8 a cord above Fort Randall. The stern-wheelers were hard to handle in high winds, unless heavily loaded, and were much less maneuverable than side-wheelers, but the nature of the Missouri dictated the use of the former type. The sailing season was quite short and varied from year to year, depending upon the amount of the spring runoff. Despite all these disadvantages, the water route was still regarded as the surest and safest way for the average traveler to approach Montana.[3]

The merchants of southern Dakota and northern Iowa were interested in additional means of communication with the country to the northwest, and were happy in their belief that the Government had committed itself to the Big Cheyenne wagon road. However, in the spring of 1867 the Dakota press began to display nervousness over the Army's apparently waning interest in defending such a route. In a report of July 1, General Sherman talked of corralling the Sioux into a vast area north of Nebraska, west of the Missouri and east of parallel 104 (crossing the mouth of the Yellowstone River).[4] A glance at the map told Dakota people that the Black Hills would be within this great reservation, and a howl of complaint echoed in the columns of local newspapers. When a Yankton paper heard that the Peace Commission favored such a recommendation, its editor professed disbelief, asserting that if this should be true the people of Dakota would have to take "prompt and forcible action." He told his readers that no greater calamity could befall Dakota than to have this valuable portion of the Territory closed to exploration and settlement.[5]

The action of which the editor spoke envisaged an expedition of civilians into the Black Hills, in defiance of the Army if necessary. In February 1867, B. M. Smith placed an advertisement in Yankton's *Union and Dakotaian* calling for one hundred men to form such a group, and during that month there were several public meetings held at Yankton to discuss the proposal. J. B. Irvine, a friend of Smith's, discounted the importance of the Army, calling the military men "altogether too slow for the age, they are too much circumscribed by theory and red tape, for the dash necessary for an enterprise of this kind." He enunciated a view widely held in the West when he commented: "If once you get a foothold in the country, the military are bound to come to the rescue and support you." It was the kind of statement that infuriated Sherman because he knew it generally proved to be true. Writing to General Terry in May, Sherman opposed such an expedition on that very ground, saying "no sooner would a settlement be inaugurated than an appeal would come for protection." He therefore instructed Terry to warn civilians against participating in the proposed venture, assuring them that if they did no Army protection would be forthcoming. Terry at once relayed the information to Governor A. J. Faulk of Dakota.[6]

The Yankton editor reflected community disappointment in the Army's attitude by making a number of disparaging remarks about that arm of the service. The paper wondered, editorially, why the Government did not store its property "down East," since it appeared to be interested only in protecting its own possessions in Dakota. The infantry used was sharply criticized for its inability to catch any Indians and for being able to do no more than defend itself against attack. The infantryman, said the paper, "can only plank himself squarely on a box of hardbread and defend it while his ammunition lasts—his comrade can do the same thing. They can only be expected to hold their own and 'save their bacon.'" Bitterly, the editor talked about "sectional prejudice and personal interest" delaying Dakota's development, especially the Black Hills region, and he promised that some day this worthy end would be reached without interference from outside forces.[7] Sherman ignored the complaints and proceeded with his plans for defending Dakota.

Reinforce the river posts, Sherman told Terry. Strengthen them against attack and give them enough mobility to move against any Sioux bands that try to turn back the river steamers. "Our troops must get amongst them, and must kill enough of them to inspire fear, and then must conduct the remainder to places where Indian Agents can and will reside amongst them, and be held responsible for their conduct." [8] As the Dakota troops prepared for a test of strength, rumors floated downriver that passage to Montana was like running a gantlet. The *Miner* was said to have been attacked during May some five hundred miles out of Sioux City, and all but two of its occupants massacred. "I never saw a hostile Indian upon the trip," wrote a traveler who arrived safely at Fort Benton aboard the vessel, "and not even a friendly one, only at the trading posts and forts." The Yankton paper, although hostile toward the Army, likewise denied such rumors, saying that the river was safe, and it was the Platte (and rival) route that was overrun by savage Indians. It confessed, however, that "we have been advised to publish nothing about Indian reports—that all agitation of the matter would result in harm." [9] The truth was that there were attacks, and more would come, but none so spectacular as rumor had it.

Such resolve was not widespread among journalists and, during the winter of 1866–1867, the wildest stories circulated about conditions along the military frontier. Fort Buford, the newest of the river forts, was the subject of the most persistent of these tales. According to published accounts, the fort was overrun by savages who then burned Colonel William G. Rankin at the stake, after which they mistreated his wife in a most uncivilized manner. The dead soldiers were said to have been scalped, while officers were cut up into manageable portions and eaten. There were a number of published variations, each differing somewhat in detail.[10]

Fort Buford was built during the summer of 1866, a single company of the Thirteenth Infantry working against time to get it in a habitable and defensible condition before winter came. That there were some disagreements between managment and labor is seen in the Post Return for July, which revealed that five men had deserted. By November, however, the records show that one of the two-story blockhouses was finished, the sawmill had been roofed over, and the fort was almost able to fend off attacks.[11] On November 29 Crow's Breast, a friendly Gros Ventre, told Rankin that eleven camps of Sioux, made up principally of Hunkpapas, Sans Arcs, Blackfeet and Two Kettles, along with some Cheyennes, had gathered along the Little Missouri where they were laying plans for a general war against the whites. "I made preparation for their reception without delay," the officer commented in his official records. On December 20 and 21 there were attacks upon working parties, but the only loss was the removal of some tools from the sawmill.

On the morning of December 23 the Indians captured the sawmill and icehouse, only to be driven off by blasts from the two twelve-pounders. The attackers were back the following day, and, once again, cannon fire drove them into the woods.[12] As one of the defenders later wrote to his brother, "I spent the holidays in shooting at the hostile Indians, who, at that time were about us here every day." He admitted that it "was pretty scary times for a while," but that cannon fire had prevented any serious threat to the fort itself. However, the harassment continued, the Indians never losing an opportunity to cut off small parties of soldiers who were haying, cutting wood or fetching water. To avoid being trapped in this manner, the men stored all the wood they could gather, and set about digging a well within the stockade. A party of miners, who were obliged to winter there, went to work on the well, and at twenty feet they struck gold-bearing sand that yielded ten cents for every quart of dirt extracted. Such "incentive pay" so excited the miners that they decided to form themselves into a company with the coming of spring, to prospect the countryside in general." [13]

On New Year's day a war party of Hunkpapas appeared before the fort and, "after a variety of evolutions doubtless meant to terrify," to use Rankin's words, they were dispersed by a single shot from one of the twelve-pounders. The raiders then retreated to Fort Union, where Larpenteur's men heard their great threats concerning their plans for Buford's occupants. Instead of attacking the troops again the Indians ranged the countryside looking for isolated travelers. In February they caught two of the resident miners who were making their way back from a visit to Fort

Union, and wounded one of them fatally. During the same month they raided the trading post at Fort Union, without success.[14]

It was during this time that rumors began to appear in the press that Fort Buford had been wiped out. Since that place had no official communication with the outside world between mid-January and the end of March, there was no way for the defenders to even know of the existence of such stories. The Yankton paper repeatedly denied all such rumors, maintaining that they were circulated merely to injure Dakota when, in truth, there was no more danger to the settled counties of the Territory "than there is in the Atlantic states." [15] However, since the paper had no more information than anyone else, such denials were set aside as an effort to brush the truth under the rug. In his official reports of March and April, Rankin stated that there had not been any attacks since early January.

When the river opened in the spring, Buford's garrison was increased by four infantry companies of about one hundred men each, giving the post a total strength of approximately five hundred. Breech-loading rifles replaced the old muzzle-loading muskets, further strengthening the command against attack. Early in August the Sioux displayed their contempt for these reinforcements by swooping down on the Colonel's family cow and filling it with arrows; about a dozen of them then sat on their horses about one thousand yards from the fort "where they performed a pantomime of gestures expressing contempt and defiance" before riding off into the nearby hills. Twenty mounted troopers immediately gave pursuit, "with wholly negative results," as the Post Surgeon explained the affair. From over at Fort Union, Larpenteur could hear the cannonading occasioned by the attack, and he gave his usual laconic report: "Nobody killed that we can learn except two cows killed and two wounded." [16] Captain Howell mentioned the raid in his report, and complained of the ease with which the Indians escaped, knowing that the infantrymen could not catch them and would not try for fear of being cut off and annihilated. He strongly recommended cavalry if the posts were to be at all effective.[17] Meantime, the war of nerves went on as the Sioux constantly sent messages to Rankin, forecasting an early attack that would wipe out the entire command.[18]

Buford's occupants spent the summer close to the protective walls of the fort. When Indian Agent Mahlon Wilkinson at Fort Berthold asked for protection against the Sioux Rankin refused, saying he feared for the safety of his own post.[19] He was practically surrounded by hostiles who longed for an opportunity to overrun Buford. The Indians, unable to cope with the fort's "big thunder," kept their distance, but they watched the cattle herd with daily interest, hoping that it would stray in search of better grass. Rankin saw the hayfields wither under the hot August sun, and he worried about the coming winter. In August he appealed to the Postmaster General for mail service, pointing out that the overland route from St. Paul to Fort Benton was of little use to him since he had no authority to open any of the bags that passed his way to see if there was any mail for Fort Buford.[20] He remembered the long period of isolation during the preceding year. Dr. James Kimball described the daily monotony as one of writing reports, of studying and, occasionally, of getting out for a brief hunt if no Indians were in evidence. The countryside, rich in game, provided mainly a meat diet: antelope chops, roast buffalo, elk steak, grouse, catfish. These were supplemented by bread, milk and an occasional pie. In the evening the Doctor studied the Sioux language and, by diligent application, learned about six hundred words, enough to make himself understood by members of several of the bands.[21]

As the men of Fort Buford prepared for their second winter, every effort was made to make the place as strong and as comfortable as possible. Fort Union, having been sold to the Government, was torn down, and its usable parts taken to the new Army post. Larpenteur noted, in August, that the kitchen had been demolished and its wood was used for fuel in the steamboat *Miner*. Social life at Fort Union, however, remained unchanged in the face of such plunging progress. "Weather very warm," said the trader. "Indians and old squaws about the establishment all drunk." [22] Dr. Kimball described Buford as a typical river fort, surrounded by a palisade that protected adobe structures which housed men, officers and such usual facilities as the bakery, hospital, blacksmith's shop, storerooms, magazine and stables.[23]

Occasionally when a steamer stopped to unload stores, Rankin would prevail upon the Captain to use his vessel as a kind of floating fort in which the men could go out to search for wood. The *Deer Lodge* performed such a service in August 1867.[24] Efforts at construction and wood-gathering were hampered about this time when the Colonel was ordered to send one hundred men to the river country's newest post, Fort Stevenson. Rankin complained that the request had kept his work almost at a standstill, and he strongly urged the return of the detail. Apparently he was asked to supply the necessary transportation, for he wrote a rather strong letter to Stevenson's recently arrived commanding officer, Colonel Phillipe Régis de Trobriand, saying that the ten teams sent to him were in no condition to travel, being in a "most wretched and worn out condition." Colonel de Trobriand, who was also commanding officer of the Middle District, Department of Dakota, promptly returned the letter and warned Rankin that any future communications would have to be couched in more respectful language for he was not accustomed to being addressed in such a manner.[25]

The close confinement of men and officers at Buford began to show its results as they faced another long winter. In October Lieutenant Thomas Little and Rankin, both drunk, got into a violent argument, with Little accusing his commanding officer of selling military supplies to passing mackinaw boats for his own personal profit. The quarrel reached its peak when Little struck Rankin and knocked him down, shortly after which each preferred charges against the other and requested a court-martial. Grimly, De Trobriand commented that whiskey, the curse of the service at these remote posts, would this time make a contribution by ridding the Army of two unworthy officers, unless somehow justice was thwarted.[26] Both officers were placed under arrest, and Captain Francis Clarke was put in command of Fort Buford. Before the affair was over, Rankin had accumulated six charges and twenty-two specifications against himself, but, to De Trobriand's dismay, he not only escaped trial but was assigned to the recruiting service "which is considered as a favor." Little, also released from arrest, continued to serve at Buford.[27]

The winter of 1867–1868 at Fort Buford was uneventful, except for internal turmoil. In November a wood wagon was attacked and one man was killed, but the driver and the remainder of the escort made it back to the fort, giving up four mules to the raiders. During the next month the mail carrier was robbed, but allowed to proceed, unharmed.[28] Other than this there were no difficulties and no further Indian threats against the fort itself. That the men moved about the neighborhood more freely was suggested by Charles Larpenteur, when he commented: "Times very brisk with the Soldiers & Indians. Soldiers received their extra duty pay amounting to near four thousand dollars of which we took in three hundred and eighty five." [29] In the custom of the country, the troops took to native dress, using buffalo hides for overshoes, gloves, coats and leggings, with beaver hats completing their attire.[30] Colonel Rankin sought to care for their intellectual needs by recommending a post library, holding that a set of carefully selected standard works would "be useful in raising the moral standard of the troops." [31] This recommendation was made at a time when he was about to lose his command for quarrelsome drunkenness and at a place where some of the officers were drunk almost continuously. By spring one of the soldiers, confined to the guardhouse for a lengthy period of time, cut his own throat to avoid further punishment and was buried with full military honors.

Despite their threats of destruction to the river forts, the Indians caused very little concern to the occupants of any forts during 1867. Southern Dakota was beginning to feel the impact of settlement, and there were only occasional complaints about Indians in the Fort Randall area. In July the commanding officer reported that he had only sixty-three men available for duty and, at the rate of desertion, he wondered if his establishment would long be capable of any defense. The Brulés made occasional raids upon Randall's livestock herds and, on one occasion, made off with a few horses and mules, some of which belonged to the Yankton Indians, leaving one herdsman with a shoulder arrow wound.

As a matter of routine, mounted troopers gave chase, with the usual negative results.[32] Neither side seemed very excited about the operation. A little higher on the river, the dismemberment of old Fort Sully went on, its buildings being used for firewood. The new fort, whose buildings were described as substantial, roomy and comfortable, was nearing completion.[33] At Fort Rice Lieutenant Colonel Elwell Otis kept his companies of the newly organized Twenty-second Infantry busy rebuilding and strengthening that place. Still farther upriver, near the mouth of Douglass Creek, several companies of the Thirty-first Infantry were encamped on the east bank of the river, hard at work on a new post that would be named after General Thomas G. Stevenson, who had lost his life at the battle of Spottsylvania in 1864.

Fort Stevenson was a link in a chain of forts along the river and in a chain that ran from the Red River of the North to the mouth of the Yellowstone. Located among the friendly Mandans, Gros Ventres and Rees, it was more a post than a fortified position and, for the most part, duty there was one of monotony rather than excitement generated by attack, as in the case of such a place as Buford. In his *Sketches of the Frontier and Indian Life,* Joseph Henry Taylor commented that the post's graveyard contained but a single headboard marked "Killed by Indians." [34] When the *Miner* stopped there in July 1867, Captain C. W. Howell noted that the quarters were being constructed of adobe, with shingled roofs, and that they presented a neat and comfortable appearance.[35] There were scattered attacks upon the workers that summer and fall, but they were so inconsequential that no casualties were inflicted. Dysentery and scurvy combined into a far more formidable enemy, with fifty-five men suffering the former ailment and, by the spring of 1868, sixty-one having been afflicted by the latter.[36] Despite illness and a loss of work days, the place was ready for occupancy in the autumn of 1867. It was designated as headquarters for the Department's Middle District, which also included Fort Buford as well as new Fort Totten, located 131 miles to the northeast at Devil's Lake.

Typical of Indian warfare, points found to be well defended normally were not attacked in force and, even when attacked, the efforts were not very determined. The Sioux, who had expressed great displeasure at a growing use of the river route, did not mount any kind of a concerted campaign against its defenders. Instead, they raided and picked away at isolated parties, whether they were herdsmen, mail carriers or transients moving from fort to fort. Such victims usually were left in an almost unrecognizable condition. For example, in May 1867 two men caught within ten miles of Fort Buford were killed and their bodies pinned to the ground with twenty-seven arrows, "scalped and horribly mutilated."[37]

Mackinaw boats, floating downriver, were attacked repeatedly, and even the more heavily armed steamboats were regular targets. As Captain Howell passed the mouth of the Big Cheyenne aboard the *Miner,* he remarked that this was a favorite place for attacking the boats. To avoid a barrage of fire descending from the high bluffs, the crewmen placed boiler iron, six feet high, on either side of the pilot house and built a temporary log breastworks along the boiler deck, fortified by a small field piece. At night, when boats had to be moored along the river bank, guards constantly patrolled the decks to prevent a surprise attack. These precautions, said Howell, were commonly taken north of Fort Randall.[38] Mrs. Wilbur Fisk Sanders, en route to Montana aboard the *Abeona* that spring, noted "alarm of Indians" as they steamed above new Fort Sully.[39] As a rule the attackers succeeded only in killing an occasional passenger with random shots, and did little other damage. More of an annoyance was their harassment of the woodchoppers and the resultant uncertainty of a fuel supply for vessels moving upriver. If the choppers were lucky, they managed to fort up in their cabins, but this did not protect their accumulations of wood from being burned before the attackers moved away. Some of the more resourceful Indians engaged in woodcutting themselves or tried to sell captured supplies to the passing steamers.

The low esteem in which the Indians held the river forts was summarized by Special Agent C. T. Campbell of the Indian Bureau in the spring of 1867. Commenting that the natives were determined to prevent what he termed the march of civilization beyond the river, Campbell described the Sioux as confident and proud, ever aware that their condition was better than that of the Indians who had yielded to the white man's blandishments, and in this mood they would not remain inactive in the vicinity of river settlements. He reiterated the commonly held view that there was nothing to prevent marauding all the way from Yankton's very outskirts to the farthest fort up the Missouri. As they moved along that route, the war parties bypassed infantry-held forts with perfect ease and paraded freshly taken scalps and plunder under the very eyes of the defenders, singing their war songs and chanting derision at the braves in blue who hid, like women, behind the protective shelter of brass cannons. The Agent assured his superiors that any Indians roaming the country between the Missouri and Platte Rivers could be attacked without fear of killing anyone who was either friendly or innocent, for there were no such red residents in the area. To him, this was strictly enemy territory and the present condition was that of war.[40]

Despite all threats by Indians, and in the face of periodic attacks upon steamboats ascending the river, forty-three vessels left St. Louis for upper river points in 1867. One vessel made two round trips. This fleet carried approximately 8,000 tons of freight, a quarter of which went to Government posts. On their return they brought back passengers, gold, hides and small peltries. Other boats started from Sioux City, now becoming an important commercial center because of its rail connection with Chicago.

By starting at Sioux City, steamers could make two trips without difficulty, for it required five or six weeks less than required for a round trip from St. Louis.[41]

During the summer of 1867 the War Department investigated the Missouri River situation, trying to ascertain the strength of the Sioux, the degree of their hostility and the seriousness of their threats against river travel. In June Generals Alfred Sully and E. S. Parker (later to be Commissioner of Indian Affairs) went up the river, taking with them the famed Father De Smet, to talk with various bands of the discontented. At Fort Sully there were about 220 lodges of different Sioux bands who willingly made known their present unhappiness. Theirs was a feeling of insubordination, said Sully, and a strong feeling against cultivating the soil. Flatly, they demanded the removal of troops from the country and an abandonment of travel routes used by the whites.[42] At Fort Rice the Generals found another large camp of Indians, "some thousand of them, very wild looking cusses,"[43] as one visitor described them, and the sentiments expressed at this council echoed those heard earlier. The group reached Fort Union early in July, where Sully had asked to have some Assiniboins brought in for a talk. Two half-breeds were dispatched on the errand but, as Larpenteur recorded, they were gloriously drunk before they were three miles away from the place. One of them staggered in that evening with a tale of attack and pursuit by the Sioux, but as the experienced trader explained it, the only enemy in the vicinity was whiskey. The following day the missing half-breed was found under a cart, still drunk; after he was restored to normal the mission proceeded. By July 7 enough natives had been rounded up to hold what Larpenteur called a "grand council," but "it amounted to very little and is not worth mentioning." The Indians who turned up for the conference were displeased that the efforts of the preceding year had, thus far, yielded no tangible results, such as supplies and presents. All Sully had to offer was talk and more questions, no hardware.[44]

Later in the summer, toward the end of August, General William T. Sherman himself went up the Missouri aboard the *St. Johns,* to find out all he could about the Indian problem in the area. He stopped at Forts Randall and Sully to listen to tribal complaints. Rather formally dressed in white gloves and a long military cape, he gravely listened at Fort Sully as members of the Two Kettles band, and others, told of their woes. His answer to charges that no food was forthcoming was that the Army fed its own soldiers and that the Indian Bureau was responsible for the natives. With reference to the Cherokees, he mentioned that some Indians owned their own farms and homes; he wondered why these people did not do the same. Long Mandan, with whom he was talking, said that if supplies and instructions were forthcoming, it might be worth a try. When asked about river travel, this particular Indian said he had no personal objection, but others did not agree with him. He even agreed to chop wood for the steamers.[45]

The Missouri River frontier of 1867, to which Commissioner Francis Walker later referred, showed little inclination to remain fixed. Steamboat traffic increased in the face of Indian threats, and Federal officials continued to investigate the possibilities of reservations somewhere beyond the Missouri, where the country was regarded as suitable for agriculture. As these developments took place, the postwar wave of immigration lapped at the edges of the river country, particularly from its southern reaches, and gave every indication that Manifest Destiny had lost none of its vigor. By the spring of 1868 a new rush of homesteaders was under way.

Community leaders in southern Dakota watched the influx of settlers with pleasure and congratulated each other upon the march of progress. "The tide of Northwestern emigration has set in this direction," said the Yankton paper, "and our fair and fertile plains are being flooded by the hardy and industrious sons of the old settled States." Hundreds of families were said to be crossing the Big Sioux River every week, searching for claim-sites upon which to build homes. In July the local press reported that 30,000 acres had been taken up by homesteading and by preemption at the Vermillion land office during the preceding month. It confidently predicted that the momentum would continue to propel "the very best class of population" into the young Territory.[46]

The Sioux living to the north and west watched the movement with increasing uneasiness and continued their defiance. They would never realize their desire to wipe out the hated posts, and the clumsy-looking stern-wheelers continued to make their tortured passages to Montana. But, for the next few years, the tribesmen made life along the northern portions of the river dangerous for small, unprotected parties. The line of posts that stood guard could do little more than defend itself and form a military frontier that, one day, would provide a launching platform for the final thrust against the proud horsemen of the North.

FOURTEEN

The Terrors of the Left Bank

By the summer of 1868 Dakota presented a picture in contrasts. Into its southern portion pushed farmers and their families, eagerly searching out homesteads in a section of the country known for its rich soil, while to the north, particularly in the vicinity of Fort Buford, the state of siege continued.

During that spring the troops at this northerly post continued their efforts to make it more comfortable, gathering adobe bricks from the Durfee and Peck store, then being demolished at Fort Union, and making additional quantities for enlarging the facilities.[1] Rarely did they venture very far from the fort, except in well-armed parties, for the Sioux kept a sharp eye open for stray travelers. In order to maintain any kind of communication with other posts, it was necessary to hire a civilian to carry dispatches to Fort Stevenson, and so dangerous was the journey that he demanded $100 a round trip.[2] The isolation was such that the troops stationed there had received no pay for a year. When the *Benton* turned up early in June, carrying a paymaster, Larpenteur said his appearance "made a glad set of soldiers" and that, shortly, "greenbacks were flying around like as though they were trash." He remarked that the soldiers came to his store "like men" and paid off their debts, which elicited the comment: "The day was delightful." [3]

On occasion, details of mounted soldiers were sent out to investigate reports of killings, to assist steamers in distress, or for other duties. Toward the middle of May Lieutenant Cornelius Cusick and sixteen men ventured forth to verify a rumor that a Northwest Fur Company wagon had been attacked. Less than ten miles away they found the bodies of two teamsters, stripped, scalped, riddled with arrows and mutilated; there were no Indians in sight.[4] During the next month Colonel A. W. Bowman, now in command, received a request from the master of a steamer, stranded on a bar, asking for a detail to protect his crewmen while they lightened the load and freed the vessel.[5] On another occasion the *Unilda* requested and received a detail to accompany the boat beyond Fort Buford because the crew was in a state of near-mutiny.[6] In late July Lieutenant Cusick took a party of fifty soldiers to Fort Stevenson to escort back a herd of 210 beef cattle intended to supply Fort Buford. The Indians did not pass up the opportunity to try for some of the "pinto buffalo," but they were driven off empty-handed.[7] Although Cusick brought in the beef supply intact, word of its arrival spread throughout the neighborhood, and the Sioux resolved to make a more serious effort at appropriating part of the fresh supplies. Within a week the opportunity presented itself.

On August 20 Buford's entire herd, 250 cattle, was grazing about a mile and a half from the fort, in the custody of twenty-five mounted soldiers. It was hot work; the thermometer at the post stood at 103° in the shade. "All at once," wrote the post surgeon, "from half a dozen ravines and on all sides Indians came tearing down on them, with their hideous yells, stampeding the herd and taking the men by surprise." As the swirling fight began, men within the fort were alerted by the lookout's alarm, and as fast as they could get hold of guns they started for the herd on the dead run. The doctor, who watched them go, thought they must have set some kind of a speed record for infantrymen. The Indians used their time to advantage, driving the herd as fast as possible toward the nearby breaks, or badlands, while part of their number formed a rear guard that charged the oncoming infantrymen repeatedly with dazzling feats of horsemanship.

Dr. Kimball thought it was the liveliest fight he had seen since the Civil War days. "It was exciting in the extreme," he later recalled, "to see the prairie covered with those splendid horsemen, hideously painted, whooping and yelling, riding at the top of their speed right into our fire, trying to break our line." Slowly the infantrymen forced back the attackers, described by the doctor as mainly Oglalas and Cheyennes, while the few available mounted troopers tried to catch the rustlers who were making off with the herd. Cusick, with eight horsemen, made a daring charge in which the Indians made every effort to capture him, officers being especially prized as prisoners. A flight of arrows filled the air around him and one lodged in his saddle, but he was not hit. The only wound he received resulted from a severe blow on the back from a war club, the Indian who delivered it immediately breaking off, since he had "counted coup." Dr. Kimball gave the decision to the Indians, saying they had won the day by making off with two hundred of the herd and thus leaving the fort to face the winter short of beef, milk and butter.

Official reports of the affair varied in detail. Captain C. J. Dickey reported to Colonel de Trobriand's office that the affair, which lasted three hours and covered five miles, cost Fort Buford 210 cattle and horses and left behind only 40 head of beef cattle, many of which were dying from wounds received in the raid. The Post Return for August gave a figure of 192 cattle and 4 horses. Dickey's casualty figure was three killed and one badly wounded; the Post Return showed two killed and two wounded. Larpenteur, who made note of the affair in his diary, agreed with Captain Dickey's statistics.[8]

As the sun came up the following day, Lieutenant Martin Hogan and a detachment of mounted troops left the fort in search of the missing cattle. He found carcasses scattered all along the trail and managed to round up twelve live strays, but there were no Indians to be found in the vicinity. Thomas Little, who had been under arrest since October 1867, was released long enough to lead another search party some eighteen miles up the Missouri, but he returned empty-handed. At the beginning of September Lieutenant Cusick, now well enough for duty, made another search that took him almost to the British line but he, too, came back having accomplished no more than a march of 130 miles.

There was nothing left to do but requisition more beef, which Captain Dickey did, and to write off the loss as one of the costs of warfare in the upper Missouri country. Later, the friendly Assiniboins said they had found forty-four head of stock, and the Captain asked that this figure be subtracted from future requisitions, but this was small comfort. The troops at Fort Buford had to face the fact that life beyond the palisades was dangerous at all times, and that even to maintain a sufficient food supply was a constant struggle.

The disappearance of the marauding Indians was only illusory. While the young officers led their men on repeated searches for missing cattle, and reported that the Sioux had literally vanished from the face of the earth, the fort was under constant surveillance by the Indians. On September 18, less than a month after the big raid, four enlisted men went out to hunt prairie chickens, without bothering to get permission, and were promptly attacked under the very eyes of the fort. Hunkpapa Sioux caught the party within a thousand yards of the cattle herd, and they killed Private W. H. See before the herders could be of assistance. The usual alarm was sounded and men rushed forth from the garrison, only to find that the Indians had escaped across the river. The soldiers found one of the bullboats, left behind, and in a manner reminiscent of Indian retribution, they promptly cut it to pieces. Their action only underscored the futility of the kind of warfare in which they were engaged and the frustration of chasing an enemy that could not be caught.[9]

Toward the latter part of November a Sioux who was living in a camp near the fort openly bragged that he had participated in the August raid. He was promptly thrown into the guardhouse by Lieutenant Cusick. After three days of confinement he was reported to have made an escape attempt that ended when the soldiers put three bullets into him, and, as Larpenteur dryly commented, that "was the last of Mr. Sioux." His fellow tribesmen heard of the affair and renewed their threats that Buford's days were numbered.[10] Since they had made such assertions before, but never had caused the establishment itself any harm, Buford's officers probably did not give the matter much thought.

With winter coming on and the morale of the men at a new low, the command at Buford faced internal problems that were of more immediate concern. During September an unspecified number of men from four of the companies had been placed in confinement for what appears in the records to have been a refusal to perform duty. After several weeks of punishment, Captain Dickey advanced the opinion that the men "were not aware of the enormity of the crime they committed, not knowing that mutiny may be passive as well as active." In their favor, he said that up to the sixth of September they had worked very faithfully.[11] Life at Buford during the cold months was more confining than usual, but to be locked up in the guardhouse for any period of time was almost maddening, as the suicide of one of the prisoners suggested. At the time, there were four privates from Company E, Thirty-first Infantry, who had been in confinement since July 1867 awaiting sentencing for general court-martial offenses; the terms of enlistment for three of them had expired. Captain Dickey seems to have understood the unusual circumstances of service at this lonely, isolated post. He was willing to forgive a little mutiny now and then to have his troops available for defense.

The Captain, who was second in command, also needed the services of all available officers. In mid-September Thomas Little, now a captain, was permanently released from arrest. Dickey's need for officers was all the more pressing since he found it necessary to prefer charges against the post commandant, Colonel Andrew W. Bowman, whose drunken orgies lasted as long as twelve to fifteen days at a stretch. By January Bowman, who was confined to his bed most of the time and unable to do anything but sign an occasional paper from a prone position, was put under arrest and Dickey took command. Before the month was out Bowman submitted countercharges, accusing Dickey of engaging in an ungentlemanly squabble with one of the other officers on a wine-filled January evening and of quarreling with two traders at the post a year earlier. Colonel de Trobriand viewed the dredging up of old offenses as purely vengeful in spirit and guessed that Dickey had been "pushed into a trap." Despite the

Colonel's sympathy for Dickey, the command on January 29 was handed on down to Captain Little, who had not yet been fully cleared of the charge that he had struck Rankin. But, as De Trobriand said, had Little not been freed from arrest, the command of a five-company post deep in Indian country would have fallen into the hands "of a simple lieutenant." Drunkenness, he concluded, and a tolerance for it, was the cause of such a state of affairs. "What an Augean stable!" he wrote in disgust.[12]

That the command at Buford was fighting a losing battle with the bottle is well documented, yet there was some disposition on the part of the officers to control its sale, presumably on the ground that the enlisted men were not gentlemen and therefore could not hold their liquor. In January 1869 Captain Little closed up Larpenteur's store, reporting to district headquarters at Fort Stevenson the discovery that the trader was dealing in this dangerous commodity. Larpenteur admitted that he had been shut down for a period of eight days, but he said it was because he had sold to the Indians "a few more loads of ammunition than regulations allowed." The Captain also suspended the operations of another trader, John B. Gerard, for selling liquor to the Indians and for trying to persuade soldiers to procure Government grain for which he was willing to pay. The latter crime was regarded as being so "incriminating and reprehensible" that Gerard was ordered off the reservation.[13] Colonel de Trobriand's office agreed with the disposition of Gerard's case, saying the trader had been evicted from Fort Stevenson for the same offense. Lieutenant J. W. Marshall, acting assistant adjutant general at Fort Stevenson, wrote that Gerard deserved no leniency and that his license should be suspended at once. He suggested that Little might destroy the confiscated liquor "if you think it is preferable." [14] There is no record of the fate of this contraband.

The necessity of temperance at Fort Buford, if not prohibition, was illustrated by the events of a drunken Christmas night when one of the soldiers undertook a one-man war against constituted authority. Lieutenant E. H. Townsend, commanding Company C of the Thirteenth Infantry, was in his quarters when someone began kicking violently at his door. Before the officer could open it to identify the visitor, the lower panels of the door were completely shattered. When the door was finally opened and the officer peered out, he took a fist hard in the face. "Who are you, and what does this mean?" he called out, only to be hit in the face two more times. "Finding that he was an active and powerful man and about to overcome me," he later wrote, "I exerted myself to the utmost, in order to get him out of the house, but in doing so, he tore out a handful of my hair and also tore my shirt almost entirely off me." Recovering from his surprise, Townsend knocked the intruder down twice, the second time jumping on him with both feet to keep him down, and then called the guard in to arrest him. Only when they hauled the soldier off to the hospital did Townsend learn that he was a private from Company H who was thoroughly drunk and bent upon expressing his displeasure with the management at Buford, nothing personal intended.[15]

All that the officers at Buford could do during the winter, when both Indians and blizzards kept the troops within the palisades, was try to keep each other sober, fill out the usual report forms, and serve out their time. Since they all lived in what amounted to a prairie Devil's Island, the only relief from boredom was occasional Indian attacks, and these came close to being welcomed by all as a diversion from the curse of idleness.

On January 13 a party of nine Sioux rode up to the southeast corner of the fort and fired a few shots, apparently in a spirit of revenge for the killing of the Indian who had tried to escape from his jailers. The attack faded before any serious shooting took place. A party of Assiniboins who had been trailing the Sioux drove them off, capturing one horse and wounding one of the warriors. Since no scalps were taken, the Assiniboins were as dissatisfied with the engagement as were the soldiers. They showed their frustration, in the manner of the troops who had recently cut up the bullboat, by exhuming the body of a Sioux killed in an earlier attack and ceremoniously scalping the corpse before hacking it to pieces. Larpenteur watched the victory dances that followed this triumph and passed it off with his usual dry comment: "Weather still very fine." [16] His years among the tribesmen had taught him how to live at such a place as Fort Buford; it was the Army men, relative newcomers, who could not adjust to it.

As spring came once more to the little island of troops marooned in a desert sea, there were signs of life and hope for the new season. Captain Little reported in March that there was sufficient firewood on hand to last until warm weather, and that the men were hauling saw logs in anticipation of resuming unfinished construction projects. Some of the buildings erected earlier, particularly those made of adobe, had not lasted very well and would have to be replaced. The Captain also revealed that the men had wintered well and were in surprisingly good health. As usual, there was a shortage of officers and he was obliged to draw one from what amounted to an officers' pool; that is, to release Second Lieutenant Charles H. Leonard of the Thirty-first Infantry from arrest so that he might be used for duty.[17] The new season would require more enlisted men; during March and April the time of enlistment for 106 of those present would expire and they would be sent downriver by an early steamer. Little was somewhat perplexed as to their status in the meantime, pondering the problem of subsisting them after discharge. This was only one of the many questions that faced young officers who searched their manuals in vain for prepared answers.[18] The promise of a possible solution came at 3 P.M. on March 27, for at that hour the ice began to break on the river, an anuual event that signaled the temporary end to isolation and always occasioned a celebration at the river posts.[19]

During March a transaction occurred that was to mark the passing of an era along the upper river. At that time the partnership that made up the North West Fur Company expired by limitation, and, by mutual consent, the firm was dissolved. It was agreed that business would continue for another year in order to liquidate corporate affairs and to dispose of stock on hand. With this move the Company retired from active business along the river from Fort Buford southward and also at Fort Totten, near Devil's Lake. Goods that were not sold would be moved farther up the river to take advantage of trading possibilities among the northern Indians. The agreement of dissolution, signed on March 9 at New York City, signified the decline of fur trading along the lower river and marked the advance of the frontier deeper into the American Northwest.[20] The firm of Durfee & Peck was left to carry on what trade remained on the Missouri below the mouth of the Yellowstone River.

The summer of 1869 was not particularly eventful at Fort Buford. When the grass turned green and the herds were put out to graze along the nearby slopes, the Indians resumed their usual sniping. In mid-May they staged a small raid and were at once driven off by the six-pounders. During the early weeks of the summer the command dwindled as the men who were being discharged took passage down the river and as others were transferred to duty at neighboring posts. Lieutenant Colonel Henry A. Morrow, who assumed command of the fort that spring, complained that the discharge of civilian employees left the establishment without a blacksmith, carpenter, engineer or sawyer, and there were no enlisted men who could fill their jobs. By late June he had only eighty-nine enlisted men on hand and, presuming that no replacements would be furnished, he faced the prospect of losing enough additional men by the first of the year to reduce his command to a mere twenty-six. By August his command was so small that Morrow did not have enough troops to guard the herd, and he was obliged to keep the animals within two hundred yards of the post. This, he said, was not to graze the livestock—for there was no grass—but to exercise and water them. He had to feed his cattle grain, an item that was hauled upriver at great expense. When, late in August, eighty-six recruits turned up, they had no arms and there were not enough at the post to supply them.[21]

The Indian attacks during the summer were not as serious as that of August 1868. The Indians made a small raid in mid-July, without doing any damage. On August 10 they caught four men within two miles of the fort and killed all of them before escaping across the river. The inability of the troops to save such parties was severely criticized by newspapers downriver, whose accounts demonstrated how people living in more settled areas did not understand the situation at Fort Buford. The *Sioux City Weekly Times,* for example, sharply attacked Colonel Morrow for not pursuing the Indians, said to number over two hundred, and it wondered why the Indians were not wiped out by the fort's cannon which were supposed to have a range of six miles. These accounts did not take into consideration the nature of the Indian menace in the Buford area, the diminished condition of the command, or the nature of the terrain over which the men had to work. Therefore, it was as easy as ever to inquire why the Army was not doing its job of protecting American citizens who chose to wander in dangerous parts.[22]

Morrow himself explained that he had no troops for any serious encounters beyond the post, and that the affair in question—which happened beyond the view of the post—was over before an effective chase could have been made. He admitted that the Indians had appeared daily before his post for two weeks prior to the event, literally inviting a chase, but he would not be lured into an ambush. He confessed freely that his post, intended to garrison five hundred men, was so weak that it was literally helpless, and the Indians knew it. All he could do was keep it from being invaded. Meanwhile the Santees were particularly bold, ranging north of the fort toward the Canadian line, engaging in hit-and-run attacks and fleeing for the international border when necessary. They hated Fort Buford with a passion and never lost a chance to raid its neighborhood. As Morrow put it, "they are the terror of the left [north] bank of the Missouri River." [23]

General Winfield Scott Hancock, who visited the river posts that summer, singled out Fort Buford as a post exceedingly offensive to the Sioux, and he made the oft-repeated comment that it had been under almost constant siege since its founding. From the first it had been able to do no more than defend itself, and that did not include protection of the herds that grazed under the very eyes of its guns. The history of Buford documented the ineffectiveness of a small infantry post deep in Indian country, and the only solution Hancock could suggest was to strengthen the place. Even this did not promise much, for as he said, "Larger or smaller, it has not heretofore commanded the respect of the Indians."[24] Lieutenant Colonel Samuel B. Holabird, who also made an inspection in the summer of 1869, agreed with Hancock. Buford was regarded by the Sioux as so offensive that many of them who traded peaceably at other posts never lost a chance to commit hostile acts when they passed this post. As the Colonel expressed it, they went to other posts to be fed, "but come up to Buford to collect scalps." He emphasized the fort's isolated position when he explained that it was 150 miles by land from Fort Stevenson and that the only means of communication, during a large part of the year, was overland. So dangerous was this route, he thought, that to cross it the soldiers would have to develop some extraordinary qualities. Even if they traveled in strong parties, the ravines were so snow-filled that dog teams would have to be used instead of horses, and few of the troops were trained in this method of transportation.[25] When driving a cattle herd to Buford, to sustain its food supply, the trip took as much as eleven days, or an average of less than ten miles a day. Such a slow-moving target was almost an unbearable temptation for Indians who watched the snail-like progress of fat beeves and thought of the long winter ahead.

Fort Stevenson was built, in part, to fill the great gap of land that stretched between forts Rice and Buford. Located a few miles from the point where the Missouri makes its westward turn, the new post was a link in the chain of river forts and a part of another fortified line that was being developed to protect the northern route from Minnesota to Montana. It was also intended as a supply base for Fort Totten, 130 miles to the east, and as a means of military protection for the village Indians living around the old trading post, Fort Berthold. The new post was located a few miles downriver from those Indians, sometimes referred to as the Three Tribes, because no suitable military reservation could be located in the vicinity of Fort Berthold that would not include their villages and corn fields. Additionally, the new location was at a point where the river passed the nearest to Fort Totten, yet was one that afforded timber, grass and a practical steamboat landing.[26]

Fort Stevenson presented visitors with the usual picture of a parade ground, 220 feet square, surrounded by one-story adobe buildings that served as barracks, warehouses, a hospital and the usual auxiliary structures. The walls, from twelve to fourteen inches thick, provided quarters that were well insulated and fire resistant. Brick chimneys lent an added protection from fire. Water from the Missouri River was used at the post, since other sources of supply were impregnated with alkali. The Surgeon General's office reported that it was "sweet, although very muddy, particularly in the spring time," but quite acceptable after it settled.[27] Colonel Holabird rated the officers' quarters as "good" when he stopped there in the summer of 1869. The floors were of tongue-and-groove pine, the walls well plastered and the chimneys built from the ground instead of being perched on cross-beams as they were in the troops' quarters. However, he complained that improvements were being made much too slowly and inefficiently. The adobe structures, he noted, soon would crumble away if they were not given a coat of stucco, and he recommended that the post plasterer, whose time was about to expire, be offered $130 a month to stay on and finish his job. In general, he thought it a satisfactory post, but it was quite costly to supply.[28] The latter complaint applied to most western forts.

The usual efforts to combat boredom and to elevate morale were evident in the well-stocked library (850 volumes) and the billiard room. The post surgeon, Dr. John V. Bean, who tried the cushions without much luck, said he preferred the game to croquet, "which is profanely called 'Presbyterian billiards.'" Despite the availability of such recreations, strong drink remained the favorite pastime. In one of his letters home, the doctor noted the passing of one of the officers, whom he called "another victim of alcohol," and later he lamented the arrival of a captain who brought to Stevenson a record of drunkenness on duty. Since the newcomer was to have a position of command, the young surgeon concluded that he would give up the position that paid him $134 a month (of which he cleared $100) and go home. There were no other attractions for him. As he said: "It is the money and nothing else that is keeping me here." Dr. Washington Matthews succeeded him in September 1869.[29]

In contrast to Fort Buford, the Sioux gave Fort Stevenson very little trouble. A traveler who went upriver on the *Miner* in the spring of 1868 said that the fort had gone through the winter completely undisturbed by Indian attacks.[30] The presence of the Three Tribes in the neighborhood may have been the deciding factor. The Sioux preferred to attack them, instead of the soldiers, as they had done for some time in the past. Dr. Bean wrote of one such assault, in June of 1869, wherein the Sioux were driven away from the Berthold villages with sharp losses. The doctor was quite pleased when one of the Gros Ventre warriors presented him with an enemy scalp. Such visits were frequently made by the Three Tribes, whose members appreciated the handouts given by the command at Stevenson and, as the doctor observed, "they thought immediately after their fight was a good time to present themselves." They were not disappointed. The soldiers watched this internecine warfare with interest, for as Bean further commented, this kind of conflict was using up the Plains Indians faster than their struggles with the whites.[31] A contemporary observer agreed with Dr. Bean that the village Indians were no contest for the Sioux in any serious battles, and he wondered how long the "poor starving ragamuffin horde cooped up in the Indian villages at Fort Berthold" would survive. Hunger, disease and Sioux attacks were thinning their ranks, and there seemed little that the Federal Government was able to do about saving them.[32]

When the Sioux were not persecuting them, the Three Tribes farmed and lived peaceably in their log-and-earthen huts, earning additional income by cutting wood for sale to passing steamers, or by trading with the soldiers. That the natives had services as well as goods to offer is seen in the report of Dr. Washington Matthews, post surgeon. He complained that the proximity to the villages resulted in an almost continual battle against venereal disease. The Army could not, as it never would, discover how to keep its men away from native women. Otherwise, said the doctor, the health of the command was excellent. Except for such expected difficulties as diarrhea during the warm months, there were very few serious diseases. Pulmonary complaints were almost unknown in the clear, dry climate; there had been but two cases of pneumonia since 1865, dating back to the command's occupation of Fort Berthold.[33] He certainly must have agreed with General Hancock, who described the villagers as "friendly to us," as he puzzled over methods of controlling ailments politely termed social diseases.

The days at Stevenson were routine, with little to break the monotony. So fixed in their way of life did the men become that they were part of another world, and they grew resigned to their lot in the manner of long-term convicts in a penal institution. Dr. Bean reflected this feeling as he watched the ice break up in the Missouri late in March 1869. Writing of this important annual event, he remarked that "in due time the steamboat will be making us its occasional visits. Those long absent representations of civilization will bring also a temporary change in the usual monotony, but perhaps it will only increase and awaken this partially latent discontent." [34]

While visiting steamers brought news from "the States," and perhaps bred homesickness, the release from winter's grip provided a change of scene and a new freedom for the men. In this land of exaggerations, the transformation often came rapidly, and, in a matter of days, the countryside shed its tawny coat and donned one of pale green. As Dr. Bean expressed it, "we have no spring, it is a mere leap from winter to summer, and the prairie is green and pretty, a thing that I thought never occurred to displace the infernal and almost eternal brown after the prairie burns black." [35] In these days of welcome, when the earth thawed and plant life sprang back into life, the men of Stevenson had chance to roam the countryside, to hunt or merely to exhilarate in their release from winter's servitude.

Spring in Dakota was a brief interlude, a reprieve from the bitter cold of winter before the hot, dry days of summer. By July Dr. Bean had lost his enthusiasm of May, and he complained that "this miserable destitute country ought to be left to the Indians anyway, it never will be settled, it never can be." The natives accepted the country as they found it, and utilized its resources as best they could. They voiced no complaints about the land. There were still buffalo to be had, but the supply was variable and often the hunt was disappointing. The coming of the forts to the river brought cattle herds intended to feed the troops, and they were regarded with interest by the hunters. Thus Stevenson's relative calm was broken occasionally when the Sioux tried to make off with a few head of stock. The raids were infrequent and usually took the garrison by surprise. Dr. Bean described the confusion of an August morning as the long roll sounded in the early hours. Officers and men, half-dressed, stumbled out to answer the alarm, unsure of the size or nature of the attack, befuddled by the swirl of horsemen mixed with milling cattle, and frustrated at their inability to come to grips with the enemy. This time the Indians were persistent, and the melee continued for over an hour during which time, said the doctor, firing was very brisk. It was not a very dangerous battle in which to participate, for even though a great deal of ammunition was expended, the only fatality was an Indian pony killed by shellfire. Three or four of the attackers were thought to have been wounded, while the soldiers reported no casualties. The official report claimed only one Indian horse killed and "probably 1 warrior." [36]

During the period that the Sioux picked on Fort Buford, and paid occasional visits to Fort Stevenson, the frontier of the white man gradually closed in upon the Indians. Each year peace commissioners came to Fort Rice to talk with tribal representatives—in 1865, 1866 and 1867—trying to persuade the wandering bands to settle down and "walk the white man's path." In 1868 a portion of them agreed to the Treaty of Fort Laramie, while others signed a similar document at Fort Rice, by which the Government promised to help Indian families learn a new way of life. Farm tools, draft animals, livestock and rations were offered to those who would settle down and take instruction in the art of agriculture. In August 1868 a piece of country that approximated the boundaries of present South Dakota was set aside for "the exclusive use of the Sioux nation of Indians," as the War Department phrased it. General W. S. Harney, the old hand who had known that part of the country for over a decade, was put in charge of disbursements and other administrative matters, while General Alfred H. Terry governed the affairs of the troops stationed there.[37]

The selection of Harney as the Indians' "white chief" was a good one. It was he who met with the Sioux at Fort Rice in July 1868, after having sent out Father De Smet and Charles Galpin to bring them in. The Indians offered their usual objections, saying that they would not talk until the steamboats ceased to ascend the river and all the troops had departed, but they came in anyway—and talked. At the conference they renewed their arguments. Running Antelope, a Hunkpapa, said he remembered Harney at Fort Pierre thirteen years back, and commented: "I never met a man of sense since, except Father De Smet, and I listen to him." He went on, outlining the grievances of his people and objecting at intervals to the presence of the forts. Magpie, another Hunkpapa, looked about him at Fort Rice, and suggested that the land would be better if the soldiers disassembled the establishment and hauled it away. But, in the end, objections faded in view of more promises made and of the prospect for more reliable table fare in the future. During 1868 and 1869 the Cheyenne River Agency and the Grand River Agency were established along the Missouri; by 1869 there were approximately 4,500 Sioux at the latter place.[38]

By 1869, also, the War Department had fixed its line of forts along the river and now, in addition to keeping open that highway to Montana, it had the additional task of policing the new Indian agencies. The duty at the forts never had been easy and, while physical conditions gradually improved, assignment to them was not much in demand. Colonel Holabird wrote that the troops who garrisoned the river posts had the worst stations occupied by the Army, "always excepting the Yuma Desert and Alaska." These were difficult posts to maintain, he added, because they were both remote and expensive. Discipline was always a problem in such conditions of isolation and, since the postwar Army did not always attract the best examples of American manhood to the recruiting stations, the job facing young officers at these outposts was unusually trying. Holabird underscored the situation in his report when he singled out Fort Buford, saying that the morals of the troops there never had been very good, but that this was the inevitable result of neglect and isolation.[39]

The series of little dots on the map that represented the Missouri River posts made up one of America's postwar frontiers. General Hancock pointed this out in 1869 when he said that in Minnesota and in that part of Dakota lying east of the Missouri River, there were no active Indian hostilities. West of that line, however, travelers still moved at their own risk and the country through which they passed was not yet considered safe. He thought that reservations should also be established on the east side of the river where more peaceful Indians could learn the ways of peace and contentment. "The river would then be a formidable barrier between the well and evil disposed—not always easily passed, and readily controlled." After a few years, he predicted, such Indians could be moved westward, at a time when "Indian matters will have become more settled."[40]

Time was foreclosing upon the future of the northern tribes. White settlement continued to creep into southern Dakota, and soon there would be a demand for shrinkage of the Indian reservations there. River trade increased as the railroads moved westward to meet it, thereby shortening the trip to Montana. The Union Pacific Railroad now spanned the High Plains and, although the Bozeman Trail to Montana had been abandoned, it would not be long before rails would be reaching out toward the mining country by way of Idaho. The circle was tightening around the Sioux, and they knew it. They did the only thing which they could do; fight, and retreat, and fight again.

Fort Buford, still remote and well within hostile country, continued to feel the full fury of their hatred. But time was running out here, too, for the Northern Pacific survey crews were out in the field, and soon more rails would make a new puncture in the Indian frontier. In the meantime the Army's task was to hold the line and to prevent the Indians from breaking through the barriers it had erected around them. To do this effectively, the War Department concluded that the river forts would have to be strengthened and maintained for some time to come.

FIFTEEN

The Reservation Frontier

The establishment of Indian agencies along the river after 1868 gave new significance to the Dakota military frontier. In that year Fort Randall, a post thought to have almost outlived its usefulness, was reinforced "in consequence of the establishment of a new Indian reservation in the immediate vicinity," as General Alfred H. Terry explained it.[1] Colonel Samuel Holabird, who inspected Randall during the next summer, admitted that the fort was in a run-down condition, but pointed out that it also had other disadvantages, such as being on the wrong side of the river. He had doubts about the wisdom of building it up again. True, he said, there was an Indian reservation nearby; however, its occupants were "of the friendly, subdued kind," and rather than being any threat, they actually formed a protective wall against the wilder Indians who lived to the north. This, in addition to the rapidly growing white population of southern Dakota, convinced the Colonel that it would be better to use available troops up in the Yellowstone country where the Sioux still posed a real threat.[2] Justification for strengthening so southerly a post may have had its origins at higher administrative levels, where leading officers showed concern over the future of the postwar Army and were happy to find additional assignments for the troops, especially at appropriations time. Whatever the necessities of the case, soldiers were to be associated with Indian reservations for the next several decades.

Local businessmen were somewhat inclined to agree with Holabird, although their feelings in the matter were mixed. While they welcomed the troops as a market for their goods, they did not want to admit the necessity of their presence, for that suggested a continued Indian menace and this was a deterrent to immigration. For example, R. F. Pettigrew wrote from Sioux Falls, Dakota, in the spring of 1870, arguing that the valley in which he lived was as safe as Sioux City and that any stories of Indian dangers ought not to be published, for they tended to frighten off prospective settlers.[3] There were other signs that civilization had come to southern Dakota. Not only was there daily stage service between Sioux City and Fort Randall, as well as a weekly run as far north as Fort Sully, but commercial establishments were beginning to appear in the vicinity. A little village named White Swan City had sprung up near Fort Randall, and it could boast of two white swans from Missouri who were offering their services to the troops. As a Sioux City paper expressed it, this pair of frontierswomen were braving the hardships of camp life and the insults of the Indians to make a living in the new land of opportunity.[4] The paper's reference to them as "White Squaws" suggests that settlement of the country had reached a state of refinement whereby the soldiers no longer were obliged to rely upon native talent for their after-hours recreation.

Despite the advance of the Anglo-Saxon frontier, the War Department decided that Fort Randall was a necessary and valuable post. In May 1870 it was heavily reinforced with ten companies of the Fourteenth Infantry, five of which soon were scattered along the river near the agencies to the north.[5] Into the log barracks of Randall went the new troops and, before long, there were the usual complaints by medical officers that the badly ventilated and crowded quarters were producing pneumonia and other pulmonary diseases. Efforts were made to provide recreational facilities for the men, but it was difficult to attract their attention to things of the mind. The post library contained some three hundred volumes, many of which were fiction and were read, but there was little call for heavier tomes. Inspecting officers complained that Appleton's Encyclopedia "has scarcely been referred to," and Prescott's historical works had been read by only one man. It was thought that if more western writings, such as the Journals of Lewis and Clark or the works of Henry Rowe Schoolcraft, were available, more men might be attracted to the printed word.[6] This was not beyond the realm of possibility, but competing with the lamps in the library was the red glow that lighted the way to White Swan City, and such lures inevitably proved stronger than browsing among the books.

Thus, the appearance of what might be called a "reservation frontier" saved Fort Randall at a time when the fighting frontier had passed it by, and it remained as the southern anchor of the line of posts scattered along the river. An examination of the monthly Post Return for the years 1868 and 1869 indicates that garrison duty predominated in life at the fort. Month after month, the report sheets show that there were no events worthy of special notice. There were a few exceptions when, on widely separated occasions, some of the Brulé Sioux attacked isolated woodcutters, but this often was more in the nature of eliminating the competition than any effort to do away with the white race.[7] Now and then trouble at the nearby Whetstone Agency arose out of internecine warfare brought on by bootleg alcohol. In the autumn of 1869 Chief Spotted Tail, a Brulé, killed Big Mouth, an Oglala, and ended a feud of long standing. Captain D. C. Poole, Agent in charge, laid the blame on strong drink and called for troops from Fort Randall to preserve order among his charges. After arresting one white man and two half-breeds who were accused by Poole, the troops returned to the routine they had followed for so long, grateful for even this small chance to break the monotony.[8]

Two hundred miles to the north stood new Fort Sully, about halfway between Randall and Rice. This four-company post, built between 1866 and 1868 as a replacement for the original Fort Sully (located some thirty miles downriver), performed a function similar to that of Fort Randall. Its occupants carried out their daily garrison duties without serious interruption from nearby tribes, and as the new reservations were located across the river, it served as another of the "reservation" forts. While its barracks were the source of constant complaint by inspecting officers, the officers' quarters were comfortable and well furnished. The tongue-and-groove flooring, walls of fine wainscoting and excellent furnishings moved Colonel Holabird to call the quarters "too elaborate." The troops, on the other hand, lived in cottonwood log barracks 350 by 17 feet in dimension and badly ventilated. There were no washrooms or bathrooms; bathing had to be performed out-of-doors, weather permitting. Considering Dakota winters, it is doubtful that personal sanitation received much attention. The average temperature for January 1869 at neighboring Fort Randall was 3°, with the warmest day recorded that month a mere 28°. Even the officers at Fort Sully were not treated to the luxury of bathrooms, since all water had to be hauled from the river. Two eight-mule teams made constant trips to keep enough water on hand for cooking and laundering.[9]

A visitor who stopped at Fort Sully in the spring of 1868 found it to be a comfortable post, commanded by General D. S. Stanley and garrisoned by three hundred troops. Around five hundred lodges of Brulé and Yanktonnais Sioux lived in the vicinity and, although some of them were not of the friendliest, they caused no trouble.[10] The establishment was well stocked with supplies of all kinds, so much so that Colonel Holabird thought the amount "greatly in excess for the size of the garrison," but this merely emphasized its role as a base and a storehouse. The Indians, often in a near-desperate condition by spring, occasionally were given part of such stores, although usually they received goods condemned by the Army as being unfit for human consumption. The natives who owned anything of value visited the establishment of Durfee & Peck, the local trading post, where they stocked up on various necessities and frequently on illicit whiskey.[11]

Dr. John Bean was quite impressed by Fort Sully. He called it a "very fine post," much larger and more comfortable than his own station at Fort Stevenson. "There were nine or ten ladies here," he wrote, "and as a consequence it is more pleasant, and society more refined." [12] Such refinements apparently were noticed by the enlisted men, some of whom were not completely satisfied with occasional visits to the tepees. One of them wrote a long letter to a Sioux City girl, inviting her to join him on a trial basis.

"You can come and live for a while," he explained, "and if, after a time, you do not like it, there will be no harm done, and you can go away again. If you do like it, and I am so happy as to succeed in gaining your affections, and you still desire then to lead a steady life, I will *marry* you." There is no record of the acceptance of this generous offer, but, as the local newspaper commented, it indicated "what desperate straits some of the male population of up-country forts are willing to resort to," a remark that was hardly complimentary to the sisters of Sioux City.[13]

Efforts to improve conditions at the river posts were reflected in comments made by visitors and various inspecting officers. Holabird was quite pleased when he stopped at Fort Rice in 1869, and he commented that the improvement there during the past two years was tremendous. The whole establishment presented a neat and efficient view to travelers who came in sight of it as they made their approach. A ten-foot stockade, made of two-inch planks, surrounded an area approximately 550 by 850 feet. It was dominated by bastions, two stories high, built of carefully squared and dovetailed logs that stood out some thirteen feet from the stockade, at opposite corners of the fort, and protected the walls from any enemy trying to scale them. In place of the old, decayed, rat-infested buildings now stood clean, comfortable barracks and storehouses. They were built of clapboards, with shingled roofs and ample window space, providing cheerful, well-ventilated quarters for the men and dry storage space for supplies. Even the guardhouse drew complimentary remarks, it being warmed by stoves and well lighted.

Just outside the stockade, about an eighth of a mile distant, stood a steam sawmill that had cut most of the lumber and shingles used in the reconstruction commenced in 1868. Near it, on a gentle slope, was the cemetery, containing approximately 140 graves. The land that stretched beyond was generally barren, having little water or timber, and it was described by Assistant Surgeon Washington Matthews as being so sterile that no crops were raised on it, "and it is doubtful if any can be." Drought and grasshoppers, he said, had stifled all attempts at raising a post garden and, consequently, he saw little future in any agricultural efforts in Dakota. These were Sioux lands, he noted, peopled by natives who were tall, muscular, enduring and healthy, but whose condition was already beginning to deteriorate. There were no settlements near the post and there were few Indians, for most of them had gone to the Grand River Agency.[14]

By now the days of excitement at Fort Rice had largely passed. No longer did the Sioux threaten the place, harry the herders who tried to protect the beef supply, or even give much trouble to the mail carriers who maintained a reasonably reliable service to the outside world on a weekly basis. Water was hauled from the river, as it was at the other posts, "good thick water from the Missouri," to use the words of one of the enlisted men, and two log icehouses with a capacity of about 150 tons kept drinks cool all through the summer. "A soldier's life at this post was, on the whole rather tiresome," wrote one of them, noting that the post trader, the barkeeper and their families were the only white people outside of the garrison.[15] In a year or so Fort Abraham Lincoln would be built, about thirty miles up the river, and the little frontier town of Bismarck would spring into existence, but still Fort Rice would remain fairly isolated and lonely as it continued its guard duty along the waterway to Montana.

Even the upper river country around forts Buford and Stevenson appeared to be quieting down by 1870. There were a few demonstrations at Buford, as Sioux raiders continued to threaten the place and to pick on woodchoppers or other small parties of whites, but the violence that accompanied the fort's establishment had begun to subside. In June Colonel Charles C. Gilbert arrived on the *Emilie La Barge* with three companies of the Seventh Infantry and relieved Colonel Morrow's Thirteenth Infantry companies.[16]

One of the first requests for assistance made to the new commanding officer suggested the changing nature of duties at the outpost. A trader named W. W. Ivey, who had an establishment in eastern Montana Territory, complained that he was having difficulty controlling the native population in his locality and he asked for help. "I have had some trouble here with Indians getting Drunk," he wrote. "They leave this place in the morning for the mouth of popular [Poplar] river and return at knight with a suply of whickey obtained at that place. I ask of you to assist mee stoping sutch operations near this trading post." [17] Another communication from the neighborhood of Poplar River also revealed a less warlike attitude on the part of the residents. Chief Black Eye, a Yanktonnais who claimed a long record of friendly relations with the whites, sent over an inquiry duly signed with a large "X", in which he asked about the Colonel's intentions. "I understand that your policy is for war and not peace, and I wish to inform you that I am for peace and not war," wrote the Chief. He asserted that he was tired of taking the blame for hostile actions of the Santees and Hunkpapas and he inquired, in passing, as to the food supply at the fort. Gilbert endorsed the letter with the comment that he had made no announcements of policy and that he had no food on hand for Indians.[18]

Requests for troops to discipline drunk and disorderly Indians, or applications to the military for groceries, did not mean that peace had come to the country around the mouth of the Yellowstone, but these developments hinted at a stabilization of the situation on that particular front. Fort Buford, with only three companies of infantry, was still undermanned except for defensive operations, and the military planners continued their requests for more troops. General Phil Sheridan expressed the belief that there would be more difficulties with the northern Sioux, and admitted that the forces under his command were not yet prepared for serious warfare. He recommended temporary concessions to the Indians "until we can get more troops on the upper Missouri," underscoring his argument with the comment that Fort Buford was still under a practical state of siege.[19]

As the officers in the Military Division of the Missouri marked time, life at Fort Buford resembled that of its sister forts. Charles Larpenteur noted the lull in activities as he wrote in his diary: "All very quiet on the Potomac." [20] To occupy their time the men turned to various forms of entertainment, ranging from baseball, cricket, hunting and theatrical performances, to poker, serious drinking or visits to the nearby Gros Ventre lodges. Dr. Kimball had strong objections to the latter activity, contending that the only way to keep his men free of disease was to remove the source, that is, to move the Indian women away. The doctor was also confronted by the other principal occupational disease at the post: drinking. Both the commanding officer and the post surgeon realized that in the case of Indian women and liquor, temperance, rather than prohibition, was the most reasonable answer. While Dr. Kimball expressed a willingness to treat some of the diseased Assiniboin women, who were apparently of a higher type than the Gros Ventres he wanted to deport, and to recognize the necessity of their services, the post commandant favored the liberal sale of beer on the ground that it had been "found to diminish drunkenness" at other posts where it was sold. In the spring of 1870 W. H. Carey, agent for Durfee & Peck, asked for permission to start a brewery. His request was favorably endorsed, the argument being advanced that beer was "less hurtful than ardent spirits and being certain that a stimulating beverage of some sort will be drank" this was the lesser of the evils. That the trading post dealt in stronger stuff was suggested in a remark Larpenteur made about the death of one of the soldiers, when he alleged that the man was poisoned by drinking whiskey bought from Durfee & Peck, a firm for which he had worked until he was fired.[21]

Although women and liquor were invariably attractive to the soldiers, these diversions were not universally acclaimed as the answer to boredom. When the enterprising Larpenteur set up a bowling alley the response was immediate and enthusiastic. The grand opening came on September 14, 1870, and the next day he wrote, in glee: "Ten Pin Alley rolling in full bloom, never stopped the whole day." His diary for the next few days carried such remarks as: "Ten Pin Alley full," "Times good," "Ten Pin Alley doing great business," "Rolling Ten Pins at a great rate." By the twentieth he had come to the conclusion, "Nothing can stop that ball in the alley."[22] The old trader even tried to branch out into other fields, requesting permission to set up what he called "a house of entertainment," promising to "keep as many as twenty boarders & no more." He did not elaborate on the nature of the proposed institution's function, and there is no record of its acceptance, although Colonel Gilbert endorsed the project.[23]

If the days at Buford were routine, at least they appear to have been more comfortable than those of a few years earlier. A visitor wrote in 1871 that, "I was there last month, and a right good post it is, many call it the finest post in Dakota." [24] Those who saw it at this time described the place stockaded on three sides, the open side facing the river, with adobe buildings that were judged to be adequate, with the exception of the enlisted men's barracks that were, as usual, dark and gloomy, and an overcrowded guardhouse. Typically, the water supply came from the river and was used primarily for cooking and laundry purposes, but not for bathing. As one inspector wrote, the water "contains a large amount of suspended matter, principally clay and sand." By adding six grains of alum per gallon and allowing the product to stand for twelve hours, it became clear and quite potable. Gardens, planted in shallow ravines paralleling the river, produced lettuce, radishes, peas, turnips, cucumbers and sweet corn in sufficient quantity to supply the garrison. Wild game, found to be much more palatable than the stringy beef from the herd, completed a table that proved highly acceptable to the troops. During winter months, when garden produce was not available, the post stocked large quantities of antiscorbutics such as molasses, pickles and sauerkraut. In the autumn of 1870, for example, the commissary had on hand 831 gallons of molasses, 807 gallons of pickles and 732 gallons of sauerkraut, enough to last until spring. Thus, the medical officer could report that the health of the command was excellent, except, of course, for the chronic problems of diarrhea and venereal disease.[25]

During the early 1870's the War Department tightened its network of fortifications in eastern Dakota, reinforced the line of river posts and placed temporary encampments of soldiers in the vicinity of the new Indian reservations. The natives, especially the nontreaty bands, continued to complain about the advance of white population and the increasing use of water and land routes. They also had new worries. The Northern Pacific Railroad was on its way west, and only the Panic of 1873 would blunt its forward thrust as it reached the new village of Bismarck, located on the banks of the river. Even the Indians knew that this was but a pause, not a termination.

Meanwhile, river trade flourished. Thirty-five different vessels reached Fort Benton in 1868, and although that figure was not equaled in the next year, so many of the boats double-tripped that the total number of arrivals was larger than ever. By then cargo capacities had increased, and in 1869 almost five thousand tons of freight, exclusive of that sent by the Government, reached Montana. New speed records were set. Grant Marsh brought the *Nile* into Sioux City after a run from Fort Benton that required only fourteen days. His record was short-lived; the *Cora* bettered it within a matter of a few days. During that exciting year of steamboat travel, seven million pounds of freight left Sioux City alone, and word came from Montana that the Territory had realized over $90,000,000 from its mineral resources. Sioux City, now enjoying rail service to Chicago, did a thriving business and proudly announced itself as the new Gateway to the West. Aside from its recent rise to commercial eminence, it was Government headquarters for shipping all stores to Dakota, Montana and Idaho territories. It was also the main port of embarkation for troops going upriver and, while the residents were glad to have the business, they were frequently happy to see the boys on their way. On one occasion a local paper reported that a group had left aboard the *Andrew Ackley* and the editor bade them farewell, saying: "We trust they will be of more benefit to people up north than they were here." Those receiving their discharges, after tours of duty at the river posts, were paid off at Sioux City. That they fed money into the local economy at various levels is revealed in a news story that told of "one unfortunate fellow [who] was eased of $285 in a house of bad repute the night before last, and he was so oblivious that he doesn't know the girl that volunteered to take such care of his finances." [26]

The Montana trade, and the demands for military transportation, were augmented by mounting numbers of settlers who now began to invade southern Dakota in earnest. A Sioux City paper, noting that a long train had just arrived by the Sioux City and Pacific Railroad, said that five of its cars were filled with immigrants and their belongings. "They were decked out in the latest Scandinavian fashion, and were gazed on with curiosity as they grouped together on the platform—about 170 of them," wrote a reporter, who watched them with interest. There were, no doubt, others who met the train, for E. W. Sargent of Richland, Dakota (Union County), already had asked his friends at Sioux City to turn "up this way" all immigrants arriving there. He promised that settlers coming to Richland could find a home, for the town promoters were willing to give a building lot to any respectable man who would erect a home on it.[27] Union county was now advertised as a place where "a trace of the full-blooded savage is no longer found," where the tepee had given way to the farmhouse, "and where the dirty savage is supplanted by the hardy, industrious Frenchman and Irishman."[28] Apparently Scandinavians were also welcome in this new land of opportunity for those whose skins were white.

The country that stretched northward for three hundred miles from the Iowa line, on both sides of the Missouri, was pronounced by Sioux City supporters as an area that not only was free of red taint, but also one into which permanent settlers were now coming in great numbers. "As the last and greatest of the public domains which offer free homes, liberal laws, and unparalleled prospective prosperity in the future to its people, Dakota stands preeminently alone," said the local newspaper. There was, of course, rich land, capable of producing enormous crops, but there were rumors of even more exciting resources. In 1871 a Sioux City paper made reference to the probable existence of gold along American Creek, which flowed into the Missouri from the east not far above Fort Randall, but even more startling was the report of a diamond, valued at $50,000, having been found along the James River, also in eastern Dakota. There was no gold or diamond rush in eastern Dakota, the settlers being more readily convinced of the long-term possibilities of extraction from the prairie soil, but such stories always added a delightful fillip to the booming of a new country. Of much more interest to immigrant farmers was the suggestion that they utilize empty steamboats, returning from trips to the upper river, to take their crops into Sioux City where higher prices awaited them.[29] With arable homesteads served by water transportation awaiting them, the newcomers did not need to have the lure of gems and gold dangled before their eyes. Just the land, said to be free of Indian depredations, was enough for Europeans who had tilled diminishing parcels of soil in the old country.

The steady pressure of settlers against the southern Dakota Indian frontier was complemented by a new threat to the upper river country. The Northern Pacific Railroad, chartered in 1864, now threatened to become a reality, as surveyors took to the field and planted a trail of stakes across the barren sod straight into the heart of Sioux country. There was resistance and, for the moment, it was effective. Secretary of the Interior Orville Browning admitted in the autumn of 1868 that the surveys of that season were given up for want of sufficient soldiers to protect the field engineers.[30] The need for troops was underscored by a report from the American Vice Consul at Winnipeg who wrote, in May 1870, of rumors that five hundred well-armed Sioux were ready to descend upon the river country west of Buford, and that in all probability this would be a summer of heavy warfare.[31] Despite repeated threats by the Indians, however, the work progressed and, as fall came in 1870, the crews neared the Montana line. In October Lieutenant William Nelson of the Seventh Infantry, with a detail of mounted soldiers and scouts, escorted Thomas Morris, Chief Engineer of the railroad's Dakota division, and his men on a reconnaissance into the Yellowstone Valley. Meanwhile, General W. S. Hancock, who headed the Department of Dakota with headquarters at St. Paul, Minnesota, warned his superiors that by spring some important changes would have to be made in the disposition of troops in the upper river country.[32] Reconnaissance parties might carry out their assignments without meeting disaster, but he felt that, sooner or later, there would be a showdown and blood would flow. The necessity of a military force in northwestern Dakota was obvious to the Army men who studied the inevitable conflict that must take place if the advance were to be made.

In the spring of 1871 the commanding officer at Fort Stevenson warned that the Sioux were again reported to be ready for a large-scale retaliation as soon as the grass was tall enough for campaigning. His informants told him that at least eight hundred warriors would join in such an attack for, as the Indians expressed it, they were "pressed as a wounded bear." [33] Departmental officers took such stories quite seriously and responded by sending reinforcements into the upper river country so that escort parties could be made sufficiently strong to protect themselves against large bodies of Indians.

In September General Hancock assigned a total of six infantry companies from forts Randall, Rice and Sully as guards for surveying parties that worked beyond Fort Buford. This force, under the command of Major J. N. G. Whistler, patrolled the country as far west as the modern town of Glendive, Montana, and returned without seeing so much as a single hostile Indian. This did not mean that the enemy had changed its mind, or that it was unaware of the invasion, but rather that the warriors would not do open battle with any force capable of striking back. Indian agents reported that the hostiles were very much agitated by the operation, as were the reservation Indians, but all were wary of an adverse result of extensive warfare at this time. Those on reservations took the philosophical view that the railroad was inevitable and confessed that they had become sufficiently accustomed to the taste of "tame buffalo" meat to stay home rather than fight. Despite this rationalization, they remained unhappy over recent developments. General Sheridan, in command of the Military Division of the Missouri, with headquarters in Chicago, understood the restlessness of the tribes and he recommended strengthening the garrison at Fort Buford in anticipation of what he regarded as certain warfare.[34]

As the Missouri River Indians watched the settlers' frontier edge forward, and saw their country not only threatened by this great army of farmers, but also by the penetration of transportation facilities that would bring more whites, they grew exceedingly restless. The establishment of reservations was another irritant, particularly to the hostiles, for this also increased the number of troops along the river. During 1870 General Hancock established temporary posts at six agencies in Dakota to provide protection for Indian Bureau employees and for the Indians themselves.[35] Although this was said to be a temporary expedient, designed to facilitate administrative matters on the reservations during a transitional period, it was generally eyed with distrust by the Sioux for they did not believe that the soldiers would leave in the near future. Time would justify their fears.

The agents and their employees at the various reservations urged the assignment of troops for their protection and criticized the War Department for moving so slowly to their aid. They pointed out that an agent and perhaps a half dozen workers were no match for several thousand Indians, who were inclined to vent their feelings upon those nearest at hand. Captain George M. Randall, in charge at the Cheyenne Agency, wrote that affairs at that place were in constant turmoil. When his Indians were not quarreling among themselves, they were fighting with the wilder natives who moved in at ration time and appropriated their food. For the white employees life was a precarious matter. Not only was Randall's life repeatedly threatened, but his men were subjected to constant indignities. For example, on one occasion his servant was caught by six Indians while on an errand to the sutler's store, "and bent over a saber and held by five, while the sixth perpetrated a deed without shame upon him, they all taking their turn in a like way," to quote a newspaper account of the affair. A young lieutenant was similarly approached, in his own quarters, "by an Indian who wanted to commit a similar deed on him, but the Lieut. got out of the room by strategy." Randall himself received the same proposition.[36]

To answer the pleas for protection made by those stationed at the Cheyenne Agency, and to exercise some measure of control of the inmates of the place, a small military post was established there in the spring of 1870. It was simply designated "Post at Cheyenne Agency" until the autumn of 1878, when it was renamed Fort Bennett in honor of Captain Andrew S. Bennett, killed in action in the Bannock Indian war that year. At the time of establishment, the little fort was manned by two companies of the Seventeenth Infantry.[37]

Despite treaties and steady handouts of food and supplies, the reservation Indians continued to grumble over their lot, many of them asserting that they never intended to sign any papers that allowed the Government to build forts or make roads west and south of the Missouri. To demonstrate their displeasure they took potshots at passing steamers and challenged the passengers to come ashore and fight. The *Farragut,* which arrived at Sioux City toward the end of May 1870, reported that several shots had been fired at it about fifteen miles above Fort Randall, one of the bullets passing within inches of the boat's captain as he slept in his berth. In another instance, two companies of soldiers tried to land above the Cheyenne Agency and were met by three thousand howling warriors, dressed and ready for battle. The attempt at a beachhead was abandoned.[38]

The Indians at the Cheyenne Agency repeatedly told Captain Randall that they would kill him if he did not leave before the next sunrise, but the days passed and no one came forward to carry out the threat. Then the reservation Sioux said they would burn down any blockhouses built at the Agency, fearing that such fortifications would put them at a disadvantage when the promised day of reckoning arrived. Again the talk bore no fruit and the soldiers erected a fortified enclosure at the Agency.[39] General Hancock acknowledged that the Indians were resentful, but he did not expect the situation to get out of hand. By the autumn of 1870 he said the reservation residents were generally quiet, and he believed that there would be no major difficulty with them. He based his conclusion, in part, upon the fact that these people were weakened by near-starvation, but since they had few horses and could not hunt, they would continue to depend upon the Government corn supply to keep them alive.[40] As the editor of a Sioux City paper put it, no one ever heard of a Sioux resigning his rations in mid-winter. Captain Poole, acting as Agent at the Whetstone Agency, confirmed the belief that there would be no uprising when he said that while the young braves talked loudly, the older ones "looked upon the matter with indifference." [41]

The reservation Sioux were not the only ones who were unhappy with the presence of the Army along the river. In 1869 the

War Department issued an order against further trespassing upon lands set aside for use by the military and, as it began to be carried out, there were loud protests from settlers. When one Tompkins, who had married an Indian woman and had settled on La Chappelle Creek (a branch of the Bad River), was burned out at the order of Colonel D. S. Stanley, commanding Fort Sully, there was a great outcry in the press. Now, said one editor, the upper Missouri country had fallen under the sway of a despotism "more autocratic and tyrannical than was ever exercised by Russia over Poland," and the situation was such that it was bound to arouse "the just indignation of every one who believes in the existence or perpetuity of a Republican form of government."[42] When "Buck Soldier," writing from Fort Rice, had some unkind words to say about his superiors, the press seized upon his story as a means of documenting its criticism of the Army. According to "Buck," the commanding officer not only had obliged one of the cooks to make home brew for him to sell at twenty cents a quart, but he also had fathered the child of a sixteen-year-old girl who was the daughter of a post musician and then had intimidated the poor man until an abortion was performed. In addition, this tyrant was accused of sending the men out to repel nonexistent Indians, while the laundresses were left to "man" the fort, so that he would have something to report to his superiors when they turned up for periodic inspections.[43]

Criticisms of the military arm were usually reported by newspapers in areas farther down the river, in places where the Army no longer had many troops, and where the economic opportunities afforded by its presence were being seized upon by civilians closer to the Indian frontier. In the case of the Sioux City press, its real reason for attacking the Army's conduct in Dakota arose not so much out of sympathy for men like Tompkins, who ordinarily would have been dismissed as just another squaw man, or for "Buck," whose complaint about the management was quite normal, but rather because the local merchants were no longer getting the lion's share of military supply orders. The *Times* of that city admitted this when it accused Durfee & Peck of being so much "on the right side" of Secretary of War William W. Belknap that the firm had deprived Sioux City of at least $50,000 worth of business. Such a development, said the paper, was the result of arbitrary, autocratic and un-American conduct on the part of "certain drunken, worthless and corrupt government officers on the Upper Missouri."[44] Such charges underscored the fact that the military frontier had, indeed, moved forward.

During the early Seventies the river forts were transformed from a front line of defense for settlements in Minnesota, southern Dakota and northwestern Iowa to the role of guarding land and water routes westward, and as a base of supplies for both the advancing military elements and the newly located Indian reservations that fronted on the river. So rapid was the advance of the settlement frontier that it took less than a decade for it to cross the river and to invade a country no one at the time believed to be useful agriculturally. The chain of river posts, regarded as vital at the time it was established, was left in the wake of the westward movement. These posts might have been abandoned sooner had it not been for the existence of the reservations and the necessity of policing them until their inhabitants no longer posed a threat to those who had taken over that part of the country.

SIXTEEN

Forts Among the Farmers

One of the characteristics of the American frontier movement was acceleration. It took the colonial settlers over 150 years after the settlement at Jamestown to establish themselves west of the Appalachians. But during the following century they fanned out in a great arc that extended from the Southwest to Oregon, after which they invaded the mineral gulches of the Rockies and then made a final assault upon the Great American Desert. During the early 1870's, as the nation prepared for a centennial celebration that was to mark a hundred years of growth and prosperity, the westward movement broke into a gallop, which even amazed Americans accustomed to plunging progress. One of the dramatic developments came in the region of the northern high plains, an area long considered useless by settlers.

General Philip Sheridan, commanding the Military Division of the Missouri which embraced much of this country, was among those who expressed constant surprise at the advance of the agricultural frontier. To him the movement was nothing short of revolutionary, and when he wrote his annual report in 1872 he commented upon the advance in such a place as Dakota which, he said, "only a year or two since was in the possession of the Indians." It seemed to him that it was only yesterday when the country between the Missouri River and the Rocky Mountains was a "barren desert, while now it is the grazing ground for stock consumed by the population of our eastern cities." Shortly, he was able to state that the natives were remarkably quiet, and that, except for scattered raids upon herds and an occasional assault upon "the poor Mandans and Rees," peace prevailed along the river. By now, he said, the task of the western army was to protect settlers from these sporadic attacks, to explore what remained as unknown territory, to aid civil authorities in maintaining law on the fringes of settlement, to protect the advancing railroads in the West, "and in fact to do everything within our power to forward the advancing wave of civilization on our frontiers." [1]

Army officers who had been stationed on the plains were surprised by the persistence of the oncoming farmers. They had long since accepted the Desert theory, as had a good many people in the East, and military planning was based upon what was regarded as a fixed fact of western aridity and sterility of soil. In 1875 Colonel W. B. Hazen wrote a book entitled *Our Barren Lands*. Based upon his experiences in northern Dakota, it maintained that this part of the country was worthless in an agricultural sense. When Colonel George A. Custer challenged his findings, Hazen responded sharply, saying that Custer had spent only one season in those parts and that the cavalryman did not know what he was talking about. General Alfred Sully, whose experience in Dakota was considerable, agreed with Hazen and called the land unfit for cultivation, with a few isolated exceptions. Writing from his station at Vancouver, Washington, in 1874, the veteran campaigner still remembered vividly his struggle against extinction in the wild country of the Dakota badlands a decade earlier. He did not even believe that cattle could be raised there with any success, due to the bad water and severe winters, and he offered the opinion that "I would not recommend it as a good country to settle in, and large portions of it never can be inhabited, not even by the Indians." [2]

As the Army officers shook their heads in puzzlement over the mysterious advance of the settlers' frontier, southern Dakota appeared to be approaching stabilization, at least from the military standpoint. Commissioner of Indian Affairs Francis A. Walker reported that, by 1872, reservations west of the river were becoming well populated and, including the older reserves, nearly 25,000

Indians had been settled at such establishments. Still at large were some 11,000 so-called hostiles. The most powerful were the Teton Sioux under Sitting Bull and Black Moon, and, rather than negotiate for rations, they had moved westward into northeastern Montana.[3] It was with these that the Army would be concerned over the coming decade. The reservation Indians, on the other hand, offered so little trouble that military protection was almost unnecessary. Agent Edmond Palmer wrote from the Grand River Agency in 1874, saying that his charges had even stopped insulting him and, in consequence of this mild behavior, he had entirely dispensed with the need of soldiers at the Agency.[4]

The confinement of what one visiting dignitary called "these wandering Arabs" brought a state of calm to the river country that began to be looked upon with mild concern by some of the Army personnel in the vicinity. Elizabeth Custer, who waited at Fort Rice while her husband took to the field in 1873, commented that she would rather stay there than go back East because everyone at the fort was interested in the activities of the troops. She recalled a summer she had spent at home and her irritation at the lack of enthusiasm there for the work of the western army. Her resentment toward the East's rising humanitarian sentiment in behalf of the Indian and its lack of interest in the Army was underscored by a New York City newspaper's suggestion that the nation had too many soldiers. Charging that the "military Ring" was determined to maintain a needlessly large force at a cost of thirty-five or forty million dollars a year, the paper asked that the Army be reduced to a maximum of 10,000 men. Talk such as this made military men almost hopeful that the Indians would rise up, now and then, to justify the need for more troops in western country.[5]

Eastern disenchantment with a large military establishment occasionally found support in western communities, particularly when the Army was engaged in duties offensive to the frontiersmen. In 1867 a number of miners had prepared a prospecting expedition into the Black Hills, only to have General Sherman recommend that this area be included in the large Sioux reservation then being considered. Sioux City papers called him a "brainless and peaky-headed vagrant" for taking such a position, but the decision stood. In 1872 Charles Collins, editor of the *Sioux City Times,* ignored the fact that the region was closed to whites and joined with three other men to organize the Black Hills Mining and Exploration Association for the purpose of examining the area for its mineral riches. Shortly, Collins' paper carried advertisements reading: "Ho! for the Black Hills. The great outfitting house of Cole & Hedges have on hand, and are constantly receiving a complete assortment of outfitting goods for the New Eldorado." The paper also carried news items quoting men who had visited the Hills and who said, in one instance, that "the mineral wealth of that country is sufficient to pay the national debt." The writer expressed his dismay that "the Government should donate such a country to a race of degraded thieves as a park, for they want it for nothing else, and feed them in the bargain." To the great irritation of Collins, both Generals Hancock and Stanley reiterated the fact that this was reservation land and they intended to evict any trespassers. Collins publicly challenged the officers and said that prospectors would go into the country regardless of any efforts to keep them out. The newspaperman showed that he understood the force of the westward movement when he predicted that after the invasion Congress would be obliged to sanction the move and the men would be vindicated.[6]

It is possible that Collins even thought that the Army would shut its eyes to a miners' invasion, although it was obliged to state publicly that such a move was against the law. The War Department was, at this time, quite hostile to the Department of the Interior, and the leading generals were doing everything they could to show that the Indians should be returned to their custody. The Indian habit of feeding on Government beef during the winter, as it was dispensed at the agencies, and taking to the field for hostile operations during the summer, was exceedingly annoying to the Army. For several years Sheridan had been convinced that a military post should be established in the Black Hills to control the raiders. This, at least, was his ostensible reason for sending Colonel Custer and six companies of the Seventh Cavalry on an expedition to the Hills during the summer of 1874. To send an officer of Custer's known aggressiveness on a mission that presumably was to examine the countryside for a fort site suggests that Sheridan's sympathies were not with the Indians. In explaining the choice of such an officer to General Terry, Sheridan commented that he thought Custer "especially fitted for such an undertaking."

Custer's summer expedition both complicated matters for the Interior Department and encouraged miners who eyed the Black Hills covetously. The press was well supplied with accounts of the military movement, and readers were treated to extensive descriptions of the beauty of the land, its agricultural fertility and its mineral resources. According to newspaper accounts, this unexplored country was an oasis in the desert, and Custer's men rode through a "fairy land, filled with bright-hued flowers of numberless varieties, whose perfume filled the air, with lovely valleys, delightful natural parks, clear limpid streams" meeting their view each day. Stories of how the men gathered bouquets of flowers, without even dismounting, and of the "entire command of horses and men . . . gaily decked with flowers" proceeding through this paradise, also excited prospective settlers who wanted to plough up a country of such unbounded fertility.

Much more exciting were the stories of gold in the area of Harney's Peak. There had been talk of its existence for a decade, and the "off limits" position taken by the Army had only confirmed the truth of the rumor to many an anxious prospector. When Custer's men returned to the river forts, they brought back talk of pay dirt in the Black Hills, and the excitement mounted to new heights. An infantryman stationed at Fort Randall wrote that their accounts "produced a sensation" at that post. Taking one of the cavalrymen aside, he asked for the whole truth in the matter, and was astonished when the trooper produced a rifle shell filled with gold dust. Further investigation revealed that many of Custer's men carried empty shells that were packed with dust. When newspapers learned of these reports their columns carried glowing accounts of new mineral riches that awaited miners. One Iowa paper announced that "Custer's Eldorado is something but little less glorious than heaven itself." Those who still doubted had only to read Sheridan's annual report, written that autumn, to discover that he not only confirmed the discoveries, but he labeled the Black Hills country as much richer in resources than heretofore believed.[7]

With the publication of this report, backed by the comments of such a well-known plainsman as Charley Reynolds who scouted for Custer, it is not surprising that a new outbreak of Black Hills fever erupted in Dakota. The expedition of miners marched forth, and the Army reluctantly carried out its orders to oppose the invasion. When the first elements of the miners eluded troops sent to intercept them, Collins' paper asserted that the Government was wasting its time and money. Before long, however, the net was cast over the interlopers and they were caught. Methodically, the troops destroyed wagons, arms, food and equipment belonging to 150 of those who had marched from Sioux City, and then placed the men under arrest. "And now," wrote a discouraged trooper, "it turns out that the arrest of the last party was illegal, they being in Nebraska and out of the Indian reservation. The people of the west are wild about the arrest, and abuse us soldiers as if we were to blame for carrying out the orders of the government. They call us such pet names as robbers. . . ." [8] The writer advised prospectors to keep out of the country, as troops were combing it carefully to prevent illegal entries. His advice was ignored, and the prediction made earlier by Collins proved to be correct. In the autumn of 1875 efforts were made to effect new treaties with the Sioux, and when these attempts failed, the War Department simply discontinued its efforts to carry out what Sheridan called "an exceedingly disagreeable and embarrassing duty." Once more the spearhead of the frontier movement had displayed its power and had demonstrated that the white advance could not be stopped, not even by the Federal Government itself.

Meanwhile, the westward push across the northern reaches of Dakota continued. The Northern Pacific Railroad, officially chartered and granted lands for construction purposes, reached the Missouri River in 1872. In answer to Indian threats, the War Department established a new post at the point where the road crossed the river, and named it after Colonel H. Boyd McKeen of the Eighty-first Pennsylvania Volunteers, who had fallen at the battle of Cold Harbor in the spring of 1864. In November 1872 the name was changed to Fort Abraham Lincoln, and it was converted to a cavalry post from which Colonel Custer sallied forth on his Black Hills expedition in 1874, and from which he left on his ill-fated Little Big Horn campaign two years later.[9] The fort was located near the little railhead town that was named Bismarck, in honor of the German chancellor then so much admired in the United States.

Fort Abraham Lincoln characterized the change that had come to the Missouri River military frontier in the brief decade that began with the construction of Fort Randall. Instead of the usual infantry post made of logs and roofed with dirt, there now stood a large cavalry establishment of lumber hauled in by the Northern Pacific Railroad. That seven hundred carloads of materials were required to complete it testified to the size and completeness of this new post.

The concentration of troops near the railhead signified the intention of the Army to support that project to the fullest extent. General Sherman, the ranking general officer, assured his old friend, Sheridan, that the work would advance no matter what the opposition. He viewed this as he had the Union Pacific: It was a national project, one that would advance white settlement and would be of great value in solving the problem of hostile Indians. Francis A. Walker, Commissioner of Indian Affairs, agreed with him and stated publicly that, within two years, the Northern Pacific Railroad "will of itself completely solve the Great Sioux problem, and leave the ninety thousand Indians ranging between the two transcontinental lines as incapable of resisting the Government as are the Indians of New York or Massachusetts. Columns moving north from the Union Pacific, and south from the Northern Pacific, would crush the Sioux and their confederates as between the upper and nether millstones."

Sherman was under no illusions as to the magnitude of the coming operations. He called the country west of Fort Stevenson "miserable" and predicted that the Sioux in that region would be "hostile in an extensive degree." Here, he said, was the probable scene of a last-ditch stand by Indians who regarded the oncoming road as a symbol of their doom. To prepare for violent resistance, the Army ordered two strong military units into the field in the spring of 1872. The first, under Colonel D. S. Stanley, was comprised of six hundred infantry supported by a battery of Gatling guns and twelve-pounders. It was ordered to move from Fort Rice to the mouth of the Powder River, while a second force of about four hundred men under Major E. M. Baker would patrol the country westward from that point.[10]

When Sheridan later reported that Baker's force was unable to carry out its assignment "on account of the demonstration of hostile Indians," military men knew that the days ahead would be violent. The Sioux made sure that there would be no misunderstanding about this by attacking Fort Abraham Lincoln itself, in the spring of 1873. Sheridan responded by transferring the Seventh Cavalry regiment to Dakota so that in the future the Indians could be followed and punished. It had taken ten years for the Sioux to convince the War Department that infantry posts alone would not be sufficient. The appointment of Colonel Custer as Fort Abraham Lincoln's new commanding officer suggested the changing nature of the river posts from defensive units to bases of supply for cavalry units that were to range deep into Montana in search of the hit-and-run hostiles.

During the next few years, as the so-called "Indian Wars" of the West were concluded, the forts lying between Randall and Buford found themselves relegated to a secondary line of defense and to serving as suppliers of men and materiel for the front. The westward movement of the military frontier and the advance of the Northern Pacific into Montana not only altered the role of the river posts, but it actually increased the isolation of several. A contemporary Army historian wrote that the arrival of the railroad had left Fort Sully to rely solely upon river steamers, a declining mode of transportation, and that it could lay claim to the category of a desirable frontier post only on the score of healthfulness. Fort Buford, lying north of the railroad, found itself in a similar situation.[11] Fort Abraham Lincoln, on the other hand, owed its existence and its current importance to the new road.

When General Custer rode out of Fort Abraham Lincoln on his last campaign, the Seventh Cavalry band played "The Girl I Left Behind Me." Not only were the wives—soon to be widows—left to watch and wait, but the personnel of the establishment took up their respective roles as housekeepers of the fort while the troopers were absent. This was the role that most of the river posts assumed during these years, and as new units were transferred in and then out again for duty in the field, the departing soldiers might well have sung "The Fort I Left Behind Me." Those who remained stood guard duty, went on occasional details to protect the whites from the Indians or the Indians from the whites at nearby reservations, and spent the remainder of their time fighting boredom. Month after month commanding officers noted "nothing of importance" in their Post Returns, and searched for something of significance to write. The breakup of the river's ice or a fire in the barracks constituted the only events worth recording.

To pass the time and to offer the men something more than solace from the bottle, there was entertainment at the typical western post. Mrs. Custer described the efforts of the men at Fort Abraham Lincoln, as they knocked together a leaky building made of warped cottonwood boards and built a small theater. Playing behind smoking tallow-candle footlights, and before backdrops painted on condemned canvas, the soldiers presented musical and dramatic offerings that amused themselves, if no one else. Now and then the soldiers drafted professionals, stranded en route to or from the West, and the quality of the production was momentarily raised. Good or bad, the performances were patronized as the soldiery turned out in numbers and sat on uncomfortable, backless benches to watch their fellow men attempt to take them on a flight from reality.

There was a similar dramatic troupe at Fort Buford, and it made the usual endeavor at offering diversion to a set of bored men and officers. Private William B. Sanford, who served there in 1874, mentioned evening concerts and efforts by the local thespians, as well as billiards or library reading for those who preferred it. He wrote also of gambling and drinking, which appeared to be equally popular among both men and officers. On one occasion he noted in his diary that he had helped one of the officers clean up his quarters after a big party, and for his trouble he got some "segurs and whiskey." Lieutenant R. H. Day of the Sixth Infantry confessed to the Post Adjutant that he could not perform his duties on a given day because he was suffering "from having drank to much the night previous." He offered the defense that he had fought a long hard battle against the affliction and that he would continue his efforts toward a better life in the hope that the commanding officer would refrain from arresting him for these temporary relapses in his war with alcohol.[12]

Efforts to elevate the morals of the military community were carried on at most of the forts, the battle growing more complicated as military inactivity grew. A branch of the Good Templars' Society was founded at Fort Randall "to combat the fearful influence of the saloon and gambling den," as one old soldier later recorded. The initial announcement of the movement was met by catcalls and jeers, but, the next night, eighteen men turned up and an organization was founded. "So effective was the lodge," wrote the Chief Templar, "that the saloon's business decreased to the point that they discharged their famous $10 a day bartender." [13] A correspondent for the *Yankton Herald* supported the contention that reform had set in when he spoke of the troops as appearing clean and sober when he visited Fort Randall. He was much pleased by the post's appearance, and he reported that his stay there had been both informative and pleasant.[14]

The problem of whiskey persisted, however, and all efforts to stamp out the trade failed. In the middle Seventies the Agent at Standing Rock complained that his Indians regularly left the reservation and went to Fort Rice, where they obtained liquor. Since soldiers stationed there could buy the article in unlimited quantities from the Post Trader, control was extremely difficult. When drunkenness became so prevalent that bottles were commonly found in the guardhouse, Colonel Elwell Otis decided that it was time to close up the bar. "Whiskey ranches" soon sprang up around the edges of the military reservation and the flow of spirits continued. Efforts to prevent the importation of liquor also failed, even when honest attempts were made by steamboat owners to cooperate with military authorities. Canned goods, purporting to contain tomatoes or peaches, came ashore filled with whiskey, and when this was discovered new methods of bootlegging were devised. Bottles were dropped overboard at night, tied to a fishing line and a float, to be gathered in later by the dealer who stationed himself at an appropriate distance downstream. He then distributed his "catch" to the Indians and soldiers.[15]

By the 1880's the day of the river fort was drawing to a close. Life at the posts was largely routine, and there was little expectancy of a call to arms for defense of the establishment. Denny Moran, who took a job as civilian driver at Fort Randall, said that the trees were now large and that the fort was "a very showy place." He talked of brisk social activity in the neighborhood, and remarked that evidence of the commingling races was easily discernible. His reference was to the fact that the Twenty-fifth Infantry (colored) had recently served at Randall and had left behind a number of children on the nearby reservation. White or black, the soldier here, and at other posts, had little choice in the way of feminine companionship. Moran himself attested to this when he told of driving the paymaster to Yankton and of being out on the town one evening with two soldier friends when the trio tried to enter the local Turner Hall where a dance was in progress. He was in civilian clothes and was admitted, but the soldiers were turned away. As he remarked, any girl seen with one of the soldiers was considered to be of low repute, and most of them tended to shun those in uniform.[16]

Dr. William C. Gorgas, later to become famous for his battle against yellow fever in Panama, was stationed at Fort Randall at this time, and from his pen came a picture of life at the post. He described the community of officers and their wives as cultivated and entertaining, but exceedingly restricted. "Life was a constant routine of going to the same dinners, listening to the same stories, laughing at the same jokes; whist and euchre parties . . . now and then afforded relaxation; the inevitable quarrels of such a small society added a little spice, and a whiff of scandal came as an occasional godsend." [17] As William Tecumseh Sherman commented on western posts in general: "Spite of 'wise counsels' and 'sage advices' officers will marry, have families, and yearn for schools, churches, and refined society. These are not to be found in the remote corners where duty compels us to post our pickets." The old officer thought that the American Army should follow the British custom of sending men out for service abroad with the distinct understanding that it would be for no more than five years. Unhappily, he confessed, this was difficult to do, especially with the cavalry, since the main duty of the Army of the Eighties was in the West.[18]

Fort Sully, made more remote than ever by the absence of rail service, typified the western post that was left behind by the westward movement of the frontier. Albert Peckham, alias Henry Hurley, who served in the Eleventh Infantry there during the Eighties, exemplified the boredom felt by young men at such places. Writing to Albert Dollenmayer, whom he called "friend Dolly," he quite freely expressed his intention to desert when a good opportunity presented itself. His principal complaint, and that of his fellow men, was the arduous manual labor that was daily performed. On one occasion he wrote that the troops had just put up three hundred tons of hay and now were requested to cut eight hundred cords of wood. He predicted that, of the forty-five new recruits, no more than ten would be on hand after payday "as they say they did not come into the Army to cut wood for they could get lots of that in civil life." This, he said, was not at all unusual, and while he did not disapprove of their actions, he criticized the result. "We work like the dickens all summer in the gardens and get a good pile of vegetables ahead for winter, when along comes a batch of recruits in the fall, eat up all the vegetables and then take a trip East for the good of their health." Each year, he said, there was a migration of "spring birds" that took away about half the men in each company. Other than the hard work and boredom, he had no serious complaint. At one time he admitted that he had not stood guard duty in two months. This was all right for those who liked it, said Peckham, but he was not one of those who cared about such duty. He was then awaiting a response to a request for discharge but had heard nothing from the officer to whom he had sent his letter. "I guess he got his a— up because I did not address him as Col.," he concluded philosophically.[19]

Officers at Fort Sully recognized the problem of morale and made an effort to provide some diversions. The band room was repaired and fitted with a new stage where concerts were given each Tuesday evening. It was also used for officers' dances, and the enlisted men were permitted to dance there twice a month. New lamps replaced candles in the library, an institution that contained 1,050 volumes by 1881. The post surgeon reported that, during a period of twelve months, there had been 3,960 withdrawals of books, periodicals and newspapers, or an average of twenty-eight per person in the garrison. Even Peckham had to admit that life under such conditions had its virtues, but, as he said, "the only thing that kills me is having the same thing over and over; now if we had a change once in a while it would not be so bad." When he discovered that a saloon and dance hall were being erected only five miles away his spirits rose, for now, he said, "we do not have so far to go to have a little fun." For a time he almost decided against desertion.[20]

Life at faraway posts became less disagreeable, particularly for the officers, as improvements continued to be made. Lieutenant Charles S. Farnsworth described Fort Buford, in the early Nineties, as a fort having ample quarters, a full supply of stores and excellent hunting. "The chickens are so plentiful that you can almost kill them with a stick," he wrote. "Deer are being brought into the post by the dozen." In 1892 he communicated with a number of electric light companies in the East, using the newly developed typewriter, and asked for bids on four hundred incandescent lamps and twenty street lights for the post. Living conditions were improving so rapidly at Buford that he wondered, in one of his letters, why more colored people did not take advantage of the service and enlist. He thought that the opportunities for them in the Army should be very attractive. He answered his own query, so far as Fort Buford was concerned, when he revealed that a number of Negro soldiers had sought discharges because they did not like the Dakota winters. It was nearly April when he wrote, yet the thermometer stood at zero each night and the river was a solid mass of ice.[21]

As quiet came to the country through which the Missouri River ran—below Fort Buford—military planners watched the change with interest. In 1878 General John Gibbon, commanding the Department of Dakota, wrote that affairs in his department had been remarkably quiet except for occasional raids in the vicinity of the Black Hills. This area, now crawling with prospectors, was referred to by General Alfred Terry as a new frontier and a place that now required protection. The commanding general, W. T. Sherman, agreed that the military frontier had moved westward, and his requests for appropriations now were pointed at the country lying between the Black Hills and northern Montana. The river country, he thought, should be used for relocated Sioux because of its proximity to the river and the economy of supplying both the Indians and the troops that guarded them in that area. He estimated that if the Indians were located near the river, the cost of maintaining agencies would be less than half that at places farther inland.[22]

Army officers, being of a normally conservative nature and not infrequently opposed to change, continued to have difficulty in comprehending the sweep of homesteaders into Dakota. General Gibbon found it hard to understand why an area, only a few years earlier described in most geographies as unexplored, should now be pierced by rails and deluged with stockmen and farmers. Sheridan talked of it too, and tried to guess the potential value to cattle interests or land investors. Sherman's reports in these years were filled with wonder, and even puzzlement, over the rapidity of advance. Secretaries of War, such as Alexander Ramsey and Robert Lincoln, watched the changing scene and formulated their plans in the light of extreme quiet among the Indians and the rapid advance of the railroads. They, too, found the plains' situation fluid to a disturbing degree.[23]

By the mid-Eighties Dakota had essentially passed from a

frontier condition to one of military stability and a relatively fixed Indian population. In 1886 Secretary of the Interior L. Q. C. Lamar revealed that settlers had purchased approximately four million acres of land in Dakota, an area larger than the states of Rhode Island and Connecticut. Almost a million and a half of this amount was taken up during the year preceding his report. In a land that only recently had been a scene of warfare stood some 82,000 farms, and the Black Hills region, another area of conflict, was contributing five million dollars a year in minerals to the nation's economy.[24] General Thomas Ruger believed that such a state of calm in Dakota was the result of relentless Army activity and the gradual acceptance by the Indians of a dependent condition. Now, he said, the hostile Indian had no place to go. The railroads had brought in an army of settlers who had finished the destruction of buffalo herds and had penetrated the last places of refuge traditionally used by the hostiles. He was satisfied that the "shifting Indian frontier," as he called it, was ended, and that all the elements for deciding what posts should be continued or abandoned were present. By 1887 the once important Fort Abraham Lincoln had but six officers and seventy-one men. Fort Buford, with about three hundred men, was the only large river post that remained. Now the problem of the War Department was to justify the existence of the chain of forts that stretched upriver from Randall to Buford, and to show cause why they should remain in the midst of the homesteaders.[25] This it was unable to do, for time had overtaken the advancing Army, and the posts had become relics of a recent past.

Forts Rice and Stevenson were the first of the principal posts to be abandoned. The Northern Pacific Railroad, which ran between them and not far from either, eliminated the need for their continued existence. Fort Rice, only twenty-eight miles south of the railroad, was recommended for abandonment early in 1878 by General Sheridan, who said that it had now fulfilled the object for which it was built. By November 25 the troops had departed, except for a small detachment left behind to transfer property and to break up the post. Within a few weeks the departmental quartermaster reported that all public buildings and other public property had been removed from Fort Rice. By August 1883 Fort Stevenson also was given up by the Army, and its buildings were turned over to the Indian Agent at Fort Berthold. Sheridan explained that the completion of the railroad now provided a speedy means of transportation in the region and, therefore, Stevenson also had outlived its usefulness.[26]

The other main river posts lasted for a decade and then died quietly. Fort Randall, no more than a skeleton post after 1884, finally was abandoned in 1892.[27] Fort Sully followed, two years later, when Secretary of War Daniel S. Lamont concluded that it was no longer needed for military purposes. On October 20, 1894, Major James A. Gageby led three companies of the Twelfth Infantry out of the place, bound for Fort Niobrara, Nebraska, and another river fort was silenced.[28]

Fort Buford, which had stood for nearly thirty years as a sentinel at the confluence of the Missouri and Yellowstone rivers, was the last of the original posts to go. General Brooks reported in 1895 that its buildings were in such a dilapidated condition that it would require a large sum to restore them. This, in addition to the fact that it was no longer useful as a military station, persuaded him to recommend abandonment. In the autumn of that year the small garrison that remained packed up the post's stores and, on October 1, detachments of the Tenth Cavalry and the Twenty-fifth Infantry left for a new assignment in central Montana by way of the recently completely Great Northern Railroad. A month later the handful of men who had remained to perform housekeeping duties also boarded a westbound train and Fort Buford stood vacant.

Nearly three decades earlier Colonel W. G. Rankin and his men had been put ashore, with instructions to build an outpost high along the river. So hostile was their reception that for a time the very existence of the fort was in doubt. But now Scandinavian farmers had replaced the fierce Sioux, and travelers on the new railroad looked out of their car windows and occasionally saw a tramp steamer flailing its way through muddy waters hauling grain or coal between rail points. It all seemed quaint to these modern folk, as they stood on the threshold of the Twentieth century, and, no doubt, many of them wondered why the Army had established a line of forts in so peaceful and pastoral a land. It seemed incredible that only a few years earlier this was the land of the Sioux, and a white minority had been obliged to fight for their existence among the natives.

The river forts that had stood along the frontier as a "picket line of civilization," to use General Sherman's words, were gone. Because of their temporary nature they had not been built as permanent structures. Abandoned, they disappeared so completely that, in a very short time, there was no evidence that they had ever existed. Even the ground upon which some of them stood would go under water at a future day, when a series of dams appeared along the Missouri, and the fort sites would be as inaccessible as the hulks of sunken ships. All that remained was a memory of a fleeting frontier where lonely flagstaffs reared their heads above palisaded walls, and blue-clad troopers responded to the brassy call of bugles when the Sioux stood upon nearby hills and taunted the strangers in their land to come forth and fight.

BIBLIOGRAPHICAL ESSAY

The most valuable materials to be found concerning the forts of the Missouri River frontier are in the original correspondence held by the National Archives at Washington, D.C. In the Records of the United States Army Commands, Letters Sent and Letters Received, will be found the official version of the origin, expansion and final disposal of these forts. These are in Record Group 98. Day-to-day events and smaller details of fort life are contained in the Post Returns, the reports of commanding officers sent forward each month.

A vast body of essential evidence is available in various printed documents, particularly the annual reports of the Secretaries of War and Interior, as well as a number of individual reports pertaining to specific events. Post surgeons, usually well educated and possessed of time to write, provide interesting and intelligent views of fort life. These are found in circulars issued from time to time by the Surgeon General's Office. Journals of officers sent out on inspections are also found in the Federal Serial set. For the earlier period, when the Army was contemplating the fortification of this frontier, see the Military Affairs volumes in the American State Papers.

There are a number of private diaries, letters, and journals pertaining to the forts, and these are noted in the citations. The most extensive and most useful among them are the C.A.R. Dimon Papers now held by the Yale University Library. State historical societies, particularly those of Montana, Minnesota and North Dakota, have original letters that are extremely revealing. Some of these have been published in the quarterlies published by the respective states. In addition, the university libraries of the region have theses and dissertations, some of which are also in printed form, that pertain to the forts or to their personnel.

In the state quarterlies also will be found a variety of articles touching upon individual forts, military campaigns, fur trade and other related subjects. Of these, *North Dakota History* is the most fruitful. Reminiscences of some of the contemporaries are in print and these range from easily available accounts, such as that of Larpenteur (published in several editions), to such scarce items as J. H. Drips' *Three Years Among the Indians in Dakota* and Captain D. C. Poole's *Among the Sioux of Dakota.* There are a number of books that tell the story of fur trading on the Missouri, or of river travel, and by supplementing with these the state histories, some of which are quite recent, one may rather easily gain a general view of the period. There is no monographic work, however, that deals specifically and in depth with the Missouri River military frontier.

Newspaper accounts contribute individual items and lend color to the overall picture, the most valuable of which are the extant copies of *The Frontier Scout* published at both Fort Union and Fort Rice. In these issues the reader will find not only the detail not otherwise available, but also a good deal of opinion and emotional impact. City newspapers, such as those of Sioux City and of Yankton, also present the point of view held by civilian contemporaries in rather strong terms.

To itemize the rather long list of sources used would be repetitious, for they are found in the specific citations that follow, and are listed according to chapter.

NOTES

Chapter 1. The Mysterious, Muddy Missouri

[1] Comments from the *Missouri Gazette* and *Niles Register* are quoted by Hiram M. Chittenden, *The American Fur Trade of the Far West* (New York, 1902), 3 volumes, II, 563–565.

[2] Ashley to O'Fallon, June 4, 1823. Condition of the Military Establishment, etc., Doc. 247, *American State Papers,* Military Affairs, Vol. 2, 587.

[3] Leavenworth to Atkinson, June 18, 1823. *Ibid.*, 586.

[4] *Ibid.*, 585.

[5] E. P. Gaines to J. C. Calhoun, July 28, 1823, *Ibid.*, 579.

[6] Report of Colonel Henry Leavenworth, August 30, 1823, *Ibid.*, 592–593.

[7] Quoted by Dale L. Morgan, *Jedediah Smith and the Opening of the West* (Indianapolis, 1953), 77.

[8] Atkinson discussed the treadmill transmission in a letter of October 11, 1823. See Russell Reid and Clell G. Gannon, "Journal of the Atkinson-O'Fallon Expedition," *North Dakota Historical Quarterly,* Vol. 4, No. 1 (October 1929), 54–55. See also Roger L. Nichols (ed.), *General Henry Atkinson: A Western Military Career* (Norman, Oklahoma, 1965), Chapter 6.

[9] Quoted by Nichols, *Atkinson,* 102.

[10] The outline of the story is told in the "Journal of the Atkinson-O'Fallon Expedition." Nichols, *Atkinson,* fills in the details, 103–4.

Chapter 2. The Fur Forts

[1] Frederick T. Wilson, "Fort Pierre and Its Neighbors," *South Dakota Historical Collections,* Vol. 1, 273 is the authority for the fort's dimensions. Travelers usually called it a square. Thaddeus Culbertson, John Palliser and Edward Harris, who accompanied Audubon in 1843, all referred to it as a square, but all of them recorded different dimensions.

[2] Thaddeus A. Culbertson, "Journal of an Expedition to the Mauvaises Terres and the Upper Missouri in 1850," ed. by John Francis McDermott, Smithsonian Institution, Bureau of American Ethnology, Bulletin 147 (Washington, 1952), 76.

[3] John Palliser, *Solitary Rambles of a Hunter in the Prairies* (London, 1853), 103.

[4] Maximilian, *Travels in the Interior of North America,* ed. by Reuben G. Thwaites, *Early Western Travels* (Cleveland, 1906), Vol. 22, 316. Editor Thwaites noted that Laidlaw was "an able trader, but of quick irascible temper, and unpopular with his subordinates."

[5] Culbertson, "Journal of an Expedition," 86.

[6] *Ibid.*, 76.

[7] E. de Giradin, "A Trip to the Badlands in 1849," *South Dakota Historical Review,* Vol. 1, No. 2 (January 1936), 46–47. It was first published in a French travel magazine, *Le Tour du Monde,* in 1864.

[8] Constant R. Marks (ed.), "Letellier's Autobiography," *South Dakota Historical Collections,* Vol. 4, 221–22.

[9] Report of Isaac I. Stevens to George Manypenny, September 16, 1854. Report of the Commissioner of Indian Affairs, 1854, *Sen. Ex. Doc.* 1, Part I, 33 Cong., 2 sess. (Serial 746), 404.

[10] John Charles Frémont, *Memoirs of My Life* (Chicago, 1887), 39, 40.

[11] "Journal of Peter Garrioch." Summary of 1842 written January 1, 1843. Film of typed copy in Minnesota Historical Society, St. Paul.

[12] De Giradin, *op. cit.,* 66.

[13] Hiram M. Chittenden, *History of Early Steamboat Navigation on the Missouri River* (New York, 1903), 1, 148.

[14] De Giradin, *op. cit.,* 67.

[15] Report of Alfred D. Vaughan from Fort Pierre, September 20, 1853. Report of the Commissioner of Indian Affairs, 1853, *Sen. Ex. Doc.* 1, 33 Cong., 1 sess. (Serial 690), 354.

[16] Report of Alfred D. Vaughan from Fort Pierre, October 19, 1854, in Report of the Commissioner of Indian Affairs, 1854, *Sen. Ex. Doc.* 1, Part I, 33 Cong., 2 sess. (Serial 746), 288.

[17] Edwin T. Denig, *Indian Tribes of the Upper Missouri* (Washington, 1930), 407–8.

Chapter 3. "We'll Never Forgive Old Harney"

[1] Thomas S. Jesup to D. H. Vinton, March 23, 1855; Vinton to Jesup, March 30, 1855; W. S. Harney to Lt. Col. L. Thomas, Assistant Adjutant General, Headquarters of the Army, April 5, 1855, in "Official Correspondence Relating to Fort Pierre," *South Dakota Historical Collections,* Vol. 1, 1902, 381–386, hereafter cited as OCRFP and *SDHC*. See also, Frederick T. Wilson, "Fort Pierre and Its Neighbors," *SDHC,* Vol. 1, 278.

[2] Adjutant General S. Cooper to Harney, April 25, 1855, OCRFP, 386–387; G. K. Warren to Major O. F. Winship, AAG of Sioux Expedition, August 7, 1855, OCRFP, 390–394.

[3] Harney to L. Thomas, AAG Army Headquarters, April 5, 1855, OCRFP, 385; Major W. R. Montgomery, Second Infantry, to Col. S. Cooper, Adjutant General of the Army, July 31, 1855, OCRFP, 389; Wilson, "Fort Pierre and Its Neighbors," 281, 282; Clement Lounsberry, *Early History of North Dakota* (Washington, 1919), 213. Lounsberry founded the *Bismarck Tribune.*

[4] Report of Alfred J. Vaughan, September 12, 1855. Report of the Commissioner of Indian Affairs, 1855, *Sen. Ex. Doc.* 1, 34 Cong., 1 sess. (Serial 810), 393.

[5] Harney to L. Thomas, AAG Army Headquarters, June 2, 1855, OCRFP, 388.

[6] Harney to L. Thomas, AAG Army Headquarters, from camp on Blue Water Creek, Nebraska Territory, September 5, 1855. Annual Report of the Secretary of War, *Sen. Ex. Doc.* 1, Part II, 34 Cong., 1 sess. (Serial 811), 49–51; Colonel St. George Cooke's report of September 5 is found in *Sen. Ex. Doc.* 58, 34 Cong., 3 sess., 1–4. He reported that when his troops recognized women in the fight they did not shoot, except when the women shot arrows at the men. His figures on casualties vary with Harney's.

[7] For a general account of the affair see LeRoy R. Hafen and Francis M. Young, *Fort Laramie and the Pageant of the West, 1834–1890* (Glendale, California, 1938), 240–243.

[8] Thomas Wright to Commissary General, September 13, 1855, OCRFP, 396.

[9] Augustus Meyers, "Dakota in the Fifties," *SDHC*, Vol. 10, 133–34.

[10] Harney to L. Thomas, AAG Army Headquarters, October 19, 1855, OCRFP, 397.

[11] Harney to L. Thomas, AAG Army Headquarters, December 14, 1855, OCRFP, 413.

[12] Meyers, *op. cit.*, 138.

[13] Harney to L. Thomas, AAG Army Headquarters, December 14, 1855, OCRFP, 413.

[14] Headquarters, Sioux Expedition, Order No. 12, October 21, 1855, OCRFP, 400.

[15] P. T. Turnley to Col. Charles Thomas, Acting Quartermaster General, November 1, 1855, OCRFP, 401.

[16] Van Vliet to Turnley, October 26, 1855, OCRFP, 400–1.

[17] C. E. Galpin to P. T. Turnley, November 1, 1855, OCRFP, 403–4.

[18] P. T. Turnley to Quartermaster Thomas S. Jesup, November 1, 1855, OCRFP, 406–7.

[19] Galpin to Turnley, November 8, 1855, OCRFP, 412.

[20] W. R. Montgomery to Turnley, September 22, 1855, OCRFP, 396.

[21] Wilson, *op. cit.*, 264.

[22] Meyers, *op. cit.*, 154, 158.

[23] Meyers, *op. cit.*, 151.

[24] Fort Pierre Post Returns, November, 1855. Adjutant General's Office, Record Group 94, Army and Navy Branch, National Archives, Washington, D.C.

[25] Meyers, *op. cit.*, 161.

[26] Meyers, *op. cit.*, 158–9; Report of the Commissary of General Subsistence, Quartermaster General's Report, Report of the Secretary of War, 1856, *Sen. Ex. Docs.*, Part II, 3 sess. (Serial 876), 258.

[27] Harney Correspondence of January 20, February 22, March 9 and June 30, 1856, OCRFP, 416, 420, 423 and 428 respectively.

[28] Harney to L. Thomas, AAG Army Headquarters, March 12, 1856, OCRFP, 425.

[29] Jefferson Davis to Harney, December 26, 1866, in "Council With the Sioux Indians at Fort Pierre," *House Ex. Doc.* 130, 34 Cong., 1 sess. (Serial 859), 4, 5.

[30] *Ibid.*, 14–16.

[31] Chittenden, *History of Early Steamboat Navigation*, I, 202–3.

[32] "Council With the Sioux Indians at Fort Pierre," *op. cit.*, 6–7; see also Logan Uriah Reavis, *The Life and Military Services of General William Selby Harney* (St. Louis, 1878), 261–4.

[33] "Council With the Sioux Indians at Fort Pierre," *op. cit.*, 10.

[34] Doane Robinson, *A History of the Dakota or Sioux Indians, SDHC*, Vol. 2, 1904, 226.

[35] Cooper to Harney, June 20, 1856, OCRFP, 427.

[36] Linda W. Slaughter, "Fort Randall," *Collections of the State Historical Society of North Dakota*, Vol. 1 (1906), 425; "Records of Events: Fort Pierre, Nebraska Territory," OCRFP, 431–2; Lounsberry, *North Dakota, op. cit.*, 218; Wilson, *op. cit.*, 291–292. See also Carleton W. Kenyon, "History of Fort Randall" (Master's thesis, University of South Dakota, 1950).

[37] Letters of W. H. McClean (Post Adjutant), September 2, and of Colonel Lee, September 3 and 29, 1856, all addressed to Headquarters, Department of the West, Fort Leavenworth. Record of the U.S. Army Commands, Letters Sent, 1856–1867, Fort Randall. Record Group 98, Army and Navy Branch, National Archives.

[38] Record of Events: Fort Pierre, Nebraska Territory, OCRFP, 432.

[39] Report of the Secretary of War, 1856. *Sen. Doc.* 5, Part II, 34 Cong., 3 sess. (Serial 876).

Chapter 4. Turbulent Tribesmen

[1] Francis Lee to Headquarters, Dept. of the West, January 19, 1857; to the Quartermaster General, January 31, 1857; to the Quartermaster General at St. Louis, February 27, 1857. Records of U.S. Army Commands, Letters Sent, 1856–1867, Fort Randall. Record Group 98, Army and Navy Branch, National Archives.

[2] Report of Surgeon T. C. Madison, September, 1857. "Statistical Report on the Sickness and Mortality in the Army of the United States," *Sen. Ex. Doc.* 52, 36 Cong., 1 sess. (Serial 1023), 40.

[3] Lee to Headquarters, Dept. of the West, Leavenworth, February 8, 1857. Records of U.S. Army Commands, Letters Sent, 1856–1867, Fort Randall. R. G. 98, Army and Navy Branch, N.A.

[4] Lee to AGO, Army Headquarters, March 3, 1857. Record of U.S. Army Commands, Letters Sent, 1856–1867, Fort Randall. R. G. 98, Army and Navy Branch, N.A.; Meyers, "Dakota in the Fifties," *op. cit.*, 187.

[5] Meyers, *Ibid.;* Lee to J. B. S. Todd, September 22, 1857. Record of U.S. Army Commands, Letters Sent, 1856–1867, Fort Randall. R. G. 98, Army and Navy Branch, N.A.

[6] *Sioux City Iowa Eagle,* July 4 and 25, 1857.

[7] *Ibid.*, August 8, 1857.

[8] *Ibid.*, December 19, 1857.

[9] Report of Alexander H. Redfield, September 1, 1858, Report of the Commissioner of Indian Affairs, 1858, *Sen. Ex. Doc.* 1, 35 Cong., 2 sess. (Serial 974), 436; *Sioux City Iowa Eagle,* June 12, 1858, March 5, 1859.

[10] *Sioux City Iowa Eagle,* August 8, 1857; Clement Lounsberry, *Early History of North Dakota* (Washington, 1919), 225.

[11] Redfield's report of September 1, 1858, *op. cit.*, 436.

[12] Lee to Mr. Stoker and Others, March 9, 1847. Records of the U.S. Army Commands, Letters Sent, 1856–1867, Fort Randall. R. G. 98, Army and Navy Branch, N.A.

[13] Reports of Alexander Redfield, September 1 and October 12, 1858, *op. cit.*, 436–445.

[14] Report of Alfred J. Vaughan, September 12, 1855. Report of the Commissioner of Indian Affairs, 1855, *Sen. Ex. Doc.* 1, 34 Cong., 1 sess. (Serial 810), 392–3; Vaughan's report for September 10, 1856, Report of the Commissioner of Indian Affairs, 1856, *Sen. Ex. Doc.* 5, 34 Cong., 3 sess. (Serial 875), 628; Reports of Alexander Redfield, September 1 and October 12, 1858, *op. cit.*

[15] See Vaughan's report of September 10, 1856, *op. cit.*, 631-7; Report of A. H. Redfield, September 9, 1857, Report of the Commissioner of Indian Affairs, *Sen. Ex. Doc.* 11, 35 Cong., 1 sess. (Serial 919), 416–8; Redfield's report of September 1, 1858, *op. cit.*, 439.

[16] Philip E. Chappell, "A History of the Missouri River," *Transactions of the Kansas State Historical Society 1905–1906,* Vol. 9 (Topeka, 1906), 291.

[17] Redfield's report of September 1, 1858, *op. cit.*, 437; H. W. Wessells to AAG, Hdq. Army of the West, July 7, 1858. Records of U.S. Army Commands, Letters Sent, 1856–1867, Fort Randall. R. G. 98, Army and Navy Branch, N.A.; Henry A. Boller, *Among the Indians: Eight Years in the Far West, 1858–1866* (Philadelphia, 1868), 24–27.

[18] Redfield's report of September 1, 1858, *op. cit.*, 438–42.

[19] Report of Alfred J. Vaughan from Fort Benton, July 24, 1859. Report of the Commissioner of Indian Affairs, 1859, *Sen. Ex. Doc.* 2, Part I, 36 Cong., 1 sess. (Serial 1023), 484; Chittenden, *History of Steamboat Navigation,* I, *op. cit.*, 237.

[20] Report of the Secretary of War, 1858, *House Ex. Doc.* 2, Part II, 35 Cong., 2 sess. (Serial 998), 13.

[21] Report of Lt. G. K. Warren, appended to Report of the Secretary of War, 1858, *ibid.*, 644.

[22] For example see comments from the *Sauk Rapids Frontiersman* (Minnesota), quoted by Francis Paul Prucha in *The Army Post on the Minnesota Frontier, 1819–1882* (Master's thesis, University of Minnesota, 1947), 144–5.

[23] Report of the Secretary of War, 1857. *House Ex. Doc.* 2, Part II, 35 Cong., 1 sess. (Serial 943), 3–5.

[24] Elias J. Marsh, "Journal of Dr. Elias J. Marsh; Account of the Steamboat Trip on the Missouri River, May-August, 1859," *South Dakota Historical Review,* Vol. 1, No. 2 (January 1936), 96.

[25] Report of A. A. Humphreys. Report of the Secretary of War, 1858, *op. cit.*, 586–587.
[26] Report of the Secretary of War, 1859, *Sen. Ex. Doc.* 2, Part II, 36 Cong., 1 sess. (Serial 1024), 13.
[27] *Sioux City Iowa Times*, June 1, 1860.
[28] Report of Alexander Redfield, September 1, 1858, *op. cit.*, 439.
[29] Report of Lieutenant Henry E. Maynadier, 1860. *Sen. Ex. Doc.* 77, 40 Cong., 1 sess. (Serial 1317), 147–9.
[30] Martin F. Schmitt (ed.), "From Missouri to Oregon in 1860. The Diary of August V. Kautz," *The Pacific Northwest Quarterly*, Vol. 37, No. 3 (July 1946), 204.
[31] Report of W. A. Burleigh, Yankton Agent, October, 1861, in Report of the Commissioner of Indian Affairs, 1861. *Sen. Ex. Doc.* 1, Part I, 37 Cong., 2 sess. (Serial 1117), 730.
[32] *Weekly Dakotian* (Yankton), September 7, 1861.
[33] Report of the Commissioner of Indian Affairs, 1861, *op. cit.*, 635–6; Post Returns, Fort Randall, September, 1861. Records of the Adjutant General's Office, R. G. 94, Army and Navy Branch, N.A.
[34] Chittenden, *Early Steamboat Navigation*, I, 217.
[35] *Sioux City Iowa Times*, May 11, July 6, August 24, 1860.
[36] John Mason Brown (ed.), "A Trip to the Northwest in 1861," *The Filson Club Quarterly*, Vol. 24, No. 20 (April, 1950), 112.

Chapter 5. Rumblings North of Randall

[1] Elias J. Marsh, "Journal of Dr. Elias J. Marsh; Account of a Steamboat Trip on the Missouri River, May-August, 1859," *South Dakota Historical Review*, Vol. 1, No. 2 (January 1936), 90; John Pattee, "Dakota Campaigns," *SDHC*, Vol. 5, 276; Albert Watkins (ed.), "Notes of the Early History of the Nebraska Country," *Publications of the Nebraska State Historical Society*, Vol. 20, 313.
[2] "Notes of the Early History of the Nebraska Country," *op. cit.*, 313. The excerpt is from an unidentified newspaper of September 18, 1858, probably the *Daily Missouri Republican*.
[3] Journal of Captain W. F. Raynolds, United States Army Corps of Engineers, 1859–1860, *Sen. Ex. Doc.* 77, 40 Cong., 1 sess. (Serial 1317), 18–19.
[4] Report of Alexander H. Redfield, October 17, 1859. Report of the Commissioner of Indian Affairs, 1859. *Sen. Ex. Doc.* 2, 36 Cong., 1 sess, Vol. 1 (Serial 1023), 494. Captain W. F. Raynolds, who stopped at Fort Randall on his way downriver in September 1860, said he had never seen finer vegetables, especially the beets which he said were "of gigantic size." Journal of Captain W. F. Raynolds, 1859–1860, *Sen. Ex. Doc.* 77, 40 Cong., 1 sess. (Serial 1317), 124.
[5] Report of Alexander H. Redfield, October 17, 1860. Report of the Commissioner of Indian Affairs, 1860. *Sen. Ex. Doc.* 1, 36 Cong., 2 sess., Vol. 1 (Serial 1078), 311.
[6] Martin F. Schmitt (ed.), "From Missouri to Oregon in 1860. The Diary

of August V. Kautz," *The Pacific Northwest Quarterly*, Vol. 37, No. 3 (July 1946), 202.

[7] Frederick T. Wilson, "Fort Pierre and Its Neighbors," *SDHC*, Vol. 1, 294; John Pattee, "Dakota Campaigns," *SDHC*, Vol. 5, 277.

[8] Post Returns, Fort Randall, December, 1861. Records of the Adjutant General's Office, R. G. 94, Army and Navy Branch, N.A.

[9] Amos R. Cherry manuscripts, in "Iowa Troops in the Sully Campaigns," *Iowa Journal of History and Politics*, Vol. 20, No. 3 (July 1922), 411 and 412.

[10] John Pattee, "Dakota Campaigns," *op. cit.*, 277.

[11] Amos R. Cherry manuscripts, *op. cit.*, 411. Captain Pattee was not satisfied with the post rations which he said cooked down from an issue of twelve ounces to a serving of only four ounces, and he called the bacon wormy and totally unfit for use. Captain John Pattee to Commissary General, January 14, 1862. Records of U.S. Army Commands, Letters Sent, 1856–1867, Fort Randall. R. G. 98, Army and Navy Branch, N.A.

[12] Amos R. Cherry manuscripts, *op. cit.*, 410–1.

[13] Pattee, "Dakota Campaigns," *op. cit.*, 280–1; Pattee to Lyman, February 4, 1862. Records of U.S. Army Commands, Letters Sent, 1856–1867, Fort Randall. R. G. 98, *op. cit.*

[14] Pattee, "Dakota Campaigns," *op. cit.*, 281; Post Returns, Fort Randall, February through May, 1862; John Pattee, *Report of Major John Pattee upon a letter of charges of J. B. S. Todd, Delegate in Congress from Dakota Territory, to the Adjutant General, U.S.A. made March 18, 1863* (Des Moines, Iowa, 1863), Coe Collection, Yale University Library; A. M. English, "Dakota's First Soldiers: History of the First Dakota Cavalry, 1862–1865," *SDHC*, Vol. 9, 241; Pattee to S. D. Sturgis, May 12, 1862. Record of U.S. Army Commands, Letters Sent, 1856–1867, Fort Randall. R. G. 98, *op. cit.*

[15] Pattee to George B. Hoffman, May 13, 1862. Records of U.S. Army Commands, Letters Sent, 1856–1867, Fort Randall. R. G. 98, *op. cit.*

[16] The foregoing paragraphs are drawn largely from Pattee, *Report of Major John Pattee upon a letter of charges of J. B. S. Todd, op. cit.*, 6, 8, 9, 10, 27, 28, 33; and from Clement Lounsberry, *Early History of North Dakota* (Washington, 1919), 218. Pattee's comments about Lyman, the "Indianized specimen," are from a letter he wrote to George B. Hoffman, July 16, 1862. Records of U.S. Army Commands, Letters Sent, 1856–1867, Fort Randall. R. G. 98, *op. cit.*

[17] "Official Correspondence Pertaining to the War of the Outbreak, 1862–1865," *SDHC*, 8, 101. These are official records reprinted from government documents, principally *Official Records of the War of the Rebellion*. The period from May 23, 1865 to October 24, 1865 is found in *SDHC*, Vol. 31, 469–563.

[18] Report of Samuel N. Latta, August 27, 1862. Report of the Commissioner of Indian Affairs, 1862. *House Ex. Doc.* 1, 37 Cong., 3 sess., Vol. II (Serial 1157), 336–337. A Passenger of the *Spread Eagle* who witnessed the deliberations said that Latta could not get along with the interpreter and he called the agent a "very stupid man." John Delany, however, was

prejudiced; he was an admirer of the Chouteaus, of whom Latta was quite critical. John E. Sunder (ed.), "Up the Missouri to the Montana Mines; John O'Fallon Delany's 'Pocket Diary for 1862,'" *Missouri Historical Society Bulletin,* Vol. 19, No. 1 (October 1962), 11.

[19] Report of Samuel Latta, August 27, 1862, *op. cit.* 337–41.

[20] Charles Primeau to Pierre Chouteau, Jr., June 20, 1862. Report of the Commissioner of Indian Affairs, 1862, *op. cit.*, 518.

[21] Report of J. B. Hoffman, September 1, 1862. Report of the Commissioner of Indian Affairs, 1862, *op. cit.*, 332.

[22] "Letter from the chief men of the Hunkpapas," Report of the Commissioner of Indian Affairs, 1862, *op. cit.*, 516.

[23] Report of Samuel Latta, August 27, 1862, *op. cit.*, 340.

[24] Report of Governor William Jayne, October 8, 1862. Report of the Commissioner of Indian Affairs, 1862, *op. cit.*, 321.

[25] The *Dakotian* (Yankton), December 23, 1862.

[26] James L. Fisk, "Expedition from Fort Abercrombie to Fort Benton (1862)," *House Ex. Doc.* 80, 37 Cong., 3 sess. (Serial 1164), 20–21.

[27] William J. Peterson (ed.), "The Log of the Henry M. Shreve to Fort Benton in 1869," *Mississippi Valley Historical Review,* Vol. 31, No. 4 (March 1945), 536. The *Dakotian,* of Yankton, reported the ascent of the four vessels, remarking that in addition to Indian goods and merchandise they carried "wealthy and influential men, who by their means and personal efforts will . . . facilitate the . . . richness of the new Eldorado." Issue of June 3, 1862.

[28] Leslie A. White (ed.), *Lewis Henry Morgan: The Indian Journals, 1859–1862* (Ann Arbor: University of Michigan Press, 1959), 141–142.

[29] Comments about the *Spread Eagle's* trip are found in White, *Lewis Henry Morgan, ibid.*, 104–42, 167; A. H. Wilcox, "Up the Missouri to Montana in the Spring of 1862," typescript, Historical Society of Montana, Helena; "Diary of James Harkness," *Contributions to the Historical Society of Montana,* II, 347; Sunder, "Up the Missouri to the Montana Mines," *op. cit.*, 12; Helen Addison Howard (ed.), "Diary of Charles Rumley from St. Louis to Portland, 1862," in *Sources of Northwest History* (Missoula, 1933), No. 28, 3; Francis McGee Thompson, "Reminiscences of Four-Score Years," *The Massachusetts Magazine,* Vol. 5 (1912), 150–67; William E. Lass, *A History of Steamboating on the Upper Missouri River* (Lincoln: University of Nebraska Press, 1962), 33. For a description of these vessels and something of their history see Philip E. Chappell's *History of the Missouri River* in which he provides a detailed list of river steamers.

[30] Report of Samuel Latta, August 27, 1862, *op. cit.*, 341. In his report of March 7, 1863, Report of the Commissioner of Indian Affairs, 1863, *House Ex. Doc.* 1, 38 Cong., 1 sess. (Serial 1182), 284, he quoted Jayne's message of 1862.

[31] Pattee to General James G. Blunt, July 21, 1862. Records of U.S. Army Commands, Letters Sent, 1856–1867, Fort Randall. R. G. 98, *op. cit.*

Chapter 6. "It Is a National War"

[1] Proclamation of Governor William Jayne, August 30, 1862, in OCPWO, *SDHC,* Vol. 8, 101–102.

[2] Nutt to Kirkwood, September 15, 1862, in OCPWO, 104; Report of William Jayne, October 8, 1862 in Report of the Commissioner of Indian Affairs, 1862, *House Ex. Doc.* 1, 37 Cong., 3 sess. (Serial 1157), 320; Linda W. Slaughter, "Fort Randall," *Collections of the State Historical Society of North Dakota,* Vol. I (1906), 428.

[3] Footnote to Nutt's letter of September 15, 1862, *op. cit.,* 104.

[4] *The Dakotian* (Yankton) September 15 and 22, 1862.

[5] Erling Theodore Jorstad, *The Life of Henry Hastings Sibley* (Doctoral dissertation, University of Wisconsin, 1957), 300–301. Kenneth Carley, *The Sioux Uprising of 1862* (St. Paul, 1961), 55.

[6] Carley, *op. cit.,* 71.

[7] The *Dakotian,* September 30, 1862.

[8] *Ibid.,* October 28, 1862.

[9] Pierre Chouteau, Jr., to William P. Dole, December 2, 1862. Report of the Commissioner of Indian Affairs, 1862, *op. cit.,* 516.

[10] Letters of Pattee to the Commissioner of Indian Affairs, September 9, 1862 and to John Pope, September 19, 1862 in Records of U.S. Army Commands, Letters Sent, 1856–1867, Fort Randall. R. G. 98, Army and Navy Branch, N.A.

[11] W. A. Burleigh to William P. Dole, November 17, 1862. Report of the Commissioner of Indian Affairs, 1862, *op. cit.,* 520. Dr. Burleigh, originally from Maine, moved to Pennsylvania and became quite successful. He was an enthusiastic Lincoln supporter in 1860 and for his efforts Lincoln offered him a foreign mission which he declined. Later, when offered the Yankton Agency, he accepted. He was twice elected delegate to Congress from Dakota.

[12] The *Dakotian,* September 30, 1862.

[13] The *Dakotian,* November 11, 1862; Primeau to Chouteau, November 4, 1862. Report of the Commissioner of Indian Affairs, 1862, *op. cit.,* 523.

[14] McFetridge to Rice, November 23, 1862. Report of the Commissioner of Indian Affairs, 1862, *op. cit.,* 552.

[15] Jayne, Burleigh and Williams to Lincoln, December 24, 1862, in OCPWO, *op. cit.,* 108–9; The *Dakotian,* December 23, 1862.

[16] Pattee to General John Cook, December 1, 1862. Records of U.S. Army Commands, Letters Sent, 1856–1867, Fort Randall. R. G. 98, Army and Navy Branch, N.A.; John Pattee, "Dakota Campaigns," *SDHC,* Vol. 5, 282–7; William G. Stewart, Quartermaster, Sioux City Cavalry to Governor Alexander Ramsey, November 16, 1862, in Report of the Commissioner of Indian Affairs, 1862, *op. cit.,* 519; A. M. English, "Dakota's First Soldiers: History of the First Dakota Cavalry, 1862–1865," *SDHC,* Vol. 9, 261–2; The *Dakotian,* November 25 and December 9, 1862.

[17] Report of William Jayne, October 8, 1862. Report of the Commissioner of Indian Affairs, 1862, *op. cit.,* 319.

[18] The *Dakotian,* January 6, 1863.

[19] *Ibid.*

[20] Frederick T. Wilson, "Fort Pierre and Its Neighbors," *SDHC,* Vol. I, 300–1; De Lorme W. Robinson, "Editorial Notes on Historical Sketch of North and South Dakota," *SDHC,* Vol. 1, 124; Jorstad, *op. cit.,* 322.

[21] The *Dakotian,* May 19 and June 9, 1863.

[22] E. Stutsman to Acting Governor John Hutchinson, April 6, 1863. Dakota Territorial Archives, Drawer 152, North Dakota Historical Society, Bismarck; Hutchinson to Cook, April 8 and May 6, 1863, and Cook to Hutchinson, May 8, 1863, in Report of the Commissioner of Indian Affairs, 1863. *House Ex. Doc.* 1, 38 Cong., 1 sess. (Serial 1182), 273–5.

[23] Pope to Sibley, February 17 and 25, 1863, OCPWO, 109–10; William P. Dole to J. P. Usher, January 26, 1863, Report of the Commissioner of Indian Affairs, 1863, *op. cit.,* 285; Jorstad, *op. cit.,* 321.

[24] Detwiler to Tufts, February 19, 1863, in the *Dakotian* of May 12. Tufts quickly became prominent in Montana, serving as Secretary to the Territory and, in 1868, briefly as Acting Governor.

[25] Report of the Secretary of the Interior, *House Ex. Doc.* 1, 38 Cong., 1 sess. (Serial 1182), v.

[26] Samuel N. Latta to William P. Dole, March 7, 1863. Report of the Commissioner of Indian Affairs, 1863, *op. cit.,* 285.

[27] Henry A. Boller, *Among the Indians: Eight Years in the Far West, 1858–1866* (Philadelphia, 1868), 354, 363–9; the *Dakotian,* June 16, 1863; John Sunder, *The Fur Trade on the Upper Missouri, 1840–1865,* 244–8; Charles Larpenteur, *Forty Years a Fur Trader on the Upper Missouri* (New York, 1898), Vol. 2, 347–352.

[28] Log of the Steamboat *Shreveport,* 1863. Documents Division, Historical Society of Montana, Helena; see also Boller's comment, *op. cit.,* 358–9.

[29] Boller, *Among the Indians, op. cit.,* 370–3.

[30] The *Dakotian,* January 27, February 3, May 19 and 26, 1863.

[31] J. H. Drips, *Three Years Among the Indians in Dakota* (Kimball, South Dakota, 1894), 26. This is a printed reproduction of a war diary, published thirty years after the events. Very scarce. Newberry Library, Chicago.

[32] Jorstad, *op. cit.,* 326–8; Helen M. White (ed.), *Ho! For the Gold Fields* (St. Paul, 1966), 79.

[33] The *Dakotian,* June 2 and July 7, 1863.

[34] Deposition of George H. Rust, April 18, 1865. In the George H. Rust Papers, 1863–1865, Minnesota Historical Society, St. Paul.

[35] The *Dakotian,* August 25, 1863.

[36] Diary of Henry W. Pierce, in Richard D. Rowen (ed.), "The Second Nebraska's Campaign Against the Sioux," *Nebraska History,* Vol. 44, No. 1 (March, 1863), 26.

[37] The *Dakotian,* August 18, 1863, quoting the *Fort Randall News.*

[38] Amos R. Cherry manuscripts. "Iowa Troops in the Sully Campaigns," *Iowa Journal of History and Politics,* Vol. 20, No. 3 (July, 1922), 418.

[39] Report of Brigadier General Alfred Sully, in Report of the Secretary of War, 1863, *House Ex. Doc.* 1, 38 Cong., 1 sess. (Serial 1184), 495.

[40] Pope to Sully, August 5, 1863, OCPWO, 112–3.

[41] OCPWO, *op. cit.,* 113.

[42] OCPWO, *op. cit.*, 118.

[43] Near modern Ellendale, North Dakota, on Elm Creek, about fifteen miles west of the James River.

[44] Taken principally from a detailed report made by Sully in Report of the Secretary of War, 1863, *op. cit.*, 495–500. See also Drips, *Three Years Among the Indians in Dakota*, 44 and 45. He was a member of the Second Nebraska and participated in the battle; *Daily Missouri Democrat*, October 7, 1863.

Chapter 7. "These Savages Block the Way"

[1] *Daily Missouri Democrat* (St. Louis), October 7, 1863.

[2] The *Dakotian*, October 6, 1863.

[3] Report of the Commissioner of Indian Affairs, 1863, *House Ex. Doc.* 1, 38 Cong., 1 sess (Serial 1182), 270–271.

[4] The *Dakotian*, December 8, 1863.

[5] Report of the Commissioner of Indian Affairs, 1863, *op. cit.*, 141. Latta's comments are found on pages 281 and 282.

[6] Henry A. Boller, *Among the Indians, op. cit.*, 355.

[7] J. H. Drips, *Three Years Among the Indians in Dakota, op. cit.*, 91.

[8] André to Sibley, August 25, 1863 in Henry H. Sibley Papers, A.S. 564, Box 11, 1863–1864, Minnesota Historical Society, St. Paul.

[9] Brown to Sibley, November 26, in Sibley Papers, *ibid.*

[10] Diary of Henry H. Sibley, June 6 to September 13, 1863. Sibley Papers, Correspondence, A.S. 564, Box 16, Minnesota Historical Society, St. Paul.

[11] OCPWO, *op. cit.*, 115–7.

[12] Report of the Secretary of War, 1863, *House Ex. Doc.* 1, 38 Cong., 1 sess. (Serial 1184), 30.

[13] Pope to Sully, August 31, 1863. OCPWO, *op. cit.*, 118–9.

[14] Order of General Alfred Sully from camp near Farm Island, September 16, 1863, the *Dakotian*, October 6, 1863; Frederick T. Wilson, "Fort Pierre and Its Neighbors," *SDHC*, Vol. 1, 310; the *Dakotian*, September 29, 1863.

[15] J. H. Drips, *op. cit.*, 64; De Lorme W. Robinson, "Editorial Notes on Historical Sketch of North and South Dakota," *SDHC*, Vol. 1, 122; Steven Hoekman, "The History of Fort Sully," *SDHC*, Vol. 26, 231.

[16] Report of W. A. Burleigh, October 12, 1863, in Report of the Commissioner of Indian Affairs, 1863, *op. cit.*, 275–7. See also Commissioner Dole's comments, *ibid.*, 140.

[17] R. C. Olin to H. H. Sibley from Milwaukee, November 20, 1863. In H. H. Sibley Papers, Correspondence, 1863–1864, A.S. 564, Box 11, Minnesota Historical Society, St. Paul.

[18] The *Dakotian*, November 17, 1863.

[19] *Ibid.*, December 8, 1863.

[20] *Ibid.*, December 1, 1863.

[21] *Ibid.*, November 17, 1863.

[22] *Ibid.*, September 29, 1863.

[23] Harold L. McElroy, "Mercurial Military: A Study of the Central Mon-

tana Frontier Army Policy," *Montana Magazine of History*, Vol. 4, No. 4 (Autumn 1954), 19.

[24] Henry Reed and LaBarge, Harkness & Company to Commissioner Dole, January 14, 1863 from Washington, D.C. Report of the Commissioner of Indian Affairs, 1863, *op. cit.*, 282–3.

[25] The *Dakotian*, November 3 and December 8, 1863.

[26] *Ibid.*, October 13, 1863.

[27] OCPWO, *op. cit.*, 154–160.

[28] Chouteau to Halleck, March 26, 1864, OCPWO, *op. cit.*, 213–4.

[29] Drips, *op. cit.*, 66.

[30] The *Dakotian*, March 29, 1864.

[31] Sully to Sibley, March 28, 1864, OCPWO, *op. cit.*, 217, 218; Pope to Sully, March 31, 1864, *ibid.*, 223, 224.

[32] Pope to Sibley, April 30, 1864. Henry H. Sibley Papers, Correspondence, 1863–1864, A.S. 564, Box 11, Minnesota Historical Society, St. Paul.

[33] Sibley to Pope, May 9, 1864, *ibid.* Charles Larpenteur, returning to his post at Fort Union, was aboard the *Benton*. On April 26 he noted in his diary that the vessel was at Fort Randall where it was learned there were 1,500 Sioux reported to be waiting at Fort Berthold to stop it. He expressed the belief, however, that "nothing but low water will prevent us from going to try there [*sic*] might." Charles Larpenteur's Journal, Vol. 2, 1864–1866. Minnesota Historical Society, St. Paul.

[34] Sibley to Sully, April 3, 1864, OCPWO, *op. cit.*, 227–9. Sully was in St. Louis at this time.

[35] Pope to Halleck, March 30, 1864, *ibid.*, 220–1.

[36] Halleck to Pope, April 4, 1864; Pope to Halleck, April 5 and Halleck to Pope, April 6, in OCPWO, *op. cit.*, 229–31.

[37] Sibley to Benson, May 10, 1864, OCPWO, *ibid.*, 261–2; Sibley to G. Renville, *ibid.*, 269.

[38] W. P. Dole to Rev. P. J. de Smet, March 21, 1864. Report of the Commissioner of Indian Affairs, 1864, *House Ex. Doc.* 1, 38 Cong., 2 sess. (Serial 1220), 419 and 421.

[39] *Ibid.*, no date, 416.

[40] "Gen. Alfred Sully's Company of Yankton Sioux Indian Scouts," memorandum in behalf of Bill S. 5151, *Sen. Ex. Doc.* 298, 57 Cong., 1 sess. (Serial 4239), 2 and 5; Sully to Pope's office, June 21, 1864, OCPWO, *op. cit.*, 303. Sully said the camp was a mixture of Upper Sioux, Yanktonnais, Two Kettles, Blackfeet Sioux, Miniconjous, Sans Arcs, Brulés and Hunkpapas.

[41] Drips, *op. cit.*, 69 and 70.

[42] Thomas to Sibley from Camp No. 18, July 2, 1864. Sibley Papers, Correspondence, 1863–1864, A. S. 564, Box 11, Minnesota Historical Society, St. Paul; Sully to Pope, July 7, 1864, OCPWO, *op. cit.*, 309. Charles E. Flandrau, who participated in the Minnesota war of 1862 as a colonel, wrote *The History of Minnesota and Tales of the Frontier* (St. Paul, 1900) in which he discussed the 1863 and 1864 Dakota campaigns from the Minnesota vantage point. See pages 187–90 regarding the march of Colonel Minor Thomas.

[43] Sully to Pope, July 7, 1864, *op. cit.*, 309.

Chapter 8. "Hell, with the Fires Put Out"

[1] There has been confusion as to whom the fort honored. In response to an inquiry by Lt. Col. Edwin Mason, Fourth Infantry, from St. Paul, March 25, 1887, the Adjutant General's Office said it was not known for whom it was named, but the opinion was volunteered that: "There can be little doubt, however, that the name of Fort Rice was given in compliment to the Hon. Henry M. Rice of Minnesota." Senator Rice was a lifelong friend of Sibley's. Mary Ann Barnes Williams, *Origins of North Dakota Place Names* (Washburn, North Dakota, 1960?) said the fort was named for "Brig. Gen. Samuel Allen Rice, U.S. Vols." The *Frontier Scout,* a newspaper published at Fort Rice, said in its July 27, 1865, issue, "This Fort was named by the Secretary of War for Brig. Gen. Rice of Mass. who fell in the Battle of the Wilderness." Francis B. Heitman, *Historical Register and Dictionary of the United States* (Washington, 1903), Vol. 1, 826, lists Brigadier General James Clay Rice of Massachusetts and New York, killed May 10, 1864 at the Battle of Laurel Hill, Virginia. Ray H. Mattison, "Fort Rice–North Dakota's First Missouri River Military Post," *North Dakota History* Vol. 20, No. 2 (April 1953), 87–109, says (page 89) that the place was named for "Gen. Clay Rice of Massachusetts." He based the claim on physician Washington Matthews' "The Medical History of Fort Rice, 1864–1878," Vol. 247, 2. Microfilm copy from Adjutant General's Office, Army and Navy Branch, National Archives. James Clay Rice is the most logical candidate for the honor.

[2] Daniel Dill, "Account of Fort Rice." Manuscript in North Dakota Historical Society, Bismarck.

[3] J. H. Drips, *Three Years Among the Indians in Dakota*, 72, 73; Charles E. de Land, "Editorial Notes on Old Fort Pierre and Its Neighbors," *South Dakota Historical Collections,* Vol. 1, 378; *Frontier Scout,* Fort Rice, July 20, 1865; Nicholas Hilger Diary, *Contributions to the Historical Society of Montana,* Vol. 2, 314; Pope to Halleck, November 3, 1864, "Official Correspondence Pertaining to the War of the Outbreak," *South Dakota Historical Collections,* Vol. 8, 351.

[4] Theodore Powell to his sister, July 27, 1864, in Powell (Oliver Stanley and family) Papers, Correspondence, 1860–1867, Minnesota Historical Society, St. Paul.

[5] Powell to his sister, August 13, 1864, *ibid.*

[6] Sully to Pope, July 17, 1864, OCPWO, *op. cit.*, 310 and 311.

[7] Diary of Gilbert Benedict, An Immigrant of 1864. Historical Society of Montana, Helena. See also the printed version in Helen M. White, *Ho! For The Gold Fields* (St. Paul, 1966), 124, 125. Comments dealing with the crossing of the troops are found in the Amos R. Cherry Manuscripts, in "Iowa Troops in the Sully Campaigns," *Iowa Journal of History and Politics,* Vol. 20, No. 3 (July, 1922), 420.

[8] Pope to Sully, August 9, 1864, OCPWO, *op. cit.*, 313.

[9] Diary of Nicholas Overholt, Vol. 1, July 29, 1864. Film, Minnesota Historical Society, St. Paul.

[10] An account of Sully's movements from July 18 through July 29, is found in Sully to Pope, July 31, 1864, OCPWO, *op. cit.*, 360–4.

[11] David L. Kingsbury, "Sully's Expedition Against the Sioux in 1864," *Collections of the Minnesota Historical Society*, Vol. 8, 451.

[12] Descriptions by Sergeant J. H. Drips, *op. cit.*, 132. Diary of Colonel Minor T. Thomas, in "General Sully's Expedition of 1864," *Contributions to the Historical Society of Montana*, Vol. 2, 322; *Frontier Scout*, Fort Union, August 17, 1864.

[13] Drips, *op. cit.*, 132.

[14] *Ibid.*, 83.

[15] Diary of Minor T. Thomas, *op. cit.*, 327. Sergeant Drips called the Yellowstone "a splendid stream" lined with a heavy growth of cottonwood timber and provided with an abundance of game. See page 85.

[16] Kingsbury, *op. cit.*, 458.

[17] Diary of Gilbert Benedict, *op. cit.*, entry for August 18.

[18] Charles Larpenteur's Journal, Vol. 2, 1864–1866. Minnesota Historical Society, St. Paul. Entry for August 21, 1864.

[19] The chronology of Sully's campaign is taken largely from letter and reports he wrote July 7, 17, and 31, August 13, 18, and 29, 1864 in OCPWO, *op. cit.*, 309–64.

[20] Sergeant Amos Cherry, who was among Sully's troops, saw the Fort as a "very pretty place indeed nice painted in fine style. Col. of 30th well contented." Amos R. Cherry manuscripts, in "Iowa Troops in the Sully Campaigns," *op. cit.*, 427.

[21] *Frontier Scout*, Fort Union, July 14, 1864.

[22] Larpenteur's Journal, Vol. 2, *op. cit.*, entry for July 14, 1864; see also Drips, *op. cit.*, 88.

[23] *Frontier Scout*, Fort Union, July 14, 1864.

[24] *Ibid.*, July 27, 1864.

[25] *Ibid.*, August 17, 1864.

[26] Larpenteur's Journal, *op. cit.*, entry for August 13, 1864.

[27] *Ibid.*, entry for August 16, 1864.

[28] *Ibid.*, entry for July 29, 1864. See also note on page 363 of Elliott Coues, *Forty Years a Fur Trader on the Upper Missouri: The Personal Narrative of Charles Larpenteur, 1833–1872*, two volumes (Minneapolis: Ross & Haines, Inc., 1962). The Lakeside Classics edition was published in 1933.

[29] Larpenteur's Journal, *op. cit.*, entry for July 16, 1864.

[30] *Ibid.*, entry for Sunday, December 25, 1865.

[31] *Ibid.*, entry for September 14, 1864.

[32] Hiram Martin Chittenden and Alfred Talbot Richardson, *Life, Letters and Travels of Father Pierre-Jean de Smet, S. J., 1801–1873* (New York, 1905), four volumes, 834 of Vol. 3; P. J. de Smet to W. P. Dole, September 23, 1864 in Report of the Commissioner of Indian Affairs, 1864, *House Ex. Doc.* 1, 38 Cong., 2 sess. (Serial 1220), 423–426. Another reason for the failure of De Smet's mission was his inability to get breed guides to take him on what they regarded as a suicidal trip. They wanted as much as twenty-five pounds sterling to guide him for as few as fifteen to twenty miles.

[33] John Buchanan, "Trip to the Gold Fields of Idaho," *The Montana Post*

(Virginia City), August 27, 1864. Buchanan was editor of the *Post.* He sold it to the better-known D. W. Tilton.

[34] Washington Matthews' description of Fort Stevenson, in *A Report on Barracks and Hospitals with Descriptions of Military Posts,* Circular No. 4, War Department, Surgeon General's Office (Washington, 1870), 394. See also Drips, *op. cit.,* 89.

[35] Much of the material concerning Sully's movements from Fort Union to Fort Rice are taken from his reports to Pope made August 29, September 9, 11 and 16 and from E. D. Townsend to E. M. Stanton, December 19, OCPWO, *op. cit.,* 323–38 and 519. See also Report of Colonel Daniel J. Dill, Fort Rice, October 4, 1864, *ibid.,* 390–2. Fisk's attempted expedition is discussed in W. Turrentine Jackson, "The Fisk Expedition to the Montana Gold Field," *The Pacific Northwest Quarterly,* Vol. 33, No. 3 (July 1942). See also Ethel A. Collins (ed.), "Pioneer Experiences of Horatio H. Larned," *Collections of the State Historical Society of North Dakota,* Vol. 7, 7–19. The most recent and best account of the Fisk expedition is found in Helen M. White, *Ho! For The Gold Fields, op. cit.* It is a complete and thoroughly documented work.

[36] Sully to Pope, October 7, 1864, OCPWO, *op. cit.,* 335.

[37] Chittenden and Richardson, De Smet, *op. cit.,* 823.

[38] Sully to Pope, October 7, 1864, OCPWO, *op. cit.,* 336. By the spring of 1865 Sully disbanded the Indian troops used during the winter and told them he thought their services worth at least $300 each (although they had been promised only $75) and that they would get it in due time. He repeated this to some of them at Washington, D.C. in 1867. They were finally paid the promised $75 each in 1878, at Fort Randall. Memorandum in Behalf of Bill S5151, *Sen. Ex. Doc.* 298, 57 Cong., 1 sess., 1902 (Serial 4239), 7.

[39] The *Dakotian* (Yankton), September 3, 1864.

[40] Pope to Edmunds, June 30, 1864, OCPWO, *op. cit.,* 305 and 306.

[41] Pope to Halleck, November 3, 1864, *ibid.,* 350 and 351.

[42] Edmunds to Commissioner William P. Dole, September 20, 1864, in Report of the Commissioner of Indian Affairs, 1864, *House Ex. Doc.* 1, 38 Cong., 2 sess. (Serial 1220), 403–6.

[43] Report of W. A. Burleigh, October 21, 1864, *ibid.,* 428–30.

[44] Deposition of George H. Rust, April 18, 1865 in George H. Rust Papers, 1863–1865. Minnesota Historical Society, St. Paul.

[45] Report of Samuel N. Latta, October 1, 1864, Report of the Commissioner of Indian Affairs, 1864, *op. cit.,* 417 and 418.

Chapter 9. "The Galvanized Yankees"

[1] Grant to General Henry Halleck, August 9, 1864, "Official Correspondence Pertaining to the War of the Outbreak," *SDHC,* Vol. 8, 428.

[2] The six regiments so raised came from Point Lookout, Rock Island, Alton and Camp Douglas, Illinois; Camp Morton, Indiana and Columbus, Ohio. Summary of U.S. Vol. Regiments, Record Group 94, AGO, P. 3793 (VS), Army and Navy Branch, National Archives.

[3] Pope to Sully, August 16, 1864, OCPWO, *op. cit.*, 442.

[4] The C. A. R. Dimon papers held by the Western Americana Library at Yale University are filled with detail describing the assignment at Fort Rice. D. Alexander Brown, *The Galvanized Yankees* (Urbana: The University of Illinois Press, 1963), used these papers extensively and has used both the Dimon Papers and Brown's book. His chapter 4 deals with the Confederate prisoners at Fort Rice.

[5] Brown, *op. cit.*, 74–77; Dimon Papers, letter of August 29, 1864.

[6] Dimon Papers, letters of September 3 and November 14.

[7] Sully to Pope, October 10, 1874, OCPWO, *op. cit.*, 339; J. H. Drips, *Three Years Among the Indians in Dakota, op. cit.*, 97.

[8] The chronology of Dimon's movements between St. Louis and Fort Rice is taken largely from the Dimon Papers and from Brown's *Galvanized Yankees, op. cit.*

[9] Letters of October 21 and November 1, 1864, Dimon Papers. Post Return, Fort Rice, November 1864.

[10] Letter of November 24, Dimon Papers.

[11] About 1901 Dimon wrote a paper entitled "Army Life Among the Hostile Indians in Dacotah Territory, 1864–1865." Typescript in Dimon Papers.

[12] The poem is found in the Dimon Papers, as are comments on sickness at the post, in a letter of April 8, 1865. For descriptions of Herrick and Adams, see *Frontier Scout*, Fort Rice, August 17, 1865.

[13] Brown, *op. cit.*, 86.

[14] Diary of William L. Larned, entries for October 29, November 8 and 11, 1864. This diary, kept from June 29, 1864 to January 31, 1866, was owned by Horatio H. Larned of Lansing, Michigan. Typescripts may be found in the Newberry Library, Chicago, and the Minnesota Historical Society, St. Paul.

[15] Poems by Adams in Dimon Papers. Many of them also were published in the post's newspaper, *Frontier Scout*.

[16] Dimon Papers; Brown, *op. cit.*, 87.

[17] Dimon Papers, February 12 and 14, 1865, Brown, *op. cit.*, 86.

[18] Letter of February 20, 1865, to Sully, in Dimon Papers. In later years Dimon admitted that his suspicions about subversion among the traders had proved to be incorrect. See "Army Life Among the Hostile Indians on Dacotah Territory, 1864–1865," Dimon Papers.

[19] Letters of May 12 and 26 and June 10, 1865, Dimon Papers.

[20] *Frontier Scout*, Fort Rice, June 29, 1865.

[21] Pope to Sully, February 1, 1865, Dimon Papers.

[22] Dimon to Sully, March 28, 1865, *ibid.*

[23] Journal of Charles Larpenteur, 1864–1868, Vol. 2, entry for May 19, 1865. Minnesota Historical Society, St. Paul.

[24] William B. Upton to Dimon, May 22, June 12 and 19, 1865, Dimon Papers. See also Dimon's letters of February 20, April 23, May 4, 26 and 31, 1865.

[25] Dimon to Sully's headquarters, January 24, 1865, OCPWO, *op. cit.*, 528–30.

[26] Captain Samuel G. Sewall to Adjutant Martin Norton, July 18, 1865, Dimon Papers. See also letters of January 24, March 9, 12 and May 22, 1865, between the Dimon brothers and from Chouteau to Sully, in Dimon Papers.

[27] Mahlon Wilkinson to Newton Edmunds, September 5, 1865. Report of the Commissioner of Indian Affairs, 1865, *House Ex. Doc.* 1, 39 Cong., 1 sess. (Serial 1248), 408–409.

[28] *Frontier Scout,* June 22, 1865; Dimon to Sully, May 26, 1865, Dimon Papers.

[29] Sully to Dimon, May 23, 1865, Dimon Papers.

[30] Dimon to Sully, June 8, 1865, Dimon Papers.

[31] Dimon to Upton, Ben Dimon and Galpin, June 7, 1865, Dimon Papers.

[32] Sully to Pope, June 10, 1865, OCPWO, *op. cit.,* 515–6. Pope to Sully, *ibid.,* 523.

Chapter 10. The Politics of War

[1] Dimon's letter to his sweetheart, October 21, 1864, and Dimon to Sully, December 1, 1864, Dimon Papers, Yale University Library, New Haven.

[2] Post Return, Fort Randall, November, 1864.

[3] Dimon to Sully's headquarters, November 11, 1864, and Dimon to Moreland, November 24, 1864, Dimon Papers.

[4] Dimon to Butler, December 8, 1864; Dimon to Sully, December 18, 1864; Sully to Dimon, January 22, 1864, Dimon Papers.

[5] Dimon to Sully, March 3, 1865, Dimon Papers.

[6] Dimon to Sully, April 3 and 14, 1865, Dimon Papers; Sully to Pope, May 13, 1865, "Official Correspondence Pertaining to the War of the Outbreak," *SDHC,* Vol. 8, 564–565.

[7] Dimon to Sully, April 29, 1865, Dimon Papers; Post Return, Fort Rice, April, 1865.

[8] Dimon to Sully, May 21, 1865, Dimon Papers; Dimon to Sully, June 2, 1865, OCPWO in *SDHC,* Vol. 31, 493; Post Returns, Fort Rice, May and June, 1865; *Frontier Scout* (Fort Rice), June 15, 1865; Brown, *Galvanized Yankees, op. cit.,* 91–93.

[9] Paul C. Phillips (ed.), "Upham Letters from the Upper Missouri," in John W. Hakola (ed.), *Frontier Omnibus* (Missoula: Montana State University Press, 1962), 281.

[10] *Frontier Scout,* June 15, 1865.

[11] *Ibid.,* June 29, 1865.

[12] Sully to Pope, May 13, 1865, OCPWO in *SDHC,* Vol. 8, 564–5.

[13] Sully to Curtis, June 6, 1865, OCPWO in *SDHC,* Vol. 31, 506. (The Official Correspondence is divided between volumes 8 and 31 of the *SDHC* and since citations from both volumes are used in this chapter the difference should be noted.)

[14] Curtis to Sully, May 26, 1865, OCPWO in *SDHC,* Vol. 31, 477; Sully to Pope, May 28, June 3, 1865, *ibid.,* 480 and 502.

[15] Sully to Pope (at St. Louis), April 15, 1865, OCPWO in *SDHC,* Vol. 8, 534 and 545.

[16] J. H. Drips, *Three Years Among the Indians in Dakota, op. cit.*, 101.

[17] Sully to Dimon, June 28, 1865, Dimon Papers.

[18] Sully to Pope, February 7, 1865, OCPWO in *SDHC*, Vol. 8, 533.

[19] Sully to Curtis, February 25, 1865, *ibid.*, 538.

[20] Sully to Pope, January 6, 1865 and Sully to Curtis, February 25, 1865, *ibid.*, 527–8 and 537–9.

[21] Pope to Sibley and Sibley to Pope, May 8, 1865, *ibid.*, 556–557.

[22] Miller to Curtis, June 2, 1865, OCPWO in *SDHC*, Vol. 31, 490–1.

[23] Pope to Sully from St. Louis and Curtis to Sully from Milwaukee, May 23, 1865, *ibid.*, Vol. 31, 471.

[24] Pope to Grant, May 23, 1865 and Grant to Pope, May 17, 1865, OCPWO in *SDHC*, Vol. 8, 579–584 and 566.

[25] See Harold E. Briggs, "Early Freight and Stage Lines in Dakota," *North Dakota Historical Quarterly*, Vol. 3, No. 4 (July, 1929), 236–237, for a discussion of Sawyer's projected road to Virginia City.

[26] A. W. Hubbard to Pope from Sioux City, May 28, 1865, OCPWO in *SDHC*, Vol. 31, 476.

[27] Sully to Pope, May 26, 1865, *ibid.*, 475.

[28] Sully to Pope, June 3, 1865, *ibid.*, 501.

[29] *Union and Dakotaian* (Yankton), May 27, July 1, 1865.

[30] Sully to Dimon, July 2, 1865, Dimon Papers.

[31] Sully to Sibley, June 27, 1865, OCPWO in *SDHC*, Vol. 31, 527.

[32] Sully to Curtis, June 17 (or 27), 1865, *ibid.*, 521.

[33] Charles Larpenteur's Journal, Vol. 2, 1864–1866, entries for April 26 and 27, 1865, Minnesota Historical Society, St. Paul.

[34] Drips, *op. cit.*, 105.

[35] Sully to Pope, July 17, 1865, OCPWO, Vol. 31, 534–5; *Frontier Scout*, July 13, 1865.

[36] Dimon to his parents, July 14, 1865, Dimon Papers; *Frontier Scout*, June 15, July 20, 1865; Statement of Post Surgeon Herrick, July 21, 1865, Dimon Papers; Pattee, "Dakota Campaigns," *SDHC*, V, 338–339.

[37] Dimon to Sully, April 8, 1865, Dimon Papers.

[38] *Frontier Scout*, June 22, 1865.

[39] Sully to Curtis, July 31, 1865, OCPWO in *SDHC*, Vol. 31, 541–4.

[40] *Frontier Scout*, August 10 and 17, 1865. Report of Alfred Sully, July 31, 1865 from Devil's Lake. Report of the Commissioner of Indian Affairs, 1865, *House Ex. Doc.* 1, 39 Cong., 1 sess. (Serial 1248), 389. See also the discussion in Erling Theodore Jorstad, "The Life of Henry Hastings Sibley" (Doctoral dissertation, University of Wisconsin, 1957), 344–354.

[41] Sully to Curtis, July 20, 1865, Report of the Commissioner of Indian Affairs, 1865, *op. cit.*, 388; OCPWO in *SDHC*, Vol. 31, 536–537.

[42] Sully to Curtis, August 8, 1865, Report of the Commissioner of Indian Affairs, 1865, *op. cit.*, 390.

[43] *Frontier Scout*, August 3, 1865; Post Return, Fort Rice, July, 1865.

Chapter 11. "SULLY'S CASE IS PECULIAR"

[1] Dimon to Major J. W. Barnes, November (no date), 1865. Dimon Papers, Yale University Library, New Haven, Conn.
[2] Charges against Adams and Upton are found in the Dimon Papers. They are undated.
[3] Dimon to his uncle, May 10, 1865, Dimon Papers.
[4] Sully to Curtis, July 23, 1865 in "Official Correspondence Pertaining to the War of the Outbreak," *SDHC*, Vol. 31, 538–9.
[5] Charles Larpenteur's Journal, Vol. 2, 1864–1866, Minnesota Historical Society, St. Paul.
[6] J. H. Drips, *Three Years Among the Indians in Dakota, op. cit.*, 109.
[7] James Boyd Hubbell Papers, 1865–1906, Minnesota Historical Society, St. Paul.
[8] *Ibid.*, Agreement of March 23, 1865; *Frontier Scout*, September 14, 1865.
[9] Charles Larpenteur's Journal, *op. cit.*, entry for August 18 and September 15.
[10] *Frontier Scout*, August 31, 1865.
[11] Dimon to Sully, December 18, 1864, Dimon Papers.
[12] *Frontier Scout*, August 24, 1865. John Pattee, in his "Dakota Campaigns," *SDHC*, Vol. 5, 344, used the identical sentence. He may have taken it from the *Scout*, or he may have written it originally for Adams' use.
[13] Grant to Sherman, July 20, 1865; Grant to Pope, July 21, 1865, OCPWO in *SDHC*, Vol. 31, 535–6.
[14] *Frontier Scout*, August 3 and 24, 1865; Drips, *Three Years, op. cit.*, 132.
[15] *Union and Dakotaian* (Yankton), July 1, 1865.
[16] Pope to Grant, July 27, 1865, OCPWO in *SDHC*, Vol. 31, 539–40.
[17] J. R. Brown to H. H. Sibley, Dec. 13, 1864, Sibley Papers, Correspondence, A.S. 564, Box 11, Minnesota Historical Society, St. Paul. In the quotation the italics are mine.
[18] Pope to Sully, August 25, 1865; Sully to Pope, August 26, 1865, OCPWO in *SDHC*, Vol. 31, 552–4.
[19] Report of Gen. Alfred Sully, September 14, 1865 in Report of the Commissioner of Indian Affairs, 1865, *House Ex. Doc.* 1, 39 Cong., 1 sess. (Serial 1248), 394; Sully to Pope, August 26, 1865, OCPWO in *SDHC*, Vol. 31, 553–4.
[20] Doane Robinson, "Ending the Outbreak," *SDHC*, Vol. 9, 409–10; Erling Theodore Jorstad, "The Life of Henry Hastings Sibley" (Doctoral dissertation, University of Wisconsin, 1957), 344–54; John Pope to Newton Edmunds, May 8, 1865, OCPWO in *SDHC*, Vol. 8, 555.
[21] Doane Robinson, *op. cit.*, 417–43.
[22] Report of the Commissioner of Indian Affairs, 1865, *op. cit.*, 196.
[23] *Union and Dakotaian* (Yankton), May 13 and 20, 1865.
[24] Harlan to Stanton, May 29, 1865, OCPWO in *SDHC*, Vol. 1, 481.
[25] Report of the Secretary of the Interior, 1865, *House Ex. Doc.* 1, 39 Cong., 1 sess. (Serial 1248), viii.

[26] Pope to Grant, June 14, 1865. Report of the Commissioner of Indian Affairs, 1865, *op. cit.*, 381.

[27] Pope to Sully, June 21, 1865, OCPWO in *SDHC*, Vol. 31, 523.

[28] Edmunds to D. N. Cooley, from Fort Sully, October 14, 1865. Report of the Commissioner of Indian Affairs, 1865, *op. cit.*, 369.

[29] John Pattee, *op. cit.*, 342–9.

[30] Pope to Sully, August 18, 1865, OCPWO in *SDHC*, Vol. 31, 552.

[31] Report of the Commission to Treat with Sioux of the Upper Missouri, in Report of the Commissioner of Indian Affairs, 1865, *op. cit.*, 721–3.

[32] Edith M. Duncan (ed.), "A Trip to the States in 1865 by J. Allen Hosmer," in John W. Hakola (ed.), *Frontier Omnibus* (Missoula, 1962), 305–8.

[33] Doane Robinson, *op. cit.*, 455; *Nebraska Daily Republican*, October 19 and 23, 1865.

[34] Report of a Special Correspondent to the *St. Paul Press*, quoted in *SDHC*, Vol. 9, 454.

[35] Edmunds to D. N. Cooley, October 14, 1865. Report of the Commissioner of Indian Affairs, 1865; *op. cit.*, 368.

Chapter 12. A Military Frontier

[1] William J. Peterson, "The Log of the *Henry M. Shreve* to Fort Benton in 1869," *Mississippi Valley Historical Review*, Vol. 31, No. 4 (March 1945), 536.

[2] *Nebraska Daily Republican*, March 16, 1866.

[3] Report by Major General John Pope, on the condition and necessities of the Department of the Missouri, February 25, 1866, *House Ex. Doc.* 76, 39 Cong., 1 sess. (Serial 1263), 1–5.

[4] *The Saint Paul Pioneer*, February 9, 1866.

[5] Report of the Northwestern Treaty Commission to the Sioux of the Upper Missouri, in Report of the Commissioner of Indian Affairs, 1866, *House Ex. Doc.* 1, 39 Cong., 2 sess. (Serial 1284), 171–3.

[6] Sherman to Col. T. S. Bowers, AAG, U.S. Army, January 13, 1866. Dakota Territorial Archives, Historical Society of North Dakota.

[7] W. T. Sherman to D. B. Sacket, April 19, 1866. "Protection Across the Continent," *House Ex. Doc.* 23, 39 Cong., 2 sess. (Serial 1288), 20.

[8] George F. Price, *Across the Continent with the Fifth Cavalry* (1883: reprinted by Antiquarian Press, New York, 1959), 248.

[9] Diary of Sarah Elizabeth Canfield, April 3, 1866. Historical Society of North Dakota. This is also published. Ray H. Mattison (ed.), "An Army Wife on the Upper Missouri: The Diary of Sarah E. Canfield, 1866–1868," *North Dakota Historical Quarterly*, Vol. 20, No. 4 (October 1953), 197.

[10] C. C. Gray to the Fort Randall Post Adjutant, August 13, 1866. Records of U.S. Army Commands, Fort Randall. Letters and Telegrams Received, 1856–1861. R.G. 98, Army and Navy Branch, National Archives.

[11] Sacket's Report in "Protection Across the Continent," *op. cit.*, 22–8.

[12] D. H. Weston Diary, Historical Society of Montana, Helena.

[13] Sacket's Report, *op. cit.*, 29–33.

[14] Steven Hoekman, "The History of Fort Sully," *SDHC*, Vol. 26, 250; Edmunds to Cooley, March 7, 1866 in Report of Commissioner of Indian Affairs, 1866, *op. cit.*, 165.

[15] Sacket's Report, *op. cit.*, 34.

[16] Post Medical Histories, Fort Sully, Record Book 145 and George S. Andrews to H. G. Litchfield, July 26, 1866, Reservation File, Fort Sully. Both in R.G. 94, AGO Files, Army and Navy Branch, N.A.; Hoekman, "History of Fort Sully," *op. cit.*, 240–1.

[17] Canfield Diary, entry for April 8, 197–8 in printed form.

[18] Weston Diary, entry for May 31, 1866.

[19] Sacket's Report, *op. cit.*, 35–43; Post Return, Fort Rice, June, 1866.

[20] William L. Larned Diary, Newberry Library, Chicago. Larned's estimate of the ferocity of the Indians around Fort Rice apparently was fairly accurate. Over a decade later its commanding officer, Captain J. S. Poland wrote a history of the place and commented that "in the spring of 1866 the Sioux war being over the Volunteers were relieved." On June 3, a few days after Sacket's departure, five companies of the Third Infantry, under Major J. N. G. Whistler, relieved the Wisconsin troops, leaving the strength at about four hundred men. See Report of Captain James S. Poland, July 20, 1878, in Department of Dakota, Letters Sent, R.G. 98, Army and Navy Branch, N.A.; Post Return, Fort Rice, July, 1866.

[21] De Lorme W. Robinson, "Editorial Notes on Historical Sketch of North and South Dakota," *SDHC*, Vol. 1, 134–5; *Contributions to the Historical Society of Montana*, Vol. 10, 289.

[22] Canfield Diary, entry for May 20, 1866, 201 in the printed version.

[23] Sacket's Report, *op. cit.*, 44–5.

[24] Weston Diary, *op. cit.*, entry for June 3, 1866.

[25] Canfield Diary, entry for June 5, 1866, 204 in the printed version.

[26] Sacket's Report, *op. cit.*, 46.

[27] Weston Diary, entry for June 3, 1866.

[28] Records of U.S. Army Posts, Camps and Stations, N.A.; Post Return, Fort Buford, October 1866. See also Robert G. Athearn, "The Fort Buford 'Massacre'," *Mississippi Valley Historical Review*, Vol. 41, No. 4 (March 1955), 678.

[29] Charles Larpenteur's Journal, Vol. 2, 1864–1866, Minnesota Historical Society, St. Paul.

Chapter 13. The Fight for the River

[1] Report of the Commissioner of Indian Affairs, 1872, *House Ex. Doc.* 1, part 5, 42 Cong., 3 sess. (Serial 1560), 398.

[2] *Saint Paul Pioneer*, February 10, 1867.

[3] Report of Captain C. W. Howell, "Improvement of the Missouri River," *House Ex. Doc.* 136, 40 Cong., 2 sess. (Serial 1337), 9.

[4] Report of W. T. Sherman, July 1, 1867 (from St. Louis). Report of the Secretary of War, 1867, *House Ex. Doc.* 1, 40 Cong., 2 sess. (Serial 1324), 67.

[5] *Union and Dakotaian*, August 17, 1867.

[6] *Ibid.*, February 9, May 18 and June 15, 1867.
[7] *Union and Dakotaian,* May 25 and June 15, 1867.
[8] Sherman to Grant, March 13, 1867, Letters and Telegrams Received, 1866–1868, Headquarters of the Army, N.A.; Sherman to Leet, March 13, 1867, *ibid.*
[9] *Union and Dakotaian,* May 18, June 22 and June 29, 1867. The *Nonpareil* of Council Bluffs, Iowa, believed the story.
[10] Philadelphia *Inquirer,* April 1, 1867; *New York Times,* April 2 and 6, 1867. For further detail see Athearn, "The Fort Buford 'Massacre,'" *op. cit.*
[11] Post Return, Fort Buford, July and November, 1866.
[12] Post Return, Fort Buford, December 1866.
[13] Charles W. Hoffman to his brother at Fort Randall, January 10. Published in the *Union and Dakotaian,* March 2, 1867; Post Return, January, 1867.
[14] Post Return, Fort Buford, January, February, 1867.
[15] *Union and Dakotaian,* March 30, April 13 and 20, May 18, 1867.
[16] Charles Larpenteur's Last Journal, entry for August 2, 1867, Minnesota Historical Society, St. Paul.
[17] Report of Captain C. W. Howell, *op. cit.*, 20.
[18] Maria Brace Kimball, *A Soldier-Doctor of Our Army* (Boston, 1917), 43–4; Post Return, Fort Buford, August 1867.
[19] Mahlon Wilkinson to Hon. A. J. Faulk from Fort Berthold, July 15, 1867. Report of the Commissioner of Indian Affairs, 1867.
[20] Lt. Cornelius Cusick to 2nd Lt. P. H. Ellis, Fort Buford, August 24, 1867. Letters Received, R.G. 94, U.S. Army Commands, Army and Navy Branch, N.A.; Rankin to Postmaster General, August 11, 1867, Letters Sent, 1867–1868, Fort Buford, R.G. 98, *ibid.*
[21] Kimball, *op. cit.*, 45–7.
[22] Larpenteur, *op. cit.*, August 2, 1867; Howell's Report, *op. cit.*, 409.
[23] Kimball, *op. cit.*, 37.
[24] "Log of the *Deer Lodge* on the Missouri River, 1867," *National Waterways* (February 1930), 45. Clipping in Montana Historical Society, Helena.
[25] Rankin to 1st Lt. James M. Marshall (AAAG for the Middle District), August 24 and September 28, 1867. Letters Sent, 1867–1868, Fort Buford, R.G. 98, *op. cit.* De Trobriand's endorsement is dated August 29.
[26] Lucile M. Kane (ed.), *Military Life in Dakota: The Journal of Phillipe Regis de Trobriand* (St. Paul, 1951) presents a full picture of life at Fort Stevenson and along the Missouri River frontier. See page 155.
[27] Kane, *ibid.*, 172, 193, 229, 296, 353; Post Return, Fort Buford, May 1868.
[28] Correspondence of November 7, 1867 and January 4, 1868. Record of U.S. Army Commands, Letters Sent, Fort Buford, R.G. 98, *op. cit.*
[29] Larpenteur, *op. cit.*, December 8, 1867.
[30] Kimball, *op. cit.*, 46.
[31] Rankin to Post Council of Administration, November 30, 1867. Record of U.S. Army Commands, Letters Received, Fort Buford, R.G. 98, *op. cit.*
[32] Post Return, Fort Randall, June, 1867; *Yankton and Dakotaian,* June 8, 1867.

[33] Report of Captain C. W. Howell, *op. cit.*, 16–17.

[34] Joseph Henry Taylor, *Sketches of Frontier and Indian Life on the Upper Missouri and Great Plains* (Bismarck, 1897), 131.

[35] Report of Captain C. W. Howell, *op. cit.*, 19.

[36] A Report on Barracks and Hospitals, Circular #4, Surgeon General's Office (Washington, 1870), 396; Post Return, Fort Stevenson, October 1867.

[37] Report of Alfred H. Terry, October 5, 1868 in Report on the Secretary of War, 1868, *House Ex. Doc.* 1, 40 Cong., 3 sess. (Serial 1367), 34.

[38] Report of Captain C. W. Howell, *op. cit.*, 397.

[39] Diary of Mrs. W. F. Sanders, Entry for May 28. Montana Historical Society, Helena.

[40] Report of C. T. Campbell, U.S. Special Agent, to N. G. Taylor, from Yankton, June 13, 1867. Report of the Commissioner of Indian Affairs, 1867, *House Ex. Doc.* 1, 40 Cong., 2 sess. (Serial 1326), 239, 240.

[41] Report of Captain C. W. Howell, *op. cit.*, 394; *Union and Dakotaian*, May 23, 1868. This item gave a figure of forty-six through trips to the head of navigation.

[42] Sully to N. G. Taylor from Fort Sully, June 9, 1867. Report of the Commissioner of Indian Affairs, 1867, *op. cit.*, 244.

[43] Journal of Stephen A. Spitzley, July 5, 1867. Montana Historical Society, Helena.

[44] Larpenteur, *op. cit.*, June 30, July 1 and July 7, 1867.

[45] Robert G. Athearn, *William Tecumseh Sherman and the Settlement of the West* (Norman, Oklahoma, 1956), 177.

[46] *Union and Dakotaian*, June 20 and July 18, 1868.

Chapter 14. The Terrors of the Left Bank

[1] Diary of Mrs. Mary E. Cook, May 18, 1868, Historical Society of Montana, Helena; Charles Larpenteur's Last Journal, May 23, 1868, Minnesota Historical Society, St. Paul.

[2] Report of Captain F. Clark, AAAG, Middle District, January, 1868. Record of U.S. Army Commands, Letters Received, Fort Buford, Doc. File 1867–1872, Army and Navy Branch, N.A. During part of the year the famed frontiersman "Yellowstone" Kelly carried the mail between Buford and Stevenson and on one trip he had to kill two attackers in order to complete the trip. Luther S. Kelly, *"Yellowstone Kelly"; The Memoirs of Luther S. Kelly*, ed. by Milo M. Quaife (New Haven, 1926), 44. See also Lucile Kane (ed.), *Military Life in Dakota: The Journal of Phillipe Regis de Trobriand* (St. Paul, 1951), 355.

[3] Larpenteur, *op. cit.*, June 4, 1868.

[4] Post Return, Fort Buford, May 1868.

[5] P. Peterson to Col. A. W. Bowman, June 9, 1868. Records of U.S. Army Commands, Letters Received, Fort Buford, File 1867–1872, *op. cit.*

[6] Lt. J. M. Marshall, AAAG, Middle District, to Col. A. W. Bowman, July 24, 1868, *ibid.*

[7] Post Returns, Fort Buford, July and August 1868.

[8] Accounts of the fight are found in Post Return, Fort Buford, August,

1868; C. J. Dickey to J. M. Marshall at Fort Stevenson, August 20, 1868, Records of U.S. Army Commands, Letters Sent, Fort Buford, R.G. 98, Army and Navy Branch, N.A.; Kimball, *Soldier-Doctor, op. cit.*, 49–51; Larpenteur, *op. cit.*, August 20, 1868.

[9] C. J. Dickey to J. M. Marshall, September 18, 1868. Records of U.S. Army Commands, Letters Sent, Fort Buford, R.G. 98, Army and Navy Branch, N.A.; Post Return, Fort Buford, September, 1868; Larpenteur, *op. cit.*, notation between 1868 and 1869 entries.

[10] Larpenteur, *op. cit.*

[11] Dickey to Lt. George Mitchell, Post Adjutant, Thirty-First Infantry, September 27, 1868. Record of U.S. Army Commands, Letters Received, Fort Buford, R.G. 98, *op. cit.*

[12] Post Return, Fort Buford, September, 1868; Kane, *op. cit.*, 352–4.

[13] Little to J. M. Marshall, February 7 and 14, 1869. Records of U.S. Army Commands, Letters Sent, Fort Buford, R.G. 98, *op. cit.;* Larpenteur, *op. cit.*, entry for January 8, 1869. John Girard was working for the firm of F. F. Girard.

[14] Marshall to Little, February 20, 1869. Records of U.S. Army Commands, Letters Received, Fort Buford, R.G. 98, *op. cit.*

[15] Statement of E. H. Townsend, Dec. 26, 1869, *ibid.*

[16] Little to Marshall, February 4, 1869, Records of U.S. Army Commands, Letters Sent, Fort Buford, R.G. 98, *op. cit.;* Larpenteur, *op. cit.*, January 13, 1869.

[17] Little to Marshall, March 6, 1869, Records of U.S. Army Commands, R.G. 98, *op. cit.*

[18] Little to Marshall, February 14, 1869, *ibid.*

[19] Larpenteur, *op. cit.*, March 27, 1869.

[20] Agreement of C. Francis Bates, James B. Hubbell and J. A. Smith & Company, March 9, 1869. Document in James Boyd Hubbell Papers, 1865–1906, Minnesota Historical Society, St. Paul.

[21] Post Return, Fort Buford, May and June, 1869; Correspondence of Henry A. Morrow, May 26, June 22, August 10 and 19, 1869; Records of U.S. Army Commands, 1869, Fort Buford, Letters Sent, R.G. 98, *op. cit.*

[22] *Sioux City Weekly Times,* April 30, 1870; Joseph Henry Taylor, *Sketches of Frontier and Indian Life on the Upper Missouri and Great Plains,* 111; Post Return, Fort Buford, August 1869.

[23] Henry A. Morrow to O. D. Green, AAG at St. Paul, August 15, 25 and November 3, 1869. Records of U.S. Army Commands, Fort Buford, Letters Sent, R.G. 98, *op. cit.*

[24] Report of Major General W. S. Hancock, October 20, 1869. Report of the Secretary of War, 1869, *House Ex. Doc.* 1, part 2, 41 Cong., 2 sess. (Serial 1412), 58.

[25] Report of Lieutenant Colonel Samuel B. Holabird of a Reconnaissance made by him in the Department of Dakota, in 1869, *Sen. Ex. Doc.* 8, 41 Cong., 3 sess. (Serial 1440), 9.

[26] A Report on Barracks and Hospitals with Descriptions of Military Posts, Circular No. 4, War Department, Surgeon General's Office, Washington, 1870, 395–6.

[27] *Ibid.*, 397–9.

[28] Report of Samuel B. Holabird, *op. cit.*, 9–11.

[29] Letters of John V. Bean, October 12 and November 24, 1868, June 22 and August 17, 1869, North Dakota Historical Society, Bismarck; A Report on Barracks and Hospitals, *op. cit.*, 399; Post Medical Histories, September 16, 1869, Fort Rice, R.G. 98, Record Book 247, Army and Navy Branch, N.A.

[30] *Union and Dakotaian*, June 6, 1868.

[31] John Bean (to Mary Bean), *op. cit.*, June 15, 1869.

[32] Taylor, *Sketches of Frontier and Indian Life, op. cit.*, 62–3.

[33] A Report on Barracks and Hospitals, *op. cit.*, 399.

[34] Bean (to James Bean), *op. cit.*, March 28, 1869.

[35] Bean (to Mrs. Mary P. Bean, his mother), *ibid.*, May 11, 1869.

[36] Bean (to Mary Bean), *ibid.*, August 3, 1869; Post Return, Fort Stevenson, August, 1869. Life at Fort Stevenson, 1867–1868, is described in detail in Kane, *op. cit.*

[37] Report of the Secretary of War, 1868, *House Ex. Doc.* 1, 40 Cong., 3 sess. (Serial 1367), 8.

[38] "Talks and Councils Held with the Indians, 1866–1869," Newberry Library, 95–104; *Union and Dakotaian*, June 6 and September 12, 1868; Elwyn B. Robinson, *History of North Dakota* (Lincoln, Nebraska, 1966), 104.

[39] Report of Lieutenant Colonel Samuel B. Holabird, *op. cit.*, 14 and 15.

[40] Report of Major General W. S. Hancock, October 20, 1869, *House Ex. Doc.* 1, 41 Cong., 2 sess. (Serial 1412), 65.

Chapter 15. The Reservation Frontier

[1] Report of Alfred H. Terry, Headquarters, Department of Dakota, St. Paul, October 5, 1868. Report of the Secretary of War, 1868, *House Ex. Doc.* 1, 40 Cong., 3 sess. (Serial 1367), 34.

[2] Report of Lieutenant Colonel Samuel B. Holabird of a Reconnaissance made by him in the Department of Dakota, in 1869, *Sen. Ex. Doc.* 8, 41 Cong., 3 sess. (Serial 1440), 13, 14.

[3] R. F. Pettigrew to the editor, *Sioux City Weekly Times*, May 28, 1870.

[4] *Sioux City Weekly Times*, May 21, 1870.

[5] Post Returns, Fort Randall, May and June, 1870.

[6] A Report on Barracks and Hospitals with Descriptions of Military Posts, Circular No. 4, War Department, Surgeon General's Office, Washington, 1870, 387.

[7] Post Return, Fort Randall, 1869, indicates that one woodcutter was killed on the tenth of that month within a mile of the post.

[8] Post Return, Fort Randall, October, 1869.

[9] Holabird, *op. cit.*, 12 and 13; Report on Barracks and Hospitals, *op. cit.*, 389.

[10] *Union and Dakotaian*, June 6, 1868; Steven Hoekman, "The History of Fort Sully," *SDHC*, Vol. 26, 234.

[11] The store, owned by George H. Durfee and C. R. Peck, both Iowans, was operated by a brother of Durfee.

[12] Bean (to Mary Bean), July 19, 1869, in Bean Letters, North Dakota Historical Society, Bismarck.

[13] *Sioux City Weekly Times,* October 15, 1870.

[14] Holabird, *op. cit.,* 11 and 12; Report on Barracks, *op. cit.,* 390–4.

[15] W. O. Taylor to O. G. Libby, February 25, 1891. Orin Grant Libby Papers, A85, Box 12, Folder 1, North Dakota Historical Society, Bismarck.

[16] Post Return, Fort Buford, June 1870.

[17] W. W. Ivey to Commanding Officer, Fort Buford, June 11, 1870. Records of U.S. Army Commands, Letters Received, Fort Buford, R.G. 98, Army and Navy Branch, N.A.

[18] Black Eye to Colonel Gilbert, August 14, 1870, *ibid.*

[19] Sheridan to the Secretary of War, quoted in *Sioux City Weekly Times,* August 28, 1871.

[20] Larpenteur's Last Journal, September 24, 1870. Minnesota Historical Society, St. Paul.

[21] Larpenteur, *ibid.,* March 3, 1871; Dr. J. P. Kimball to Post Adjutant, Letters Received, Fort Buford, R.G. 98, *op. cit.;* W. H. Carey to Henry Morrow, February 16, 1870, *ibid.*

[22] Larpenteur, *op. cit.,* September 14–20, 1870.

[23] Charles Larpenteur to O. D. Greene, August 18, 1870, Records of U.S. Army Commands, Letters Received, Fort Buford, R.G. 98, *op. cit.*

[24] Letter to G. Ray Ham in *Sioux City Weekly Times,* June 10, 1871.

[25] A Report on Barracks and Hospitals, *op. cit.,* 400–3; William Logan to William English, September 27, 1870, Record of U.S. Army Commands, Letters Received, Fort Buford, R.G. 98, *op. cit.*

[26] *Sioux City Daily Times,* June 15, August 3, October 12, December 29, 1869 and April 30, 1870; William Peterson, "The Log of the *Henry M. Shreve* to Fort Benton in 1869," *Mississippi Valley Historical Review,* Vol. 31, No. 4 (March 1945), 539.

[27] *Sioux City Weekly Times,* May 21, 1870.

[28] *Sioux City Daily Times,* March 28, 1870.

[29] *Sioux City Daily Times,* September 5, 22 and December 22, 1869; *Sioux City Weekly Times,* September 23, 1871.

[30] Report of the Secretary of the Interior, 1868, *House Ex. Doc.* 1, 40 Cong., 3 sess. (Serial 1366), xv.

[31] H. M. Robinson to Hon. J. C. B. Davis, Acting Secretary of State, from Winnipeg, May 30, 1870. Copy No. 38 in Records of U.S. Army Commands, Letters Received, Fort Buford, R.G. 98, *op. cit.*

[32] Larpenteur, *op. cit.,* September 25 and November 5, 1870, Report of W. S. Hancock, November 1, 1870 in Report of the Secretary of War, 1870, *House Ex. Doc.* 1, part 2, 41 Cong., 3 sess. (Serial 1446), 28 and 29; Post Return, Fort Buford, October 1870.

[33] S. B. Hayman to Department of Dakota, St. Paul, March 21, 1871. Records of U.S. Army Commands, Letters Sent, 1871–1876, Fort Stevenson, R.G. 98, *op. cit.*

[34] J. B. Irvine, "New Fort Sully," in *History of Sully County* (Onida, S.D.,

1939), 24; Hoekman, *op. cit.*, 253; Post Returns, Fort Randall, August and October, 1871; Report of U.S. Indian Agent J. C. O'Connor, Grand River Agency, September 9, 1871 in Report of the Commissioner of Indian Affairs, 1871, *House Ex. Doc.* 1, part 4, 41 Cong., 3 sess. (Serial 1449), 526; Report of Lieutenant General P. H. Sheridan, November 4, 1871, Annual Report of the Secretary of War, 1871, *House Ex. Doc.* 1, part 2, 42 Cong., 2 sess. (Serial 1503), 22; Diary of William P. Zahn, September 9, 1871, Zahn Manuscript B67, North Dakota Historical Society, Bismarck; Captain D. C. Poole, *Among the Sioux of Dakota: Eighteen Months Experience as an Indian Agent* (New York, 1881), 111.

[35] Report of W. S. Hancock, November 1, 1870, *op. cit.*, 26.

[36] *Sioux City Weekly Times,* April 30, 1870; Harry H. Anderson, "A History of the Cheyenne River Indian Agency and its Military Post, Fort Bennett, 1878–1891," *SDHC*, Vol. 28 (1956), 390–551; James S. Foster, *Outlines of the History of the Territory of Dakota and Emigrant's Guide to the Free Lands of the Northwest, SDHC,* Vol. 14, 175–6.

[37] Records of U.S. Army Posts, Camps and Stations, Vol. I, n.p., Army and Navy Branch, N.A.

[38] *Sioux City Weekly Times,* May 28, 1870.

[39] *Ibid.*, April 30, 1870.

[40] Report of Captain W. Clifford, Indian Agent at Fort Berthold, August 1, 1870, in Report of Commissioner of Indian Affairs, 1870, *House Ex. Doc.* 1, part 4, 41 Cong., 3 sess. (1870), 687.

[41] Poole, *Among the Sioux, op. cit.*, 111.

[42] *Sioux City Weekly Times,* August 26, 1871.

[43] *Ibid.*, November 18, 1871.

[44] *Ibid.*, July 22, August 12 and 26, 1871.

Chapter 16. Forts Among the Farmers

[1] Reports of Philip H. Sheridan, October 12, 1872 and October 1, 1874 in Reports of the Secretary of War for those years.

[2] W. B. Hazen to *New York Tribune,* February 27, 1874 and Alfred Sully to Hazen, June 18, 1874, in W. B. Hazen, *Our Barren Lands* (Cincinnati, 1875), 7, 14, and 15.

[3] Statement of F. A. Walker, January 19, 1872, copy in Letters Received, Fort Buford, R.G. 98, Records of United States Army Commands, N.A.

[4] Report of Edmond Palmer, September 8, 1874, in Report of the Commissioner of Indian Affairs, 1874, 246–247.

[5] Elizabeth B. Custer, *Boots and Saddles or Life in Dakota with General Custer* (New York, 1885), 88; in *Sioux City Weekly Times,* February 14, 1874.

[6] Robert G. Athearn, *William Tecumseh Sherman and the Settlement of the West* (Norman, Oklahoma, 1956), 179; *Sioux City Weekly Times,* March 16 and 30, 1872 and March 6, 1875.

[7] Sergeant John E. Cox, "Soldiering in Dakota Territory in the Seventies: A Communication," *North Dakota Historical Quarterly,* Vol. 6, No. 1 (October 1931), 65; *Sioux City Weekly Times,* August 15 and 29, 1874; Post

Return, Fort Abraham Lincoln, August 1874; Report of P. H. Sheridan, October 1, 1874, Report of the Secretary of War, 1874, *House Ex. Doc.* 1, part 2, 43 Cong., 2 sess. Vol. I (Serial 1634), 24. See also Watson Parker, *Gold in the Black Hills* (Norman, 1966), Chapter 2.

[8] Cox, *op. cit.*, 66 and 67; Post Returns, Fort Randall, May, June, July and August 1875.

[9] Russell Reid, "Fort Lincoln State Park," *North Dakota Historical Quarterly,* Vol. 8, No. 2 (January 1941), 101–13; Report of W. S. Hancock, October 3, 1872, in Report of Secretary of War, 1872, *House Ex. Doc.* 1, part 2, 42 Cong., 3 sess. (Serial 1558), 39 and 43; J. B. Irvine, "New Fort Sully," in *History of Sully County* (Onida, S.D., 1939), 27; Clement Lounsberry, *Early History of North Dakota* (Washington, 1919), 338; Post Returns, Fort Abraham Lincoln, 1872–1891.

[10] Sherman to Sheridan, October 7, 1872, Philip H. Sheridan Papers, Library of Congress; Report of the Commissioner of Indian Affairs, 1872, *House Ex. Doc.* 1, part 5, 42 Cong., 2 sess. (Serial 1460), 397; Report of W. S. Hancock, October 3, 1872, *op. cit.*, 39 and 40; Post Returns, Fort Rice, July and August 1872; Post Returns, Fort Randall, July 1872.

[11] Excerpt from "Locality and History of the Post." Post Medical Histories, Fort Sully, R.G. 94, Book 147 (1873–1881), Army and Navy Branch, N.A.

[12] Diary of William P. Sanford, Yale Americana Collection, Yale University; R. H. Day to Post Adjutant, November 27, 1873, Letters Received, Fort Buford, R.G. 98, *op. cit.*

[13] John E. Cox, *op. cit.*, 78–9.

[14] Charles F. Hackett, "Along the Missouri in the 70s", *SDHC,* Vol. 8, 31.

[15] John Burke to Captain James Humbert, June 3 and 5, 1876, Letters Received, Fort Rice, R.G. 98, *op. cit.;* F. M. Gibson (Post Adjutant) to J. B. Pitts (Post Trader), January 18, 1878 and Elmer Otis to AAG, March 1, 1878, Letters Sent, Fort Rice, *ibid.;* William Welsh, *Report of a Visit to the Sioux and Ponka Indians on the Missouri River* (Washington, 1872), 30.

[16] Will G. Robinson, "Benny Moran's Reminiscences of Fort Randall," *SDHC,* Vol. 23, 268–70.

[17] Marie D. Gorgas and Burton J. Hendrick, *William Crawford Gorgas* (New York, 1924), 53 and 56.

[18] Report of W. T. Sherman, November 6, 1882, Report of the Secretary of War, 1882, *House Ex. Doc.* 1, part 2, Vol. 1, 47 Cong., 2 sess. (Serial 2091), 8.

[19] Frank Peckham to Albert Dollenmayer from Fort Sully, September 18, October 15, 1883 and January 14, 1884. Albert Dollenmayer Papers, Letters, 1868–1884. Minnesota Historical Society, St. Paul.

[20] Report of Benjamin F. Pope, Post Surgeon, February and December, 1881. Post Medical Histories, Fort Sully, R.G. 94, *op. cit.;* Peckham, *op. cit.*, December 17, 1883.

[21] Charles S. Farnsworth Letters, December 30, 1891, January 14, March 4, 27 and November 6, 1892. Farnsworth Letter Book, North Dakota Historical Society, Bismarck.

[22] Report of John Gibbon, October 4, 1878, Report of the Secretary of War, 1878, *House Ex. Doc.* 1, part 2, Vol. 1, 45 Cong., 3 sess. (Serial 1843),

65 and 66; Report of Alfred Terry, November 12, 1877, Report of the Secretary of War, 1877, *House Ex. Doc.* 1, part 2, Vol. 1, 45 Cong., 2 sess. (Serial 1794), 519; Report of W. T. Sherman, Report of the Secretary of War, 1876, *House Ex. Doc.* 1, part 2, 44 Cong., 2 sess. (Serial 1742), 39.

[23] Gibbon's Report of 1878; Sheridan's Report of 1880; Report of Secretary Alexander Ramsey, 1880 and Report of Robert T. Lincoln, 1884.

[24] Report of the Secretary of the Interior, 1886, *House Ex. Doc.* 1, part 5, 49 Cong., 2 sess. (Serial 2467), 68.

[25] Reports of Thomas H. Ruger, August 30, 1887, Report of the Secretary of War, 1887, *House Ex. Doc.* 1, part 2, Vol. 1, 50 Cong., 1 sess. (Serial 2533), 137 and September 15, 1888 in Report of the Secretary of War, 1888, *House Ex. Doc.* 1, part 2, Vol. 1, 50 Cong., 2 sess. (Serial 2628), 158.

[26] Abandoned Military Reservations. Letter from the Secretary of War, Relative to the Disposition of Abandoned Military Reservations, *House Ex. Doc.* 90, 46 Cong., 3 sess. (Serial 1978), 16 and 17; Reports of Alfred Terry, October 8, 1883 and P. H. Sheridan, October 17, 1883, both in report of the Secretary of War, 1883, *House Ex. Doc.* 1, part 2, Vol. 1, 48 Cong., 1 sess. (Serial 2182), 104 and 116; Post Returns, Fort Stevenson, August, 1883.

[27] Report of General John R. Brooke, Headquarters of the Platte, August 10, 1893, Report of the Secretary of War, 1893, *House Ex. Doc.* 1, part 2, Vol. 1, 53 Cong., 2 sess. (Serial 3198), 131.

[28] Post Return, Fort Sully, October 20, 1894; Steven Hoekman, "History of Fort Sully," *SDHC,* Vol. 26, 269–70; Report of General John R. Brooke, August 23, 1894, Report of the Secretary of War, 1895, *House Ex. Doc.* 2, Vol. 1, 54 Cong., 1 sess. (Serial 3370), 132.

Index